Praise for *Psychological Therapies for Adults*

"This book is edited by four professors who are the leading ... field of intellectual disabilities. Their collective expertise and experience are extremely impressive. This book will undoubtedly make an important contribution to the understanding and treatment of the range of difficulties encountered in this population."

Roz Shafran, Professor of Clinical Psychology at the School of Psychology and Clinical Language Sciences, Reading University

"The editors have brought together an impressive, international group of contributors to present psychological therapies for people with intellectual disabilities. The volume is rich in clinical examples which are extremely valuable in illustrating the therapeutic techniques in action. The chapters on preparing people with intellectual disability for psychological treatment and adapting therapies for persons with intellectual disabilities will be useful for therapists from all theoretical orientations."

Betsey Benson, Ph.D., Associate Professor of Clinical Psychiatry and Psychology, Nisonger Center UCEDD, Ohio State University

"Without doubt, *Psychological Therapies for Adults with Intellectual Disabilities* is the best book available at present on this topic. Its chapters span different theoretical frameworks, with an emphasis on cognitive behaviour therapy for a range of emotional and behavioural problems often encountered in people with intellectual disabilities. It provides guidance on many practical issues that come with adapting psychological therapies to people with intellectual disabilities. The editors and contributors are all leading experts in their field, which has resulted in a book that should be standard for practitioners, researchers and students working with people with intellectual disabilities and mental health problems."

Prof. Dr. Robert Didden, Radboud University Nijmegen, The Netherlands

"The book gives a thorough account of the current state of science in psychological therapies for people with learning disabilities and outlines a plausible way forward for clinicians and researchers to develop a stronger evidence base for such interventions. The chapters on lesser known interventions, e.g. mindfulness were very useful and informative. The authors are all well-known experts and have presented the material persuasively and with clarity."

Angela Hassiotis, Reader in Psychiatry of Intellectual Disabilities, Mental Health Sciences Unit, Faculty of Brain Sciences, University College London

Psychological Therapies for Adults with Intellectual Disabilities

Edited by John L. Taylor, William R. Lindsay, Richard P. Hastings and Chris Hatton

A John Wiley & Sons, Ltd., Publication

This edition first published 2013
© 2013 John Wiley & Sons, Ltd.
Reprinted with Corrections July 2014.

Wiley-Blackwell is an imprint of John Wiley & Sons, formed by the merger of Wiley's global Scientific, Technical and Medical business with Blackwell Publishing.

Registered Office
John Wiley & Sons Ltd, The Atrium, Southern Gate, Chichester, West Sussex, PO19 8SQ, UK

Editorial Offices
350 Main Street, Malden, MA 02148-5020, USA
9600 Garsington Road, Oxford, OX4 2DQ, UK
The Atrium, Southern Gate, Chichester, West Sussex, PO19 8SQ, UK

For details of our global editorial offices, for customer services, and for information about how to apply for permission to reuse the copyright material in this book please see our website at www.wiley.com/wiley-blackwell.

The right of John L. Taylor, William R. Lindsay, Richard P. Hastings and Chris Hatton to be identified as the authors of the editorial material in this work has been asserted in accordance with the UK Copyright, Designs and Patents Act 1988.

Wiley also publishes its books in a variety of electronic formats. Some content that appears in print may not be available in electronic books.

Designations used by companies to distinguish their products are often claimed as trademarks. All brand names and product names used in this book are trade names, service marks, trademarks or registered trademarks of their respective owners. The publisher is not associated with any product or vendor mentioned in this book. This publication is designed to provide accurate and authoritative information in regard to the subject matter covered. It is sold on the understanding that the publisher is not engaged in rendering professional services. If professional advice or other expert assistance is required, the services of a competent professional should be sought.

Library of Congress Cataloging-in-Publication Data
Psychological therapies for adults with intellectual disabilities / Edited by John L. Taylor, William R. Lindsay, Richard P. Hastings, Chris Hatton.
      pages cm
   Includes bibliographical references and index.
   ISBN 978-0-470-68346-0 (hbk.) – ISBN 978-0-470-68345-3 (pbk.)   1. People with mental disabilities–Psychology.   2. People with mental disabilities–Counseling of.
   RC451.4.M47P777 2013
   362.2–dc23
                              2012031380

A catalogue record for this book is available from the British Library.

Cover image: Wooden posts in sea at high tide. Image © James Ross / Getty.
Cover design by www.cyandesign.co.uk

Set in 10/12.5 pt Galliard by Toppan Best-set Premedia Limited

1 2013

Contents

About the Editors

John L. Taylor (john2.taylor@northumbria.ac.uk)
Professor of Clinical Psychology, Consultant Clinical Psychologist and Psychological Services Professional Lead
Northumbria University and Northumberland, Tyne & Wear NHS Foundation Trust, UK

John Taylor qualified as a clinical psychologist from Edinburgh University and has worked mainly in intellectual disability and forensic services in a range of settings in the United Kingdom (community learning disability services, and high, medium, and low secure services). Dr. Taylor has authored or coauthored over 90 publications related to his clinical research interests in the assessment and treatment of mental health and emotional problems and offending behavior associated with intellectual disabilities in a range of research journals, professional publications, and books. He is a Past President of the British Association of Behavioural & Cognitive Psychotherapies (BABCP). Previously, Dr. Taylor was Chair of the BPS Faculty for Forensic Clinical Psychology, the BPS Mental Health Working Group, and the Department of Health National Forensic Mental Health R&D Programme – Learning Disability Steering Group. Currently, he chairs the BPS Approved Clinicians Peer Review Panel.

William R. Lindsay (billlindsay@castlebeck.com)
Consultant Clinical Forensic Psychologist, Professor of Learning Disabilities and Forensic Psychology, Honorary Professor
Castlebeck; University of Abertay, Dundee; and Bangor University, UK

Bill Lindsay is Consultant Psychologist and Clinical Director in Scotland for Castlebeck. He was previously Head of Psychology (LD) in NHS Tayside and a Consultant Psychologist in the State Hospital. He is Professor of Learning Disabilities and Forensic Psychology at the University of Abertay, Dundee; Honorary Professor at Bangor University; and Honorary Professor at Deakin University, Melbourne. Dr. Lindsay has published over 300 research articles and book chapters, and given many presentations and workshops on cognitive therapy and the assessment and treatment of offenders with intellectual disability.

Richard P. Hastings (r.hastings@bangor.ac.uk)
Professor of Psychology
Bangor University, UK

Richard Hastings is Professor of Psychology at Bangor University in Wales where he is the research director of the clinical psychology training program and codirector of the masters training program in Applied Behaviour Analysis. Dr. Hastings engages in research and teaching primarily in the field of intellectual and developmental disabilities. He has authored or coauthored more than 150 journal papers, chapters, and other publications, and currently holds grants with a value in excess of £4 million. He is currently an associate editor/editorial board member for 13 research journals. Dr. Hastings' research interests focus on mental health in intellectual disability, challenging behavior, caregivers' adaptation and distress, and psychoeducational intervention for children with autism.

Chris Hatton (chris.hatton@lancaster.ac.uk)
Professor of Psychology, Health and Social Care
Lancaster University, UK

Chris Hatton is Professor of Psychology, Health and Social Care at the Centre for Disability Research, Lancaster University, UK, where he has worked since 2000. Before that, he was a researcher at the Hester Adrian Research Centre, University of Manchester, UK. He has also been Research Director of the Lancaster University Doctoral Programme in Clinical Psychology, and is a cofounder of the Public Health Observatory concerning people with intellectual disabilities. Over the past 20 years, Dr. Hatton has had a consistent research interest in the mental health and well-being of people with intellectual disabilities and their families, including work on understanding the social determinants of inequalities in mental health and well-being, and evaluating assessment tools, psychosocial interventions, and broader innovations in social policy designed to improve mental health and well-being. He has been an author on over 100 peer-reviewed journal articles and over 20 book chapters, and has jointly edited or authored 10 books.

List of Contributors

Alastair L. Barrowcliff
Consultant Clinical Psychologist and Clinical Lead (Learning Disabilities)
Five Boroughs Partnership NHS Foundation Trust, UK

Nigel Beail
Professor of Psychology, Consultant Clinical Psychologist and Professional Head of Psychological Services
University of Sheffield and South West Yorkshire Partnership NHS Foundation Trust and Barnsley Metropolitan Borough Council, UK

Dave Dagnan
Honorary Professor and Clinical Director
Lancaster University and Cumbria Partnership NHS Trust, UK

Alan Dowey
Consultant Clinical Psychologist, Deputy Head of Adult Learning Disabilities
Betsi Cadwaladr University Health Board and Bangor University, UK

Eric Emerson
Professor of Disability & Health Research and Professor of Disability Population Health
Lancaster University, UK and University of Sydney, Australia

Anna J. Esbensen
Assistant Professor of Pediatrics
Cincinnati Children's Hospital Medical Center, Cincinnati, Ohio, USA

Gillian Haddock
Professor of Clinical Psychology and Head of Division of Clinical Psychology
University of Manchester, UK

Dougal Julian Hare
Senior Lecturer in Clinical Psychology
University of Manchester, UK

Sigan L. Hartley
Assistant Professor
University of Wisconsin-Madison, Wisconsin, USA

Tom Jackson
Consultant Clinical Psychologist
South West Yorkshire Partnership NHS Foundation Trust and Barnsley
Metropolitan Borough Council, UK

Andrew J. Jahoda
Professor of Learning Disabilities and Honorary Consultant Clinical Psychologist
University of Glasgow and NHS Greater Glasgow and Clyde, UK

Robert S.P. Jones
Academic Director and Honorary Professor, North Wales Clinical Psychology
Programme and Head of Learning Disability (Clinical Psychology)
Bangor University and Betsi Cadwalader University Health Board, UK

Amy Kilbane
Clinical Psychologist
University of Glasgow and NHS Greater Glasgow and Clyde, UK

Martin Knapp
Professor of Social Policy and Director, LSE Health and Personal Social Services
Research Unit (PSSRU)
London School of Economics, UK

Giulio E. Lancioni
Professor, Department of Neuroscience and Sense Organs
University of Bari, Italy

Stephen J. Noone
Consultant Clinical Psychologist
Northumberland, Tyne & Wear NHS Foundation Trust, UK

Raymond W. Novaco
Professor of Psychology and Social Behavior
University of California, Irvine, California, USA

Stephen C. Oathamshaw
Consultant Clinical Psychologist and Head of Specialty
Scottish Borders Learning Disability Service, NHS Borders, UK

Angela D.A. Singh
Chief Executive Officer
American Health and Wellness Institute, Long Beach, California, USA

Ashvind N.A. Singh
Chief Clinical Officer
American Health and Wellness Institute, Long Beach, California, USA

Judy Singh
Chief Program Evaluation Officer
American Health and Wellness Institute, Raleigh, North Carolina, USA

Nirbhay N. Singh
Chief Learning and Development Officer
American Health and Wellness Institute, Raleigh, North Carolina, USA

Peter Sturmey
Professor of Psychology
Queens College and The Graduate Center, City University of New York, USA

Paul Willner
Emeritus Professor of Psychology
Swansea University, UK

Alan S.W. Winton
Senior Lecturer
School of Psychology
Massey University, Palmerston North, New Zealand

Foreword

I first became involved in working with persons with intellectual and developmental disabilities while in graduate school (many years ago!). It was not a burning desire to work in this field nor was it even an interest area at the time. I was simply a starving graduate student and I was offered a position as coordinator of a deinstitutionalization project based at the university. By way of context, I had grown up in a small town in upstate New York (USA) where the major employer was a large state institution for persons with intellectual and developmental disabilities. The institution was at the edge of town and fairly isolated from the rest of the community. Integration with the community and interaction with the town's residents was minimal at best. As a result, many of my peers (and myself included) grew up with very stereotypic, biased, and inaccurate attitudes toward persons with disabilities.

My involvement in the deinstitutionalization project ended up having profound impact on my career. My role in the project was mulifaceted. I was involved in direct care, supervision of staff, cooking (scary!), transportation, overnights, and community integration activities. Many days I would work with the project participants from early morning to bedtime. I very soon realized that my prior attitudes and expectations about persons with intellectual and developmental disabilities were terribly off base. I became particularly interested in the array of social–emotional issues of persons with disabilities. The term "dual diagnosis" had not become part of our vernacular at that time, but I realized that was my interest. At that point, I had also completed several courses in counseling and psychotherapy. It struck me as odd that none of these courses included any content on counseling persons with intellectual disabilities. If mentioned, the guidance in those courses was that counseling and psychotherapy was not appropriate for persons with intellectual disabilities. Clearly, we have come a long way, and *Psychological Therapies for Adults with Intellectual Disabilities* is a strong evidence of this.

More recently, I spent several weeks in Fall 2011 at the University of Glasgow and was hosted by Dr. Andrew J. Jahoda (thank you again, Andrew) of their Centre for Excellence in Development Disabilities and Department of Mental Health and Wellbeing. Dr. Jahoda is coauthor of several chapters in this book. I also had the

opportunity to spend a day with Dr. John L. Taylor. The overall goal of my trip was
to get a better understanding of the intellectual and developmental disability services
in the National Health Service, particularly in the dual diagnosis area. I was
very impressed with the service delivery in the United Kingdom. During my visit
with Dr. Taylor, he told me about this forthcoming book and asked if I would consider writing a foreword for the book. I was extremely honored, and after having
read the manuscript, I was very pleased to have a small association with this outstanding book.

This book will be an invaluable resource both to professionals who work with
persons with intellectual and developmental disabilities as well as more general mental
health professionals. In fact, I believe this book will go a long way in encouraging
general mental health professionals to offer a fuller and broader array of psychotherapeutic interventions for adults with disabilities. This book emphasizes "think broadly
and creatively" in planning services for adults with disabilities.

The first chapters in the book deal primarily with the context of mental health
issues with persons with intellectual disabilities – these chapters alone provide an
excellent overview of issues in the dual diagnosis area, again providing a broad perspective. The next set of chapters describes various approaches and strategies for
preparing clients for psychotherapy and how to make developmental adaptations in
therapeutic techniques (e.g., how to encourage expression, monitor thoughts, and
use appropriate language). These chapters provide an outstanding overview of various
clinical techniques and considerations and cut across theoretical perspectives. Taken
alone, these chapters provide a highly useful clinical guidebook.

The remainder of the book focuses on specific theoretical approaches and specific
problems areas. These chapters provide an excellent balance of practice issues and
review of research. The major theoretical approaches are addressed (cognitive–behavioral, mindfulness, behavioral, psychodynamic) as well as primary presenting problem
areas (anxiety disorders, mood disorders, autism spectrum disorders, psychosis, psy-
chosexual problems). The chapters parallel many books on providing therapeutic
services for the general population, and the references cited in these chapters are an
incredible resource.

For years, I have been an unabashed supporter and advocate for the provision of
psychotherapeutic services for persons with intellectual disabilities. And, I have also
been a critical reviewer of the research literature base in this area. *Psychological Therapies for Adults with Intellectual Disabilities* provides an excellent base for both practitioners and researchers in this area. While the chapter authors are predominantly
from the United Kingdom, the resources and literature represent an international
perspective. In particular, my North American colleagues will find great value in this
book. I have not seen a better summary of both the research and clinical issues than
those covered in this book. For those professionals who already work with adults
with intellectual disabilities, this book will expand your knowledge base and skill
repertoire. For general mental health professionals, you will be better able to intervene with your clients with intellectual disabilities with more confidence and a
broader perspective.

In my mostly cluttered and marginally organized office, I reserve one bookshelf
for those books that I consult frequently and/or highly value – sort of my own per-

sonal "hall of fame" for books. *Psychological Therapies for Adults with Intellectual Disabilities* has a space reserved on that shelf!!!

H. Thompson Prout, PhD
Professor, University of Kentucky
Lexington, Kentucky, USA
July 2012

Preface

It has been estimated that one in six people suffer from mental health problems such as anxiety and depression at any one time. The UK government has stated that this is the single largest cause of disability and illness in England accounting for nearly 40 percent of people receiving incapacity benefits. The effects of these conditions on individuals, their families and carers can be chronic and devastating. Economists have estimated the total cost to the economy of anxiety and depression in terms of lost productivity, sick and other benefits to add up to billions of pounds and equates to one per cent of the national income.

Only one in four of those whose condition is recognised receive effective treatment. Although medication can be a successful treatment for many people, many others would prefer alternative forms of treatment. Psychological therapies have proved to be as effective as drugs in tackling many mental health problems and are often more effective in the longer term. The National Institute for Health and Clinical Excellence (NICE), an independent government advisory body in the UK, has recommended psychological therapies as effective and long-lasting treatments for a wide range of mental health conditions in its clinical guidelines. Subsequently the National Health Service in England has invested heavily in improving access to these interventions through funding new services, training courses and thousands of specially trained therapists.

The situation for people with intellectual disabilities who experience mental health and emotional problems is arguably far worse. People with intellectual disabilities are more likely than others to experience living circumstances and life events that are known to be associated with increased risks for mental health problems. Although mental health and emotional problems are common amongst people with intellectual disabilities, they often go undetected and thus untreated. Despite policy and legislative developments designed to enable people with intellectual disabilities to access mainstream mental health services and effective treatments, there is no evidence that this group is in fact reaping any of the benefits of the large scale investment in improved psychological therapy services.

The reasons – historical, cultural, attitudinal, economic – that people with intellectual disabilities are disadvantaged and excluded in this way are complex and varied.

It is the case though that the evidence for the effectiveness of psychological therapies has been slow to develop and hard to come by for clinicians working in routine service settings. This is especially difficult for mental health practitioners who may see people with intellectual disabilities and mental health problems only occasionally or in small numbers.

This volume is aimed at such colleagues and others working in mental health and primary care fields. It sets out the social, policy and economic context, the evidence base, and examples of good clinical practice to assist clinicians and practitioners in providing effective psychological therapies to people with intellectual disabilities who experience mental health problems. Psychological therapies including cognitive, behavioural, psychodynamic and mindfulness-based interventions for a range of mental health and emotional problems including anxiety, depression, anger and psychotic disorders are covered. There are also chapters on working with carers and with clients with autistic spectrum disorders. In addition to guiding good practice in treating these problems and client groups, issues including assessment, adaptation of therapy techniques, and preparing patients for therapy are addressed.

We hope that in bringing this up-to-date material together in a single volume clinicians will be better able to provide effective psychological therapies to adults with intellectual disabilities. It should also be a useful resource to students and therapists in training in the use of psychological therapies and thus over time help to reduce the inequality in access to effective treatments for this client group.

Finally, we would like to thank our colleagues Andy Peart and Kathy Syplywczak at Wiley-Blackwell for their encouragement and help at the beginning and end stages of this project respectively. Particular thanks go to Karen Shield, Senior Project Editor (Psychology) for her forbearance and encouragement during the substantive writing stage this venture.

John L. Taylor, William R. Lindsay,
Richard P. Hastings & Chris Hatton
September 2012

Chapter 1

Mental Health and Emotional Problems in People with Intellectual Disabilities

John L. Taylor
Martin Knapp

Historically, there has been a general lack of regard for the mental health needs of people with intellectual disabilities (e.g., Stenfert Kroese, 1998). This is despite clear evidence that people in this population have higher levels of unmet needs and receive less effective treatment for their mental health and emotional problems, and despite the promotion of government policies and the introduction of antidiscrimination legislation designed to break down these barriers. For example, in England, the *National Service Framework for Mental Health* (Department of Health, 1999) applied to all working age adults and aimed at improving quality and tackling variations in access to care. Its successors, *New Horizons: A Shared Vision for Mental Health* (HM Government, 2009) and *No Health without Mental Health* (HM Government and Department of Health, 2011), prioritized better access to psychological therapies (especially cognitive therapy) for socially excluded groups and improved outcomes in mental health by promoting equality and reducing inequalities. The report on *Services for People with Learning Disabilities and Challenging Behaviour or Mental Health Needs* (Department of Health, 2007) recommended that "[mental health] services available to the whole community increase their ability to meet the needs of people with learning disabilities whose behaviour presents challenges and who have a diagnosed mental illness" (p. 17). In terms of primary legislation, people with intellectual disabilities who experience mental health problems should be able to access services and receive the same treatment as others with reasonable modifications being made in accordance with relevant legislation (e.g., the Disability Discrimination Act 1995, incorporated into the Equality Act 2010).

Despite this raft of policy and legislation, there are a number of reasons for the continuing inequality of access to mental health services and effective treatment for people with intellectual disabilities. These include (a) a lack of knowledge and awareness of mental health and emotional problems experienced by people with intellectual disabilities; (b) some reluctance on the part of therapists to provide these

Psychological Therapies for Adults with Intellectual Disabilities, First Edition.
Edited by John L. Taylor, William R. Lindsay, Richard P. Hastings, and Chris Hatton.
© 2013 John Wiley & Sons, Ltd. Published 2013 by John Wiley & Sons, Ltd.

interventions to people in this population; (c) a lack of good quality evidence to guide practice with this client group; and (d) the difficulty of making an economic case in an increasingly challenging fiscal context. These and related issues are explored further in the following sections.

Identifying Mental Health and Emotional Disorders in People with Intellectual Disabilities

As a group, people with intellectual disabilities are more likely than people in the general population to experience living circumstances and life events associated with an increased risk of mental health problems, including birth trauma, stressful family circumstances, unemployment, debt, stigmatization, lack of self-determination, and lack of meaningful friendships and intimate relationships (Martorell *et al.*, 2009). People with intellectual disabilities report experiencing stigma and negative beliefs about themselves and their social attractiveness (MacMahon & Jahoda, 2008), and the stigma and discrimination so often associated with mental health problems add to these challenges (Thornicroft, 2006). In addition, people in this population are likely to have fewer psychological resources available to cope effectively with stressful events, as well as poorer cognitive abilities including memory, problem-solving, and planning skills (van den Hout *et al.*, 2000).

Prevalence

Despite these apparent disadvantages, it is not clear whether people with intellectual disabilities experience more mental health and emotional problems than those without disabilities. Studies of mental health problems among samples of people in this population report large variations in prevalence depending on the methodology used, such as the use of case note reviews versus clinical evaluation, the nature and type of diagnostic assessment used, the location of the study sample (e.g., inpatient vs. generic community services), and, importantly, the inclusion of challenging behavior as a mental health problem or not (see Kerker *et al.*, 2004 for a brief review).

Studies of populations of people with intellectual disabilities using *screening* instruments to identify potential cases report rates of mental health problems (excluding challenging behavior) of between 20 percent and 39 percent and studies involving clinical assessment of psychiatric diagnosis in people with intellectual disabilities have reported point prevalence rates of between 17 percent and 22 percent when behavior problems are excluded (see Table 1.1). These figures are quite similar to the rates between 16 percent and 25 percent for mental health problems found in the general population (e.g., McManus *et al.*, 2009; Singleton *et al.*, 2001). Although the overall rates of mental health problems (excluding behavior problems) among people with intellectual disabilities appear to be broadly consistent with those found in the general population, the profiles for types of disorders differ. In particular, the rates for psychosis and affective disorders are somewhat higher among people with intellectual disabilities, while those for personality, alcohol/substance use, and sleep disorders are considerably lower (Cooper *et al.*, 2007; Singleton *et al.*, 2001). Hatton and

Table 1.1 Selected Studies of the Prevalence of Mental Health Problems Experienced by Adults with Intellectual Disabilities Using (a) Screening Instruments and (b) Clinical Assessments

	N	Prevalence (%)
(a) Studies using screening instruments		
Taylor *et al.* (2004)	1155	20
Deb *et al.* (2001)	90	22
Roy *et al.* (1997)	127	33
Reiss (1990)	205	39
Iverson and Fox (1989)	165	36
(b) Studies involving clinical assessments[a]		
Cooper *et al.* (2007)	1023	18
Cooper and Bailey (2001)	207	22
Lund (1985)	302	17
Corbett (1979)	402	21

[a]Rates excluding behavior problems calculated using the data presented by Cooper *et al.* (2007) in Table 6, p. 33.

Taylor (2010) present a more detailed discussion of the prevalence of specific types of mental health and emotional disorders (anxiety, depression, psychosis, dementia, substance misuse, and anger) among people with intellectual disabilities.

Diagnostic overshadowing

Although case recognition is a crucial step in meeting the mental health needs of people with intellectual disabilities, many of these needs are not detected and so remain untreated. There can be several reasons for this.

Reiss *et al.* (1982) used the term "diagnostic overshadowing" to describe the phenomenon in which carers and professionals misattribute signs of mental health problems, such as social withdrawal as a result of feelings of depression, to an aspect of a person's intellectual disability, for example, poor social skills. Although it is likely that causes and maintaining factors overlap, the relationship between mental health problems and challenging behavior in people with intellectual disabilities remains unclear (Emerson *et al.*, 1999) and requires further elucidation. Taylor (2010) reported that correlations between scores on a challenging behavior schedule and the three subscales of the Psychiatric Assessment Schedule for Adults with Developmental Disability (PAS-ADD) Checklist mental health screening tool (Moss *et al.*, 1998) were statistically significant (all $p < 0.001$), but relatively small in magnitude (0.32 affective disorder, 0.31 organic disorder, and 0.28 psychotic disorder) for 740 adults with intellectual disabilities. These data are consistent with the suggestion that while challenging behaviors and mental disorders experienced by people in this population are associated, they are distinct problems.

The issue of diagnostic overshadowing can be exacerbated by the values base and ethos of the training of many staff working in intellectual disability services. Staff in these services tend to use a conceptual framework built around challenging behavior rather than one focused on mental health to understand problematic behavior. Consequently, they may be antithetic to viewing a person's behavior as indicative of a mental health problem rather than a form of challenging behavior (Costello, 2004). Furthermore, services for people with intellectual disabilities and those for people with mental health problems are often organizationally and functionally separate and have distinct cultures that can lead to gaps in the provision of diagnostic and treatment services (Hassiotis *et al.*, 2000).

Assessment of mental health problems

An additional obstacle to the identification of mental health and emotional problems experienced by people with intellectual disabilities is clinical assessment. The assessment measures available to detect mental health problems among people in this client group are not well developed and often lack reliability and validity. Although in its early stages, work is under way to develop measures for a range of purposes and conditions (e.g., screening and detailed diagnostic assessments for multiple mental health problems, anxiety, depression, psychosis, and trauma) using adapted and *de novo* measures that can be self or informant. The issues concerning the assessment of mental health problems in adults with intellectual disabilities and a description of a range of tools available to assess these problems are set out in more detail in Chapter 3 of this book.

Therapeutic Disdain

Therapist attitudes and beliefs

In the past, many therapists have been reluctant to offer individual psychotherapy, including cognitive–behavioral therapy (CBT), to clients with intellectual disabilities. Offering these treatment approaches requires the development of close working relationships with clients who may be thought to be unattractive because of their disabilities, which make the therapeutic endeavor more challenging and the achievement of quick treatment gains more difficult. Bender (1993) used the term "the unoffered chair" to describe this "therapeutic disdain" (p. 7). In addition, therapists may have assumed that people with intellectual disabilities do not have the cognitive abilities required to understand or benefit from psychological therapy. There is, however, no evidence in the intellectual disabilities field that deficits in particular cognitive abilities result in poorer outcomes, and studies involving children show that it is not necessary to have mature adult cognitive structures to benefit from CBT (Durlak *et al.*, 1991).

A further reason for therapists and services routinely failing to offer psychological therapy to people with intellectual disabilities is the lack of research evidence to support its use with these clients. The lack of good quality research is in part due to difficulties in obtaining funding for research in this area from established grant-giving bodies. Another issue is research ethics committees' reticence about approving research studies involving participants with intellectual disabilities due to concerns about their capacity to give valid consent to take part in clinical research. Although some people with intellectual disabilities may not be able to comprehend all of the information required to participate in research (Arscott *et al.*, 1998), there is evidence that research participants of average intellectual ability do not fully comprehend key aspects of treatment studies they have consented to take part in either (Featherstone & Donovan, 2002). Thus, we risk discriminatory practices in excluding people with intellectual disabilities from potentially beneficial or benign treatment outcome research based on erroneous assumptions about their capacity to consent compared with the general population.

Cognitive impairments

Over the last 30 years, psychological therapies, especially CBT, have become established in the treatment of common mental health problems and some severe mental health problems such as psychosis. More recently, this development has been underpinned by the inclusion of CBT for a range of mental health conditions in the National Institute for Health and Clinical Excellence (NICE) guidance. NICE is an independent organization in England that provides advice to the government on the evidence supporting interventions for the promotion of good health and the prevention and treatment of ill-health (www.nice.org.uk). Historically, it has been assumed that people with intellectual disabilities have cognitive impairments that hinder their ability to engage successfully in and benefit from CBT and other evidence-based psychotherapies.

Despite the concern that people with intellectual disabilities may have difficulties in coping with the complexity of interventions aimed at modifying cognitive distortions, experimental evidence shows that people with mild intellectual disabilities can recognize emotions (Joyce *et al.*, 2006; Oathamshaw & Haddock, 2006; Sams *et al.*, 2006); label emotions (Joyce *et al.*, 2006); discriminate thoughts, feelings, and behaviors (Sams *et al.*, 2006); and link events and emotions (Dagnan *et al.*, 2000; Joyce *et al.*, 2006; Oathamshaw & Haddock, 2006). However, there is some research showing that the majority of these participants with intellectual disabilities were unable to do an experimental task involving understanding of the mediating role of cognitions, particularly when the complexity of the task was increased (Dagnan *et al.*, 2000; Joyce *et al.*, 2006; Oathamshaw & Haddock, 2006). However, it is not clear whether this phenomenon is simply a function of the complexity of the experimental tasks presented to study participants or if it would be observed in routine treatment settings.

Changes in professional attitudes

There are encouraging signs that provision of evidence-based psychological therapies, and CBT in particular, to people with intellectual disabilities is increasing. Nagel and Leiper (1999) found that approximately one-third of British psychologists who responded to a survey on the use of psychotherapy with people with intellectual disabilities reported using these approaches frequently. An edited book on CBT for people with intellectual disabilities (Stenfert Kroese *et al.*, 1997) and a special issue of the *Journal of Applied Research in Intellectual Disabilities* devoted to CBT (Willner

& Hatton, 2006) point to increasing interest in the use of these therapeutic approaches with these clients. A special issue of *Behavioural and Cognitive Psychotherapy* – the official scientific journal of the *British Association for Behavioural and Cognitive Psychotherapies* (BABCP) – concerning contemporary developments in the theory and practice of CBT included a paper on applications for people with intellectual disabilities (Taylor *et al.*, 2008).

There is also emerging evidence that practitioners in the field are beginning to offer CBT interventions aimed at identifying and modifying cognitive distortions rather than relying on techniques that focus on ameliorating cognitive skills deficits. For example, Lindsay (1999) reported on successful outcomes of CBT interventions for people referred for a range of clinical problems including anxiety, depression, and anger that explicitly incorporated work on the content of cognitions underpinning and maintaining their emotional difficulties. Willner (2004) and Stenfert Kroese and Thomas (2006) used imagery rehearsal therapy, a technique that deals with dream imagery in the same way as cognitive distortions, to successfully treat a man and two women, respectively, who were experiencing postabuse traumatic nightmares. Haddock *et al.* (2004) reported a case series of five people with mild intellectual disabilities and psychosis who showed improvements following a cognitive–behavioral intervention adapted from an established therapy that included a cognitive restructuring component.

The Evidence for Psychological Therapies for People with Intellectual Disabilities

The difficulties in developing an evidence base to support psychological (and other forms of) treatments for people with intellectual disabilities have been discussed previously (e.g., Oliver *et al.*, 2003; Sturmey *et al.*, 2004) and are covered in some depth in Chapter 17 of this book. In the following section, an overview of the evidence for psychological therapies for this client group is provided to frame the detailed discussion of the application of these approaches to particular types of disorders and client groups in succeeding chapters.

Reviews of reviews of the evidence

Gustafsson *et al.* (2009) surveyed systematic reviews that evaluated the effects of psychosocial interventions for adults with intellectual disabilities who experienced mental health problems. They found 55 reviews that concerned the effectiveness of psychotherapy (mainly behavioral and cognitive behavioral interventions) for adults with intellectual disabilities published between 1969 and 2005. Only two reviews met the survey inclusion criteria. The results of these reviews showed that interventions based on cognitive–behavioral approaches appear to reduce aggression at the end of treatment, although the reviews included studies judged to be of low quality.

In a narrative review of reviews that focused more specifically on psychotherapy for people with intellectual disabilities, Prout and Browning (2011a) described the conclusions of seven reviews published between 2000 and 2011. Prout and

Browning found that research on psychotherapy with this client group continues to lack a critical mass of studies with robust designs (particularly randomized controlled trials (RCTs)) required to establish the efficacy of these approaches. This lack of rigor notwithstanding, they concluded that psychotherapy is "at least moderately beneficial" for people with intellectual disabilities and a range of mental health problems (p. 57). They suggested that in addition to RCT studies, future research needs to consider the active ingredients of effective treatments, and the adaptations and process variables (e.g., therapeutic alliance) that contribute to successful outcomes.

Reviews and commentaries

There have been numerous narrative reviews and commentaries that have considered the effectiveness of psychotherapy for people with intellectual disabilities who have mental health and emotional problems. A summary of some of the key themes and conclusions from these reviews is given in the following discussion.

Prout and Nowak-Drabik (2003) reported on perhaps the most comprehensive review of psychotherapy for people with intellectual disabilities. Using a clear definition of psychotherapy, they considered 92 studies published over a 30-year period between 1968 and 1998. The pool of 92 studies was rated systematically by "experts" with regard to outcome and effectiveness. The studies in this pool involved behavioral (33 percent), cognitive–behavioral (13 percent), analytic/dynamic (15 percent), humanistic/person centered (2 percent), and "other" (37 percent) types of psychotherapy. Just 9 of the 92 study reports were found to meet the study criteria and provided sufficient information to be used in a meta-analysis of treatment effectiveness; this yielded a mean effect size of 1.01. Exploratory analyses suggested that published studies involving manual-guided individual treatment and behaviorally orientated therapies (excluding behavior modification) yielded higher outcome and effectiveness ratings. Prout and Nowak-Drabik (2003) concluded from their analysis that psychotherapy for people with intellectual disabilities produces moderate outcomes and benefits for clients. Although many of the studies included in the review lacked methodological rigor, the authors suggested that psychotherapeutic interventions should be more frequently considered in treatment plans for these clients.

Beail (2003) provided a commentary comparing "self-management" approaches, cognitive therapy, and psychodynamic psychotherapy outcome studies in the intellectual disabilities field. Numerous case studies, case series, and a small number of uncontrolled group studies concerning self-management approaches were identified, especially in the forensic intellectual disability field. Only a few attempts at controlled studies were cited – two studies in the area of problem-solving reported mixed results in terms of outcome, and three studies in the anger management field produced significant improvements.

Although the literature pertaining to cognitive–behavioral self-management approaches reviewed by Beail (2003) is quite limited, this contrasts with the evidence available for psychodynamic psychotherapy with this client group. Four pre-post treatment open trials of psychodynamic psychotherapy were included, which were successful in reducing behavioral and offending problems among people with intellectual disabilities. Very little evidence was available to support the use of cognitive therapy as means of targeting distorted cognitions that underpin problem behavior, attitudes, and emotional distress in this population.

Beail (2003) concluded that the evidence base for cognitive behavioral psychotherapy had progressed a little in the previous five or six years, but more than that for psychodynamic psychotherapy. However, the paucity and quality of the outcome research in this area was such that claims for the effectiveness of these types of interventions could only be tentative. It was suggested that the potential of these emerging therapies warranted more thorough evaluation using more robust methodologies.

Sturmey (2004) selectively reviewed and critiqued cognitive therapy for people with intellectual disabilities with anger, depression, and sex-offending problems. He concluded that the evidence to support CBT approaches is weak when compared with the extensive evidence base for behavioral interventions based on an applied behavioral analysis paradigm. This view was reinforced in a later critique of cognitive therapy for people with intellectual disabilities (Sturmey, 2006). However, Prout and Browning (2011a) suggested that Sturmey's position is based on a "misunderstanding" (p. 56) of what defines psychotherapy and an attempt to separate out behavioral and cognitive elements of empirically supported multicomponent treatments in order to defend a particular conceptual view.

Willner (2005) critically reviewed psychotherapeutic interventions for people with intellectual disabilities. He found that CBT interventions utilizing cognitive skills training (e.g., self-management, self-monitoring, self-instructional training) show promise for a range of mental health and emotional control problems. Approaches focusing on cognitive distortions were considered to have only a very limited evidence base. Willner concluded that there is a "wealth of evidence" (p. 82) from methodologically weak studies that psychological therapies (chiefly CBT) can benefit people with intellectual disabilities with emotional problems for which there is no realistic alternative.

Dagnan (2007) considered "recent research" (unfortunately the time period is not specified) concerning individual interventions as part of a wider review of psychosocial interventions for people with intellectual disabilities and mental health problems. He concluded that although there is some limited evidence to support cognitive therapy for a range of problems (anxiety, depression, anger, obsessive–compulsive disorder, and trauma-related symptoms), there are significant gaps in the literature. There were, for example, few high-quality randomized trials, a lack of process research on the mechanisms for change for people with intellectual disabilities, and limited evidence for interventions for people with more severe and enduring mental health problems (e.g., psychosis).

Prout and Browning (2011b) looked at psychological treatment studies involving people with intellectual disabilities published between 2006 and 2011. They concluded that the published studies present generally positive results supporting the use of psychotherapy with this client group. Both individual and group approaches show benefits for clients, and anger reduction approaches are the most researched interventions in this population. Prout and Browning also reviewed doctoral dissertations completed between 1993 and 2009 to examine the *file draw* phenomenon that proposes a bias toward studies showing positive outcomes being presented in peer-reviewed journals. They concluded that these research dissertation study results provide further support for the effectiveness of psychotherapeutic interventions for people with intellectual disabilities.

Making the "Economic Case" for Interventions

A final reason for the continuing inequity of access to appropriate interventions to meet mental health needs could be the difficulty in demonstrating that such actions are "economically attractive." Of course, the fundamental purpose of psychological and other therapies is not to save money or to achieve cost-effectiveness; it is to improve the health and well-being of individuals with (in this case) mental health needs, as well as the well-being of significant others, such as family members. However, as fiscal austerity comes to dominate decision making at every level within health and social care systems, it is inevitable that questions will be asked with increasing frequency (and indeed, increasing urgency) about the costs of interventions, any future savings they might generate, and the balance between amounts expended and outcomes achieved. Those questions are being asked by decision makers locally and nationally, frontline and strategic, as they each face unprecedented cuts to their budgets.

Local commissioners within health, housing, social care, and other systems, for example, must work within annual budgets to purchase services and treatments that best meet the needs of their populations. Although they will be acutely aware of the wider impacts of decisions they take, that is beyond their own budget boundaries, pressures on them to manage their resources make it inevitable that they focus primarily on their own concerns and balances. Thus, a group of people such as those with intellectual disabilities and mental health needs, whose needs might spread beyond the health system into social care, welfare benefits, specialist housing, and beyond, may lose out because of this tendency to withdraw back into "silos" at the time of acute fiscal austerity. Even strategic decision makers at the highest level of government, for example, within the Treasury, will be particularly focused on public sector expenditure and associated borrowing, and so may be less concerned about the spillover consequences of decisions for private individuals, particularly for families. Decisions taken by a local or central decision maker to place more reliance on unpaid family carers will appear relatively "costless" because the impact will be felt by the family, perhaps by the employers of family members and so on.

The difficulty that the field of intellectual disabilities and mental health faces is that the interventions that are available and for which there is an evidence base that they work (in terms of improving health and well-being) cannot point to cost savings for public budgets. There might in due course be a reduction in the need for expensive interventions, but to date, there has been little investigation of this area. Another consequence of the current fiscal austerity, over and above the focus on own budgets, is short-termism, with budget holders desperate to achieve savings from their investments within the current or maybe the following financial year, but not to be so heavily influenced by savings that might follow over a number of years.

The territory has also changed in the last few years. At a time when budgets were growing, albeit relatively slowly in many cases, it was often sufficient to point to the outcome advantages of interventions that actually increased expenditure rather than reduced it, on the grounds that the better outcomes were worth the additional expenditure necessary to achieve them. In a context where there is no margin for "additional expenditure," this algorithm of cost-effectiveness gains but without cost savings often looks somewhat out of place.

Conclusions

People with intellectual disabilities are potentially more vulnerable than others to the risk of experiencing mental health problems. Despite this increased susceptibility, their assessment and treatment needs have often not been recognized, and they have experienced significant obstacles in accessing appropriate services. Although the picture is gradually improving, and despite the various policy developments and government guidelines concerning inclusion of those with disabilities, some basic issues concerning access to and delivery of mental health services for people with intellectual disabilities have yet to be resolved (Michael, 2008). For example, the Department of Health *Improving Access to Psychological Therapies* (IAPT) program is focused on the implementation of NICE guidelines for common mental health problems in England (www.iapt.nhs.uk). The *Learning Disabilities Positive Practice Guide* (Department of Health, 2009) indicates that IAPT services need to be flexible in providing effective psychological therapies for people with intellectual disabilities. This could include offering treatment information in easy-to-understand formats, using easy-read or therapist-administered self-report assessments, and utilizing NICE-approved psychological interventions modified to meet the needs of people with intellectual disabilities. However, despite this guidance, and the hundreds of millions of pounds invested in this program, it is not known, and no data are being systematically collected to indicate whether or not people with intellectual disabilities are accessing or benefitting from these highly resourced new psychological therapy services.

In the past, psychological therapists have avoided engaging with clients with intellectual disabilities in order to provide effective interventions aimed at reducing symptoms and alleviating subjective distress associated with their conditions. Based on the emerging evidence concerning the effectiveness of psychological interventions for the emotional problems experienced by this client group, this historical "therapeutic disdain" can surely no longer be justified. From work described in the professional and academic literature, the picture is gradually changing from one of professional indifference to one of increasing interest in and concern for the needs of clients with intellectual disabilities who experience mental health difficulties.

The research literature supporting the use of psychological therapies with clients with intellectual disabilities is developing, albeit at a slow rate. Reviewers and commentators consistently call for significant gaps in the evidence base to be filled, including

- more rigorous outcome studies, including RCTs, to establish the efficacy of clearly defined psychotherapeutic interventions for specific types of problems with distinct patient populations;

- process research into the active ingredients of psychological therapies and mechanisms of change for people with intellectual disabilities experiencing mental health problems;
- follow-up research examining sustainability of treatment effects over time and the generalizability of gains from treatment settings into routine care conditions;
- an understanding of the economic consequences of delivering these treatments.

Developments in service provision, professional practice, and research and evaluation concerning psychological therapies for adults with intellectual disabilities who experience an array of mental health and emotional problems in a variety of contexts are described by experts from a range of perspectives in the remainder of this book.

References

Arscott, K., Dagnan, D. & Stenfert Kroese, B. (1998). Consent to psychological research by people with an intellectual disability. *Journal of Applied Research in Intellectual Disabilities, 11*, 77–83.

Beail, N. (2003). What works for people with mental retardation? Critical commentary on cognitive-behavioural and psychodynamic psychotherapy research. *Mental Retardation, 41*, 468–472.

Bender, M. (1993). The unoffered chair: The history of therapeutic disdain towards people with a learning difficulty. *Clinical Psychology Forum, 54*, 7–12.

Cooper, S.-A. & Bailey, N.M. (2001). Psychiatric disorders amongst people with learning disabilities: Prevalence and relationship to ability level. *Irish Journal of Psychological Medicine, 18*, 45–53.

Cooper, S.-A., Smiley, E., Morrison, J., Williamson, A. & Allan, L. (2007). Mental ill-health in adults with intellectual disabilities: Prevalence and associated factors. *The British Journal of Psychiatry, 190*, 27–35.

Corbett, J.A. (1979). Psychiatric morbidity and mental retardation. In F.E. James & R. Snaith (Eds.) *Psychiatric illness and mental handicap* (pp.11–25). London: Gaskell.

Costello, H. (2004). *Does training carers improve outcome for adults with learning disabilities and mental health problems?* PhD thesis, King's College, University of London.

Dagnan, D. (2007). Psychosocial interventions for people with intellectual disabilities and mental ill-health. *Current Opinion in Psychiatry, 20*, 4456–4460.

Dagnan, D., Chadwick, P. & Proudlove, J. (2000). Towards and assessment of suitability of people with mental retardation for cognitive therapy. *Cognitive Therapy and Research, 24*, 627–636.

Deb, S., Thomas, M. & Bright, C. (2001). Mental disorder in adults with intellectual disability. I: Prevalence of functional psychiatric illness among a community-based population aged between 16 and 64 years. *Journal of Intellectual Disability Research, 45*, 495–505.

Department of Health (1999). *National Service Framework for Mental Health: Modern standards and service models*. London: Department of Health.

Department of Health (2007). *Services for People with Learning Disabilities and Challenging Behaviour or Mental Health Needs*. London: Department of Health.

Department of Health (2009). *Learning disabilities positive practice guide*. London: Department of Health.

Durlak, J., Fuhrman, T. & Lampman, C. (1991). Effectiveness of cognitive-behavior therapy for maladaptive children. *Psychological Bulletin, 110*, 204–214.

Emerson, E., Moss, S. & Kiernan, C. (1999). The relationship between challenging behaviour and psychiatric disorders in people with severe developmental disabilities. In N. Bouras (Ed.) *Psychiatric & behavioural disorders in developmental disabilities & mental retardation* (pp.38–48). Cambridge, UK: Cambridge University Press.

Featherstone, K. & Donovan, J. (2002). "Why don't they just tell me straight, why allocate it?" The struggle to make sense of participating in a randomised controlled trial. *Social Science & Medicine, 55*, 709–719.

Gustafsson, C., Ojehagen, A., Hansson, L., Dandlund, M., Nystrom, M., Glad, J. *et al.* (2009). Effects of psychosocial interventions for people with intellectual disabilities and mental health problems: A survey of systematic reviews. *Research on Social Work Practice, 19*, 281–290.

Haddock, G., Lobban, F., Hatton, C. & Carson, R. (2004). Cognitive-behaviour therapy for people with psychosis and mild intellectual disabilities: A case series. *Clinical Psychology & Psychotherapy, 11*, 282–298.

Hassiotis, A., Barron, P. & O'Hara, J. (2000). Mental health services for people with learning disabilities: A complete overhaul is needed with strong links to mainstream services. *British Medical Journal, 321*, 583–584.

Hatton, C. & Taylor, J.L. (2010). Promoting healthy lifestyles – Mental health and illness. In G. Grant, P. Ramcharan, M. Flynn & M. Richardson (Eds.) *Learning disability: A life cycle approach to valuing people* (2nd edn, pp. 381–408). Maidenhead: Open University Press.

HM Government (2009). *New Horizons: A Shared Vision for Mental Health*. London: Department of Health.

HM Government and Department of Health (2011). *No Health without Mental Health: Cross-government mental health outcomes strategy for people of all ages*. London: Department of Health.

Iverson, J.C. & Fox, R.A. (1989). Prevalence of psychopathology among mentally retarded adults. *Research in Developmental Disabilities, 10*, 77–83.

Joyce, T., Globe, A. & Moody, C. (2006). Assessment of the component skills for cognitive therapy in adults with intellectual disabilities. *Journal of Applied Research in Intellectual Disabilities, 19*, 17–23.

Kerker, B.D., Owens, P.L., Zigler, E. & Horwitz, S.M. (2004). Mental health disorders among individuals with mental retardation: Challenges to accurate prevalence estimates. *Public Health Reports, 119*, 409–417.

Lindsay, W.R. (1999). Cognitive therapy. *The Psychologist, 12*, 238–241.

Lund, J. (1985). The prevalence of psychiatric disorder in mentally retarded adults. *Acta Psychiatrica Scandinavica, 72*, 563–570.

MacMahon, P. & Jahoda, A. (2008). Social comparison and depression: People with mild and moderate intellectual disabilities. *American Journal of Mental Retardation, 113*, 307–318.

Martorell, A., Tsakanikos, E., Pereda, A., Gutierrez-Recacha, P., Bouras, N. & Ayosu-Mateos, J.L. (2009). Mental health in adults with mild and moderate intellectual disabilities: The role of recent life events and traumatic experiences across the life span. *The Journal of Nervous and Mental Disease, 197*, 182–186.

McManus, S., Meltzer, H., Brugha, T., Bebbington, P. & Jenkins, R. (2009). *Adult psychiatric morbidity in England, 2007. Results of a household survey*. London: The Health & Social Care Information Centre.

Michael, J. (2008). *Healthcare for all: Report of the independent inquiry into access to healthcare for people with learning disabilities*. London: Department of Health.

Moss, S., Prosser, H., Costello, H., Simpson, N., Patel, P., Rowe, S. *et al.* (1998). Reliability and validity of the PAS-ADD Checklist for detecting psychiatric disorders in adults with intellectual disability. *Journal of Intellectual Disability Research, 42*, 173–183.

Nagel, B. & Leiper, R. (1999). A national survey of psychotherapy with people with learning disabilities. *Clinical Psychology Forum, 129*, 14–18.

Oathamshaw, S. & Haddock, G. (2006). Do people with intellectual disabilities and psychosis have the cognitive skills required to undertake cognitive behavioural therapy? *Journal of Applied Research in Intellectual Disabilities, 19*, 35–46.

Oliver, P.C., Piachaud, J., Done, D.J., Cooray, S.E. & Tyrer, P. (2003). Difficulties developing evidence-based approaches in learning disabilities. *Evidence-Based Mental Health, 6*, 37–39.

Prout, H.T. & Browning, B.K. (2011a). Psychotherapy with persons with intellectual disabilities: A review of effectiveness research. *Advances in Mental Health and Intellectual Disabilities, 5*, 53–59.

Prout, H.T. & Browning, B.K. (2011b). The effectiveness of psychotherapy for persons with intellectual disabilities. In R.J. Fletcher (Ed.) *Psychotherapy for individuals with intellectual disability* (pp.265–287). Kingston, NY: NADD Press.

Prout, R. & Nowak-Drabik, K.M. (2003). Psychotherapy with persons who have mental retardation: An evaluation of effectiveness. *American Journal of Mental Retardation, 108*, 82–93.

Reiss, S. (1990). Prevalence of dual diagnosis in community-based day programs in the Chicago metropolitan area. *American Journal of Mental Retardation, 94*, 578–585.

Reiss, S., Levitan, G.W. & McNally, R.J. (1982). Emotionally disturbed mentally retarded people: An underserved population. *The American Psychologist, 37*, 361–367.

Roy, A., Martin, D.M. & Wells, M.B. (1997). Health gain through screening – Mental health: Developing primary health care services for people with an intellectual disability. *Journal of Intellectual and Developmental Disability, 22*, 227–239.

Sams, K., Collins, S. & Reynolds, S. (2006). Cognitive therapy abilities in people with learning disabilities. *Journal of Applied Research in Intellectual Disabilities, 19*, 25–33.

Singleton, N., Bumpstead, R., O'Brien, M., Lee, A. & Meltzer, H. (2001). *Psychiatric morbidity among adults living in private households, 2000*. London: The Stationery Office.

Stenfert Kroese, B. (1998). Cognitive-behavioural therapy for people with learning disabilities. *Behavioural and Cognitive Psychotherapy, 26*, 315–322.

Stenfert Kroese, B., Dagnan, D. & Loumidis, K. (Eds.) (1997). *Cognitive-behaviour therapy for people with learning disabilities*. London: Routledge.

Stenfert Kroese, B. & Thomas, G. (2006). Treating chronic nightmares of sexual assault survivors with an intellectual disability – Two descriptive case studies. *Journal of Applied Research in Intellectual Disabilities, 19*, 75–80.

Sturmey, P. (2004). Cognitive therapy with people with intellectual disabilities: A selective review and critique. *Clinical Psychology and Psychotherapy, 11*, 222–232.

Sturmey, P. (2006). On some recent claims for the efficacy of cognitive therapy for people with intellectual disabilities. *Journal of Applied Research in Intellectual Disabilities, 19*, 109–117.

Sturmey, P., Taylor, J.L. & Lindsay, W.R. (2004). Research and development. In W.R. Lindsay, J.L. Taylor & P. Sturmey (Eds.) *Offenders with developmental disabilities* (pp.327–350). Chichester: Wiley.

Taylor, J.L. (2010). *CBT for adults with intellectual disabilities*. Paper presented to the NADD International Congress and Exhibit Show, Toronto, Canada, April 2010.

Taylor, J.L., Hatton, C., Dixon, L. & Douglas, C. (2004). Screening for psychiatric symptoms: PAS-ADD Checklist norms for adults with intellectual disabilities. *Journal of Intellectual Disability Research, 48*, 37–41.

Taylor, J.L., Lindsay, W.R. & Willner, P. (2008). CBT for people with intellectual disabilities: Emerging evidence, cognitive ability and IQ effects. *Behavioural and Cognitive Psychotherapy, 36*, 723–733.

Thornicroft, G. (2006) *Shunned: Discrimination against people with mental illness.* Oxford: Oxford University Press.

van den Hout, M., Arntz, A. & Merckelbach, H. (2000). Contributions of psychology to the understanding of psychiatric disorders. In M.G. Gelder, J.L. Lopez-Ibor & N.C. Andreasen (Eds.) *New Oxford textbook of psychiatry* (pp.277–292). Oxford: Oxford University Press.

Willner, P. (2004). Brief cognitive therapy of nightmares and post-traumatic ruminations in a man with learning disabilities. *The British Journal of Clinical Psychology, 43,* 459–464.

Willner, P. (2005). The effectiveness of psychotherapeutic interventions for people with learning disabilities: A critical overview. *Journal of Intellectual Disability Research, 49,* 73–85.

Willner, P. & Hatton, C. (Eds.) (2006). Special issue: Cognitive behavioural therapy. *Journal of Applied Research in Intellectual Disabilities, 19,* 1–129.

Chapter 2

Social and Psychological Factors as Determinants of Emotional and Behavioral Difficulties

Eric Emerson
Andrew J. Jahoda

Introduction

One of the main characteristics of the paradigms (biological, behavioral, cognitive, or psychotherapeutic) that dominate thinking about the emotional and behavioral needs of people with intellectual disability is their focus on identifying the proximal or immediate causes of distress. Whether the specific processes involve neurotransmitters, cognitive schema, or contingencies of reinforcement, there exists a common belief that the closer we can get to understanding the *immediate* causes of a phenomena, the more credible our explanations (and the greater our chances of designing effective interventions or supports). Of course, the identification of mediating pathways and immediate (or proximal) causes is critically important in developing a nuanced understanding of any phenomena and does open up the possibility of designing "downstream" interventions that seek to alter these proximal causes.

It is an error, however, to consider that evidence of mediation reduces the scientific significance or social importance of background (or distal) variables. Indeed, a radically different view is often taken in contemporary public health research where the focus is often on explicitly identifying the distal (or remote) causes of more proximal events, or, in the words of Professor Sir Michael Marmot, "the causes of the causes" (The Marmot Review, 2010; World Health Organization, 2008). Such an approach opens up the possibility of developing "upstream" interventions that address background (or distal) variables that may have a broad and pervasive impact on the mental health and well-being of populations.

In this chapter, we will argue that understanding and effectively responding to the emotional and behavioral needs of people with intellectual disabilities requires that we address the importance of both "upstream" *and* "downstream" determinants of the emotional and behavioral health of people with intellectual disabilities.

Psychological Therapies for Adults with Intellectual Disabilities, First Edition.
Edited by John L. Taylor, William R. Lindsay, Richard P. Hastings, and Chris Hatton.
© 2013 John Wiley & Sons, Ltd. Published 2013 by John Wiley & Sons, Ltd.

Upstream Determinants: Socioeconomic Position and Poverty

All societies are hierarchically structured, and in all societies, a person's position in the social hierarchy will shape his or her (and his or her children's) access to and control over key resources that play an important role in determining health and well-being (Graham, 2007; The Marmot Review, 2010; World Health Organization, 2008). People occupying lower socioeconomic positions may have difficulty accessing resources that are necessary to enable them to live lives that are considered appropriate or decent within their society. That is, they experience *poverty* (Graham, 2007; Lister, 2004; Spicker, 2007). Of course, societies differ in many important ways. Culture and economic development both shape what may be considered a standard of living consistent with human dignity and social decency. Key social institutions (e.g., educational and legal systems) determine the extent of social mobility that is possible (Graham, 2007; National Equality Panel, 2010; Nunn *et al.*, 2007). Some societies are more hierarchical than others leading to greater or lesser levels of inequality (Wilkinson, 2005; Wilkinson & Pickett, 2009).

Of course, in all societies, families supporting a child with intellectual or developmental disabilities are located at all points across the social hierarchy. They are, however, significantly more likely than other families to be located in lower socioeconomic positions and to experience poverty (Chapman *et al.*, 2008; Durkin, 2002; Emerson, 2007, 2012; Emerson *et al.*, 2009; Leonard & Wen, 2002). The strength of association between socioeconomic position and intellectual and developmental disabilities does vary significantly by type and severity of disability. Stronger associations are found as the severity of intellectual disability *decreases*, with much weaker or no association between socioeconomic position and the prevalence of autistic spectrum disorder or profound multiple intellectual disability (Baird *et al.*, 2006; Chapman *et al.*, 2008; Emerson, 2012). Thus, for some people with intellectual or developmental disabilities (e.g., autistic spectrum disorders, profound multiple intellectual disability), rates of exposure to low socioeconomic position or poverty in childhood will be similar to that in the wider population. For others, and especially for children with less severe intellectual disabilities, rates of exposure will be considerably greater than in the wider population.

Why is this important? There now exists a wealth of evidence documenting (in the general population) the negative impact of exposure to low socioeconomic position and/or poverty *especially in childhood* on behavioral health and well-being (Cohen *et al.*, 2010; Graham, 2007; Hertzman & Boyce, 2010; Shonkoff, 2010; Shonkoff *et al.*, 2009; World Health Organization, 2008). There is also considerable evidence to suggest that exposure to low socioeconomic position and/or poverty (and factors associated with low socioeconomic position and/or poverty) is related to the development *and persistence* of some emotional and behavioral difficulties in children and adults (Broidy *et al.*, 2003; Jenkins, 2008; Maughan *et al.*, 2004; Tremblay, 2000, 2006; Tremblay *et al.*, 2004).

Three important themes emerge from these literatures; in that the negative psychological and behavioral outcomes associated with low socioeconomic position or poverty:

- are related to the duration, depth, and breadth of exposure (Ackerman *et al.*, 2004; Evans & Kim, 2010; Jarjoura *et al.*, 2002; Lynch *et al.*, 1997; McLeod & Shanahan, 1996; Petterson & Albers, 2004);
- are mediated through a multiplicity of pathways including, but not limited to, increased risk of exposure to a range of material and psychosocial hazards such as poorer educational and occupational opportunities, adverse life events, poorer health and welfare services, and poorer quality neighborhoods (Bradley *et al.*, 2001; Cohen *et al.*, 2010; Evans & Kantrowitz, 2002; Evans & Kim, 2010; Kawachi & Berkman, 2003). Many of these pathways, however, are rooted in family functioning and parenting practices (Bradley & Corwyn, 2002; Conger & Donnellan, 2007; Linver *et al.*, 2002); and
- may be moderated by a range of factors. Put simply, some children (and their families) are more resilient than others.

Indeed, there exists a wide-ranging and extensive literature on the issues of vulnerability and resilience in the face of adversity (Grant *et al.*, 2006; Haskett *et al.*, 2006; Luthar, 2006; Luthar & Brown, 2007; Rutter, 2000; Sandberg & Rutter, 2008; Schoon, 2006). A key message from this literature is that resilient functioning in children and young people is likely to reflect the complex interplay between individual characteristics and attributes (e.g., temperament, intelligence, personality, coping style, religiosity), their relationships with and characteristics of their families (e.g., supportive parenting style, family cohesion), and their relationships with and characteristics of the wider social context in which they are living (e.g., sense of belongingness to the local community, quality of educational and leisure services, neighborhood safety). It is notable that many of the factors associated with resilient functioning are also related to socioeconomic position and/or poverty. As a result, the impact of low socioeconomic position/poverty on well-being is likely to operate through both increasing the cumulative risk of exposure to a variety of material and psychosocial hazards *and* by undermining the resilience of the person so exposed.

Socioeconomic position, poverty, and the well-being of people with intellectual or developmental disabilities

In the preceding section, we summarized evidence indicating that (1) exposure to low socioeconomic position and/or poverty in childhood has a pervasive negative impact on behavioral health and well-being; and (2) people with intellectual disabilities are more likely than their nondisabled peers to be exposed to low socioeconomic position and/or poverty in childhood. Unless people with intellectual disabilities are somehow immune to the types of process that link socioeconomic position/poverty to health and well-being in the general population, we should expect exposure to low socioeconomic position/poverty to be at least as important in understanding the well-being of people with intellectual disabilities as it is for understanding the well-being of other people. Unsurprisingly, there is no evidence to suggest that such immunity exists (Emerson & Hatton, 2007b, 2010). While some studies have suggested that the form of the relationship between breadth of exposure to socioeconomic risk and the prevalence of mental health problems is very similar for children

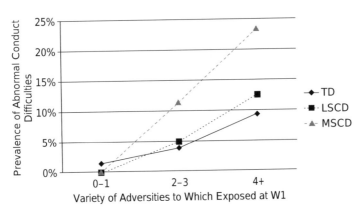

Figure 2.1 Exposure to environmental risk at age 4/5 and the prevalence of persistent conduct difficulties at ages 4/5, 6/7, and 8/9 for children with and without cognitive delay at age 4/5. TD, "typically developing"; LSCD, less severe cognitive delay; MSCD, more severe cognitive delay.

with and without intellectual disabilities (Emerson & Hatton, 2007b), others have suggested that children with intellectual disability may be *less resilient* when exposed to higher levels of adversity (Emerson *et al.*, 2011). For example, Figure 2.1 shows the prevalence of *persistent* conduct difficulties (significant levels of conduct difficulties being shown at ages 4/5, 6/7, and 8/9) among a nationally representative sample of Australian children with and without borderline or intellectual disability (estimated IQ < 85) exposed to varying levels of adversity at age 4/5. Under conditions of no or low adversity, there is no difference at all between the two groups. As levels of adversity increase, so does the gap between children with and without borderline or intellectual disability. What is quite startling in these data is the difference in prevalence rates across differing levels of exposure to social and economic adversity. While persistent conduct difficulties were shown by less than 2 percent of children exposed to no or just one adversity, they are shown by 24 percent of children with "more severe" cognitive delay (estimated IQ < 78) when exposed to four or more adversities (Emerson *et al.*, 2011).

If exposure to low socioeconomic position and/or poverty has a pervasive detrimental impact on well-being, *and* if people with intellectual disabilities are more likely to be exposed to such circumstances, it is hardly rocket science to suggest that the poorer emotional and behavioral well-being of people with intellectual disabilities may, *in part*, be attributable to their poorer socioeconomic position. Indeed, recent research suggests that increased exposure to low socioeconomic position/poverty may account for (1) 20–50 percent of the increased risk for poorer health and mental health among two nationally representative cohorts of British children and adolescents with intellectual disabilities (Emerson & Hatton, 2007a, 2007b, 2007c); (2) 29–43 percent of the increased risk for conduct difficulties and 36–43 percent of the increased risk for peer problems among a nationally representative cohort of six- to seven-year-old Australian children with intellectual disabilities or borderline intellectual functioning (Emerson *et al.*, 2010); (3) a significant proportion of increased rates of self-reported antisocial behavior among adolescents with intellectual disability

(Dickinson *et al.*, 2007); and (4) 32 percent of the increased risk for conduct difficulties and 27 percent of the increased risk for peer problems among a nationally representative cohort of three-year-old British children with developmental delay (Emerson & Einfeld, 2010). These results also provide evidence that exposure to poverty or low socioeconomic position accounts for part of the variation in well-being *among* people with intellectual disabilities (Emerson, 2003b; Emerson & Hatton, 2007b, 2008a, 2008b; Emerson, Robertson *et al.*, 2005; Emerson et al., 2007; Koskentausta *et al.*, 2006).

As noted above, however, the effects of low socioeconomic position or poverty on the well-being of people with intellectual disabilities are likely to be mediated through a number of distinct pathways that may themselves be linked to (but not unique to) low socioeconomic position. Current evidence suggests that emotional or behavioral difficulties in people with intellectual disabilities may be associated with the following potential mediating pathways:

- cumulative exposure to acute life stresses or adverse "life events" (Coe *et al.*, 1999; Cooper *et al.*, 2007; Esbensen & Benson, 2006; Hamilton *et al.*, 2005; Hastings *et al.*, 2004; Hatton & Emerson, 2004; Hulbert-Williams & Hastings, 2008; Monaghan & Soni, 1992; Owen *et al.*, 2004);
- exposure to specific life events such as abuse (Beail & Warden, 1995; Murphy *et al.*, 2007; Sequeira *et al.*, 2003), parental death (Bonell-Pascual *et al.*, 1999; Esbensen *et al.*, 2008), and placement outside the home (Esbensen *et al.*, 2008);
- poorer family functioning (Chadwick *et al.*, 2008; Emerson, 2003b; Hardan & Sahl, 1997; Wallander *et al.*, 2006); and
- being brought up by a single parent (Dekker & Koot, 2003; Emerson, 2003a; Hardan & Sahl, 1997; Koskentausta *et al.*, 2006).

Upstream Determinants: Disablism

Social position is not, of course, solely determined by socioeconomic factors. It is also determined by a range of factors associated with pervasive inequalities (e.g., ethnicity, gender, age, disability status). Indeed, people with intellectual disabilities are at risk of experiencing systemic and overt discrimination associated with their disability (disablism). The impact of disability discrimination on health and well-being is likely to be mediated by multiple processes (Emerson & Baines, 2010):

- First, the existence of systemic or institutionalized disablism may prevent people with intellectual disabilities gaining access to timely, appropriate, and effective health and mental health care (Disability Rights Commission, 2006; Michael, 2008).
- Second, discriminatory systems and practices contribute to the social exclusion of people with intellectual disabilities. As a result, they are more likely than their peers to be exposed to living conditions (poverty, unemployment, social adversity, low control, low status, poor housing) associated with poor health outcomes (Graham, 2007; The Marmot Review, 2010).
- Finally, direct exposure to disablism (e.g., through bullying or hate crime) is likely to have a negative impact on the person's mental and physical health (Emerson, 2010; Pascoe & Richman, 2009; Sherry, 2010).

A parallel may be drawn here with the research investigating the determinants of the health inequalities experienced by people from minority ethnic groups. Here, a growing body of research has highlighted the association between exposure to overt acts of racism and poorer health outcomes (Dressler *et al.*, 2005; Gee *et al.*, 2009; Krieger, 1999; Mays *et al.*, 2007; Myers, 2009; Nazroo, 2003; Pascoe & Richman, 2009; Williams & Mohammed, 2009). Exposure to overt acts of *disablism* (discrimination on the basis of disability) is a relatively common experience for many people with intellectual (and other) disabilities (Emerson, Malam *et al.*, 2005; Mencap, 2007; Norwich & Kelly, 2004; Sheard *et al.*, 2001; White *et al.*, 2003; Williams *et al.*, 2008) and may plausibly be related to poorer health outcomes (Emerson, 2010).

Downstream Determinants: Psychological Factors as Mediating and Moderating Processes

Robert Edgerton published a book of case studies concerning individuals he had followed up since they had been discharged from an institution in California in the 1960s (Edgerton & Ward, 1991). A striking description was given of one individual who was desperately poor, with limited informal support or access to even basic health care. Yet the authors commented on how remarkably positive this man remained, despite his dreadful social circumstances. This contrasts with accounts by Reiss and Benson (1984) of people with learning disabilities who attended their outpatient mental health clinic, and expressed an acute awareness of the discrimination they faced and a sense of hopelessness about their futures. These very different outcomes raise questions about issues of resilience and vulnerability, and the individual and interpersonal processes that might mediate or moderate the impact of powerful social factors like deprivation and disablism.

The historical view was that people with intellectual disabilities lacked awareness of their social circumstances. An assumed lack of insight was one of the reasons that there was a reluctance to acknowledge that people with intellectual disabilities could become depressed, and this diagnosis remained a matter of debate up until the 1980s (McBrien, 2003). However, there is a large body of evidence showing that people with mild to moderate intellectual disabilities *are* aware of their social circumstances and, in particular, their stigmatized status (Beart *et al.*, 2005; Cooney *et al.*, 2006; Reiss & Benson, 1984). This leads one to question how awareness of their social status might affect them. Long before current symbolic interactionist theories of the self were developed, Adam Smith (1759/2002) pointed to the inextricable link between the social and personal sense of self:

> Were it possible that a human creature could grow up to manhood in a solitary place, without any communication with his one species, he could no more think of his own character or the propriety or demerits of his sentiments and conduct, or the beauty of his own mind, than of the beauty or deformity of his own face. All these are objects which he cannot easily see . . . and with regard to which he is provided with no mirror which can present them to his view. Bring him into society, and he is immediately provided with the mirror he wanted before. (p. 129)

Internalizing disablist stereotypes

Discriminatory treatment takes many forms. Recent high-profile examples of hate crimes in the United Kingdom, leading to the death or serious injury of people with intellectual disabilities, are indicative of a much wider picture of social rejection and bullying (Ali *et al.*, 2008; Sherry, 2010). However, the effects of discriminatory treatment can be more subtle, for example, through being overprotected by families seeking to shelter their offspring from harm.

If social and interpersonal exchanges are a means by which people learn who they are, then there is the possibility that individuals with mild intellectual disabilities might internalize stigmatized views about themselves. Increased awareness of stigma has been shown to be associated with low self-esteem and a tendency for young people with intellectual disabilities to compare themselves negatively with others (Szivos-Bach, 1993). Consistent with these findings, Dagnan and Sandhu (1999) also reported that negative social comparison was associated with greater levels of depression and poor self-esteem. A further exploration of the association between social cognitive factors and depression examined the links between experience of stigma, core evaluative beliefs about self, and the nature of social comparisons made by 39 individuals with intellectual disabilities (Dagnan & Waring, 2004). Regression analyses found links between the participants' experience of stigma, the nature of their core evaluative beliefs about themselves, and the inferences that they made when comparing themselves with others. Although the analyses could not prove a causal link, the implication was that people who internalized negative evaluations of self were likely to make negative social comparisons. In turn, these social comparisons reinforced the individuals' poor self-evaluations. It is interesting to note that there is growing evidence from the study of health inequalities in the general population that psychosocial factors, such as having a sense of control, mastery, and self-esteem, appear to be important mediators of the impact of socioeconomic position of physical health (Matthews *et al.*, 2010).

Adam Smith's quote from 1790 also implies that internalizing a social sense of self is a developmental process. There is a body of developmental work that provides powerful evidence about the possible impact of the early social experience of people with mild intellectual disabilities, such as frequent experience of failure, on how they think and behave (Zigler *et al.*, 2002). Surprisingly, little consideration has been given to the possible clinical relevance of this work. Zigler described how such negative experience can shape the "personality" of children with intellectual disabilities. However, these "personality" dimensions might equally be viewed as reflecting underlying schema or the beliefs that people hold about themselves and their world. Children with mild disabilities are thought to differ from their nondisabled peers on the following dimensions: (1) a greater "motivation" to depend on a "supportive adult"; (2) a sense of uneasiness about meeting new adults; (3) less optimism about succeeding with new challenges; (4) being more likely to rely on others to help them solve problems; and (5) obtaining less satisfaction from addressing and finding solutions to difficulties.

An awareness of difference might result in people being aware of their stigmatized status and vigilant to social threats. Hartley and McLean found that depressed individuals with intellectual disabilities reported a greater number of stressful social interactions than nondepressed individuals and produced more global, negative, and internal attributions about the cause of these difficult social situations (Hartley & Maclean, 2009). It is not hard to imagine that coming to see oneself as stupid or someone who is not valued, could increase the social stresses and make it more likely that one might blame oneself for interpersonal difficulties, thereby increasing the likelihood of low mood and depression. Research concerning frequent aggression and people with intellectual disabilities also suggests that it can be people's awareness of their social position, rather than a lack of social insight, that contributes to their sensitivity to threat, leading to increased conflict (Jahoda *et al.*, 2006a, 2006b).

Resilience

As self-aware individuals, people with mild learning disabilities are not merely shaped by their social circumstances but also play an active role in negotiating their identities and coping with environmental challenges. Just as internalizing disablist stereotypes might negatively influence people's attributions, having a relatively positive sense of self or self-esteem might help to counteract the impact of stigma. For example, Finlay and Lyons (2000) interviewed people from learning disability day services and found that the participants did not talk about themselves in relation to their intellectual disabilities; rather, they used downward social comparisons to emphasize their positive identities. Their findings are consistent with those found for other stigmatized groups, where people tend to downplay their weaknesses and emphasize their strengths (Crocker & Major, 1989). This would constitute what social identity theory designates as social creativity (Tajfel & Turner, 1979), but it can also be seen as a genuine disagreement with the dominant comparisons that dictate a stigmatized status. Internalizing the same social norms through the process of socialization means that individuals with intellectual disabilities will also have a sense of what is fair. In a study examining the self-perceptions of individuals with mild intellectual disabilities, the participants did not deny their impairments in relation to particular difficulties such as with reading or writing. However, they rejected discriminatory views of them as inferior persons (Jahoda *et al.*, 2010).

Michael Marmot pointed out that life skills and cognitive abilities play an important part in determining health and social outcomes (The Marmot Review, 2010). Consequently, "distal" social and economic factors are likely to have a more pronounced impact on the well-being of people with intellectual disabilities. However, it is not only ability that allows one to achieve personal goals, but also having sufficient autonomy and self-belief to work toward those goals. Wehmeyer and Garner found that a sense of self-determination was not necessarily associated with IQ scores. Therefore, being more self-determined might help individuals to pursue areas of interest or activities that are intrinsically rewarding or satisfying. It might also help people in their efforts to obtain employment (Wehmeyer & Garner, 2003), or to develop intimate and supportive relationships, also known to be protective to people's well-being (Lunsky, 2003). Resilience relates not only to internal individual strengths or processes, but also to people's reflections on the success of their actions in the world (Markova, 1987).

A personal sense of success is also linked to how others view our actions. For example, an individual's achievements, however modest, may mean little unless they are recognized as such by others (Jahoda *et al.*, 2010). Having a range of valued social roles or positions is thought to protect against psychological distress. It means that failure or difficulty in one area of a person's life is less likely to have a devastating impact on their self-esteem, if they can continue to reflect positively about other roles they fulfill (Linville, 1987). However, people's intellectual impairments are likely to mean that even as they move into adulthood, they will continue to rely on the support of others to achieve personal goals such as employment. Consequently, as the Marmot report eloquently states, "achieving individual empowerment requires social action."

Conclusions

This chapter has largely been concerned with "upstream factors" that have a detrimental effect on mental health, including poverty and social marginalization. Those reading this book for ideas about therapeutic interventions might be asking themselves about the relevance of these wider social influences. However, we would contest that an awareness of these issues has a number of practical implications for therapeutic work.

In the first instance, therapists need to be careful that their practices do not increase health inequalities and further disadvantage individuals with intellectual disabilities who are harder to reach and support. For example, it might be a mistake to move toward more strictly clinic-based approaches while therapeutic colleagues working in adult mental health move toward models that reach out to individuals who are more deprived or marginalized. In addition, group-based parent training programs have been shown to be less effective for poorer and single-parent families (Lundahl *et al.*, 2006). Taking seriously these broader social factors means holding onto established systemic and multidisciplinary approaches. Services for people with intellectual disabilities were among the first in the United Kingdom to adopt collaborative working across health and social care settings.

Awareness of "upstream" social determinants of psychological distress could also influence the content of therapists' interventions. Therapeutic work might address the impact of some kinds of social adversity, such as being socially marginalized or stigmatized (Jahoda *et al.*, 2009). While it would be unrealistic to expect therapists to change the social odds stacked against many of the individuals they work with, therapists need to acknowledge their existence in order to give the clients that they work with a better chance of beating them.

Recognizing the developmental impact of social factors on the well-being of people with intellectual disabilities should also cause pause for thought in terms of the most effective use of therapeutic resources. The emphasis on competency-based models in therapeutic interventions means that the more skilled the therapist, the more "complex" the presentations they are thought able to deal with. In other words, the energies of the most skilled practitioners are drawn toward crisis interventions at an individual level. This might go some way to explaining an almost complete absence of work concerning the resilience of people with intellectual disabilities. Investing in work to foster resilience and well-being among young people who face social adversity requires not only organizational change, but also a will from therapists to tackle the social causes of psychological distress.

References

Ackerman, B.P., Brown, E.D. & Izard, C.E. (2004). The relations between persistent poverty and contextual risk and children's behavior in elementary school. *Developmental Psychology, 40*(3), 367–377.

Ali, I., Strydom, A., Hassiotis, A., Willima, R. & King, M. (2008). A measure of perceived stigma in people with intellectual disability. *The British Journal of Psychiatry, 193,* 410–415.

Baird, G., Simonoff, E., Pickles, A., Chandler, S., Loucas, T., Meldrum, D. *et al.* (2006). Prevalence of disorders of the autism spectrum in a population cohort of children in South Thames: The Special Needs and Autism Project (SNAP). *Lancet, 368,* 210–215.

Beail, N. & Warden, S. (1995). Sexual abuse of adults with learning disabilities. *Journal of Intellectual Disability Research, 39,* 382–387.

Beart, S., Hardy, G. & Buchan, L. (2005). How people with intellectual disabilities view their social identity: A review of the literature. *Journal of Applied Research in Intellectual Disabilities, 18,* 47–56.

Bonell-Pascual, E., Huline-Dickens, S., Hollins, S., Esterhuyzen, A., Sedgwick, P. & Abdel-noor, A. (1999). Bereavement and grief in adults with learning disabilities: A follow-up study. *The British Journal of Psychiatry, 175,* 348–350.

Bradley, R.H. & Corwyn, R.F. (2002). Socioeconomic status and child development. *Annual Review of Psychology, 53,* 371–399.

Bradley, R.H., Corwyn, R.F., McAdoo, H.P. & Garcıa, C.C. (2001). The home environments of children in the United States: Part I. Variations by age, ethnicity, and poverty status. *Child Development, 72,* 1844–1867.

Broidy, L.M., Nagin, D.S., Tremblay, R.E., Bates, J.E., Brame, B. & Dodge, K. (2003). Developmental trajectories of childhood disruptive behaviours and adolescent delinquency: A six site, cross national study. *Developmental Psychology, 39,* 222–245.

Chadwick, O., Kusel, Y. & Cuddy, M. (2008). Factors associated with the risk of behaviour problems in adolescents with severe intellectual disabilities. *Journal of Intellectual Disability Research, 52,* 864–876.

Chapman, D., Scott, K. & Stanton-Chapman, T. (2008). Public health approach to the study of mental retardation. *American Journal of Mental Retardation, 113*(2), 102–116.

Coe, D.A., Matson, J.L., Russell, D.W., Slifer, K.J., Capone, G. & Baglio, C. (1999). Behavior problems of children with Down syndrome and life events. *Journal of Autism and Developmental Disorders, 29,* 149–156.

Cohen, S., Janicki-Deverts, D., Chen, E. & Matthews, K.A. (2010). Childhood socioeconomic status and adult health. *Annals of the New York Academy of Sciences, 1186,* 37–55.

Conger, R.D. & Donnellan, M.B. (2007). An interactionist perspective on the socioeconomic context of human development. *Annual Review of Psychology, 58,* 175–199.

Cooney, G., Jahoda, A., Gumley, A. & Knott, F. (2006). Young people with learning disabilities attending mainstream and segregated schooling: Perceived stigma, social comparisons and future aspirations. *Journal of Intellectual Disability Research, 50,* 432–445.

Cooper, S.A., Smiley, E., Finlayson, J., Jackson, A., Allan, L., Williamson, A. *et al.* (2007). The prevalence, incidence and factors predictive of mental ill-health in adults with profound intellectual disabilities. *Journal of Applied Research in Intellectual Disabilities,* 20, 493–501.

Crocker, J. & Major, B. (1989). Social stigma and self-esteem: The self-protective properties of stigma. *Psychological Review, 96*, 608–630.

Dagnan, D. & Sandhu, S. (1999). Social comparison, self-esteem and depression in people with intellectual disability. *Journal of Intellectual Disability Research, 43*, 372–379.

Dagnan, D. & Waring, M. (2004). Linking stigma to psychological distress: A social-cognitive model of the experience of people with learning disabilities. *Clinical Psychology & Psychotherapy, 11*, 247–254.

Dekker, M.C. & Koot, H.M. (2003). DSM-IV disorders in children with borderline to moderate intellectual disability. II: Child and family factors. *Journal of the American Academy of Child and Adolescent Psychiatry, 42*(8), 923–931.

Dickinson, H., Parkinson, K., Ravens-Sieberer, U., Schirripa, G., Thyen, U., Arnaud, C. *et al.* (2007). Self-reported quality of life of 8-12-year-old children with cerebral palsy: A cross-sectional European study. *Lancet, 369*, 2171–2178.

Disability Rights Commission (2006). *Equal treatment – Closing the gap.* London: Disability Rights Commission.

Dressler, W.W., Oths, K.S. & Gravlee, C. (2005). Race and ethnicity in public health research: Models to explain health disparities. *Annual Review of Anthropology, 34*, 231–252.

Durkin, M. (2002). The epidemiology of developmental disabilities in low-income countries. *Mental Retardation & Developmental Disabilities Research Reviews, 8*(3), 206–211.

Edgerton, R.B. & Ward, T.M. (1991). I gotta put my foot down. In R.B. Edgerton & M.A. Gaston (Eds.) *I've seen it all! Lives of older persons with mental retardation in the community.* Baltimore, MD: Paul Brookes.

Emerson, E. (2003a). Mothers of children and adolescents with intellectual disability: Social and economic situation, mental health status, and the self-assessed social and psychological impact of the child's difficulties. *Journal of Intellectual Disability Research, 47*(Pt 4–5), 385–399.

Emerson, E. (2003b). Prevalence of psychiatric disorders in children and adolescents with and without intellectual disability. *Journal of Intellectual Disability Research, 47*(Pt 1), 51–58.

Emerson, E. (2007). Poverty and people with intellectual disability. *Mental Retardation and Developmental Disabilities Research Reviews, 13*, 107–113.

Emerson, E. (2010). Self-reported exposure to disablism is associated with poorer self-reported health and well-being among adults with intellectual disabilities in England: Cross sectional survey. *Public Health, 124*, 682–689.

Emerson, E. (2012). Household deprivation, neighbourhood deprivation, ethnicity and the prevalence of intellectual and developmental disabilities. *Journal of Epidemiology and Community Health, 66*, 218–224.

Emerson, E. & Baines, S. (2010). *Health inequalities and people with learning disabilities in the UK: 2010.* Durham, NC: Improving Health & Lives: Learning Disabilities Observatory.

Emerson, E. & Einfeld, S. (2010). Emotional and behavioural difficulties in young children with and without developmental delay: A bi-national perspective. *Journal of Child Psychology and Psychiatry, and Allied Disciplines, 55*, 583–593.

Emerson, E., Einfeld, S. & Stancliffe, R. (2010). The mental health of young Australian children with intellectual disabilities or borderline intellectual functioning. *Social Psychiatry and Psychiatric Epidemiology, 45*, 579–587.

Emerson, E., Einfeld, S. & Stancliffe, R. (2011). Predictors of the persistence of conduct difficulties in children with borderline or intellectual disabilities. *Journal of Child Psychology and Psychiatry, and Allied Disciplines, 52*(11), 1184–1194.

Emerson, E., Graham, H., McCulloch, A., Blacher, J., Hatton, C. & Llewellyn, G. (2009). The social context of parenting three year old children with developmental delay in the UK. *Child: Care, Health & Development, 35*(1), 63–70.

Emerson, E. & Hatton, C. (2007a). Poverty, socio-economic position, social capital and the health of children and adolescents with intellectual disabilities in Britain: A replication. *Journal of Intellectual Disability Research, 51*(11), 866–874.

Emerson, E. & Hatton, C. (2007b). The mental health of children and adolescents with intellectual disabilities in Britain. *The British Journal of Psychiatry, 191*, 493–499.

Emerson, E. & Hatton, C. (2007c). The contribution of socio-economic position to the health inequalities faced by children and adolescents with intellectual disabilities in Britain. *American Journal of Mental Retardation, 112*(2), 140–150.

Emerson, E. & Hatton, C. (2008a). The self-reported well-being of women and men with intellectual disabilities in England. *American Journal of Mental Retardation, 113*(2), 143–155.

Emerson, E. & Hatton, C. (2008b). Socioeconomic disadvantage, social participation and networks and the self-rated health of English men and women with mild and moderate intellectual disabilities: Cross sectional survey. *European Journal of Public Health, 18*, 31–37.

Emerson, E. & Hatton, C. (2010). Socio-economic position, poverty and family research. In L.M. Glidden & M.M. Seltzer (Eds.) *On families: International review of research on mental retardation.* New York: Academic Press.

Emerson, E., Malam, S., Davies, I. & Spencer, K. (2005). *Adults with learning difficulties in England 2003/4.* Leeds: Health & Social Care Information Centre.

Emerson, E., Robertson, J. & Wood, J. (2005). The mental health needs of children and adolescents with intellectual disabilities in an urban conurbation. *Journal of Intellectual Disability Research, 49*, 16–24.

Emerson, E., Robertson, J. & Wood, J. (2007). The association between area-level indicators of social deprivation and the emotional and behavioural needs of black and South Asian children with intellectual disabilities in a deprived urban environment. *Journal of Applied Research in Intellectual Disabilities, 20*, 420–429.

Esbensen, A.J. & Benson, B.A. (2006). A prospective analysis of life events, problem behaviours and depression in adults with intellectual disability. *Journal of Intellectual Disability Research, 50*, 248–258.

Esbensen, A.J., Seltzer, M.M. & Krauss, M.W. (2008). Stability and change in health, functional abilities and behavior problems among adults with and without Down syndrome. *American Journal of Mental Retardation, 113*, 263–277.

Evans, G.W. & Kantrowitz, E. (2002). Socioeconomic status and health: The potential role of environmental risk exposure. *Annual Review of Public Health, 23*, 303–331.

Evans, G.W. & Kim, P. (2010). Multiple risk exposure as a potential explanatory mechanism for the socio-economic status-health gradient. *Annals of the New York Academy of Sciences, 1186*, 174–189.

Finlay, W.M. & Lyons, E. (2000). Social categorisations, social comparisons and stigma: Presentations of self in people with learning difficulties. *The British Journal of Social Psychology, 39*, 129–146.

Gee, G.C., Ro, A., Shariff-Marco, S. & Chae, D. (2009). Racial discrimination and health among Asian Americans: Evidence, assessment, and directions for future research. *Epidemiologic Reviews, 31*, 130–151.

Graham, H. (2007). *Unequal lives: Health and socioeconomic inequalities.* Maidenhead: Open University Press.

Grant, K.E., Compas, B.E., Thurm, A.E., McMahon, S.D., Gipson, P.Y., Campbell, A.J. *et al.* (2006). Stressors and child and adolescent psychopathology: Evidence of moderating and mediating effects. *Clinical Psychology Review, 26,* 257–283.

Hamilton, D., Sutherland, G. & Iacono, T. (2005). Further examination of relationships between life events and psychiatric symptoms in adults with intellectual disability. *Journal of Intellectual Disability Research, 49,* 839–844.

Hardan, A. & Sahl, R. (1997). Psychopathology in children and adolescents with developmental disorders. *Research in Developmental Disabilities, 18,* 369–382.

Hartley, S.L. & Maclean, W.E. (2009). Stressful social interactions experienced by adults with mild intellectual disability. *American Journal on Intellectual and Developmental Disabilities, 114,* 71–84.

Haskett, M.E., Nears, K., Ward, C.A. & McPherson, A.V. (2006). Diversity in adjustment of maltreated children: Factors associated with resilient functioning. *Clinical Psychology Review, 26,* 796–812.

Hastings, R.P., Hatton, C., Taylor, J.L. & Maddison, C. (2004). Life events and psychiatric symptoms in adults with intellectual disabilities. *Journal of Intellectual Disability Research, 48,* 42–46.

Hatton, C. & Emerson, E. (2004). The relationship between life events and psychopathology amongst children with intellectual disabilities. *Journal of Applied Research in Intellectual Disabilities, 17*(2), 109–118.

Hertzman, C. & Boyce, T. (2010). How experience gets under the skin to create gradients in developmental health. *Annual Review of Public Health, 31,* 329–347.

Hulbert-Williams, L. & Hastings, R.P. (2008). Life events as a risk factor for psychological problems in individuals with intellectual disabilities: A critical review. *Journal of Intellectual Disability Research, 52,* 883–895.

Jahoda, A., Dagnan, D., Stenfert Kroese, B., Pert, C. & Trower, P. (2009). Cognitive behavioural therapy: From face to face interaction to a broader contextual understanding of change. *Journal of Intellectual Disability Research, 53,* 758–771.

Jahoda, A., Pert, C. & Trower, P. (2006a). Frequent aggression and attribution of hostile intent in people with mild to moderate mental retardation: An empirical investigation. *American Journal of Mental Retardation, 111,* 90–99.

Jahoda, A., Pert, C. & Trower, P. (2006b). Socioemotional understanding and frequent aggression in people with mild to moderate intellectual disabilities. *American Journal of Mental Retardation, 111,* 77–89.

Jahoda, A., Wilson, A. & Stalker, K. (2010). Living with stigma and the self-perceptions of people with mild intellectual disabilities. *The Journal of Social Issues, 66,* 521–534.

Jarjoura, G.R., Triplett, R.A. & Brinker, G.P. (2002). Growing up poor: Examining the link between persistent childhood poverty and delinquency. *Journal of Quantitative Criminology, 18*(2), 159–187.

Jenkins, J. (2008). Psychosocial adversity and resilience. In M. Rutter, D. Bishop, D. Pine, S. Scott, J. Stevenson, E. Taylor *et al.* (Eds.) *Rutter's child and adolescent psychiatry* (5th edn). Oxford: Blackwell.

Kawachi, I. & Berkman, L.F. (2003). *Neighborhoods and health.* Oxford: Oxford University Press.

Koskentausta, T., Iivanainen, M. & Almqvist, F. (2006). Risk factors for psychiatric disturbance in children with intellectual disability. *Journal of Intellectual Disability Research, 51,* 43–53.

Krieger, N. (1999). Embodying inequality: A review of concepts, measures, and methods for studying health consequences of discrimination. *International Journal of Health Services, 29,* 295–252.

Leonard, H. & Wen, X. (2002). The epidemiology of mental retardation: Challenges and opportunities in the new millennium. *Mental Retardation and Developmental Disabilities Research Reviews, 8,* 117–134.

Linver, M.R., Brooks-Gunn, J. & Kohen, D.E. (2002). Family processes as pathways from income to young children's development. *Developmental Psychology, 38*(5), 719–743.

Linville, P.W. (1987). Self-complexity as a cognitive buffer against stress-related illness and depression. *Journal of Personality and Social Psychology, 52,* 663–676.

Lister, R. (2004). *Poverty.* Cambridge, UK: Polity Press.

Lundahl, B., Risser, H.J. & Lovejoy, M.C. (2006). A meta-analysis of parent training: Moderators and follow-up effects. *Clinical Psychology Review, 26,* 86–104.

Lunsky, Y. (2003). Depressive symptoms in intellectual disability: Does gender play a role? *Journal of Intellectual Disability Research, 47,* 417–427.

Luthar, S.S. (2006). Resilience in development: A synthesis of research across five decades. In D. Cicchetti & D.J. Cohen (Eds.) *Developmental psychopathology, Vol. 3: Risk, disorder, and adaptation.* Hoboken, NJ: John Wiley & Sons.

Luthar, S.S. & Brown, P.J. (2007). Maximizing resilience through diverse levels of inquiry: Prevailing paradigms, possibilities, and priorities for the future. *Development and Psychopathology, 19,* 931–955.

Lynch, J.W., Kaplan, G.A. & Shema, S.J. (1997). Cumulative impact of sustained economic hardship on physical, cognitive, psychological, and social functioning. *The New England Journal of Medicine, 337*(26), 1889–1895.

Markova, I. (1987). *Human awareness.* London: Hutchinson.

Matthews, K.A., Gallo, L.C. & Taylor, S.E. (2010). Are psychosocial factors mediators of socioeconomic status and health connections? A progress report and blueprint for the future. *Annals of the New York Academy of Sciences, 1186,* 146–173.

Maughan, B., Rowe, R., Messer, J., Goodman, R. & Meltzer, H. (2004). Conduct disorder and oppositional defiant disorder in a national sample: Developmental epidemiology. *Journal of Child Psychology and Psychiatry, and Allied Disciplines, 45,* 609–621.

Mays, V.M., Cochran, S.D. & Barnes, N.W. (2007). Race, race-based discrimination, and health outcomes among African Americans. *Annual Review of Psychology, 58,* 201–225.

McBrien, J.A. (2003). Assessment and diagnosis of depression in people with intellectual disability. *Journal of Intellectual Disability Research, 47,* 1–13.

McLeod, J.D. & Shanahan, M.J. (1996). Trajectories of poverty and children's mental health. *Journal of Health and Social Behavior, 37,* 207–220.

Mencap (2007). *Bullying wrecks lives: The experiences of children and young people with a learning disability.* London: Mencap.

Michael, J. (2008). *Healthcare for all: Report of the independent inquiry into access to healthcare for people with learning disabilities.* London: Independent Inquiry into Access to Healthcare for People with Learning Disabilities.

Monaghan, M.T. & Soni, S. (1992). Effects of significant life events on the behaviour of mentally handicapped people in the community. *British Journal of Mental Subnormality, 38,* 114–121.

Murphy, G.H., O'Callaghan, A.C. & Clare, I.C.H. (2007). The impact of alleged abuse on behaviour in adults with severe intellectual disabilities. *Journal of Intellectual Disability Research, 51,* 741–749.

Myers, H.F. (2009). Ethnicity- and socio-economic status-related stresses in context: An integrative review and conceptual model. *Journal of Behavioral Medicine, 32,* 9–19.

National Equality Panel (2010). *An anatomy of economic inequality in the UK.* London: Government Equalities Office.

Nazroo, J. (2003). The structuring of ethnic inequalities in health: Economic position, racial discrimination and racism. *American Journal of Public Health, 93*(2), 277–284.

Norwich, B. & Kelly, N. (2004). Pupils' views on inclusion: Moderate learning difficulties and bullying in mainstream and special schools. *British Educational Research Journal, 30*, 43–65.

Nunn, A., Johnson, S., Monro, S., Bickerstaffe, T. & Kelsey, S. (2007). *Factors influencing social mobility.* London: DWP.

Owen, D.M., Hastings, R.P., Noone, S.J., Chinn, J., Harman, K. & Roberts, J. (2004). Life events as correlates of problem behavior and mental health in a residential population of adults with developmental disabilities. *Research in Developmental Disabilities, 25*, 309–320.

Pascoe, E.A. & Richman, L.S. (2009). Perceived discrimination and health: A meta-analytic review. *Psychological Bulletin, 135*, 531–554.

Petterson, S.M. & Albers, A.B. (2004). Effects of poverty and maternal depression on early child development. *Child Development, 72*(6), 1794–1813.

Reiss, S. & Benson, B.A. (1984). Awareness of negative social conditions among mentally retarded, emotionally disturbed outpatients. *The American Journal of Psychiatry, 141*, 88–90.

Rutter, M. (2000). Psychosocial influences: Critiques, findings, and research needs. *Developmental Psychopathology, 12*, 119–144.

Sandberg, S. & Rutter, M. (2008). Acute life stresses. In M. Rutter, D. Bishop, D. Pine, S. Scott, J. Stevenson, E. Taylor *et al.* (Eds.) *Rutter's child and adolescent psychiatry.* Oxford: Blackwell.

Schoon, I. (2006). *Risk and resilience: Adaptations in changing times.* Cambridge, UK: Cambridge University Press.

Sequeira, H., Howlin, P. & Hollins, S. (2003). Psychological disturbance associated with sexual abuse in people with learning disabilities: Case-control study. *The British Journal of Psychiatry, 183*, 451–456.

Sheard, C., Clegg, J., Standen, P. & Cromby, J. (2001). Bullying and people with severe intellectual disability. *Journal of Intellectual Disability Research, 45*, 407–415.

Sherry, M. (2010). *Disability hate crimes: Does anyone really hate disabled people?* Burlington, VT: Ashgate.

Shonkoff, J.P. (2010). Building a new biodevelopmental framework to guide the future of early childhood policy. *Child Development, 81*, 357–367.

Shonkoff, J.P., Boyce, W.T. & McEwen, B.S. (2009). Neuroscience, molecular biology, and the childhood roots of health disparities: Building a new framework for health promotion and disease prevention. *JAMA: The Journal of the American Medical Association, 301*, 2252–2259.

Smith, A. (1759/2002). *The theory of moral sentiments.* Cambridge, UK: Cambridge University Press.

Spicker, P. (2007). *The idea of poverty.* Bristol: Policy Press.

Szivos-Bach, S.E. (1993). Social comparisons, stigma and mainstreaming: the self esteem of young adults with a mild mental handicap. *Mental Handicap Research, 6*, 217–236.

Tajfel, H. & Turner, J. (1979). An integrative theory of intergroup conflict. In W.G. Austin & S. Worchel (Eds.) *The social psychology of intergroup relations.* Monterey, CA: Brooks/Cole.

The Marmot Review (2010). *Fair society, healthy lives: Strategic review of health inequalities in England post-2010.* London: The Marmot Review.

Tremblay, R.E. (2000). The development of aggressive behavior during childhood: What have we learned in the past century? *International Journal of Behavioral Development, 24*, 129–141.

Tremblay, R.E. (2006). Prevention of youth violence: Why not start at the beginning? *Journal of Abnormal Child Psychology, 34*(4), 481–487.

Tremblay, R.E., Nagin, D.S., Seguin, J.R., Zoccolillo, M., Zelazo, P.D., Boivin, M. *et al.* (2004). Physical aggression during early childhood: Trajectories and predictors. *Pediatrics*, *114*(1), e43–e50.

Wallander, J.L., Dekker, M.C. & Koot, H.M. (2006). Risk factors for psychopathology in children with intellectual disability: A prospective longitudinal population-based study. *Journal of Intellectual Disability Research*, *50*, 259–268.

Wehmeyer, M.L. & Garner, N.W. (2003). The impact of personal characteristics of people with intellectual and developmental disability on self-determination and autonomous functioning. *Journal of Applied Research in Intellectual Disabilities*, *16*, 255–265.

White, C., Holland, E., Marsland, D. & Oakes, P. (2003). The identification of environments and cultures that promote the abuse of people with intellectual disabilities: A review of the literature. *Journal of Applied Research in Intellectual Disabilities*, *16*, 1–13.

Wilkinson, R.G. (2005). *The impact of inequality.* New York: The New Press.

Wilkinson, R.G. & Pickett, K.E. (2009). *The spirit level: Why more equal societies almost always do better.* London: Penguin.

Williams, B., Copestake, P., Eversley, J. & Stafford, B. (2008). *Experiences and expectations of disabled people.* London: Office for Disability Issues.

Williams, D.R. & Mohammed, S.A. (2009). Discrimination and racial disparities in health: Evidence and needed research. *Journal of Behavioral Medicine*, *32*, 20–47.

World Health Organization (2008). *Closing the gap in a generation: Health equity through action on the social determinants of health.* Final report of the Commission on the Social Determinants of Health. Geneva: World Health Organization.

Zigler, E., Bennett-Gates, D., Hodapp, R. & Henrich, C.C. (2002). Assessing personality traits of individuals with mental retardation. *American Journal of Mental Retardation*, *107*, 181–193.

Chapter 3

The Assessment of Mental Health Problems in Adults with Intellectual Disabilities

Chris Hatton
John L. Taylor

Introduction

Any effective formulation and psychological intervention rests on the foundation of reliable and valid assessment of a person's mental health problems. Such assessment is crucial in guiding clinical decisions, particularly when deciding the nature and style of the psychological intervention to be attempted. Assessment is an equally crucial first step when considering psychological interventions with adults with intellectual disabilities, although there is less evidence concerning the assessment of mental health problems in this group and little consensus concerning mental health assessment tools (Hatton & Taylor, 2010).

In this chapter, we will introduce some fundamental issues concerning the identification and assessment of mental health problems in adults with intellectual disabilities, describe the range of tools available to assess mental health problems in this population, and outline some factors to consider when deciding on which tool to use. Before discussing these issues in depth, it is important to define the scope of this chapter.

First, this chapter will focus on the assessment of mental health problems in adults with intellectual disabilities. Psychopathology classification systems and consequently assessment tools for children and adults have a number of important differences, and cognitive–behavioral therapy is less advanced with children with intellectual disabilities than it is with adults with intellectual disabilities. Commonly used measures assessing psychopathology relevant to mental health in children with intellectual disabilities include the Development Behaviour Checklist (Einfeld & Tonge, 1995; Einfeld *et al.*, 2006), the Strengths and Difficulties Questionnaire (see Emerson, 2005; Emerson *et al.*, 2010; Kaptein *et al.*, 2008), and the Development and Well-Being Assessment (see Emerson, 2003; Emerson & Hatton, 2007).

Psychological Therapies for Adults with Intellectual Disabilities, First Edition.
Edited by John L. Taylor, William R. Lindsay, Richard P. Hastings, and Chris Hatton.
© 2013 John Wiley & Sons, Ltd. Published 2013 by John Wiley & Sons, Ltd.

Second, this chapter does not include assessments of mental health problems specifically designed for adults with autism. Very few autism-specific assessments of mental health problems have been developed (see LoVullo & Matson, 2009; Matson & Boisjoli, 2008; Smith & Matson, 2010, for research using one such measure, the autistic spectrum disorder-classroom assistant (ASD-CA)), probably because mental health assessments and diagnostic criteria suitable for people with intellectual disabilities are likely to be equally valid for adults with autism (see Melville *et al.*, 2008; Tsakanikos *et al.*, 2006).

Finally, this chapter is explicitly concerned with assessments of mental health problems rather than assessments of challenging behavior. Causal relationships between mental health problems and challenging behaviors are notoriously tangled and unclear (Emerson & Einfeld, 2011; see this text also for a discussion of the assessment of challenging behavior). However, it is at least clear that signs of mental health problems are not best conceptualized and treated solely as instances of challenging behavior, and also that challenging behaviors are not solely signs of mental health problems (see Felce *et al.*, 2009; Myrbakk & von Tetzchner, 2008a; Sturmey *et al.*, 2010).

Fundamental Issues in the Identification and Assessment of Mental Health Problems in Adults with Intellectual Disabilities

Question 1: How does identification occur for adults with intellectual disabilities?

The first issue influencing the identification and assessment of mental health problems in adults with intellectual disabilities is the social context within which identification and assessment occur. For example, typical referral pathways to mental health services, through a general practitioner (GP) due to a person having problems fulfilling social roles (e.g., spouse, parent, employee) (Goldberg & Huxley, 1980), may be less common for people with intellectual disabilities. People with intellectual disabilities are less likely to be in social roles where problems would be apparent, environments for people with intellectual disabilities may be so restricted that a mental health problem may not be activated or displayed (e.g., a specific phobia), and some mental health problems may not manifest themselves in behaviors that are seen as problematic by carers or professionals (e.g., depression manifesting in social withdrawal and loss of energy) (Edelstein & Glenwick, 2001). In contrast, people with intellectual disabilities may be referred to mental health services when their behavior is construed as a problem by other people rather than being a problem for the person themselves (e.g., anger in response to restrictions on autonomy and choice). This makes the development of valid and reliable screening assessment tools particularly important for use by family carers and professionals working with people with intellectual disabilities (Oliver *et al.*, 2005) as well as clinicians.

Question 2: Do standard psychiatric diagnostic criteria apply to (some or all) people with intellectual disabilities?

Over the past 30 years, persistent problems in the general identification of mental health have led to the development of internationally recognized standard psychiatric classification systems such as the Diagnostic and Statistical Manual of Mental Disorders (fourth edition; American Psychiatric Association, 1994) and the International Classification of Diseases Classification of Mental and Behavioural Disorders (tenth edition; World Health Organization, 1993). While these classification systems may have increased the reliability of psychiatric diagnoses for the general population, it is unclear how applicable they are to people with intellectual disabilities (Sturmey, 2007).

First, it is possible that these ways of classifying mental health problems may not be applicable to the experiences of people with severe and complex intellectual disabilities, who frequently have little or no symbolic language skills (Cooper *et al.*, 2007; Dagnan, 2007; Sturmey, 2007). For example, can a person with no symbolic language experience auditory hallucinations, or have the cognitive skills necessary to conceptualize and plan a suicide attempt?

Second, these classification systems are categorical; to reach a threshold for a mental health problem, a person needs to experience a pattern of symptoms at a certain level of frequency and severity. Many people with intellectual disabilities may show clear signs of a mental health problem, but not show a sufficient range of signs to trigger a diagnosis of a mental health problem (Langlois & Martin, 2008; Moss, Prosser, Goldberg *et al.*, 1996). There are also broader questions about how useful categorical diagnostic systems are in guiding psychological clinical work with people with mental health problems.

Third, these classification systems contain some assumptions that might be difficult to apply to people with intellectual disabilities. For example, these systems often diagnose a mental health problem as a change from the usual, when a person with intellectual disabilities may have had unrecognized mental health problems for months or years. These systems also assume a usual level of functioning that may be difficult to apply to people with intellectual disabilities; for example, criteria for depression include a diminished ability to think or concentrate.

Within the International Statistical Classification of Diseases and Related Health Problems, 10th Revision (ICD-10) system, there have already been modified diagnostic criteria produced for people with mild intellectual disabilities (World Health Organization, 1996) and people with moderate to severe intellectual disabilities (Royal College of Psychiatrists, 2001), called the Diagnostic Criteria for Psychiatric Disorders for Use with Adults with Learning Disabilities/Mental Retardation (DC-LD). However, both of these modifications have been the subject of some debate (Cooper, 2003; Einfeld & Tonge, 1999) and are based on informal expert consensus methods with limited validity. An alternative diagnostic system, the Diagnostic Manual for Intellectual Disabilities (DM-ID) has also been developed using expert consensus methods (Fletcher *et al.*, 2007) in North America; less extensive field testing results have been reported (Fletcher *et al.*, 2009).

Question 3: Is it possible to accurately assess mental states in people with intellectual disabilities?

Identifying a mental health problem almost always involves gaining some access to the mental state of the person (Sims, 1988). Many mental states, whether perceptions, emotions, or beliefs, can really only be accessed by the person describing what his or her mental state is; inferring a mental state from a person's behavior can be highly questionable.

Research evidence suggests that most people with intellectual disabilities and good functional communication skills can give accurate descriptions of their own mental states, as long as interview schedules are sensitively adapted (Dagnan & Lindsay, 2004; Finlay & Lyons, 2001). There are many examples of self-report mental health measures that have been successfully developed or adapted for people with mild or moderate intellectual disabilities (see next section). However, there is little or no research evidence demonstrating that asking people with more severe and complex intellectual disabilities about their mental states produces reliable or valid responses (Ross & Oliver, 2003a).

Question 4: To what extent can we use information from other people to assess mental health problems in people with intellectual disabilities?

Many measures to assess mental health problems in people with intellectual disabilities have been designed to be used with an informant (typically a paid carer or a family member) rather than with the person themselves (see Question 5). There is some convergence between the self-reports of people with mild or moderate intellectual disabilities and informants using highly structured clinical interview schedules, with informants more likely to pick up behavioral signs and unlikely to reliably report mental state (Moss, Prosser, Ibbotson *et al.*, 1996). However, people with intellectual disabilities and carers are less likely to agree using less structured interviews concerning emotional distress (Bramston & Fogarty, 2000).

Question 5: To what extent can we use observational information to assess mental health problems in people with intellectual disabilities?

Many mental health problems are considered to have distinctive patterns of behavior associated with them, although relying on behavioral observations alone is unlikely to reliably identify most mental health problems. For example, self-reports and behavioral observations often do not agree (Rojahn *et al.*, 1995). Moreover, the frequent reporting of "atypical" behavioral symptoms in people with severe and complex intellectual disabilities suggests that reliable behavioral markers of mental health problems are unlikely in this group (Ross & Oliver, 2003a).

Mental Health Assessment Tools for Use with Adults with Intellectual Disabilities

The development of reliable and valid mental health screening measures for adults with intellectual disabilities is in its early stages, with a proliferation of measures and little evidence on the reliability or validity of any of them (Beail, 2004; Dagnan & Lindsay, 2004; Mohr & Costello, 2007; Novaco & Taylor, 2004). Different measures vary according to:

- whether they are measures developed for the general population and then used or adapted for people with intellectual disabilities, or whether they are specifically designed for people with intellectual disabilities;
- whether they are designed as self-report measures to be completed by people with intellectual disabilities (almost always in an interview format), or whether they are designed to be completed by informants about the person with intellectual disabilities (in either a questionnaire or interview format);
- whether they are designed primarily for people with mild/moderate intellectual disabilities, people with severe/profound intellectual disabilities, or the whole range of people with intellectual disabilities;
- whether they are designed to act as a screen across a wide range of mental health problems, or whether they focus in more detail on a particular mental health problem;
- how much training and knowledge of mental health issues is needed to use the measure;
- the length of time they take the professional, person with intellectual disabilities, and/or the informant to complete;
- the time frame they use to assess mental health problems – measures using a longer time frame (e.g., symptoms in the past year) may be less suitable for repeated administration to evaluate a therapeutic intervention than measures using shorter time frames (e.g., symptoms in the last two weeks).

Information on a wide range of mental health measures is presented in Tables 3.1 and 3.2. For measures of multiple health problems (Table 3.1) and measures of specific mental health problems (Table 3.2), information is provided on the name of the measure and associated references, whether the measure has been designed for the general population (and potentially adapted) or specifically for people with intellectual disabilities, whether the measure is designed for self-report or informant report, the number of items in the measure, evidence of the measure's reliability and validity, and the time frame the measure uses for reporting signs of mental health problems (e.g., symptoms in the last week).

As yet, there is little consensus on which measures are preferred, although systematic reviews of assessment tools in specific areas such as depression are beginning to emerge (Hermans & Evenhuis, 2010). The measures in Tables 3.1 and 3.2 have most often been tested in terms of their reliability (internal consistency, and sometimes test–retest and inter-rater reliability for informant measures). Tests of validity have been less frequently and less stringently conducted, partly because of the lack of "gold standard" methods for determining mental health problems in people with intellectual disabilities against which new assessment measures can be tested (as seen in previous section). Among measures of multiple mental health problems (Table 3.1), the range of mental health problems included can be idiosyncratic and partial in their coverage, with a lack of stability concerning which items group together into coherent scales (see, e.g., Hatton & Taylor, 2008). Due to the proliferation of new measures, few measures have been subject to extensive testing over time by research groups independent of the developers of the measure, and sample sizes for testing are often relatively small, particularly across the whole range of potential scores for the measure. Finally, there are serious questions about the validity of mental health classification systems, and mental health measures derived from them, in assessing psychopathology among people with severe and profound intellectual disabilities.

Table 3.1 Assessment Measures: Multiple Mental Health Problems

Measure	General population measure or specific for people with intellectual disabilities	Self-report or informant report	Areas assessed	Number of items	Reliability, validity, time frame for assessing symptoms
Reiss Screen for Maladaptive Behavior (Reiss, 1988a, 1988b)	Specific	Informant	Total Aggressive behavior Psychosis Paranoia Depression (behavioral signs) Depression (physical signs) Dependent personality disorder Avoidant behavior Autism	36 items	Adequate reliability Adequate sensitivity Poor specificity (Myrbakk & von Tetzchner, 2008b; Sturmey & Bertman, 1994) Assesses symptoms in the last three months
Diagnostic Assessment for the Severely Handicapped (DASH) (Matson et al., 1991) DASH-II (Matson, 1995)	Specific	Informant	Total Anxiety Depression Mania Autism Schizophrenia Stereotypies/tics Self-injury Elimination disorders Eating disorders Sleep disorders Psychosexual disorders Organic syndromes Impulse control/miscellaneous	83 items (DASH) 84 items (DASH-II)	Designed for people with severe intellectual disabilities Adequate reliability Some evidence for adequate sensitivity (DASH-II; Bamburg et al., 2001) Poor specificity (DASH-II; Myrbakk & von Tetzchner, 2008b) Frequency of symptoms assessed in the last two weeks Duration of symptoms assessed up to 12+ months

Instrument	Type	Subscales	Respondent	Items	Properties
Psychopathology Instrument for Mentally Retarded Adults (PIMRA) (Matson et al., 1984; Senatore et al., 1985)	Specific	Total Schizophrenic disorder Affective disorder Psychosexual disorder Adjustment disorder Anxiety disorder Somatoform disorder Personality disorders	Self or informant	56 items	Adequate reliability Questionable sensitivity and specificity (Masi et al., 2002; Sturmey et al., 1991) Assesses symptoms in the last six months
PAS-ADD Checklist (Moss, Prosser, Costello et al., 1996)	Specific	Total Affective/neurotic disorder Organic condition Psychotic disorder	Informant	29 items	Adequate reliability Reasonable sensitivity Questionable specificity (Hatton & Taylor, 2008; Moss et al., 1998) Assesses symptoms in the last four weeks
Mini PAS-ADD (Prosser et al., 1997)	Specific	Total Anxiety and phobia Depression Expansive mood Obsessions and compulsions Psychoses Dementia Autistic features	Informant	86 items	Good reliability Good sensitivity Questionable specificity (Deb et al., 2001; Myrbakk & von Tetzchner, 2008b; Prosser et al., 1998) Assesses symptoms in the last four weeks
Symptom Checklist 90 (revised) (SCL-90-R) (Derogatis, 1983; Kellett et al., 1999)	General (adapted)	Global severity index Positive symptom distress index Positive symptom total Somatization Obsessive–compulsive Interpersonal sensitivity Depression Anxiety Hostility Phobic anxiety Paranoid ideation Psychoticism	Self	90 items	Adapted by using an assisted completion format Good reliability Adequate sensitivity and specificity (Kellett et al., 1999) Assesses symptoms in the last seven days

(Continued)

Table 3.1 (*Continued*)

Measure	General population measure or specific for people with intellectual disabilities	Areas assessed	Self-report or informant report	Number of items	Reliability, validity, time frame for assessing symptoms
Brief Symptom Inventory (Derogatis, 1993; Kellett *et al.*, 2003, 2004)	General (adapted)	Global severity index Positive symptom distress index Positive symptom total Somatization Obsessive–compulsive Interpersonal sensitivity Depression Anxiety Hostility Phobic anxiety Paranoid ideation Psychoticism	Self	53 items	Adapted by using an assisted completion format Good reliability Adequate sensitivity, questionable specificity (Endermann, 2005; Kellett *et al.*, 2003, 2004) Assesses symptoms in the last seven days
Developmental Behaviour Checklist – Adults (Mohr *et al.*, 2005)	Specific	Total Self-absorption Disruption Anxiety Depression Communication disturbance Problems in social relating	Informant	106 items	Some evidence on sensitivity and specificity for depression (Torr *et al.*, 2008) Good reliability and validity (Mohr *et al.*, 2005) Assesses symptoms over the last six months

Instrument	Type	Respondent	Format	Criteria	Notes
Psychiatric Assessment Schedule – Adults with Developmental Disability (PAS-ADD) (Moss et al., 1997)	General (adapted)	Self and informant	Semistructured interview, core 145 questions	To ICD-10 criteria: Schizophrenia Depression Phobic anxiety disorders Other anxiety disorders Autism screen	Comprehensive adaptation of Schedules of Clinical Assessment in Neuropsychiatry (World Health Organization, 1992) Extensive rewording and redesign for use with both person with intellectual disabilities and an informant Uses ICD-10 standard psychiatric classification system for diagnosis (World Health Organization, 1993) Adequate reliability and validity (Costello et al., 1997; Deb et al., 2001; Moss, Prosser, Goldberg et al., 1996; Moss, Prosser, Ibbotson et al., 1996; Moss et al., 1997) Assesses symptoms in relation to an established "anchor event" approximately one month before the interview
Mood and Anxiety Semi-structured (MASS) Interview (Charlot et al., 2007)	Specific	Informant	35 symptom items with behavioral descriptions	To DSM-IV criteria: Anxiety disorders (generalized anxiety disorder (GAD), panic disorder, obsessive–compulsive disorder (OCD), anxiety disorder not otherwise specified) Major depressive disorder Mania	Good reliability Adequate sensitivity and specificity (Charlot et al., 2007) Assesses symptoms in the past month

(Continued)

Table 3.1 (*Continued*)

Measure	General population measure or specific for people with intellectual disabilities	Areas assessed	Self-report or informant report	Number of items	Reliability, validity, time frame for assessing symptoms
Psychopathology Checklists for Adults with Intellectual Disability (Hove & Havik, 2008)	Specific	Derived from DC-LD criteria (Royal College of Psychiatrists, 2001): Dementia Psychosis spectrum Depression Mania Anxiety disorders (agoraphobia, social phobia, specific phobia, generalized anxiety, panic anxiety) OCD Problem behavior (verbal aggression, physical aggression, destructive behavior, self-injurious behavior, sexually inappropriate behavior, opposition behavior, demanding behavior, wandering behavior)	Informant	Psychopathology checklists 218 items Problem behavior checklists 52 items	Adequate reliability Adequate sensitivity, poor specificity (Hove & Havik, 2008) Time frame for assessment of symptoms varies according to DC-LD guidelines (Royal College of Psychiatrists, 2001)

Table 3.2 Assessment Measures: Specific Mental Health Problems

Measure	General population measure or specific for people with intellectual disabilities	Areas assessed	Self-report or informant report	Number of items	Reliability, validity, time frame for assessing symptoms
Hospital Anxiety and Depression Scale (Dagnan et al., 2008; Zigmond & Snaith, 1983)	General (adapted)	Depression (7 items) Anxiety (7 items)	Self	14 items (7 for depression, 7 for anxiety)	Adapted with wording changes and standardized response format (Dagnan et al., 2008) Good reliability, encouraging validity (Dagnan et al., 2008) Assesses symptoms in the last week
Zung Depression Scale (Dagnan & Sandhu, 1999; Kazdin et al., 1983; Lindsay et al., 1994; Prout & Schaefer, 1985; Zung, 1965)	General (adapted)	Depression	Self or informant	20 items	Original measure used (Prout & Schaefer, 1985) Adapted with wording changes and fewer response options (Dagnan & Sandhu, 1999; Kazdin et al., 1983; Lindsay et al., 1994) For adapted informant version (Gordon et al., 2007) Good reliability, encouraging validity (Dagnan et al., 2008; Gordon et al., 2007; Powell, 2003) Assesses symptoms in the last several days

(Continued)

Table 3.2 (Continued)

Measure	General population measure or specific for people with intellectual disabilities	Areas assessed	Self-report or informant report	Number of items	Reliability, validity, time frame for assessing symptoms
Beck Depression Inventory (Beck et al., 1961)	General (adapted)	Depression	Self	21 items	Original measure used (Prout & Schaefer, 1985)
Beck Depression Inventory II (Beck et al., 1996)					Adapted with wording changes and fewer response options (Helsel & Matson, 1988; Kazdin et al., 1983; Nezu et al., 1995); Good reliability and validity (Lindsay & Skene, 2007; Powell, 2003); Assesses mood in the last two weeks
Glasgow Depression Scale (Cuthill et al., 2003)	Specific	Depression	Self or informant (carer supplement)	20 items; Carer supplement 16 items	Good reliability (Dagnan et al., 2008); Good sensitivity and specificity (Cuthill et al., 2003); Assesses symptoms in relation to an anchor event one week before
Self-Report Depression Questionnaire (Esbensen & Benson, 2007; Esbensen et al., 2005)	Specific	Depression	Self	32 items	Adequate reliability and validity (Esbensen & Benson, 2007; Esbensen et al., 2005); Assesses symptoms in the last two weeks
Birleson Depressive Short Form Self-Rating Scale (Birleson, 1981; Hartley & McLean, 2009)	General	Depression	Self	18 items	Adequate reliability and validity (Benson & Ivins, 1992; Hartley & McLean, 2009); Assesses symptoms in the last week

Scale	Type	Construct	Informant	Items	Notes
Zung Self-Rating Anxiety Scale (Lindsay et al., 1994; Zung, 1971)	General (adapted)	Anxiety	Self	20 items	Adapted with wording changes and fewer response options (Lindsay et al., 1994) Adequate reliability, encouraging validity (Ramirez & Lukenbill, 2008)
Beck Anxiety Inventory (Beck & Steer, 1990; Lindsay & Lees, 2003)	General (adapted)	Anxiety	Self	21 items	Assesses symptoms in the last week Adapted (Lindsay & Lees, 2003) Adequate reliability and validity (Lindsay & Skene, 2007)
Glasgow Anxiety Scale (Mindham & Espie, 2003)	Specific	Anxiety	Self	27 items	Assesses symptoms in the last week Good reliability Good sensitivity and specificity (Mindham & Espie, 2003)
Mood, Interest & Pleasure Questionnaire (Ross & Oliver, 2002, 2003b)	Specific	Mood: Interest and pleasure	Informant	25 items	Assesses symptoms in relation to an anchor event one week before Designed for people with severe intellectual disabilities Good reliability, adequate validity (Ross & Oliver, 2002, 2003b)
Positive and Negative Syndrome Scale (PANSS) (Hatton et al., 2005; Kay et al., 1989)	General	Psychotic experiences: Positive symptoms Negative symptoms General symptoms	Self	28 items	Assesses symptoms in the last two weeks Good reliability Good validity on positive symptoms and general symptoms, inadequate validity on negative symptoms (Hatton et al., 2005)
Psychotic Rating Scales (PSYRATS) (Haddock et al., 1999; Hatton et al., 2005)	General	Psychotic experiences: Auditory hallucinations Delusions	Self	17 items	Assesses symptoms in the last week Good reliability Good validity on auditory hallucinations, unknown validity on delusions (Hatton et al., 2005) Assesses symptoms in the last week

(Continued)

Table 3.2 (*Continued*)

Measure	General population measure or specific for people with intellectual disabilities	Areas assessed	Self-report or informant report	Number of items	Reliability, validity, time frame for assessing symptoms
Complicated Grief Questionnaire for People with Intellectual Disabilities (CGQ-ID) (Guerin *et al.*, 2009; Prigerson *et al.*, 1995)	Specific (adapted from general measure for children)	Complicated grief reactions: Separation distress Traumatic grief	Informant	23 items	Original measure Inventory of Complicated Grief (Prigerson *et al.*, 1995) Adapted measure (Guerin *et al.*, 2009) Good reliability, some evidence for validity (Guerin *et al.*, 2009) Assesses symptoms since bereavement (variable time frame)
Novaco Anger Scale (NAS) (Novaco, 2003; Novaco & Taylor, 2004)	General (adapted)	Anger: Disposition and experience in the cognitive, arousal, and behavioral domains	Self	48 items	Original measure (Novaco, 2003) Adapted for people with mild–borderline intellectual disabilities and to be administered as a structured interview (Novaco & Taylor, 2004) Good reliability and validity Assesses present state
Provocation Inventory (PI) (Novaco, 2003; Novaco & Taylor, 2004)	General (adapted)	Anger: Reactivity across a range of potentially provoking situations	Self	25 items	Original measure (Novaco, 2003) Adapted for people with mild–borderline intellectual disabilities and to be administered as a structured interview (Novaco & Taylor, 2004) Good reliability and validity Assesses anger responses to hypothetical situations

Measure	Type	Description	Items	Properties
Anger Inventory (AI) (Benson & Ivins, 1992; Rose & Gerson, 2009)	Specific	Anger: Reactivity across a range of potentially provoking situations	35 items	Self or informant	Original self-report measure (Benson & Ivins, 1992) Adapted for informants (Rose & Gerson, 2009) Good internal reliability, good validity for self-report measure (Rose & West, 1999) Questionable validity for informant measure Assesses anger responses to hypothetical situations
Ward Anger Rating Scale (WARS) (Novaco, 1994; Novaco & Taylor, 2004)	General	Anger: A two-part scale regarding (a) verbal and physical behaviors associated with anger and aggression, and (b) anger attributes displayed during the previous seven days	25 items	Informant	Original measure (Novaco, 1994) Good reliability and validity (Novaco & Taylor, 2004; Steptoe et al., 2008) Assesses behaviors in the last week
Imaginal Provocation Test (IPT) (Taylor et al, 2004)	General (adapted)	Anger: An idiographic measure of anger reactivity in terms of emotional and behavioral responses and attempts to regulate these	10 items (administered in two parallel forms)	Self	Original measure (Novaco, 1975) Adapted for use with people with ID (Taylor et al., 2004) Good reliability and validity (Taylor et al., 2004) Assesses anger responses to hypothetical situations

When considering which assessment measures are likely to be most suitable for your purposes, the following factors should be important in your decision making:

- Do you require a diagnostic measure or a continuous measure of severity of mental health problem? It is important to check whether your assessment is intended as a diagnostic tool that principally categorizes someone as experiencing a mental health problem or not, or if it is intended as a continuous measure of symptoms of a mental health problem that will be sensitive to change over time. For research reporting purposes or for determining eligibility for a service, a diagnostic tool may be useful. For evaluating change associated with a psychosocial intervention, a continuous measure may be more appropriate.
- Do you need to screen across a wide range of mental health problems or focus on a specific mental health problem? If assessing across a range of mental health problems, it is important to consider whether the measure covers the range of mental health problems you are interested in and how long the measure will take to administer – screening in this way can be useful for establishing the mental health needs of a population and establishing potentially comorbid mental health problems, although the specificity of the screening tools outlined in Table 3.1 can be problematic. Measures of specific mental health problems are more often used to establish rates of specific mental health problems and to focus on the progress of individuals throughout a therapeutic intervention, as they are usually quicker to administer, particularly over time.
- How much time do you have to administer the measure? As mentioned above, measures of multiple mental health problems, measures requiring information from both the person with intellectual disabilities and informants, and measures requiring semi-structured interview schedules will all tend to take longer to administer than short measures of specific mental health problems. However, it is important to note that all self-report measures will require some form of interview with the person with intellectual disabilities (although some informant measures can be completed by questionnaire). This is particularly important to consider when using mental health assessments as part of routine therapeutic interventions – you do not want the entire therapy session to be taken up with assessment!
- Will you be repeatedly administering the measure over time, particularly in evaluating an intervention? When using a measure over repeated time points to evaluate a therapeutic intervention, it is particularly important to consider the time frame the measure uses to assess symptoms of mental health problems. For example, measures using standard psychiatric diagnostic criteria may require people to report their symptoms over the past month, three months, or even a year. Such a measure is of little use when evaluating a relatively brief cognitive behavioral intervention, where measures assessing symptoms in the last week or two weeks may be more appropriate. It is also important to consider how sensitive the measure is likely to be to changes in the severity of a mental health problem over time; for example, does scoring on the measure have substantial ceiling or floor effects, and are items scored in simpler ways that may be less sensitive to change (e.g., is a symptom present or not?) or more complex ways that allow gradations of severity (e.g., is a symptom not present at all, present a little bit, present a lot, present all the time?).
- Will you be working with people with intellectual disabilities who can provide self-report data, and are reliable informants accessible? It is important to establish early on whether the person with intellectual disabilities you are working with has the

capacity to reliably complete a measure of mental health status, and different measures have different demands of the language, cognitive, emotion recognition, and memory capacities of the person completing them. If you are intending to collect data from informants, it is important to establish which informants will be in the best position to provide reliable and valid information. You may need to collect information from more than one informant to cover different aspects of a person's life – for example, a day center worker may know the person very well but he or she would not have the information on sleep disturbance that could be gained from a parent or a residential carer.

- Pragmatic issues. It is important to check whether the administration of the measure requires specific training, and whether the measure is copyrighted and requires you to purchase the measure.

A final point is that the measures discussed in this chapter only represent a set of standardized measures for psychological problems that have been used with adults with intellectual disabilities. When conducting a psychological intervention with an individual, they are no substitute for the range of individualized clinical measures and tools used during therapy, as illustrated throughout this book (see also Taylor & Novaco, 2005, for numerous examples of individualized materials that can be used in anger treatment with people with intellectual disabilities).

Conclusions

As this chapter has hopefully shown, the picture concerning the assessment of mental health problems among adults with intellectual disabilities is rapidly developing. Although there are substantial methodological challenges in developing reliable and valid mental health assessment tools, particularly for adults with severe and profound intellectual disabilities, substantial progress has been made, to the point whether the major problem is becoming the proliferation of measures rather than a lack of them. Given the increasing range of mental health assessment tools available for use with adults with intellectual disabilities, there are now no barriers to the use of such measures for the identification and assessment of psychological problems and the evaluation of treatment effectiveness in routine professional practice.

References

American Psychiatric Association (1994). *Diagnostic and statistical manual of mental disorders* (4th edn). Washington, DC: American Psychiatric Association.

Bamburg, J.W., Cherry, K.E., Matson, J.L. & Penn, D. (2001). Assessment of schizophrenia in persons with severe and profound mental retardation using the diagnostic assessment for the severely handicapped (DASH-II). *Journal of Developmental and Physical Disabilities, 13*, 319–331.

Beail, N. (2004). Methodology, design, and evaluation in psychotherapy research with people with intellectual disabilities. In E. Emerson, C. Hatton, T. Thompson & T.R. Parmenter (Eds.) *The international handbook of applied research in intellectual disabilities* (pp. 531–547). Chichester: Wiley.

Beck, A.T. & Steer, R.A. (1990). *Manual for the Beck Anxiety Inventory*. San Antonio, TX: The Psychological Corporation.

Beck, A.T., Steer, R.A. & Brown, G.K. (1996). *Beck Depression Inventory – 2nd edition manual*. San Antonio, TX: The Psychological Corporation.

Beck, A.T., Ward, C.H., Mendelsohn, M., Mock, J. & Erbaugh, J. (1961). An inventory for measuring depression. *Archives of General Psychiatry, 4*, 561–571.

Benson, B.A. & Ivins, J. (1992). Anger, depression and self-concept in adults with mental retardation. *Journal of Intellectual Disability Research, 36*, 169–175.

Birleson, P. (1981). The validity of depressive disorder in childhood and the development of a self-rating scale: A research report. *Journal of Child Psychology and Psychiatry, and Allied Disciplines, 22*, 73–88.

Bramston, P. & Fogarty, G. (2000). The assessment of emotional distress experienced by people with an intellectual disability: A study of different methodologies. *Research in Developmental Disabilities, 21*, 487–500.

Charlot, L., Deutsch, C., Hunt, A. & McIlvane, W. (2007). Validation of the Mood and Anxiety Semi-structured (MASS) Interview for patients with intellectual disabilities. *Journal of Intellectual Disability Research, 51*, 821–834.

Cooper, S.A. (Ed.) (2003). Diagnostic Criteria for Psychiatric Disorders for Use with Adults with Learning Disabilities (DC-LD). *Journal of Intellectual Disability Research, 47*(Suppl. 1), 50–61.

Cooper, S.A., Smiley, E., Finlayson, J., Jackson, A., Allan, L., Williamson, A. *et al.* (2007). The prevalence, incidence and factors predictive of mental ill-health in adults with profound intellectual disabilities. *Journal of Applied Research in Intellectual Disabilities, 20*, 493–501.

Costello, H., Moss, S., Prosser, H. & Hatton, C. (1997). Reliability of the ICD 10 version of the Psychiatric Assessment Schedule for Adults with Developmental Disability (PAS-ADD). *Social Psychiatry and Psychiatric Epidemiology, 32*, 339–343.

Cuthill, F.M., Espie, C.A. & Cooper, S.-A. (2003). Development and psychometric properties of the Glasgow Depression Scale for people with a learning disability: Individual and carer supplement versions. *The British Journal of Psychiatry, 182*, 347–353.

Dagnan, D. (2007). Commentary: The prevalence, incidence and factors predictive of mental ill-health in adults with profound intellectual disabilities. *Journal of Applied Research in Intellectual Disabilities, 20*, 502–504.

Dagnan, D., Jahoda, A., McDowell, K., Masson, J., Banks, P. & Hare, D. (2008). The psychometric properties of the hospital anxiety and depressions scale adapted for use with people with intellectual disabilities. *Journal of Intellectual Disability Research, 52*, 942–949.

Dagnan, D. & Lindsay, W.R. (2004). Research issues in cognitive therapy. In E. Emerson, C. Hatton, T. Thompson & T.R. Parmenter (Eds.) *The international handbook of applied research in intellectual disabilities* (pp.517–530). Chichester: Wiley.

Dagnan, D. & Sandhu, S. (1999). Social comparison, self-esteem and depression in people with learning disabilities. *Journal of Intellectual Disability Research, 43*, 372–379.

Deb, S., Thomas, M. & Bright, C. (2001). Mental disorder in adults with intellectual disability. I: Prevalence of functional psychiatric illness among a community-based population aged between 16 and 64 years. *Journal of Intellectual Disability Research, 45*, 495–505.

Derogatis, L.R. (1983). *SCL-90-R: Administration, scoring and procedures: Manual II*. Towson, MD: Clinical Psychometrics Research.

Derogatis, L.R. (1993). *Brief symptom inventory: Administration, scoring and procedures manual* (3rd edn). Minneapolis, MN: National Computer Systems.

Edelstein, T.M. & Glenwick, D.S. (2001). Direct-care workers' attributions of psychopathology in adults with mental retardation. *Mental Retardation, 39*, 368–378.

Einfeld, S.L., Piccinin, A.M., Mackinnon, A., Hofer, S.M., Taffe, J., Gray, K.M. *et al.* (2006). Psychopathology in young people with intellectual disability. *JAMA: The Journal of the American Medical Association, 296*, 1981–1989.

Einfeld, S.L. & Tonge, B.J. (1995). The Development Behaviour Checklist: The development and validation of an instrument to assess behavioural and emotional disturbance in children and adolescents with mental retardation. *Journal of Autism and Developmental Disorders, 25*, 81–104.

Einfeld, S.L. & Tonge, B.J. (1999). Observations on the use of the ICD-10 guide for mental retardation. *Journal of Intellectual Disability Research, 43*, 408–413.

Emerson, E. (2003). Prevalence of psychiatric disorders in children and adolescents with and without intellectual disability. *Journal of Intellectual Disability Research, 47*, 51–58.

Emerson, E. (2005). Use of the Strengths and Difficulties Questionnaire to assess the mental health needs of children and adolescents with intellectual disabilities. *Journal of Intellectual and Developmental Disability, 30*, 14–23.

Emerson, E., Einfeld, S. & Stancliffe, R. (2010). The mental health of young children with intellectual disabilities or borderline intellectual functioning. *Social Psychiatry & Psychiatric Epidemiology, 45*, 579–587.

Emerson, E. & Einfeld, S.L. (2011). *Challenging Behaviour* (3rd edn). Cambridge, UK: Cambridge University Press.

Emerson, E. & Hatton, C. (2007). Mental health of children and adolescents with intellectual disabilities in Britain. *The British Journal of Psychiatry, 191*, 493–499.

Endermann, M. (2005). The Brief Symptom Inventory (BSI) as a screening tool for psychological disorders in patients with epilepsy and mild intellectual disabilities in residential care. *Epilepsy & Behavior, 7*, 85–94.

Esbensen, A.J. & Benson, B.A. (2007). An evaluation of Beck's cognitive theory of depression in adults with intellectual disability. *Journal of Intellectual Disability Research, 51*, 14–24.

Esbensen, A.J., Seltzer, M.M., Greenberg, J.S. & Benson, B.A. (2005). Psychometric evaluation of a self-report measure of depression for individuals with mental retardation. *American Journal of Mental Retardation, 110*, 469–481.

Felce, D., Kerr, M. & Hastings, R.P. (2009). A general practice-based study of the relationship between indicators of mental illness and challenging behaviour among adults with intellectual disabilities. *Journal of Intellectual Disability Research, 53*, 243–254.

Finlay, W.M. & Lyons, E. (2001). Methodological issues in interviewing and using self-report questionnaires with people with mental retardation. *Psychological Assessment, 13*, 319–335.

Fletcher, R., Loschen, E., Stavrakaki, C. & First, M. (Eds.) (2007). *Diagnostic Manual – Intellectual Disability (DM-ID): A textbook of diagnosis of mental disorders in persons with intellectual disability*. Kingston, NY: NADD Press.

Fletcher, R.J., Havercamp, S.M., Ruedrich, S.L., Benson, B.A., Barnhill, L.J., Cooper, S.A. *et al.* (2009). Clinical usefulness of the diagnostic manual-intellectual disability for mental disorders in persons with intellectual disability: Results from a brief field survey. *The Journal of Clinical Psychiatry, 70*, e1–e8.

Goldberg, D.P. & Huxley, P. (1980). *Mental illness in the community: The pathway to psychiatric care*. Tavistock: London.

Gordon, M.S., Shevlin, M., Tierney, K.J., Bunting, B. & Trimble, T. (2007). Correspondence between self-ratings and key-workers' ratings of depression in adults with mild learning disabilities. *The British Journal of Clinical Psychology, 46*, 491–495.

Guerin, S., Dodd, P., Tyrell, J., McEvoy, J., Buckley, S. & Hillery, J. (2009). An initial assessment of the psychometric properties of the Complicated Grief Questionnaire for People with Intellectual Disabilities (CGQ-ID). *Research in Developmental Disabilities, 30*, 1258–1267.

Haddock, G., McCarron, J., Tarrier, N. & Faragher, E.B. (1999). Scales to measure dimensions of hallucinations and delusions: The psychotic symptom rating scales (PSYRATS). *Psychological Medicine, 29*, 879–899.

Hartley, S.L. & McLean, W.E. Jr. (2009). Depression in adults with mild intellectual disability: Role of stress, attributions, and coping. *American Journal on Intellectual and Developmental Disabilities, 114*, 147–160.

Hatton, C., Haddock, G., Taylor, J.T., Coldwell, J., Crossley, R. & Peckham, N. (2005). The reliability and validity of general psychotic rating scales with people with mild and moderate intellectual disabilities: An empirical investigation. *Journal of Intellectual Disability Research, 49*, 490–500.

Hatton, C. & Taylor, J.L. (2008). The factor structure of the PAS-ADD Checklist with adults with intellectual disabilities. *Journal of Intellectual and Developmental Disability, 33*, 330–336.

Hatton, C. & Taylor, J.L. (2010). Promoting healthy lifestyles: Mental health. In G. Grant, P. Goward, M. Richardson & P. Ramcharan (Eds.) *Learning disability: A life-cycle approach* (2nd edn, pp.381–408). Maidenhead: Open University Press/McGraw Hill Educational.

Helsel, W.J. & Matson, J.L. (1988). The relationship of depression to social skills and intellectual functioning in mentally retarded adults. *Journal of Mental Deficiency Research, 32*, 411–418.

Hermans, H. & Evenhuis, H.M. (2010). Characteristics of instruments screening for depression in adults with intellectual disabilities: Systematic review. *Research in Developmental Disabilities, 31*, 1109–1120.

Hove, O. & Havik, O.E. (2008). Psychometric properties of Psychopathology Checklists for Adults with Intellectual Disability (P-AID) on a community sample of adults with intellectual disability. *Research in Developmental Disabilities, 29*, 467–482.

Kaptein, S., Jansen, D.E.M., Vogels, A.G.C. & Reijneveld, S.A. (2008). Mental health problems in children with intellectual disability: Use of the strengths and difficulties questionnaire. *Journal of Intellectual Disability Research, 52*, 125–131.

Kay, S.R., Opler, L.A. & Lindenmayer, J.P. (1989). The Positive and Negative Syndrome Scale (PANSS): Rationale and standardisation. *The British Journal of Psychiatry, 155*(Suppl. 7), 59–65.

Kazdin, A.E., Matson, J.L. & Senatore, V. (1983). Assessment of depression in mentally retarded adults. *The American Journal of Psychiatry, 140*, 1040–1043.

Kellett, S., Beail, N., Newman, D.W. & Frankish, P. (2003). Utility of the Brief Symptom Inventory in the assessment of psychological distress. *Journal of Applied Research in Intellectual Disabilities, 16*, 127–134.

Kellett, S., Beail, N., Newman, D.W. & Hawes, A. (2004). The factor structure of the Brief Symptom Inventory: Intellectual disability evidence. *Clinical Psychology and Psychotherapy, 11*, 275–281.

Kellett, S., Beail, N., Newman, D.W. & Mosley, E. (1999). Indexing psychological distress in people with intellectual disabilities: Use of the Symptom Checklist-90-R. *Journal of Applied Research in Intellectual Disabilities, 12*, 323–334.

Langlois, L. & Martin, L. (2008). Relationship between diagnostic criteria, depressive equivalents and diagnosis of depression among older adults with intellectual disability. *Journal of Intellectual Disability Research, 52*, 896–904.

Lindsay, W.R. & Lees, M.S. (2003). A comparison of anxiety and depression in sex offenders with intellectual disability and a control group with intellectual disability. *Sexual Abuse*, 15, 339–345.

Lindsay, W.R., Michie, A.M., Baty, F.J., Smith, A.H.W. & Miller, S. (1994). The consistency of reports about feelings and emotions from people with intellectual disability. *Journal of Intellectual Disability Research*, 38, 61–66.

Lindsay, W.R. & Skene, D.D. (2007). The Beck Depression Inventory II and the Beck Anxiety Inventory in people with intellectual disabilities: Factor analyses and group data. *Journal of Applied Research in Intellectual Disabilities*, 20, 401–408.

LoVullo, S.V. & Matson, J.L. (2009). Comorbid psychopathology in adults with autism spectrum disorders and intellectual disabilities. *Research in Developmental Disabilities*, 30, 1288–1296.

Masi, G., Brovedani, P., Mucci, M. & Favilla, L. (2002). Assessment of anxiety and depression in adolescents with mental retardation. *Child Psychiatry and Human Development*, 32, 227–237.

Matson, J.L. (1995). *The diagnostic assessment for the severely handicapped – II*. Baton Rouge, LA: Scientific Publishers.

Matson, J.L. & Boisjoli, J.A. (2008). Autism spectrum disorders in adults with intellectual disability and comorbid psychopathology: Scale development and reliability of the ASD-CA. *Research in Autism Spectrum Disorders*, 2, 276–287.

Matson, J.L., Gardner, W.I., Coe, D.A. & Sovner, R. (1991). A scale for evaluating emotional disorders in severely and profoundly mentally retarded persons: Development of the Diagnostic Assessment for the Severely Handicapped (DASH) Scale. *The British Journal of Psychiatry*, 159, 404–409.

Matson, J.L., Kazdin, A.E. & Senatore, V. (1984). Psychometric properties of the Psychopathology Instrument for Mentally Retarded Adults. *Applied Research in Mental Retardation*, 5, 881–889.

Melville, C.A., Cooper, S.-A., Morrison, J., Smiley, E., Allan, L., Jackson, A. *et al.* (2008). The prevalence and incidence of mental ill-health in adults with autism and intellectual disabilities. *Journal of Autism and Developmental Disorders*, 38, 1676–1688.

Mindham, J. & Espie, C.A. (2003). The Glasgow Anxiety Scale for People with an Intellectual Disability (GAS-ID): Development and psychometric properties of a new measure for use with people with mild intellectual disability. *Journal of Intellectual Disability Research*, 47, 22–30.

Mohr, C. & Costello, H. (2007). Mental health assessment and monitoring tools for people with intellectual disabilities. In N. Bouras & G. Holt (Eds.) *Psychiatric and behavioural disorders in intellectual and developmental disabilities* (2nd edn, pp. 24–41). Cambridge, UK: Cambridge University Press.

Mohr, C., Tonge, B.J. & Einfeld, S.L. (2005). The development of a new measure for the assessment of psychopathology in adults with intellectual disability. *Journal of Intellectual Disability Research*, 49, 469–480.

Moss, S., Ibbotson, B., Prosser, H., Goldberg, D., Patel, P. & Simpson, N. (1997). Validity of the PAS-ADD for detecting psychiatric symptoms in adults with learning disability (mental retardation). *Social Psychiatry and Psychiatric Epidemiology*, 32, 344–354.

Moss, S., Prosser, H., Costello, H., Simpson, N., Patel, P., Rowe, S. *et al.* (1998). Reliability and validity of the PAS-ADD Checklist for detecting psychiatric disorders in adults with intellectual disability. *Journal of Intellectual Disability Research*, 42, 173–183.

Moss, S., Prosser, H. & Goldberg, D. (1996). Validity of the schizophrenia diagnosis of the Psychiatric Assessment Schedule for Adults with Developmental Disability (PAS-ADD). *The British Journal of Psychiatry*, 168, 359–367.

Moss, S., Prosser, H., Ibbotson, B. & Goldberg, D. (1996). Respondent and informant accounts of psychiatric symptoms in a sample of patients with learning disability. *Journal of Intellectual Disability Research, 40*, 457–465.

Moss, S.C., Prosser, H., Costello, H., Simpson, N. & Patel, P. (1996). *PAS-ADD Checklist*. Manchester: Hester Adrian Research Centre, University of Manchester.

Myrbakk, E. & von Tetzchner, S. (2008a). Psychiatric disorders and behaviour problems in people with intellectual disability. *Research in Developmental Disabilities, 29*, 316–332.

Myrbakk, E. & von Tetzchner, S. (2008b). Screening individuals with intellectual disability for psychiatric disorders: Comparison of four measures. *American Journal of Mental Retardation, 113*, 54–70.

Nezu, C.M., Nezu, A.M., Rothenberg, J.L. & Dellicarpini, L. (1995). Depression in adults with mild mental retardation: Are cognitive variables involved? *Cognitive Therapy and Research, 19*, 227–239.

Novaco, R.W. (1975). *Anger control: The development and evaluation of an experimental treatment*. Lexington, MA: Lexington Books, D.C. Heath. Reviewed by Konecni, V. (1976). Good news for angry people. *Contemporary Psychology, 21*, 397–398.

Novaco, R.W. (1994). Anger as a risk factor for violence among the mentally disordered. In J. Monahan & H. Steadman (Eds.) *Violence and mental disorder: Developments in risk assessment* (pp. 21–59). Chicago, IL: University of Chicago Press.

Novaco, R.W. (2003). *The Novaco Anger Scale and Provocation Inventory Manual (NAS-PI)*. Los Angeles, CA: Western Psychological Services.

Novaco, R.W. & Taylor, J.L. (2004). Assessment of anger and aggression in male offenders with developmental disabilities. *Psychological Assessment, 16*, 42–50.

Oliver, M.N.I., Miller, T.T. & Skillman, G.D. (2005). Factors influencing direct-care paraprofessionals' decisions to initiate mental health referrals for adults with mental retardation. *Mental Retardation, 43*, 83–91.

Powell, R. (2003). Psychometric properties of the Beck Depression Inventory and the Zung Self Rating Depression Scale in adults with mental retardation. *Mental Retardation, 41*, 88–95.

Prigerson, H.G., Maciejewski, P.K., Reynolds, C.F., Bierhals, A.J., Newsom, J.T., Fasiczka, A. *et al.* (1995). Inventory of Complicated Grief: A scale to measure maladaptive symptoms of loss. *Psychiatry Research, 59*, 65–79.

Prosser, H., Moss, S., Costello, H., Simpson, N. & Patel, P. (1997). *The Mini PAS-ADD: An assessment schedule for the detection of mental health needs in adults with learning disability (mental retardation)*. Manchester: Hester Adrian Research Centre, University of Manchester.

Prosser, H., Moss, S., Costello, H., Simpson, N., Patel, P. & Rowe, S. (1998). Reliability and validity of the Mini PAS-ADD for assessing psychiatric disorders in adults with intellectual disability. *Journal of Intellectual Disability Research, 42*, 264–272.

Prout, H.T. & Schaefer, B.M. (1985). Self-reports of depression by community based mildly mentally retarded adults. *American Journal of Mental Deficiency, 90*, 220–222.

Ramirez, S.Z. & Lukenbill, J. (2008). Psychometric properties of the Zung Self-Rating Anxiety Scale for adults with intellectual disabilities (SAS-ID). *Journal of Developmental and Physical Disabilities, 20*, 573–580.

Reiss, S. (1988a). *Reiss Screen for maladaptive behavior*. Worthington, OH: IDS.

Reiss, S. (1988b). The development of a screening measure for psychopathology in people with mental retardation. In E. Dibble & D. Gray (Eds.) *Assessment of behavior problems in persons with mental retardation living in the community*. Rockville, MD: National Institute of Mental Health.

Rojahn, J., Rabold, D.E. & Schneider, F. (1995). Emotion specificity in mental retardation. *American Journal of Mental Retardation, 99*, 477–486.

Rose, J.L. & Gerson, D.F. (2009). Assessing anger in people with intellectual disability. *Journal of Intellectual and Developmental Disability, 34,* 116–122.

Rose, J.L. & West, C. (1999). Assessment of anger in people with intellectual disabilities. *Journal of Applied Research in Intellectual Disabilities, 12,* 211–224.

Ross, E. & Oliver, C. (2002). The relationship between mood, interest and pleasure and "challenging behaviour" in adults with severe and profound intellectual disability. *Journal of Intellectual Disability Research, 46,* 191–197.

Ross, E. & Oliver, C. (2003a). The assessment of mood in adults who have severe or profound mental retardation. *Clinical Psychology Review, 23,* 225–245.

Ross, E. & Oliver, C. (2003b). Preliminary analysis of the psychometric properties of the Mood Interest and Pleasure Questionnaire (MIPQ) for adults with severe and profound learning disabilities. *The British Journal of Clinical Psychology, 42,* 81–93.

Royal College of Psychiatrists (2001). *DC-LD: Diagnostic Criteria for Psychiatric Disorders for Use with Adults with Learning Disabilities/Mental Retardation (Occasional Paper OP 48).* London: Gaskell.

Senatore, V., Matson, J.L. & Kazdin, A.E. (1985). An inventory to assess psychopathology in mentally retarded adults. *American Journal of Mental Retardation, 89,* 459–466.

Sims, A. (1988). *Symptoms in the mind: An introduction to descriptive psychopathology.* London: Bailliere Tindall.

Smith, K.R.M. & Matson, J.L. (2010). Psychopathology: Differences among adults with intellectually disabled, comorbid autism spectrum disorders and epilepsy. *Research in Developmental Disabilities, 31,* 743–749.

Steptoe, L.R., Lindsay, W.R., Murphy, L. & Young, S.J. (2008). Construct validity, reliability and predictive validity of the dynamic risk assessment and management system (DRAMS) in offenders with intellectual disability. *Legal and Criminological Psychology, 13,* 309–321.

Sturmey, P. (2007). Diagnosis of mental disorders in people with intellectual disabilities. In N. Bouras & G. Holt (Eds.) *Psychiatric & behavioural disorders in intellectual and developmental disabilities* (2nd edn, pp.3–23). Cambridge, UK: Cambridge University Press.

Sturmey, P. & Bertman, L.J. (1994). Validity of the Reiss Screen for maladaptive behaviors. *American Journal of Mental Retardation, 99,* 201–206.

Sturmey, P., Laud, R.B., Cooper, C.L., Matson, J.L. & Fodstad, J.C. (2010). Challenging behaviours should not be considered depressive equivalents in individuals with intellectual disabilities. II. A replication study. *Research in Developmental Disabilities, 31,* 1002–1007.

Sturmey, P., Reed, J. & Corbett, J. (1991). Psychometric assessment of psychiatric disorders in people with learning difficulties (mental handicap): A review of the measures. *Psychological Medicine, 21,* 143–155.

Taylor, J.L. & Novaco, R.W. (2005). *Anger treatment for people with developmental disabilities: A theory, evidence and manual based approach.* Chichester: Wiley.

Taylor, J.L., Novaco, R.W., Guinan, C. & Street, N. (2004). Development of an imaginal provocation test to evaluate treatment for anger problems in people with intellectual disabilities. *Clinical Psychology & Psychotherapy, 11,* 233–246.

Torr, J., Iacono, T., Graham, M.J. & Galea, J. (2008). Checklists for general practitioner diagnosis of depression in adults with intellectual disability. *Journal of Intellectual Disability Research, 52,* 930–941.

Tsakanikos, E., Costello, H., Holt, G., Bouras, N., Sturmey, P. & Newton, T. (2006). Psychopathology in adults with autism and intellectual disability. *Journal of Autism and Developmental Disorders, 36,* 1123–1129.

World Health Organization (1992). *Schedules of clinical assessment in neuropsychiatry, version 1*. Geneva: World Health Organization.

World Health Organization (1993). *The ICD-10 classification of mental and behavioural disorders*. Geneva: World Health Organization.

World Health Organization (1996). *ICD-10 guide for mental retardation*. Geneva: World Health Organization.

Zigmond, A.S. & Snaith, R.P. (1983). The hospital anxiety and depression scale. *Acta Psychiatrica Scandinavica, 67*, 361–370.

Zung, W.K. (1965). A self-rating depression scale. *Archives of General Psychiatry, 12*, 63–70.

Zung, W.K. (1971). A rating instrument for anxiety disorders. *Psychosomatics, 12*, 371–379.

Chapter 4

Preparing People with Intellectual Disabilities for Psychological Treatment

Dave Dagnan
Andrew J. Jahoda
Amy Kilbane

Introduction

Assessing factors that might affect therapy process and outcome and ensuring that potential clients have information about therapy are activities that are prevalent in many forms of therapy. Addressing these factors presents particular challenges when working with people with intellectual disabilities, and a number of authors have written regarding readiness and preparation for therapy for people with intellectual disabilities. For example, Willner (2006) considered readiness for therapy based on Rollnick's (1998) distinction of willingness and ability. In this chapter, we provide a further perspective on this issue and consider preparation for therapy using Lambert's (1992) categorization of common factors in therapies: client factors, therapeutic relationship factors, expectancy, and techniques. We consider this as a useful framework for considering preparation for therapy with people with intellectual disabilities. Thus, this chapter will first consider the issue of client expectations, particularly considering how people with intellectual disabilities access therapy and their understanding of what therapy is for. We will then consider the therapeutic alliance with a focus on cognitive–behavioral therapy (CBT), and consider how people with intellectual disabilities' previous experience may affect this and how we can prepare clients to maximize therapeutic alliance. We will discuss client characteristics with an emphasis on the cognitive and emotional resources that people will have and how we can assess these. Finally, we will consider therapist skills and techniques and consider how mainstreaming approaches may put demands on therapists who do not specialize in working with people with intellectual disabilities and how these should be addressed.

Psychological Therapies for Adults with Intellectual Disabilities, First Edition.
Edited by John L. Taylor, William R. Lindsay, Richard P. Hastings, and Chris Hatton.
© 2013 John Wiley & Sons, Ltd. Published 2013 by John Wiley & Sons, Ltd.

Client Expectations

Clients' views and expectations of therapy predict therapeutic outcome. Garfield (1994) defined therapy expectancies as anticipatory beliefs about what will happen during or because of therapy and separates the expectancy construct into outcome, process, and role categories. Client outcome expectations are those beliefs about whether therapy will be beneficial and will result in change; role expectations are beliefs about what behaviors the client and therapist will engage in during therapy; process expectations refer to those beliefs about the procedures, experience, and duration of therapy.

Outcome expectancy

People's expectations of therapy as they enter the process may be significantly affected by the way in which therapy is offered. In general adult mental health services in the United Kingdom, most people are referred via their general practitioner, having sought help for their problems and have the option of whether or not to agree to a referral and also the option of whether or not to turn up to an appointment once offered. In contrast, people with intellectual disabilities are usually referred and brought to specialist services by someone else, often without being consulted (Stenfert Kroese, 2008; Willner, 2003); thus, preparation for therapy might involve helping potential clients to understand why they are being offered therapy. Moreover, their beliefs about the potential for change may be quite subtle. The authors carried out a recent study into process issues concerning CBT with people who have intellectual disabilities and interviewed individuals receiving therapy. The participants did not just think that therapy was more or less likely to achieve change, but it was found that many of the participants also felt that any change was likely to be fragile or unlikely to be maintained in the longer term (Jahoda *et al.*, 2007). Obtaining this kind of insight can help to prepare the participant for therapy, perhaps beginning by addressing the participants' belief in their ability to achieve and sustain change. Moreover, it might also have implications on how the therapist prepares for therapy, something that will be addressed later in this chapter.

Role expectations

People with intellectual disabilities are likely to have a limited understanding of the role they will be expected to take in therapy. They are likely to have had experience of a variety of professionals working with them, and if they have significant problems at the time of referral, then there may well be a considerable number of professionals providing input at that point in time. This can make it difficult for the person to understand what is going to be different about the CBT therapist's contribution. Past experience of receiving help from education, health, and social care professionals will shape the participants' beliefs about the potential of therapy to help them achieve change. Exploring clients' views of other past and present input may therefore be an important part of the preparatory phase of therapy.

Process expectations

People with intellectual disabilities probably differ little from their nondisabled peers in their knowledge of how they are going to work with the CBT therapist. However, the nature of helping relationships they are used to, both formal and informal, might be rather different. Even relationships with family and others who provide emotional and practical help may be unequal and rather didactic, with the person with intellectual disabilities being a rather passive recipient of assistance (Jahoda *et al.*, 2006). Thus, it might be difficult for the clients to imagine or have a sense of what it means to work collaboratively with the therapist, and it is important to present an initial explanation of what is likely to happen in CBT sessions and the types of activity it may involve. However, Jahoda *et al.* (2009) reported the degree to which CBT for people with intellectual disabilities can be seen within a collaborative framework. Using detailed coding of transcriptions from therapy with people with intellectual disabilities, they identified that therapy is indeed an equal process although the contribution of the therapist and client is different, with the therapist providing structure through questioning but the client providing content through his or her responses.

From the outset, care needs to be taken to ensure that the participants understand the limits of the therapeutic relationship. This is a complex topic that requires professional judgment and personal sensitivity on the part of the therapist. However, therapists might mistakenly believe that clients will intuit the bounds of the relationship from their behavior and the nature of the therapeutic encounters. In the research on therapy process issues already alluded to (Jahoda *et al.*, 2007), a number of the clients we interviewed did not regard the therapeutic relationship, nor the therapy, as time limited. Instead, some believed that the positive therapeutic relationship they enjoyed would be open ended and offer them someone to speak to and obtain help from when they faced difficulties in their lives. Once again, given these individuals' histories of dealing with adversity, and the lack of continuity in the support that they have received in their lives, this may be a reasonable aspiration. Even if the participants find the time-limited nature of therapy difficult to grasp, the idea of an ending should be explicitly addressed with clients when preparing to start.

The match of the clients' understanding of the causes of their distress and their engagement with particular therapeutic approaches has been studied in mainstream populations (Meyer & Garcia-Roberts, 2007; Thwaites *et al.*, 2004) but has not yet been researched with people with intellectual disabilities. It would seem that this is a particularly useful paradigm to explore how we should address the therapeutic expectations of this client group.

The Therapeutic Relationship

Therapeutic relationships may present particular challenges to people with intellectual disabilities. Early caregiving experiences are internalized into a cognitive model that guides what a person expects of and does within his or her subsequent relationships (Bowlby, 1984). Less secure attachment styles may be characterized by higher levels of interpersonal distrust, difficulty in depending on another person for support, or preoccupation with concerns about possible abandonment. Researchers such as Weinberger (1995) and Mischel and Shoda (1995) have identified that development and maintenance of the therapeutic relationship may be particularly challenging for individuals with less secure attachment.

Bordin (1979) identified three elements to the therapeutic alliance: the assignment of tasks, the agreement of goals, and the development of a bond. Within CBT, the therapeutic alliance has some specific features. Waddington (2002) identified key areas that are typical of the therapeutic alliance in CBT. She suggested that CBT therapists do not assume that the relationship is sufficient alone to produce change but that the relationship is a powerful source for social influence. In fact, Beck (1995) suggested that the therapeutic relationship can be rewarding for those people where technical change is slow; that positive change will predict improvement in therapeutic relationship rather than the relationship needing to be strong in order to produce change; that the relationship in the earlier stages of therapy is more predictive of outcomes than the relationship at the later stages; and that partnership and confidence in the therapist will be higher for CBT than psychodynamic or interpersonal therapies.

The research we carried out investigating process issues with individuals with intellectual disabilities engaged in CBT supports the relevance of some of these points for people with intellectual disabilities (Jahoda *et al.*, 2007). Interviews with these participants and video reviews of therapy sessions by the individuals themselves suggested that they regarded their relationship with the therapist as one of the most positive aspects of therapy. Not only did positive relationships prove motivating to the clients to attend sessions and engage in the process, but these also gave them a sense of being properly understood and respected by therapists, boosting their confidence.

Both Bordin and Waddington's accounts of general and specific factors in the therapeutic alliance stress the importance of shared achievements and goals. Thus, it is important that in preparation for therapy, the therapist should be attempting to foster a sense of the client's self-efficacy. As stated above, readiness to engage in any therapeutic activity requires both the ability and the motivation to take part (Keijsers *et al.*, 1999; Krause, 1966; Rollnick, 1998). Therefore, an important phase of preparatory work might involve attempting to increase clients' sense of self-efficacy and highlighting their strengths and past successes, rather than merely focusing on problem areas. This will be fostered through careful attention to achievements within therapy, particularly in the early stages of the interactions. The careful use of agendas has been previously emphasized for CBT with people with intellectual disabilities (Lindsay, 1999). Agreeing goals for each element of interaction and celebrating the small successes of the interactions within therapy will create a sense of shared success, which will strengthen the alliance.

Client Factors

There are challenges and limits to using talking therapies such as CBT with people who have intellectual disabilities. They are likely to have some difficulties with comprehension and may struggle to express their thoughts and feelings verbally. Thus, it is important to establish the person's cognitive and emotional skills with respect to the core tasks of therapy. Assessment in this area may serve a number of functions. The assessment may be used to identify how therapy should be adapted for the individual and inform the particular approach to cognitive therapy adopted (Dagnan & Lindsay, 2004), as therapies derived from self-monitoring (Korotitsch & Neslon-Gray, 1999) or Socratic meaning-based approaches (e.g., Beck, 1995) may require different skills. The assessment may be used to identify whether clients would benefit from the opportunity to further develop specific skills prior to therapy. For example, there are a number of examples of training and developmental curricula that have demonstrated the development of emotional recognition and language skills (e.g., McKenzie *et al.*, 2000) and understanding of cognitive mediation (Bruce *et al.*, 2010). The assessment may be used to offer formulation insight into the problems facing a person. For example, it is possible that although referred for anger problems or anxiety, the person may prove to have problems associated with a profound misinterpretation of emotional communication. A clinical case where an apparently able person was interpreting any raised voice as anger is an illustration of this point. Finally, assessment may identify that cognitive therapy is not suitable or necessary for the individual, either because the assessment suggests that the issue presenting is not one that would benefit from a therapeutic intervention or because the cognitive therapy cannot be adapted sufficiently to match the person's abilities.

The above discussion assumes that formal assessment will be more informative than relying on impressions gained by the clinician during an equivalent time spent in a less structured interaction. It is also based on an assumption that formal assessment does not interfere with the therapeutic relationship. In fact, it can be argued that cognitive therapy is a highly structured approach for people with intellectual disabilities, and that this is effectively modeled in a structured intervention that creates an expectation of the nature of the therapeutic activity and the relationship with the therapist and offers repeated opportunities to model the small shared successes that will contribute to the development of a therapeutic alliance.

Assessment structure

CBT is clearly a language-based approach. There is evidence that people who work with people with intellectual disabilities routinely overestimate the communicative ability of their clients (Bradshaw, 2001). This tends to happen because in the routines of daily living, language may be used in a repetitive routine manner. There is no similar evidence for the judgments of therapists in respect to the language of people with intellectual disabilities; however, the tendency for people with intellectual disability to mask their disability or to attempt to "pass" (Edgerton, 1993) should not be underestimated.

Our assessments broadly examine cognitive emotional tasks. In developing assessments in this area, we have considered the core process through which cognitive therapists access cognition. Safran *et al.* (1986) carried out observations of cognitive therapy in action and noted that when isolating cognitions, therapists first identified the emotional or behavioral outcome, then located this outcome within the activating event, and finally explored the cognitive experience specific to that event and emotional or behavioral outcome. Similarly, we have developed assessment approaches that first consider a range of skills regarding the recognition and understanding of emotion, simple assessments of the person's ability to link emotions and behavioral outcomes to activating events, and finally assessments of the person's ability to generate mediating cognitions and to demonstrate an understanding that these cognitions link to emotions and behavior. Assessments of factors associated with a positive outcome in cognitive therapy have been described within mainstream literature. Safran *et al.* (1993) described a comprehensive questionnaire of factors associated with a positive outcome in cognitive therapy; a number of elements of this assessment have still not been fully explored with respect to people with intellectual disabilities.

Language

Our initial assessment structure begins with a simple assessment of language and other core skills. For example, we would routinely assess comprehension using assessments such as the British Picture Vocabulary Scale (Dunn *et al.*, 1997) or the Test for Reception of Grammar (Bishop, 2003); both are simple to administer and relatively quick assessments of comprehension. In particular, the Test for Reception of Grammar is an assessment that offers face validity in determining the number of words and sentence structures that people with intellectual disabilities are able to understand reliably. Where possible, it may be worth considering an IQ assessment as this offers a number of dimensions of language and problem solving that may inform clinical decisions and processes.

Recognition of emotion

In assessing a person's understanding of emotions, there are a number of dimensions to be considered. First, there is the potential to assess a person's recognition of emotion, through facial expressions or through other nonverbal signs. It may also be useful to assess the person's recognition of degrees of emotion in faces. Subsequently, we can assess the person's understanding of his or her own emotions; this may be done through direct questionnaire or through assessment of the person's ability to generate emotion-related words. It is notable that there is considerable literature regarding the recognition of emotion in people with intellectual disabilities (e.g., Rojahn *et al.*, 1995). Much of this literature has not developed from a therapeutic stance; however, there is significant literature describing methods and normative data for this type of assessment.

In clinical practice, we would recommend using simple, standardized assessments of recognition of emotion with more comprehensive individualized assessment using material that has direct relevance or is of particular interest to the client. For example, with a recent client, following the use of Makaton faces (Dagnan & Proudlove, 1997), we used photographs of characters from a well-known soap opera. The client was able to label emotions in these characters more readily than in less familiar standardized materials. In fact, although not the purpose of the specific assessment, the client was able to also identify the current story lines associated with the character and relate those to the emotions in the characters' faces in the photographs, demonstrating a more sophisticated understanding of emotions than simple labeling.

Many materials routinely used with people with intellectual disability are not photographic but rather cartoon or drawing representations of important factors in the lives of people with intellectual disability. While the ecological validity of certain types of line drawing can be questioned, there is little evidence regarding the relative performance using these materials by people with intellectual disability. It is also notable that many of the traditionally used research materials, such as the Ekman (1993) faces, present people showing "archetypally" clear emotions. It is important to recognize that day-to-day emotional expression is rarely as clear and that the idea that happiness is only associated with a big beaming smile may not be helpful in discussing positive and negative emotional experiences with a person with intellectual disability.

A final area with respect to emotion recognition that is poorly researched in people with intellectual disability is the recognition of degrees of emotion. Cognitive therapy is rarely concerned with shifting people from feeling extremely sad to feeling extremely happy. Rather cognitive therapy is concerned with ensuring "appropriate" emotional responses to certain types of experience. With this in mind, recognition of degrees of happiness, sadness, anxiety, or anger becomes potentially important. There is little literature within the intellectual disability research that describes the ability of people with intellectual disabilities to recognize and gradate degrees of emotion. Because there is an absence of research in this area, there is also an absence of appropriate material to test this aspect of emotional recognition in people with intellectual disability.

Recognition of emotion is only one aspect of emotional ability that is important in therapeutic work. It is equally important to understand the person's use of emotional language. There is relatively little literature regarding the use of emotional language in people with intellectual disability. There is therefore an interesting theoretical and practical question regarding the degree of language sophistication regarded as necessary to carry out this type of work. We have developed core tasks in the generation of recognition of emotional language (Mellor & Dagnan, 2005). In the first task, clients are presented with a simple face representing a key emotion (in our task, happy, sad, angry, and frightened); they are then given a single prompt word such as happy, sad, anger, or fear and asked to generate as many words as possible that mean those words in relation to each face. Our results suggest that people with intellectual disability are relatively poor at generating emotion-related words. The possible link between less variation in emotional labels and problems in emotion regulation deserves further exploration with people with intellectual disability. Having identified core words that people with intellectual disability tend to report as emotion-related words, we can then generate recognition tasks based on these materials. For example, we present each of the words generated by clients for happy and sad and ask the client to sort them into happy and sad words, possibly using piles on top of a happy and sad face. We would assume that clients' expressive and receptive ability for language associated with emotion will be roughly equal, although it is likely that clients' receptive ability will be slightly higher, and that they will appropriately identify a number of words that they may not routinely use within their day-to-day vocabulary.

The clinical implications of these assessments within therapy include the very careful recording of emotional language used by the client within clinical notes so that it can be used by the therapist with a degree of precision and reliability in future sessions. We can identify a number of cases where clients have used idiosyncratic words to describe important emotions that if not used reliably by the therapist would create confusion and misunderstanding (e.g., one man who used the word "bored" to describe a range of negative experiences). Finally, we can report some initial research regarding self-awareness of language understanding difficulties (Dagnan & Mellor, manuscript in preparation). We presented people with intellectual disability simple questions regarding their own difficulties in recognizing emotion and compared their answer with those questions with their actual performance on a task involving the generation of emotional language. We found a high association between the clients' statement that they find it difficult to talk about emotion with their actual performance on emotion generation language tasks. Thus, although detailed assessments can be particularly useful for some clients, their self-report in these areas can also be regarded as relatively reliable.

Recognition of the link between activating events and emotional and behavioral consequences

In assessing the clients' ability to recognize that events in their lives affect the way they feel, we use an assessment from Reed and Clements (1989) that presents a simple task where people with intellectual disability are asked to point to an emotion that might accompany a particular scenario. Thus, for example, one scenario is presented as "It's a very hot day, you want an ice cream, the ice cream shop is closed." The client's task is to point to one of two faces (happy or sad) and identify which would be his or her face in that situation. Repeated clinical use of this assessment in a number of research studies (e.g., Dagnan *et al.*, 2000, 2009) has identified that about 75 percent of people with mild and moderate intellectual disability are able to successfully complete this type of task. However, it is notable that, therefore, 25 percent of people have some difficulty with appropriately identifying emotions that would accompany particular scenarios. It is important to note in clinical practice that if a person identifies an unusual emotion in response to a scenario, then it would be important to ask the client why he or she might feel this way. It may be that the person is already using a cognitive model and has very particular reasons that are logical and appropriate to link a scenario with a paradoxical emotion. For example, in the ice cream shop example already given, some clients may say they feel happy if they are on a diet and thus are relieved that they are not going to be tempted to buy an ice cream! We have described previously how we would build on this type of assessment using unique associations between events and emotions that would occur within the person's own life (Dagnan *et al.*, 2007). Thus, questions and tasks such as "what makes you feel happy or sad," "when was the last time you felt happy or sad," "what makes other people in your life feel happy or sad," and "what makes characters in your favorite soap operas or television programs feel happy or sad," can lead into extensive discussion regarding the links between events and emotions that will help understand a person's ability in these areas.

Previous research has suggested that people's ability in these tasks is associated with language skills more than it is associated with core recognition of emotion (Dagnan *et al.*, 2000). This suggests that these tasks are highly language biased:

however, because CBT is a language-based therapy, this would seem an appropriate assessment bias in this context.

Assessing understanding of the cognitive mediation of emotion

Dagnan and Chadwick (1997) and Dagnan *et al.* (2000) introduced tasks designed to assess the understanding that people with intellectual disability have of cognitive mediation. Dagnan and Chadwick (1997) introduced a simple clinical task where a person is presented with a scenario and an associated emotion and asked to suggest what the person might be "thinking or saying to themselves" in that situation. This is a clinically interpreted task, and recently, Dagnan *et al.* (2009) have published examples of client responses to this task to guide therapists in thinking about the meaning of the responses they generate in this task. Dagnan *et al.* (2000) have reported a more complex version of this task that offers either/or options of evaluative beliefs, which suggests that people with intellectual disabilities will have significant difficulties with this type of task. This paper has been replicated on a number of occasions with similar results (Joyce *et al.*, 2006; Oathamshaw & Haddock, 2006; Sams *et al.*, 2006). Dagnan *et al.* (2009) suggested that this task is too complex for routine clinical use and that the simpler task described by them and Dagnan and Chadwick (1997) should be used in preference.

Technique Factors: Preparing Therapists

Current policy in mainstream mental health services in the United Kingdom emphasizes that people with intellectual disabilities should access the same services as people without intellectual disabilities. A key document in English services in recent years has been "Green Light" (Foundation for People with Learning Disabilities, 2004), which offers an audit tool to review whether people with intellectual disabilities are offered mental health services that meet the standards set out in the Mental Health National Service Frameworks. Mental health trusts in England have been required to meet this standard through CQC standards, which have contributed to quality ratings for NHS trusts (http://www.cqc.org.uk/periodicreview/nationalcommitmentsandpriorities2009/10/mentalhealthtrusts/bestpracticeinmentalhealthservicesforpeoplewithalearningdisability.cfm).

However, there are wider benefits in ensuring that mental health services are accessible to people with intellectual disabilities. While we have focused on people with intellectual disabilities in this chapter, we should recognize that the clinical definition of intellectual disability is predominantly a social construction and does not represent a qualitative distinction between those people who meet the diagnostic criteria and those who do not. Thus, we can point out that, while, in a population of 500 000 people there will be approximately 10 000 people with IQ scores below 70, most intellectual disability services know no more than 20 percent of this possible population, which leaves some 8000 people in this group with IQ scores probably below 70 who are already receiving mainstream services. It is likely that many of these people will not warrant a formal diagnosis of intellectual disability because their adaptive behavior is sufficient for them to cope with day-to-day demands of life. However, when they present to mainstream mental health services, they are likely to need considerable support to use many of the literacy and intellectually based interventions they would be offered. For example, in low-intensity Improving Access to Psychological Therapies (IAPT) primary health care structures (Care Services Improvement Partnership, 2008), there is a reliance on guided self-help, bibliotherapy, and referral to other social support agencies. The therapy structures offered are often simple and structured and would often benefit people with lower ability; however, some are structured around very literacy-based recording and intervention techniques. For example, the cognitive restructuring element requires people to record the situation, an associated feeling and a rating of this feeling, the associated thought and a rating of the thought, a revised thought and a rating of this thought, and a feeling associated with the revised thought; the clients are then asked to complete an exercise where they record evidence for and against the beliefs associated with the event. This is a very literacy-based approach.

If we then remind ourselves that there is actually very little functional difference between someone with an IQ score of 70 and someone with an IQ score of 75, then the techniques for assessment and adaptation identified for people with intellectual disabilities become very important for a much wider group. If we suggest that people with IQ scores below 85 might be worth considering for the assessment of core cognitive, emotional, and functional academic skills required for therapy, then some 16 percent (around one in six people) of the population might benefit from these approaches. However, mainstream mental health services do not receive referrals that are representative of the total population. Mental ill-health and problems with well-being are far more likely in groups of people with lower socioeconomic status (Jenkins *et al.*, 2008; Marmot, 2010), and difficulties with literacy, numeracy, and other cognitive–emotional skills are also associated with lower socioeconomic status. Analysis of the Health Survey for England in 2006 and 2008 suggests that the risk of mental ill-health in people in the upper quintile of income is around 5 percent for men and 8 percent for women; in the lowest quintile, however, the risk is 20 percent for men and 23 percent for women (http://www.poverty.org.uk/62/index.shtml). Thus, we could expect a significant overrepresentation of people with lower IQ scores in mainstream mental health services; we have suggested to services that this might be at least one in five referrals if not as high as one in four.

Clearly, adapting referral pathways, clinical protocols, and individual therapy for people with lower ability and functional academic difficulties is an important issue. Access to therapy needs to be seen as a function of the skills of the therapist and not just about the abilities of the person who has been referred. A failure to be able to adapt therapeutic approaches should be seen equally as a failure of the therapist rather than primarily as a failure on the part of the person referred. Within a CBT framework, a clear set of competencies for working with people with anxiety and depression exists for the training and supervision of therapists and the development of services (available online at http://www.ucl.ac.uk/clinical-psychology/CORE/CBT_Competences/CBT_Competence_List.pdf). These outline basic CBT competencies, specific CBT intervention techniques, and other problem-specific competencies; however, they also outline "generic therapeutic competencies" and "CBT meta-competencies," which include generic and CBT-specific meta-competencies. This is a valuable framework for considering the development of therapist skills in working with people with lower ability or intellectual disability. The framework highlights a number of areas such as "ability to foster and maintain a good therapeutic alliance, and to grasp the client's perspective and 'world view'" for which the under-lying competencies involve understanding of issues of therapeutic alliance as discussed in this chapter. The meta-competencies describe areas such as the "capacity to for-mulate and to apply CBT models to the individual client," which references issues of balancing simplification without becoming "reductionist" in the application of therapy and the "capacity to select and skilfully to apply the most appropriate Behav-ioural Therapy and CBT intervention method." The full application of these com-petencies within the framework taking into account socioeconomic covariates such as lower ability and functional academic skills would be important in meeting the needs of this group.

We propose that focusing the development of skills in the adaptation of therapy on therapists who work primarily with people with intellectual disabilities will inevi-tably limit access to therapy for people with intellectual disabilities, as the pool of potential therapists will always tend to be small. It is only through ensuring that "mainstream" therapists are confident in working with people with lower ability that this client group will begin to get equitable access to therapy services. On this basis, we would suggest that training for therapists to work with individuals of lower ability should be embedded within mainstream CBT courses to ensure that "mainstream" therapists are equipped to assess and adapt therapies for this client group. We also suggest that specific courses for people working only with those with intellectual disabilities should be available to those who have already completed training to an appropriate professional standard in CBT approaches (e.g., to the British Association for Behavioural and Cognitive Psychotherapies (BABCP) accreditation standards in the United Kingdom) or who have been trained to a specific role and model (such as low-intensity therapists).

Conclusions

This chapter has begun a discussion of preparing people with intellectual disabilities for therapy using a structure that is derived from an understanding of the nonspecific change agents within psychotherapy. This has not only identified a range of issues that have begun to be considered within the intellectual disability literature, but has also identified a number of areas where research and clinical practice are relatively poorly developed. We have specifically argued that these issues are core competencies for all therapists who will, inevitably, need to adapt therapy to the needs of a wide range of clients. We have suggested that, by focusing on the issues identified in this chapter, we can make therapy more accessible not only to those people with clear and identified intellectual disabilities, but also to those people who do not fully meet intellectual disability diagnostic criteria but who would certainly benefit from the approaches to assessment and adaptations to intervention that have been developed by intellectual disability clinicians and researchers.

References

Beck, J. (1995). *Cognitive therapy: Basics and beyond*. London: Guilford Press.

Bishop, D. (2003). *Test for reception of grammar* (2nd edn). London: Pearson Assessment.

Bordin, E.S. (1979). The generalizability of the psychoanalytic concept of the working alliance. *Psychotherapy: Theory, Research & Practice, 16*, 252–260.

Bowlby, J. (1984). *Attachment and loss*, Vol. 1 (2nd edn). London: Penguin.

Bradshaw, J. (2001). Complexity of staff communication and reported level of understanding skills in adults with intellectual disability. *Journal of Intellectual Disability Research, 45*, 233–243.

Bruce, M., Collins, S., Langdon, P.E., Powlitch, S. & Reynolds, S. (2010). Does training improve understanding of core concepts in cognitive behaviour therapy by people with intellectual disabilities? A randomised experiment. *The British Journal of Clinical Psychology, 49*, 1–13.

Care Services Improvement Partnership (2008). *Improving Access to Psychological Therapies implementation plan: Curriculum for low intensity therapies workers*. London: Department of Health.

Dagnan, D. & Chadwick, P. (1997). Components of cognitive therapy with people with learning disabilities. In B. Kroese, D. Dagnan & K. Loumidis (Eds.) *Cognitive therapy for people with learning disabilities*. London: Routledge.

Dagnan, D., Chadwick, P. & Proudlove, J. (2000). Towards an assessment of suitability of people with mental retardation for cognitive therapy. *Cognitive Therapy and Research, 24*, 627–636.

Dagnan, D., Jahoda, A. & Stenfert Kroese, B. (2007). Cognitive behavioural therapy and people with intellectual disabilities. In G. O'Reilly, J. McEvoy & P. Walsh (Eds.) *Handbook of clinical psychology and intellectual disability practice*. London: Routledge.

Dagnan, D. & Lindsay, W.R. (2004). Cognitive therapy with people with learning disabilities. In E. Emerson, C. Hatton, T. Parmenter & T. Thompson (Eds.) *International handbook of research and evaluation in intellectual disabilities*. New York: Wiley.

Dagnan, D., Mellor, K. & Jefferson, C. (2009). Assessment of cognitive therapy skills for people with intellectual disability. *Advances in Mental Health and Learning Disabilities, 3*, 25–30.

Dagnan, D. & Proudlove, J. (1997). Using Makaton drawings to assess the ability to recognise facial expression of emotion in people with learning disabilities. *Clinical Psychology Forum, 105*, 3–5.

Dunn, L.M., Dunn, L.M., Whetton, C. & Burley, J. (1997). *British picture vocabulary scale – II* (2nd edn). Windsor: NFER-Nelson.

Edgerton, R.B. (1993). *The cloak of competence revised and updated edition*. Berkeley, CA: University of California Press.

Ekman, P. (1993). Facial expression and emotion. *The American Psychologist, 48*, 384–392.

Foundation for People with Learning Disabilities (2004). *Green light for mental health. How good are your mental health services for people with learning disabilities? A service improvement kit*. London: Foundation for People with Learning Disabilities.

Garfield, S.L. (1994). Research on client variables in psychotherapy. In A.E. Bergin & S.L. Garfield (Eds.) *Handbook of psychotherapy and behaviour change* (4th edn, pp.190–228). New York: Wiley.

Jahoda, A., Dagnan, D., Jarvie, P. & Kerr, W. (2006). Depression, social context and cognitive behavioural therapy for people who have intellectual disabilities. *Journal of Applied Research in Intellectual Disabilities, 19*, 81–89.

Jahoda, A., Pert, C., Trower, P., Stenfert-Kroese, B., Burford, B. & Dagnan, D. (2007). *Establishing the building blocks of cognitive behavioural therapy for people with mild learning disabilities: An exploration of key process issues.* Final Report. Chief Scientist's Office, The Scottish Government.

Jahoda, A., Selkirk, M., Trower, P., Pert, C., Dagnan, D. & Stenfert-Kroese, B. (2009). The balance of power in therapeutic interactions with individuals who have intellectual disabilities. *The British Journal of Clinical Psychology, 48,* 63–77.

Jenkins, R., Meltzer, H., Jones, P.B., Brugha, T., Bebbington, P., Farrell, M. *et al.* (2008). *Foresight mental capital and wellbeing project. Mental health: Future challenges.* London: The Government Office for Science.

Joyce, T., Globe, A. & Moody, C. (2006). Assessment of the component skills for cognitive therapy in adults with intellectual disability. *Journal of Applied Research in Intellectual Disabilities, 19,* 17–23.

Keijsers, G.P.J., Schaap, C.P.D.R., Hoodguin, C.A.L., Hoogesteyns, B. & de Kemp, E.C.M. (1999). Preliminary results of a new instrument to assess patient motivation for treatment in cognitive-behaviour therapy. *Behavioural and Cognitive Psychotherapy, 27,* 165–179.

Korotitsch, W.J. & Neslon-Gray, R.O. (1999). An overview of self-monitoring research in assessment and treatment. *Psychological Assessment, 11,* 415–425.

Krause, M.S. (1966). A cognitive theory of motivation for treatment. *The Journal of General Psychology, 75,* 9–19.

Lambert, M.J. (1992). Psychotherapy outcome research: Implications for integrative and eclectic therapists. In J.C. Norcross & M.R. Goldfried (Eds.) *Handbook of psychotherapy integration* (pp.94–129). New York: Basic books.

Lindsay, W.R. (1999). Cognitive therapy. *The Psychologist, 12,* 238–241.

Marmot, M. (2010). *Fair society, healthy lives: A strategic review of health inequalities in England post-2010.* London: Department of Health.

McKenzie, K., Matheson, E., McKaskie, K., Hamilton, L. & Murray, G.C. (2000). Impact of group training on emotion recognition in individuals with a learning disability. *British Journal of Learning Disabilities, 28,* 143–147.

Mellor, K. & Dagnan, D. (2005). Exploring the concept of alexithymia in the lives of people with intellectual disabilities. *Journal of Learning Disabilities, 9,* 229–239.

Meyer, B. & Garcia-Roberts, L. (2007). Congruence between reasons for depression and motivations for specific interventions. *Psychology and Psychotherapy: Theory, Research and Practice, 80,* 525–542.

Mischel, W. & Shoda, Y. (1995). A cognitive-affective system theory of personality: Reconceptualising situation, dispositions, dynamics and invariance in personality structure. *Psychological Review, 102,* 248–268.

Oathamshaw, S.C. & Haddock, G. (2006). Do people with intellectual disabilities and psychosis have the cognitive skills required to undertake cognitive behavioural therapy? *Journal of Applied Research in Intellectual Disabilities, 19,* 35–46.

Reed, J. & Clements, J. (1989). Assessing the understanding of emotional states in a population of adolescents and young adults with mental handicaps. *Journal of Mental Deficiency Research, 33,* 229–233.

Rojahn, J., Rabold, D.E. & Schneider, F. (1995). Emotion specificity in mental retardation. *American Journal of Mental Retardation, 99,* 477–468.

Rollnick, S. (1998). Readiness, importance and confidence: Critical conditions of change in treatment. In W.R. Millar & N. Heather (Eds.) *Treating addictive behaviours* (2nd edn, pp.49–60). New York: Plenum.

Safran, J.D., Segal, Z.V., Vallis, T.M., Shaw, B.F. & Samstag, L.W. (1993). Assessing patient suitability for short-term cognitive therapy with an interpersonal focus. *Cognitive Therapy and Research, 17,* 23–38.

Safran, J.D., Vallis, T.M., Segal, Z.V. & Shaw, B.F. (1986). Assessment of core cognitive processes in cognitive therapy. *Cognitive Therapy and Research, 10*, 509–526.

Sams, K., Collins, S. & Reynolds, S. (2006). Cognitive therapy abilities in people with learning disabilities. *Journal of Applied Research in Intellectual Disabilities, 19*, 25–33.

Stenfert Kroese, B. (2008). Carers' expectations and views of cognitive behavioural therapy for adults with intellectual disabilities. *Journal of Intellectual Disability Research, 52*, 732.

Thwaites, R., Dagnan, D., Huey, D. & Addis, M. (2004). The reasons for depression questionnaire (RFD): UK standardization for clinical and non-clinical populations. *Psychology and Psychotherapy: Theory, Research and Practice, 77*, 363–374.

Waddington, L. (2002). The therapy relationship in cognitive therapy: A review. *Behavioural & Cognitive Psychotherapy, 30*, 179–191.

Weinberger, J. (1995). Common factors aren't so common: The common factors dilemma. *Clinical Psychology: Science and Practice, 2*, 45–69.

Willner, P. (2003). Assessing prior consent: An audit of referral into a clinical psychology service for people with learning disabilities. *Clinical Psychology, 30*, 25–28.

Willner, P. (2006). Readiness for cognitive therapy in people with intellectual disabilities. *Journal of Applied Research in Intellectual Disabilities, 19*, 5–16.

Chapter 5

Adapting Psychological Therapies for People with Intellectual Disabilities I:

Assessment and Cognitive Deficit Considerations

William R. Lindsay
Andrew J. Jahoda
Paul Willner
John L. Taylor

Introduction

In this chapter and the following chapter, we will deal with ways in which psychological assessments and therapies require to be adapted so that people with intellectual disabilities (IDs) can engage more effectively with the processes. In this chapter, we will consider ways in which assessments might become more accessible without losing the integrity of the test and the psychometric properties. We will also review certain specific cognitive deficits and their implications for therapy. The adaptations described in these chapters are common to all psychological therapies and include the way in which therapy should be structured and the way in which the therapist can communicate the treatment approach to clients. Because much of the work on the adaptation of therapeutic techniques has been done in the context of cognitive–behavioral therapy (CBT), we will make more reference to CBT than other treatment modalities. However, these adaptations are relevant to all forms of psychological therapy with this client group.

Assessment of Individuals with Intellectual Disabilities

Assessment for specific problems such as anxiety, depression, and anger will be dealt with in subsequent chapters. However, we will say something on the general

Psychological Therapies for Adults with Intellectual Disabilities, First Edition.
Edited by John L. Taylor, William R. Lindsay, Richard P. Hastings, and Chris Hatton.
© 2013 John Wiley & Sons, Ltd. Published 2013 by John Wiley & Sons, Ltd.

principles underlying assessment for people with IDs. Successful interventions are underpinned by good-quality formulations, which in turn require reliable and valid assessment. When considering psychological treatment for people with IDs, appropriate clinical assessment tools should be identified to assist formulation and evaluate outcome. It is important that clients can understand the assessments used. This client group is characterized by limitations in literacy, and comprehension skills assessments must be suitably adapted to allow for any language and conceptual limitations (Taylor & Lindsay, 2012).

Even when assessments have been adapted for appropriate language, it is likely that it will still be necessary to read the items and response options to clients who have the greatest difficulty in reading even the simplest material. This will have two major consequences. The first is that the assessment is likely to take considerably longer than it would with an adult outpatient population. With non-ID populations, it is often possible to send assessment schedules to clients prior to their initial appointment so that they can arrive for their first session with primary assessments already completed. This is not possible in clients with IDs. Similarly, it is often not possible to give clients with IDs a series of questionnaires to take away and bring back completed to the next appointment. The second consequence is that because each item is read to clients, assessments take the form of a structured interview. The respondent's reactions to questions, tangential comments, and emotional responses are all available to the assessor as part of the process. This is a considerable strength of conducting assessments with this client group, and it provides information that can add to the richness of the assessment, formulation, and treatment planning process.

Finlay and Lyons (2001) reviewed the available literature on the assessment of emotion and other therapeutic issues in people with IDs and concluded that there was ample evidence that suitably adapted assessments could be understood and used appropriately by this client group. As adaptations to the content and administration of assessment measures used with clients with IDs can be extensive, it is important that the psychometric properties of the instruments remain intact and that the integrity of the assessment process is not undermined or invalidated by the adaptations (Taylor & Lindsay, 2012). One of the first studies to investigate the reliability and validity of the assessments of emotion in people with IDs was conducted by Lindsay *et al.* (1994). They investigated the consistency of responding across measures of related emotions including the Zung Depression Scale (Zung, 1965), the Zung Anxiety Scale (Zung, 1971), and Goldberg General Health Questionnaire (Goldberg & Williams, 1988). They found a high degree of convergent validity of reported emotions and concluded that suitably adapted forms of self-report could be reliable and valid with this client group.

Several studies have found that the patterns of responses from people with IDs on self-report of depression show the same orderly statistical pattern as with the client groups. Dagnan and Sandhu (1999) administered the Zung Depression Scale (Zung, 1965), the Rosenberg Self-Esteem Scale, and Social Comparison Scale (Rosenberg, 1989) to 18 women and 25 men with mild IDs. The numbers involved in this study are small, and the results should be treated with caution. They reported that the factor structure of these instruments was consistent with that of the original scales. This conclusion is supported by recent stronger evidence from Kellet *et al.* (1999,

2003) on the Brief Symptom Inventory (BSI: Derogatis, 1993). They first demonstrated the efficacy of an assisted completion format. Instructions were simplified and the responses were aided with numerical and pictorial representations. They then administered the 53-item questionnaire to 335 participants with IDs. They found that the BSI factor structure corresponded broadly to that originally reported in the standardization (Derogatis, 1993). With reference to the present chapter and material presented later, it is notable that six of the scales replicated the item allocation of the original statistical analysis with five scales retaining their original labels: depression, anxiety, somatization, hostility, and paranoia. The one scale that was quite different was that of obsessive–compulsive disorder. This scale deals with cognitive difficulties associated with obsession and compulsion such as having to check and double check, having difficulty in making decisions, having trouble concentrating, and having some trouble remembering things. Kellet *et al.* (2003) wrote that for this client group, these difficulties appeared related to cognitive deficits rather than obsessive or ruminative thinking. However, apart from these notable differences, they concluded that there was considerable overlap between the general adult and the ID population factor structures.

In reviews of the assessments for use with clients who have ID, Hatton and Taylor (2010; this book) and Dagnan and Lindsay (2004) have concluded that relatively sophisticated question formats such as analogue scales can be used by people with ID with a reasonable degree of reliability and validity. Lindsay and Skene (2007), with particular reference to depression, have found that certain items on the Beck Depression Inventory (BDI) require not only linguistic ability but also the ability to understand changes in concept. In some items, there are subtle changes in concept across the grading of the scale. The item on self-criticism moves from blaming oneself (I am more critical of myself than I used to be) to a concept of universal responsibility (I blame myself for everything bad that happens). This requires not only an understanding of increasing degrees of self-criticism, but also an understanding of the nonlogical shift from self-criticism to universal blame. The item on self-dislike moves from losing confidence in oneself to disliking oneself. These differences in concept can introduce unnecessary complexity. Therefore, Lindsay and Skene (2007) simplified the internal conceptual consistency of each item so that they related only to one concept, for example, an increase in degree of self-blame. Using this methodology, they found that the underlying psychometric properties of the Beck Anxiety Inventory (BAI) (Beck *et al.*, 1988) and the BDI (Beck *et al.*, 1996) were similar to those found in the original standardization studies.

Two assessments have been developed specifically for people with IDs suffering from anxiety and depression. The Glasgow Depression Scale (GDS: Cuthill *et al.*, 2003) is a 20-item scale based on Diagnostic and Statistical Manual of Mental Disorders, Fourth Edition (DSM-IV) criteria. It was designed as a self-report measure to be filled out during interview in the manner described above by people with mild or moderate IDs. In order to check the validity, the GDS also has a carer rating for 16 of the items. The Glasgow Anxiety Scale (GAS: Mindham & Espie, 2003) contains three sections of generalized worry, specific fears, and anxiety symptoms. The questionnaire differentiated between individuals referred for anxiety and a control group of nonanxious people with IDs, although their numbers in the two groups were small at 19 and 16, respectively. The GAS correlated significantly with the BAI with large effect size. Therefore, these two scales, available free with the articles, have good reliability and validity and have been developed for people with IDs.

There are now a number of assessments that have been developed for this client group and a number of assessments that have been adapted successfully for use with people with IDs who have emotional problems. As mentioned at the beginning of this section, reliable and valid assessment is necessary both for formulation and for monitoring the progress and outcome of therapy. The fact that there are now a number of usable instruments for assessing emotion allows clinicians and researchers to evaluate psychological symptoms with some confidence.

Adaptations to Compensate for Cognitive Deficits

In order to work effectively with a person with IDs, a conscious effort is needed to adjust the style of presentation to take account of the client's limited information-processing abilities. As noted further on in this title, the major adaptation is the use of straightforward language and short sentences. There is also a greater use of nonverbal techniques such as gesture and pictorial materials: for example, estimations of the intensity of experiences or the importance of events would typically be elicited using either gestures (e.g., hand separation) or a visual scale made up of three to five shapes of increasing size (see, e.g., Marshall & Willoughby-Booth, 2010). The need for these adaptations is obvious, albeit that experience may be needed to implement them consistently.

However, difficulties also arise from other less obvious sources, which, if not recognized and addressed, are equally detrimental to engagement with CBT. A useful distinction has been drawn between cognitive distortions and cognitive deficits: cognitive distortions are the inaccuracies in the content of thoughts, assumptions, and beliefs that are the target for CBT interventions, while cognitive deficits are deficiencies in the processes by which information is acquired and processed (Dagnan & Lindsay, 2004; Kendall, 1985; Willner, 2006). Cognitive deficits can create severe problems in therapy if ignored, and this goes far wider than a simple focus on IQ. Table 5.1 summarizes deficits that may be encountered in four domains of cognition: intellect, emotional literacy, memory, and executive functioning. The table also lists some of the potential solutions to the problems that these deficits cause. The case formulation for a person with IDs is likely to include intellectual limitations as a predisposing factor, but should also include other cognitive deficits, provided they have been identified (see Willner & Goodey, 2006). These are important issues to consider during the assessment phase, because they are likely to have a damaging effect on the course of therapy if appropriate adaptations are not implemented.

Issues of emotional literacy have been extensively discussed. Many people with IDs have a limited emotional vocabulary (Joyce *et al.*, 2006; Reed & Clements, 1989), for example, difficulty in expressing feelings verbally, or a poor understanding of the difference between, for example, "sad" and "angry," and this may require some preliminary psychoeducational input before attempting to work on emotional problems (McKenzie *et al.*, 2000). Less obviously, people with IDs are generally poor at

Table 5.1 Cognitive Deficits That Can Cause Difficulty in CBT if Not Addressed

Cognitive domains	Specific processes	Implications for therapy
Intellect	Verbal understanding and reasoning	Simple words and short sentences
	Nonverbal understanding and reasoning	Use of nonverbal techniques and materials
Emotional literacy	Emotional vocabulary	Psychoeducation
	"CBT skills"	Psychoeducation and provision of ideas
Memory	Assimilation	Frequent repetition and more sessions
	Recall of experiences	Involvement of carers
	Prospective memory	Use of reminders and involvement of carers
Executive functioning	Working memory	Chunking of information
	Behavioral inhibition	Greater use of behavioral self-control techniques
	Initiative	Provision of ideas

recognizing the central role of cognitions as mediating between situations and emotions. Indeed, a minority of people with mild IDs have difficulty in recognizing the relationship between antecedents and emotional consequences, without even considering cognitions (Dagnan *et al.*, 2000; Reed & Clements, 1989). The ability to recognize the mediating role of cognitions varies greatly within the general population (Safran& Goldbers, 1986), and the majority of people with IDs have difficulty in doing this reliably (Dagnan & Chadwick, 1997; Dagnan *et al.*, 2000; Joyce *et al.*, 2006; Oathamshaw & Haddock, 2006; Sams *et al.*, 2006). All of the cited studies reported significant relationships between "cognitive therapy skills" and measures of receptive language ability. However, it is not clear whether this is a real phenomenon or a function of the complexity of the experimental tasks presented to study participants. There is a danger in extrapolating from failure on experimental cognitive tasks to an inability to engage with cognitive components of CBT in a therapeutic context (Taylor *et al.*, 2008).

It has been suggested that if a client cannot demonstrate an understanding of the mediating role of cognitions, then perhaps a simpler form of therapy, such as self-instructional training, should be offered (Dagnan & Chadwick, 1997). It is certainly true that Socratic questioning is very uphill work in these circumstances, with frequent blocks when the client can only answer "Don't know." However, the inability to articulate thoughts can often be circumvented by the therapist suggesting answers for the client to consider (e.g., "In a situation like this, some people might be thinking . . ."). This represents a dilution of the "guided exploration" component of cognitive therapies, but has the merit of allowing the conversation to continue (Willner & Goodey, 2006).

People with IDs are also likely to have memory deficits. As with emotional literacy, scores on memory tests tend to correlate positively with scores on tests of verbal ability, but again, this relationship accounts for only 40–50 percent of the variance in memory scores (e.g., Willner *et al.*, 2010), so there is a great deal of individual variability. Memory problems interfere with CBT in several different ways. Most obviously, problems in assimilating new material mean that there is a need for frequent repetition and recapitulation, both within and between sessions. This means that progress is likely to be much slower than for a more intellectually able client, and therefore that more sessions may be needed to achieve a comparable outcome. As a result, people with IDs need flexibility over the number of sessions that are available, rather than the fixed session lengths provided by some brief intervention services. Also, a more intensive treatment schedule (e.g., two sessions per week) can offset some of the cognitive limitations of this client group, which can result in problems with assimilation and recall of information from session to session (Taylor & Novaco, 2005). This in turn can enhance clients' motivation to remain engaged in treatment by maintaining momentum and preventing therapy drift.

A second problem is that people with IDs may have great difficulty in remembering and recounting their experiences, both remote and recent, which form the foundations on which a CBT session is built. In order to address this problem, it may be necessary to involve a carer to discuss the events with the client so as to aid recall. This could involve a preliminary discussion after which the carer withdraws from the session, or, with the client's consent, the carer might even be present throughout the session (see Willner & Goodey, 2006). Third, people with IDs have problems with prospective memory – remembering to do things: specifically, homework. Research has shown that completion of homework assignments is an important component of effective CBT, but one with which even intellectually able people have difficulty (Rees *et al.*, 2005). Here, the fact that people with IDs are typically supported by carers means that they are potentially at an advantage, because carers can be recruited to support clients to remember to complete their homework assignments. This can be achieved by inviting the carer to join the final part of the session when homework is being discussed. Homework can also be supported by providing aides memoire, such as reminder notes or calendars. While carers can provide invaluable assistance, involving them is not entirely straightforward, since carers, like clients, can vary in their ability and willingness to take on the tasks they are allocated (Willner, 2006). Careful assessment and sensitivity is needed when engaging carers in supporting therapy.

Impairments of executive functioning are common among people with IDs, and unlike emotional literacy and memory deficits, the severity of executive functioning deficits is largely unrelated to verbal ability within the "mild learning disability" range (Willner *et al.*, 2010). Executive functioning is a complex area that includes three broad sets of skills: (a) monitoring of one's own behavior using working memory, (b) inhibition of impulsive responding, and (c) initiating actions or changing strategies under internal control (Miyake *et al.*, 2000). Problems in the first of these areas present as a short attention span, which means that particular care is needed to keep ideas simple and short, so that they are presented in easily assimilated chunks. Problems with impulsiveness can mean that a far greater proportion of therapy time is taken up with teaching behavioral self-control skills to prevent the occurrence of crises. For example, if an angry client commits an act of physical aggression, this preempts the use of cognitive strategies aimed at avoiding such outbursts, so the priority must be to help the client to maintain self-control. Finally, a problem with the initiation of self-directed behavior can result in the client having difficulty in generating the ideas around which a Socratic dialogue is built. Just as when this problem arises from a limitation of emotional literacy, the solution is for the therapist to provide active support by suggesting ideas for the client to consider. This can easily lead to a situation in which the therapy appears more directive and less collaborative than standard CBT. Therapists may find this an uncomfortable position to adopt but accept it as inevitable in cases where the alternative would be to decline the referral.

General Adaptations to Treatment Techniques

There is no doubt that assessment and treatment methods require adaptation in order to be accessible for individuals with lower intellectual functioning. There are two fundamental aspects in relation to these adaptations and developments. The first is that effective communication is an essential requirement for any interpersonal process including therapeutic interactions. It is axiomatic, but nevertheless requires to be said, that if a person with IDs is misunderstanding the process, the whole exercise is invalid. Therefore, one of the first requirements is to adapt the process to allow for understanding and engagement by the client. Following on from this, a second fundamental requirement is that the integrity of the collaborative cognitive–behavioral approach (e.g., agenda setting, guided discovery, cognitive mediation) is not undermined or reduced by these adaptations. Therefore, we need to ensure that the processes of therapy are adhered to while the therapist's style and approach are modified to allow for the cognitive constraints presented by the client.

Communication

Simplifying one's language is not a natural or easy process. There is a significant danger in becoming patronizing and even dismissive. It requires constant adjustment of vocabulary and syntax in addition to continuing self-monitoring. There are a number of fairly basic recommendations, which, if followed, will allow for clear unambiguous communication in order to help the person with IDs engage in the process. The first is to try to use short sentences that contain a single concept. The second is what we might call "the three-syllable rule." The therapist should attempt to use words of fewer than three syllables. Constant self-monitoring of one's utterances is difficult but necessary. Whenever the therapist hears himself or herself using a word of three or more syllables, he or she should automatically review the sentence for its linguistic and syntactical complexity. Although this may sound straightforward, some professionals with many years of experience continue to use complex syntactical structures and words while conducting didactic explanations of therapeutic and other concepts. In these cases, it may be fairly obvious that clients are not understanding the information fully or engaging with the process. However, and importantly, they may appear to be participating because they have had many years of learning how to mask their lack of understanding in order to mix with normally able peers. It is good practice to ask clients to summarize previous sections of a session in order to assess their understanding and retention.

While these adaptations often promote better understanding, it should be remembered that, counterintuitively, this does not always work. One example of this is the use of simplifying pictures of facial effects. Such simple drawings can be ambiguous and difficult to follow, while richer, dynamic, and contextual cues can be easier to grasp (Matheson & Jahoda, 2005). Normally, the context for the facial expression will be part of the discussion for any particular session, but it is worthwhile remembering that additional contextual cues can sometimes be helpful in clarifying matters.

The use of Socratic or inductive methods (see "The Socratic Process/Guided Discovery") is helpful in guiding the therapist to avoid didactic explanations or presentations of information. Lengthy presentations of information are likely to become boring and tedious and may overload the client with too much information in too short a time. This can be especially true if therapists feel they should work to a time-tabled program where they need to conduct certain sessions within a certain time frame. Because of this, it is better to be reasonably flexible in the amount of time taken for each section of any program and to avoid as far as possible didactic methods. The Socratic dialogue allows the therapist to develop a series of questions that will lead patients to appropriate information. When introducing entirely new concepts, this is not always possible, but in such instances, a small amount of introductory information can begin the inductive process.

One caveat to this approach is that clients may expect to be told what to do or say because they may have had repeated experience of directed interactions. They may also be worrying about "giving the wrong answer" as a result of experiencing repeated failure and negative self-evaluation. Therefore, the therapist should be aware of the temptation to lead the session or provide the answers and information. Allow clients to review their own evidence in the development of arguments. In this way, they will gain an understanding through their own cognitive processes rather than attempting to grasp information presented by someone else. A significant drawback of this process (as with all processes in psychological therapy for people with IDs) is that it is much slower than providing the person with information. However, the therapist can have greater confidence that the client has understood the concepts with a greater length of retention.

By helping to generate the information through guided discovery, the clients are more likely to consider that they have ownership of the content of the session. A further method to promote ownership is to encourage clients to record the information themselves. Figure 5.1 shows the recording from a session of CBT in which the client has reviewed the physical, cognitive, and behavioral experiences related to her own emotions.

Case study: Emily

Emily is a 31-year-old woman who was referred for a constellation of difficulties including depression, chronic problems with self-esteem, anger, and self-harm. Her mother had evicted her from the family home some six years earlier after she had stolen money repeatedly from family members. She stayed in homeless accommodation prior to moving into her own permanent tenancy. However, the tenancy was in jeopardy because of Emily's self-harm and aggression toward her carers. She had been

Figure 5.1 Emily's record of the session exploring the emotion of sadness.

apprehended by the police on a number of occasions in relation to aggression and threats of self-harm, and there were many reports about her defensiveness and difficulties in interpersonal relationships. Intellectual assessment revealed a full-scale IQ of 64 with no particular discrepancies in her intellectual index scores. Figure 5.1 is a record in relation to the emotion of sadness. It can be seen that Emily recorded a number of actions, thoughts, and physiological reactions during the session that begin to explain the relationships between her thoughts and her emotions. The information is in a very immediate form and was photocopied and retained by her as she compiled a treatment log for continual reference. The treatment log consisted of a number of simple diagrams illustrating concepts and accompanying notes developed by Emily herself. This particular session came from the section on the preparation for CBT when the model of emotion was explored with some time taken to apply it to each client's own situation. It serves only to illustrate the method of recording information to allow greater ownership by clients themselves.

Setting an agenda

Although setting an agenda for sessions is generally considered to be a CBT technique, it is the method that can be helpful for any form of psychotherapy. It allows a relatively complex process to become more predictable and controlled. It is likely that an agenda, once established, will be repetitive, and it may be that in later sessions, the therapist and client tend to assume the agenda. In the Jahoda *et al.* (2009) analysis of the CBT process for people with IDs, setting the agenda was the method to which therapists adhered least frequently; for example, some aspects of the agenda setting were omitted on almost 50 percent of occasions. This is understandable since once the agenda has been set over the first few sessions, it will tend to follow the following format:

- Monitor current emotional state.
- Review of the past week.
- Review of homework.
- Analysis of one particular incident cognition, behavior, emotion, and arousal.
- Review implications for future and other settings.
- Exercise for the session.
- Setting homework tasks.

In Chapter 6, the way in which CBT is adapted for people with IDs will be used to illustrate the general principles of adaptation for psychological therapy.

The socratic process/guided discovery

As we have mentioned, when working with clients with IDs, therapists should attempt not to employ any didactic methods. Instead, they should follow a line of guided discovery using Socratic methods to elicit the information from participants. In this way, clients will generate the appropriate information themselves, and are more likely to retain the information. This is one of the basic principles of collaborative empiricism (Beck *et al.*, 1979; see Chapter 6) in that clients will be supported to generate their own information and data, and will reach adaptive conclusions that challenge cognitive distortions and maladaptive schema. For clients with IDs, this approach can be extremely difficult at first because they may expect therapists to outline the procedures, methods, modules, rules, and so on. Some clients may be worried about making mistakes, "giving the wrong answer," "doing the wrong thing," or "making a fool of themselves." These methods can be used in a supportive manner, but therapists should try and resist the urge to conform to expectations that they will lead or direct sessions. Inductive methods encourage participants to follow through the arguments themselves, develop their own evidence, and review pieces of information available to them. In this way, clients develop information that might challenge their dysfunctional cognitions and, more basically, dysfunctional schemas.

It is very important to use guided discovery and exploration when working with clients with IDs. They may feel that the therapist is an expert and will have the answers to any difficulties they are experiencing. It is unlikely that they will have clearly defined the problem they are experiencing, and the guided discovery method allows them to explore various aspects of their difficulties. As mentioned earlier, they are likely to have had years of acquiescence and compliance in an effort to mask their learning disability by feigning understanding. It can be tempting to use didactic methods to tell clients exactly what the problem is and what they need to do. However, such an authoritarian role will be counterproductive for the reasons discussed.

Occasionally, Socratic questioning can be difficult for some people with IDs to follow, and it is possible to help "scaffold" this approach when people are stuck. For example, it is quite legitimate for therapists to suggest alternative possible interpretations of situations to clients. If the client says that a member of the staff has been deliberately nasty when asking him or her to do his or her household chores, the therapist may not be able to come up with an alternative explanation. The therapist could ask "What if you thought the staff member was trying to help you rather than being nasty?" The therapist would then follow a number of interchanges on how it was possible to interpret that the staff member was trying to be helpful and how that would make the client feel. Once this alternative interpretation has been established with the accompanying alternative responses from the client, treatment can continue with a discussion on how he or she would respond. This can also be role played.

Therapists should also be aware that Socratic questioning can be difficult when the client with IDs is stuck on his or her antecedent to consequences manner of thinking. In the example given earlier, the client perceives the staff member as being nasty and the response is maladaptive. The therapist could suggest different possible more charitable interpretations for the staff member's actions, and the client could continue to say that he or she feels angry with the staff member and believes that the staff member was being nasty. On these occasions, a different approach should be considered. Therapist and client might use role play where the client is asked to take the part of the staff member and the therapist take the part of the client. Such role reversal is a common useful technique employed in CBT with people with IDs. Through this exercise, the client as the staff member might suggest that he or she was simply asking the other person to remember to carry out the tasks. There are a range of techniques for facilitating understanding, and all of these should be employed as treatment is progressing.

Monitoring thoughts and feelings

There is a developing technology for the valid and reliable assessment of thoughts and feelings for clients with IDs. Figure 5.2 shows a section from Emily's treatment where she monitored her feelings over a period of several weeks as treatment was

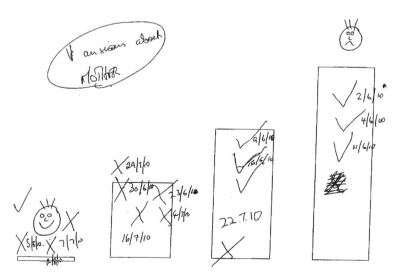

Figure 5.2 Weekly records of Emily's feelings.

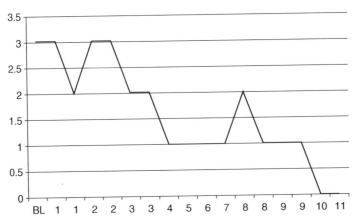

Figure 5.3   This figure graphs the information on Figure 5.2 and shows Emily's weekly ratings of how depressed she felt over the weeks of treatment. The graph shows her ratings at baseline and at all assessments over the following treatment period. A three-month follow-up is also inserted.

progressing. A formal, weekly assessment of progress has been recommended by several authors including Beck *et al.* (1979). In their session-by-session detail on a typical course of cognitive therapy, they noted the client's scores on the BDI (Beck *et al.*, 1996). This client completed the BDI between all sessions up to session 22 and at one, two, and six months' follow-up. Her scores on the BDI fell from 41 and 43 at sessions 1 and 2, respectively, through 15 and 20 at sessions 12 and 13, to 6 and 7 at sessions 21 and 22. Her self-report on the BDI continued to show improvement at six months' follow-up when her score fell to 2. With this client, there were weeks when she returned to higher scores on the BDI. For example, following an improvement to a score of 22 at session 10, she returned to a score of 30 at session 11. However, the overall trend was for an improvement in her self-reports of depression.

Clients with IDs require assistance in order to complete such an inventory, and this process might take up to 45 minutes. It is therefore difficult to complete a full BDI or BAI (Beck *et al.*, 1988) because of the amount of time required. However, it is possible to take a summary rating of how the client has felt over the previous week as is clear in Figure 5.3.

We have observed earlier the use of pictorial materials to aid assessment processes, and Figure 5.2 contains a four-point scale drawn on a piece of A4 paper that was used repeatedly throughout sessions. Emily herself drew the faces (pictorial aids) of someone feeling extremely depressed and someone who felt fine (OK). The scale moves from no feelings of depression to some feelings of depression, to quite a lot of feelings of depression to extreme feelings of depression. It can be seen from the repeated measures on Figure 5.2 that her weekly reports at the beginning of the treatment suggested that she experienced severe feelings of depression for the first few weeks. These reduced quite swiftly after the first three weeks of treatment that was taken up with an exploration of Emily's difficulties, explaining the relationship between cognition, emotion, behavior, and arousal and developing this framework for monitoring her mood. It can be seen that the method for regular monitoring of mood is immediate, straightforward, and easily accessible. This simple method of regular, weekly review of treatment progress is well established in CBT for people with IDs (Dagnan & Lindsay, 2004).

Summary

In this chapter, we have reviewed the ways in which psychological assessment of emotion can be adapted to suit the requirements of people with IDs. There are now a number of appropriate assessments that fulfill the psychometric requirements of reliable and valid assessment and are readily accessible to people with IDs. These include assessments of anxiety, depression, self-esteem, and the sequelae of traumatic incidents. For a number of reasons, cognitive difficulties should be addressed during both the assessment and treatment, and we have outlined several ways in which therapists can make allowances for the cognitive limitations in the client group. These include ways to address difficulties in understanding, simplifying procedures, repeated practice, and the use of pictorial aids to assist understanding. We have also emphasized that certain approaches inherent in CBT procedures are eminently suitable for people with IDs in therapy. Notably, these are the use of an agenda for therapy that helps to make the procedure understandable and predictable, and the use of modified Socratic procedures that may reduce the tendency in people with IDs toward acquiescence.

References

Beck, A.T., Epstein, N., Brown, G. & Steer, R.A. (1988). An inventory for measuring clinical anxiety: Psychometric properties. *Journal of Consulting and Clinical Psychology, 56,* 893–897.

Beck, A.T., Rush, A.J., Shaw, B.F. & Emery, G. (1979). *Cognitive therapy of depression.* New York: The Guilford Press.

Beck, A.T., Steer, R.A. & Brown, G.K. (1996). *Beck Depression Inventory – 2nd edition manual.* San Antonio, TX: The Psychological Corporation.

Cuthill, F., Eslie, C.A. & Cooper, S. (2003). The development and psychometric properties of the Glasgow Depression Scale for people with a learning disability. Individual and carer supplement versions. *The British Journal of Psychiatry, 182,* 347–353.

Dagnan, D. & Chadwick, P. (1997). Cognitive-behavioural therapy for people with learning disabilities: Assessment and intervention. In B. Stenfert Kroese, D. Dagnan & K. Loumidis (Eds.) *Cognitive-behaviour therapy for people with learning disabilities* (pp. 110–123). London: Routledge.

Dagnan, D., Chadwick, P. & Proudlove, J. (2000). Towards an assessment of suitability of people with mental retardation for cognitive therapy. *Cognitive Therapy and Research, 24,* 627–636.

Dagnan, D. & Lindsay, W.R. (2004). Research issues in cognitive therapy. In E. Emerson, C. Hatton, T. Thompon & T.R. Parmenter (Eds.) *The intenational handbook of applied research in intellectual disabilities* (pp.517–420). Chichester: Wiley.

Dagnan, D. & Sandhu, S. (1999). Social comparison, self-esteem and depression in people with intellectual disability. *Journal of Intellectual Disability Research*, 43, 372–379.

Derogatis, L.R. (1993). *Brief Symptom Inventory: Administrative scoring and procedures manual* (3rd edn). Minneapolis, MN: National Computer Systems.

Finlay, W.M. & Lyons, E. (2001). Methodological issues in interviewing and using self-report questionnaires with people with mental retardation. *Psychological Assessment*, 13, 319–335.

Goldberg, D. & Williams, P. (1988). *A user's guide to the general health questionnaire*. Windsor, UK: NFER-Nelson.

Hatton, C. & Taylor, J.L. (2010). Promoting healthy lifestyles – Mental health and illness. In G. Grant, P. Ramcharan, M. Flynn & M. Richardson (Eds.) *Learning disability: A life cycle approach to valuing people* (2nd edn, pp.381–408). Maidenhead: Open University Press.

Jahoda, A., Selkirk, M., Trower, P., Pert, C., Srenfert-Kroese, B., Dagnan, D. *et al.* (2009). The balance of power in therapeutic interactions with individuals with intellectual disabilities. *The British Journal of Clinical Psychology*, 48, 63–78.

Joyce, T., Globe, A. & Moodey, C. (2006). Assessment of the component skills for cognitive therapy in adults with intellectual disability. *Journal of Applied Research in Intellectual Disabilities*, 19, 17–23.

Kellet, S.C., Beail, N., Newman, D.W. & Frankish, P. (2003). Utility of the Brief Symptom Inventory (BSI) in the assessment of psychological distress. *Journal of Applied Research in Intellectual Disabilities*, 16, 127–135.

Kellet, S.C., Beail, N., Newman, D.W. & Mosley, E. (1999). Indexing psychological distress in people with an intellectual disability: Use of the Symptom Checklist-90-R. *Journal of Applied Research in Intellectual Disabilities*, 12, 323–334.

Kendall, P.C. (1985). Toward a cognitive-behavioral model of child psychopathology and a critique of related interventions. *Journal of Abnormal Child Psychology*, 13, 357–372.

Lindsay, W.R., Michie, A.M., Baty, F.J., Smith, A.H.W. & Miller, S. (1994). The consistency of reports about feelings and emotions from people with intellectual disability. *Journal of Intellectual Disability Research*, 38, 61–66.

Lindsay, W.R. & Skene, D. (2007). Use of the Beck anxiety and depression inventories in people with intellectual disabilities. *Journal of Applied Research in Intellectual Disabilities*, 20, 401–408.

Marshall, K. & Willoughby-Booth, S. (2010). Modifying the clinical outcomes in routine evaluation measure for use with people who have a learning disability. *British Journal of Learning Disabilities*, 35, 107–112.

Matheson, E. & Jahoda, A. (2005). Emotional understanding in aggressive and nonaggressive individuals with mild or moderate mental retardation. *American Journal of Mental Retardation*, 110, 57–67.

McKenzie, K., Matheson, E., McKaskie, K., Hamilton, L. & Murray, G.C. (2000). Impact of group training on emotion recognition in individuals with a learning disability. *British Journal of Learning Disabilities*, 28, 143–147.

Mindham, J. & Espie, E.A. (2003). The Glasgow Anxiety Scale for people with an intellectual disability (GAS-ID): Development and psychometric properties of a new measure for use with people with mild intellectual disability. *Journal of Intellectual Disability Research*, 47, 22–30.

Miyake, A., Friedman, N.P., Emerson, M.J., Witzki, A.H., Howerter, A. & Wager, T.D. (2000). The unity and diversity of executive functions and their contributions to complex "Frontal Lobe" tasks: A latent variable analysis. *Cognitive Psychology*, 41, 49–100.

Oathamshaw, S. & Haddock, G. (2006). Do people with intellectual disabilities and psychosis have the cognitive skills required to undertake cognitive behavioural therapy? *Journal of Applied Research in Intellectual Disabilities, 19*, 35–45.

Reed, J. & Clements, J. (1989). Assessing the understanding of emotional states in a population of adolescents and young adults with mental handicaps. *Journal of Mental Deficiency Research, 33*, 229–233.

Rees, C.S., McEvoy, P. & Nathan, P.R. (2005). Relationship between homework completion and outcome in cognitive behaviour therapy. *Cognitive Behaviour Therapy, 34*, 242–247.

Rosenberg, M. (1989). *Society and the adolescent self-image* (Rev. edn). Middletown, CT: Wesleyan University Press.

Safran, J.D. & Goldbers, L.S. 1986. Hot cognition and psychotherapy process: An information processing/ecological approach. In P. Kendall (Ed.) *Advances in cognitive-behavioural research and therapy* (Vol. 5, pp.143–177). New York: Academic Press.

Sams, K., Collins, S. & Reynolds, S. (2006). Cognitive therapy abilities in people with learning disabilities. *Journal of Applied Research in Intellectual Disabilities, 19*, 25–33.

Taylor, J.L. & Lindsay, W.R. (2012). CBT for people with intellectual and developmental disabilities. In W. Dryden, R. Branch, A. Grant & M. Townend (Eds.) *The CBT handbook.* London: Sage.

Taylor, J.L., Lindsay, W.R. & Willner, P. (2008). CBT for people with intellectual disabilities: Emerging evidence, cognitive ability and IQ effects. *Behavioural and Cognitive Psychotherapy, 36*, 723–733.

Taylor, J.L. & Novaco, R.W. (2005). *Anger treatment for people with developmental disabilities: A theory, evidence and manual based approach.* Chichester: Wiley.

Willner, P. (2006). Readiness for cognitive therapy in people with intellectual disabilities. *Journal of Applied Research in Intellectual Disabilities, 19*, 5–16.

Willner, P., Bailey, R., Parry, R. & Dymond, S. (2010). Evaluation of executive functioning in people with intellectual disabilities. *Journal of Intellectual Disability Research, 54*(4), 366–379.

Willner, P. & Goodey, R. (2006). Interaction of cognitive distortions and cognitive deficits in the formulation and treatment of obsessive-compulsive behaviours in a woman with an intellectual disability. *Journal of Applied Research in Intellectual Disabilities, 19*, 57–63.

Zung, W.K. (1965). Self-Rating Depression Scale. *Archives of General Psychiatry, 12*, 63–70.

Zung, W.K. (1971). A rating scale for anxiety disorders. *Psychosomatics, 12*, 371–379.

Chapter 6

Adapting Psychological Therapies for People with Intellectual Disabilities II:

Treatment Approaches and Modifications

William R. Lindsay
Andrew J. Jahoda
Paul Willner

Introduction

As for Chapter 5, in this chapter we will review the way in which psychological therapy can be adapted for people with intellectual disability (ID) and we will use cognitive–behavioral therapy (CBT) as our primary exemplar. There is little doubt that among "the talking therapies," CBT has had the greatest impact and is most frequently used with people with ID (Nagel & Leiper, 1999). Therefore, it makes sense to refer to this relatively extensive body of work in adapting CBT techniques for people with ID in this chapter on the adaptation of psychological therapy in general.

We will deal with a number of issues that have been found to be important aspects of the therapeutic process in mainstream psychological treatment including (a) the client–therapist relationship, (b) methods for accessing clients' core beliefs about themselves and their environment, (c) ways in which these core beliefs (or schema) can manifest in the person's thinking and in his or her behavior, (d) approaches to facilitating transfer of progress made in the treatment to the client's life in general, and finally, (e) methods that promote resilience. We will illustrate key points by using new case material, but we will also refer to the case of Emily outlined in the previous chapter.

Several authors have written about the way in which the client–therapist relationship is central to progress made during treatment. Indeed, a number of therapies promote this relationship as a core concept in the methods and process of treatment. For example, in their seminal volume on cognitive therapy for depression, Beck *et al.* (1979) outlined the basic methods of cognitive therapy, and these have remained

Psychological Therapies for Adults with Intellectual Disabilities, First Edition.
Edited by John L. Taylor, William R. Lindsay, Richard P. Hastings, and Chris Hatton.
© 2013 John Wiley & Sons, Ltd. Published 2013 by John Wiley & Sons, Ltd.

the nucleus of therapeutic techniques to the present day. They included sharing the formulation as a collaborative exercise between client and therapist, which was incorporated under the crucial client–therapist relationship that has been important to many psychological therapies since their conception. In this and subsequent books (e.g., Beck *et al.*, 2003), Beck has noted that a central feature of CBT is a collaborative relationship between the therapist and the client. They need to develop a shared formulation, organize the program of treatment around the client's needs, and work toward therapeutic goals. Power (2009) reviewed a range of studies that investigated the importance of client–therapist relationships across a range of therapeutic modalities. He concluded that in all systematic psychotherapies (e.g., CBT, interpersonal therapy), the nature of the therapeutic relationship was a necessary source for therapeutic change that accounted for a large proportion of the variance in positive clinical outcomes.

Keijsers *et al.* (2000) reviewed aspects of the client–therapist relationship such as the extent and positive nature of the therapeutic alliance and found that it had a highly significant and positive influence on treatment outcome. In this regard, the therapist needs to help the clients to understand and become familiar with the therapeutic model so that they can then go on to become actively engaged in the therapeutic process. Beck (Beck *et al.*, 1979) has termed this component of therapy "collaborative empiricism," which is developed through the Socratic process and guided discovery.

Since, as we shall explain, CBT techniques have been extensively adapted in order to be accessible to people with IDs, one might expect that the establishment of a therapeutic alliance will require adaptation also. Unfortunately, there are no guidelines for developing therapeutic relationships when working with people with ID, and generally, therapists develop these skills through practice, modeling, and supervision. Therefore, it is possible that many therapists are unable to adjust their interpersonal and therapeutic style sufficiently to successfully engage clients with ID. Thus, whether or not therapists are generally able to adapt their style and approach in order to establish therapeutic relationships with these clients is an empirical question.

To shed some light on this issue, Jahoda *et al.* (2008) conducted an extensive analysis of the therapeutic process in 15 clients with ID who received CBT. They completed initiative–response analyses on the dialogues of 30 separate treatment sessions to ascertain the extent to which the balance of power within the therapeutic relationships was equal or biased toward the therapist. They found that even in early sessions, power was evenly distributed between therapist and client and that the predicted reductions in therapist dominance were not found because of high levels of symmetry in the early sessions. Throughout the sessions, the therapist used more solicitations indicating the use of the Socratic process. These authors also investigated the extent to which therapists adhered to treatment principles during sessions (in this case, treatment was CBT). They found high levels of adherence to CBT structures and processes throughout all sessions. The components they analyzed were setting an agenda, employing appropriate feedback, conveying understanding toward the client, the interpersonal effectiveness of the therapists, collaboration, guided discovery, focusing on key cognitions, choosing appropriate interventions, and employing homework. Key cognitive processes such as guided discovery were found to be present in 94 percent of sessions indicating a high fidelity with treatment procedures. From the point of view of the therapeutic process, understanding the client's needs, interpersonal effectiveness, and employment of the collaborative process are the most relevant components. Across 90 ratings, therapists employed guided discovery in 93 percent of ratings, they demonstrated appropriate interpersonal effectiveness 95 percent of the time, and there was appropriate collaboration on 94 percent of instances. This indicates a high level indeed of effective therapist–client relationships in a technical and difficult area for therapists where they have to modify their language and delivery for the whole of the interaction.

We have already dealt with two general processes for psychological therapy in the previous chapter. We considered that the establishment of an agenda for the treatment sessions was an important and helpful procedure that could be used for all psychological therapy so that the course of treatment could become more predictable and understandable. We also outlined the use of the Socratic process, which is extremely helpful in helping clients with ID to engage with the process in a meaningful manner. It also enables the therapist to minimize some of the pitfalls in working with people with ID such as any propensity toward acquiescence on the part of clients or any tendency to be overly didactic on the part of the therapist. We will now continue with some of the processes of CBT with a view to illustrating the way in which psychological therapy can be adapted for people with ID in order to help them understand the way in which emotion and cognition will affect and in turn be affected by behavior and physiological arousal.

Identifying automatic thoughts

Guided discovery and Socratic methods are clearly seen in the way therapists elicit automatic thoughts associated with difficulties from clients. It is often easy to identify negative self-statements in clients with ID. The case study from the previous chapter (Emily) illustrates some aspects of this therapeutic process. In Emily's case, she simply said "What do you want to talk to me for? Nobody wants to talk to me." This negative self-statement – "nobody wants to talk to me" – is a powerful disincentive for engaging with others and is likely to evoke strong feelings of stigmatization. Therefore, straightforward interviewing is one of the most important methods for eliciting negative self-statements in this client group. In fact, they can be so straightforward that there is a danger of missing them. In one or two quick sentences, clients will sometimes reveal a number of negative self-statements, which if used repeatedly, can be quite debilitating in the individual's everyday life. Therapists have to be careful to isolate them and make them explicit as the client is revealing them. They can be analyzed later for their accuracy, for the way in which they evoke negative emotions and the way in which they activate underlying assumptions or schemas. In the following extract, taken from an early session with Emily, a number of automatic thoughts are elicited while she, at the same time, suggests that she is not experiencing any dysfunctional thoughts:

T: *How were you feeling when you went into the room at first?*
E: *I was feeling fine, I didn't have a problem. I had had a drink and I was feeling good.*
T: *What were you thinking when you went into the room?*

E: *I wasn't thinking anything. I was looking forward to the party and I saw her straight away and I know she doesn't like me because we had an argument two weeks ago and she was accusing me of being drunk and she would say I was drunk again and she's got friends and her friends are always talking about people behind their back.*

This short exchange reveals the way in which automatic thoughts can come tumbling out from the client's description of events. In this case, the following thoughts have been established:

She doesn't like me.
She will talk to others (negatively).
She spreads rumors about me being drunk.
She may say I was drunk before and I am drunk now.

It is also possible that these thoughts will be part of a longer and more pernicious sequence that continue to undermine Emily's emotion during the evening and will promote feelings of stigmatization. These thoughts might be the following:

Other people will start talking about me while I am here.
Lots of people at this party will be saying bad things about me.
They might start laughing at me.
They will all be looking at me to see if I am drunk.

This latter series of cognitions involves some speculation on the part of the therapist, but given that Emily has a history of depression and a history of feelings of stigmatization, it is worth exploring the extent to which these immediate self-statements become more generalized in the course of the evening in this social situation. It should be remembered that for the therapist, guided exploration is not done without considerable preparation. The therapist will have a number of hypotheses based on her knowledge of the client and her history. The questions posed by the therapist are, therefore, deliberately "guiding."

While dealing with "hot cognitions" related to recent situations is thought to be a critical aspect of CBT, the emotional element contained in the client's experience is especially important in working with people with ID. This is because it can be difficult to talk about the personal meaning of events in the absence of the emotion. The emotion can be discussed in a more immediate fashion, making it easier to find out what the person thinks and the nature of his or her reaction. In other words, it may be easier to begin talking about how one feels about an event with the prospect of subsequently moving on to cognitions about the event and cognitions about the client's response.

Eliciting automatic thoughts through role play

One effective method for eliciting negative automatic thoughts is through role play. The therapist and client can reenact some of the difficult situations that have taken place in the client's recent past.

Case study: John

John was a 29-year-old man with a measured IQ of 60. It was thought that his measured IQ was an underestimate and that his intellectual functioning was probably at the top of the range of mild ID. He had been brought up by his parents and had attended special education classes in a normal school. There have been no reports of behavioral problems either at home or at school. Some 12 months prior to his referral, he had been apprehended for a series of thefts in a local supermarket and had appeared in court. He pled guilty and was given an 18-month probation sentence. Assessment on the Brief Symptom Inventory (BSI; Derogatis, 1993) found that he had high scores on both anxiety and interpersonal sensitivity and further assessment revealed similarly high scores on the Beck Anxiety (Beck *et al.*, 1988) and Depression (Beck *et al.*, 1996) Scales. He also reported some obsessional symptoms during interviews and on the BSI. He was referred because of increasing difficulties in interpersonal situations at his day center. These interpersonal difficulties included an increase in verbal aggression and persistent arguments with staff and other attendees.

John was experiencing significant negative self-evaluations concerning being apprehended by the police and appearing in court. We role played him speaking to a member of his day center staff and his thoughts emerged in a simple uncluttered fashion with statements such as "he's going to see me as a criminal," "he's going to think I am a bad person," and "people are never going to believe me now and he doesn't believe me." By contrast, Emily was extremely reluctant throughout all of the sessions to engage in any role play sessions. She felt embarrassed and self-conscious, and so it should be remembered that it may be difficult to employ role play with some clients.

Occasionally, clients will say that they are unable to identify any thoughts. They will say only that "I don't know what I am thinking I just feel bad" or "I don't know what I am thinking I just want you to go away." These statements themselves are indeed self-statements that can be used during therapy taken at face value. If somebody is saying to himself or herself "I feel bad" or "just go away," these self-statements can be dealt with during treatment. Often, the very clarity of self-statements and feelings in people with ID is an asset to therapy and, conversely, makes them more debilitating to the individual in question. The fact that thoughts may be accessed easily should not be taken as an indication that they are not particularly important; rather, the reverse is the case. It is doubtful that clients will say to themselves "I feel bad" in situations resulting in depression. It may be that the individual's self-statements can become enmeshed into emotions and do not reach the level of conscious thought, or it may be that the person does not have the language to express his or her emotional state. It can also be the case that there is no negative thought or self-statement; people just feel bad and so do not engage with others. However, the fact that mediated self-statements are possible means that they can either be inserted into the chain of responses if they are absent, or changed to more adaptive self-statements if they are present in the sequence. In his development of the theoretical framework for self-statements, Meichenbaum (1977) wrote that it is unlikely that clients actively talk to themselves prior to treatment. Nevertheless, he recommended the employment of self-statements as a proactive treatment procedure by challenging an individual's elicited self-statements; therapists can increase their importance to a level where they may be able to employ them as a positive technique in therapy.

Another technique, reported in Lindsay *et al.* (1993), is that of role reversal. The client and therapist reverse roles and the client as therapist has to ask what "the patient" is thinking. We find that the client as therapist may ask a very leading question of the "patient," such as "do you worry that everyone is watching you when you go out of your house?" or "do you think you are a bad person?" In this way, clients can either reveal very clearly the nature of thoughts that they consider to be important in their own lives or confirm thoughts that have been elicited previously during interview. This can be the beginning of a more generalized technique in which the client is asked to review his or her circumstances from the point of view either of the therapist or of a dispassionate observer such as a friend. This technique can be used to help the client review his or her situation and views in general and will be dealt with in more detail later.

Testing the accuracy of cognitions

From the preceding sections in this chapter, it is clear that collaborative empiricism is a central method for CBT. At the same time, the clarity of procedures is important for clients with ID. The first way of embarking on collaborative empiricism is to review the direct evidence for and against the various elicited self-statements. With John, he had a number of self-statements about negative evaluation from others and feeling that others would consider him a criminal. He also stated that he was a terrible person and a bad person. As treatment developed, we were able to set John's statements on one side of a flip chart, and on the other side, we placed the number of competencies against these statements. He was a sociable man and was able to get on well with other service users in the day center. He could cook simple meals for himself, use public transport, and was quite fastidious in keeping his room and himself tidy. He was also able to review the context of his theft and knew that he had not been in a similar situation, or thought about stealing things for some months. All of these were placed on the other side of the flip chart against the generalized catastrophizing nature of his feelings of worthlessness. In this way, the empirical information gathered through Socratic questioning was employed as a direct challenge to his negative automatic thoughts and his emotions. At an intermediate stage in treatment, we therefore began to challenge directly his cognitions and, in turn, his underlying schemas.

Another common method for challenging the accuracy of cognitions is to employ reattribution methods in the manner mentioned previously through role reversal or having the client imagine himself as an independent or dispassionate observer. This is a commonly used exercise whereby the therapist asks the client to make an appraisal of an individual who has exactly the same characteristics and circumstances. In Emily's case, the therapist asked her to make an appraisal of an individual using the following procedure:

- Emily drew a female on the flip chart and gave her a name.
- She was called Mary.

- She was then asked to give Mary a number of attributes that included all of the previously agreed competencies and positive attributes that Emily considered herself to possess.
- These were duly written on the flip chart so that they could not later be negated. Therefore, at this stage, a number of positive aspects of Emily and a number of competencies were quite explicit.
- The therapist then asked her whether it was sensible for Mary to think "nobody likes me" or "everybody is talking about me" or "they all think I am a useless drunk."

There can be two results from this exercise: either the client can accept the challenges on his or her cognitions or he or she may offer further justification for them. If the latter occurs, this can be added to the list of automatic thoughts and negative cognitions that might lead to underlying assumptions and schemas that can be dealt with later in treatment. In general, this method of reattribution can be an effective means to review the outcomes for negative self-statements or to develop a clearer picture of the client's matrix of negative cognitions.

Eliciting underlying schemas and assumptions about self

Many psychological therapies rely heavily on the concept of schemas and underlying assumptions. These are thought patterns that develop early in life and become filters that organize and process incoming information. In various fields, schemas or "world views" have been employed to explain the way in which individuals approach interpersonal situations, solve personal problems, and generally deal with events in life. For example, in a completely different field, Palmer (2003) outlined theoretical approaches to explaining criminal behavior in young adult men by postulating fundamental schemas about the world. The first is a world view based on egocentricity, and this again will determine the way in which the individual carries out all interactions and exchanges with his or her surroundings. Flowing from this is a series of schemas including that the world is a hostile place, and all subsequent transactions with the world will reflect this fundamental assumption. In relation to persecutory beliefs and depression, Trower and Chadwick (1995) proposed an understanding of schemas in the context of an interpersonal theory of the self. They proposed two fundamental schemas the first of which was "poor me" paranoia that was a reflection of an insecurely constructed self. Here, the individual maintains self-esteem by viewing the persecutor as bad and inferior, and this world view permeates interpersonal style. In contrast, a proportion of people with persecutory beliefs behaved more like depressive individuals tending to have low self-esteem and blaming themselves for their presumed persecution. This schema was labeled "bad me" whereby the individual feels he or she deserves to be punished for misdemeanors resulting in associated feelings of worthlessness, perceived disapproval, and depression.

In the field of ID, the work on negative self-image and stigma (Dagnan & Sandhu, 1999; Dagnan & Waring, 2004), the relationship between social development and depression (Payne & Jahoda, 2004), and the relationship between social support and depression (Benson *et al.*, 1985; Richards *et al.*, 2001) indicate that these schemas can be of primary importance for this client group. Young *et al.* (1993) have outlined a number of maladaptive schema domains several of which seem particularly relevant to people with ID. Instability and disconnection refer to the expectations that one's basic needs for nurturance and safety may not be met by one's social support network. This leads to schemas involving abandonment, mistrust, and emotional deprivation. The domain of impaired autonomy refers to a perception that one cannot function independently and adequately within society. This is associated with schematic concepts of dependence, personal vulnerability, and under development. The domain of undesirability indicates negative social comparisons with others across a range of features including social skills, achievement, socioeconomic background, and physical and personal attractiveness. Schemas involved with undesirability are basic beliefs supporting feelings of shame, defectiveness, social undesirability, and failure. As has been seen elsewhere in this book (Chapters 7 and 8), these schemas have resonance with the work of a number of clinicians in the field of ID.

In order to identify underlying schemas, it is important to identify certain themes emerging from the therapeutic process and that are common to problematic self-statements, avoidant actions, and emotionality in individuals. As therapy progresses, it usually becomes apparent that there are certain representations or underlying assumptions that underpin the way in which the client interacts with his or her world. In the case of Emily, determining this was not difficult because she was quite open about the way she viewed the world from a very early stage in therapy. Both her self-statements and her underlying assumptions reflect the view that she felt people were stigmatizing her and had very low opinions of her from an early age. Her self-image and self-esteem were extremely low leading her to turn to alcohol abuse, self-harm, and expressing surprise at others' interest in her. In almost all of the early treatment sessions with her, she would say "what do you want to see me for?" or "why are you interested in anything about me?"

This series of statements clearly express a belief that she is not worthy of others interests, that others will view her as uninteresting or irrelevant and that others have no interest in her as a friend. This is a fundamental schema that affected all of her interactions and her behavioral patterns toward herself.

Readers may recognize aspects of avoidant personality disorder whereby individuals often have a string of self-critical automatic thoughts when they are in social situations and when they are considering their own behavior. Emily had a number of cognitions typical of avoidant individuals including thoughts such as "I'm a boring person," "I'm a stupid person," and particularly "I am ugly and unattractive." She had a number of automatic thoughts prior to social interaction that were both critical of herself and critical of others such as "he'll think I'm stupid and get onto me" while at the same time thinking "he's an idiot and I don't like him." This led to two related underlying assumptions, the first around the belief that she was basically an unlikable individual and the second concerning the belief that "others are hostile to me." In this way, the basic beliefs that individuals may have about themselves can be induced from the information given by the clients themselves.

The case of John is interesting because although the dysfunctional cognitions and maladaptive self-statements are very similar to that in Emily's case, the formulation was very different. Prior to his theft offenses, John was relatively well adjusted both within his family and with a few friends. He had attended the day center for several years, and although there had been indications of some interpersonal difficulty with minor behavioral problems when he isolated himself for short periods, there had been no evidence of aggression or serious interpersonal conflict; there had certainly been no suggestions of a negative self-concept with poor self-esteem. Following the incident with the police and court, he clearly had a number of self-statements such as "I'm a bad person" and "I'm a terrible person," but crucially, his view was dependent on his perception of others. At early stages in treatment, he said "people are just not interested in what I have got to say anymore" and "people don't believe me and they'll never believe me." Here, he seemed to be catastrophizing the reaction of others to the incident. He had become convinced that others' estimation of him would be drastically altered because of the theft. In reaction to his perception of others, he had now developed severe problems with his own self-image resulting in frequent bouts of depressed mood leading to interpersonal conflicts and verbal aggression. His basic schema of the world had changed from one that was reasonably adaptive to an underlying assumption that people hated him and that his social contacts had now changed irreversibly for the worst. This was clear from his perception of life prior to the court appearances where he said "Before that everything was on the up . . . life was ok, it was a real life . . . I had everything I wanted and I was happy." While nothing had changed overtly in his life, he still maintained his home placement and his daily routines, and still had the same circle of relationships; his perception of everything had deteriorated. Therefore, John's formulation was very different to that of Emily and centered more on one particular precipitating incident rather than a developmental history of negative self-evaluation and perception of stigma.

Identifying and testing maladaptive schemas

At this point, the process of treatment will be around halfway, and the majority of the subsequent procedures are aimed at recalling information from previous sessions and gathering further information that will challenge these maladaptive schemas. The therapist and client will have gained much understanding through the collaborative process about the clients' developmental history, their problematic behavior, and the relationship between their cognitions, their behavior, their arousal, and their emotions. It should be noted that the information on schemas is not considered to be immutable. Rather, they may evolve and change as treatment continues or they may indeed be established for the rest of the treatment sessions.

Emily's personal schemas were challenged through evidence of her interaction with others. It was possible for staff in the home to furnish information about various successful interactions and events that she participated in. One particularly important event was when she asked a friend to go to the cinema with her. They also asked a member of the support staff if she would go with them and the three of them had a highly successful outing to the cinema and afterward they all went for a burger. It was possible to analyze this outing in detail because information came from the friend and from the support worker independent of Emily's evaluation. Emily's personal evaluation was fairly neutral, but the evaluations of the other two were extremely positive. During the next treatment session, we placed Emily's evaluation alongside the evaluations of the other two, and the stark contrast between them came as something of a surprise to her. It acted as a reference point for future sessions, and Emily began to understand that her self-evaluation and her evaluation of others' perceptions were more negative than the evidence would suggest.

This repeatedly challenged her negative schema of "I'm an unlikable person" and her schema that "people are antagonistic toward me because they don't like me." She began to speculate; quite openly that she might not be as unlikable as she thought and that she might have been misinterpreting the views of others. As she began to change her beliefs about her likability, she began to enter into more interactions with her support workers and with others in the house. She was wary of these during treatment sessions, and her conversation suggested that she was expecting failure at any time. She would say "somebody's going to give me a knock back" or "they're going to say what they really think" periodically during sessions 12–16 (well over halfway through treatment). However, she was also becoming more comfortable with the obvious, positive feedback from others. In fact, support workers were delighted about the way Emily was interacting saying things like "it's great the way that girl's coming out of herself," "she's really fun to be with just now," and "she's got a great sense of humor." All of these utterances were used as evidence throughout the later stages of treatment as challenges to her negative schemas.

One important aspect of treatment was to emphasize that from time to time, others may be critical or rude for whatever reason. It was stressed throughout sessions that Emily should build resilience to periodic negative feedback from others because we all experience this from time to time. The importance of resilience was a major feature in protecting her against relapse when negative incidents might happen.

For John, the process was somewhat more straightforward. Because he could remember clearly his feelings prior to the court appearance, it was possible to contrast them with his feelings and thoughts after the court appearance. This was done explicitly on the flip chart. In the latter half of therapy, he repeatedly made statements linking the various aspects of response indicating his clear understanding of the way his thoughts and feelings were interrelated. He said "if I think correctly, I feel different and act different," "if I think bad, I feel bad and I talk a lot of bollocks (rubbish)," and "when I think a lot of bollocks (rubbish) I feel really bad." This clear understanding of the links between his cognition and his emotion helped him to reorganize his daily routines in order to control his thoughts, feelings, and subsequent behavior more clearly. It is unusual for someone with ID to gain such an explicit understanding of the link between cognition and emotion, but in John's case, it was obviously helpful in the way he made a determined effort to control his cognitions and their effect on his emotion. Once again, it is important to establish resilience in relation to improvements. This was somewhat easier with John because he became so clear about the effect his thinking had on his emotions. He developed a number of strategies for blocking his thoughts that people were evaluating him negatively. He went for a walk in the garden and had a cigarette, he listened to some particular pieces of music that made him feel better, and, in relation to specific CBT techniques, he would write down some of the countermanding information that was developed during treatment sessions. He wrote down:

People are not going to change how they see me because of one mistake.
You don't become a bad person because of one mistake.
There are lots of things in me that people like.

We also employed the technique of dispassionate observation whereby the therapist asked John to consider his own friends and his view of them. This was written down so that he rehearsed their various attributes explicitly. He was then asked to imagine that they had now committed a theft and had been to court and was asked to consider the extent to which his view of them would change on the basis of one aspect. In every case, he agreed that his perception of them would not alter in the long term. In fact, quite realistically, he repeatedly expressed the view that he would be concerned about them. His concern would include worries about why they had behaved in this manner, the effect it would have on his friends and their families, how they would feel about the incident over the next few months, and how they would overcome the effects. All of this was robust evidence that could be employed to challenge his schema about his self-worth and others' perceptions.

Homework

Homework is an integral part of many structured psychotherapies and, as part of the agenda; homework is usually set for consideration at the end of each session. Homework can be difficult for people with ID, and tasks should be kept as simple and clear as possible. Tasks can range from a piece of behavioral rehearsal, through interaction with others to rehearsal of thoughts and attitudes considered during the treatment session. The important point about homework is that it should have been discussed or practiced during the session in order to help the client develop some skills for use in the real-life setting. Behavioral rehearsal might be to approach an individual with whom the person has had difficulty in the past and engage in a piece of interaction that has been practiced during role play sessions. Clients should be encouraged to think about tasks between sessions as part of treatment rather than an optional task or a burden. However, therapists should be careful that clients are not made to feel guilty for not completing homework tasks because people with ID may find it difficult to remember the homework or to consider it during critical periods where it might be used. It is difficult to focus on an abstract task decided a few days ago when one is faced the demands of the present situation.

Having said this, we encourage clients to learn effective ways of dealing with present situations both in terms of behavior and thought and when homework assignments are effective; they can be one of the most important aspects of treatment. They encourage the client to consider the positive effects of treatment because of the potential successes inherent in carrying out homework tasks, and they also provide a great deal of reflective information for the following sessions. The way in which homework tasks have been carried out and the relative success of the incident can be used to structure future sessions and to reflect on the importance the material being dealt with during treatment.

Homework tasks are a continuation of the collaborative empiricism central to CBT. The reason for carrying out each task should be clear and the methods for carrying out tasks should be specific and rehearsed. Because of the collaborative nature of treatment, therapist and client will develop these tasks together and the clients will see them as directly relevant to their situation. In this way, it can also affect motivation because the reason for the task is linked to the reason for therapy. It is important to keep homework straightforward – that is, one particular behavioral or interactional task or one particular way of thinking in a familiar situation. Because the therapeutic techniques outlined are accessible and uncluttered, they can be much more powerful in their implementation. Clients should not be faced with a number of conditions or caveats to tasks, for example,

> If this happens then this is how you should behave but only when these circumstances are in the situation and only when you are in this place.

Such an instruction would be difficult for many of us, and for a person with ID who might have difficulty remembering the demands of the homework task in the first place, the nature of it should be kept as clear and accessible as possible.

Although it can be difficult to support the completion of homework tasks because of the reasons already mentioned, it is essential to make the effort. Not only is it a way of generalizing treatment gains, but it also helps people make the links between what has been talked about during sessions and its relevance to their daily lives. Involving significant others in treatment can make a considerable difference to the completion of homework tasks. If carers or family members are involved and knowledgeable about the progress of treatment, their help can be enlisted at key points in encouraging clients to act, interact, and think in specific ways. In this way, they can be supported in the successful implementation of behavioral and cognitive techniques in their general lives.

One important aspect of homework is self-monitoring. If clients are able to self-monitor using a form that can be adapted during treatment sessions, then the feedback from the self-monitoring tasks is invaluable. Of course, what is achieved in sessions can only be considered a success in so far is it makes a difference to people's everyday lives. Clients may lack the autonomy or ability to carry out these homework tasks on their own. They may need help to complete monitoring forms or someone to accompany them to an activity. A carer or relative may be able to support the client to employ cognitive thinking styles that have been developed during treatment so that he or she is able to challenge maladaptive styles of thinking when he or she arises in everyday life. This kind of support needed by clients may be an important consideration when deciding whether or not to include significant others in therapy sessions.

In addition to eliciting the support or help of significant others in people's lives, there are other practical steps that can be taken to increase the possibility that clients will complete self-monitoring and homework tasks between sessions. Clients can be given visual timetables to put on their kitchen wall, or telephone prompts can be given between sessions. Where clients lack literacy skills, other means of recording what they have done can be helpful. For example, they can be given Dictaphones or digital cameras to take photographs of activities they have carried out. Alternatively, significant others can have the camera to take photographs at crucial times. These ways of recording give clients an active role in the monitoring process and their recordings listened to in sessions or their photographs viewed on laptop computers. This allows the therapist to access far more information during sessions than would be the case if the clients were only to give verbal feedback or rely on their memory of events.

Relapse prevention: employing carers and significant others

The process of generalizing treatment gains from the individual therapy session into the wider aspects of the person's life can present significant challenges to the clinician.

This is because it is not only expected that the client's own views will change or become more adaptive, there is also an underlying implicit assumption that the person will take the new skills and world view developed in therapy out to the real world and act upon them and that in many cases, the real world or other people in the person's life will begin to reflect the different perspective that the client is presenting. However, for people with ID, the degree of control that is typically exerted over them within their service and social structures may either stop them acting in a different way or mean that their actions have limited impact. So when we discuss the importance of tackling issues such as stigma or social exclusion, the therapist can work to improve the person's confidence or resilience, but it may not be possible to stop others calling them names in the street or to make other people friendlier. In community settings, the therapist can have little influence over the client's living environment. By working alongside significant others in the person's life, it might be possible to begin to look at ways of reducing someone's isolation and increasing protection against, for example, name calling.

Rose *et al.* (2002, 2005) found that those clients who were accompanied to treatment by a carer made better progress than those who were not. The mechanism for this finding is presumably that carers are able to support clients in developing their skills and cognitions, in practicing the techniques developed during treatment, and in identifying target situations.

Where carers and relatives are involved, target situations can be identified with practical strategies worked out to support clients in these aspects of homework. Consistency is crucial at this point because the carer must work within the same principles and the same strategies as have been dealt with during treatment sessions. If the support worker were to deviate significantly from the agreed strategy, the client will simply become confused with competing messages. However, occasionally, when carers are involved, it can become clear that the agreed strategies are very difficult to implement because of unforeseen demands of the situation. Again, this is extremely helpful information to feedback into the therapy session so that the strategies can be adjusted to become more effective and relevant to the particular situation.

It should be remembered that there are difficulties with confidentiality when one involves carers and family members in therapy. Carers will be in sessions with agreement of the client and will be subject to the same conventions of confidentiality as the therapist. A therapist should also be very mindful that a carer who accompanies the client may have been allocated to that person irrespective of choice of preference. One of the ways of overcoming this particular difficulty is to have, in treatment, a module toward the end of treatment in which the clients can nominate an individual whom they would wish to contribute to their treatment progress. This can be discussed with the client as the sessions progress and can be arranged in advance so that an individual of the person's choice (if he or she wants to have someone accompany him or her) can be asked to contribute.

Relapse prevention: Resilience

Resilience should be built into each session and each situation dealt with. It should be part of routine procedure for the therapist and the client to consider what might happen should the predicted response not occur. Therefore, the therapists might review with the clients what they would do with a range of responses when they practice a new skill or employ a new approach to situations. These responses would vary from a good outcome through a neutral outcome to an unexpectedly bad outcome. Clients can be encouraged to develop personal resilience in the face of negative outcomes. In this way, self-appraisal to a negative outcome will be practiced in therapy. This is another important aspect of treatment, and one purpose is to equip the clients with a range of self-appraisal skills for a range of positive and negative outcomes that will serve them over their future life when therapy has ended.

Another aspect of this part of treatment is to consider what the client will do when a completely unexpected and unpredictable outcome occurs. While some of these can be suggested, by their very nature, it is difficult to either discuss them or rehearse them during treatment sessions. The important aspect is to review the way in which the client will appraise the situation and emphasize the importance of maintaining self-concept and self-esteem in unpredictable situations.

Where significant others are involved, relapse prevention can be reviewed in the context of the social network. Practically, a number of potential scenarios will be reviewed and rehearsed with both the client and the significant other. These can be based both on previous experiences and upon speculation concerning the kinds of situations that might arise in the future. The final few sessions of treatment can be used to discuss, rehearse, and possibly role play some of these potential situations. In addition, the effect of changing circumstances might be brought into the setting characteristics for future situations. For example, if these difficult interpersonal encounters were to occur while the client was on holiday rather than in usual settings, how would that affect the outcome? Here, we are altering the setting characteristics for a familiar difficulty emphasizing that even predicted situations can occur in settings that may present additional unsettling variables.

Another method for promoting resilience and maintenance of improvements is to employ follow-up sessions or booster sessions. These can be placed into treatment as a matter of routine in order to check on the extent to which any improvements in the client's functioning have been maintained. In cases where the person continues to cope successfully with people and events in his or her life, these sessions can be a routine review with encouragement to maintain these adaptive procedures. In some cases, there may have been deterioration or setbacks that present some difficulty in the case. In these instances, the client and the therapist can revisit the methods that have been used throughout the treatment in order to reestablish coping strategies. In extreme cases, another treatment course can be started. In these instances, it is likely that the course of treatment will be shorter because the client has already become familiar with the aspects of whatever treatment has been previously employed.

Conclusions

We have outlined the techniques used over the past 30 years in CBT, and, as an example for psychological therapies in general, we have indicated the way in which these techniques can be changed and adapted for people with ID. The changes require a good knowledge of their client group and also require the development of technical expertise on the part of the therapist. The structure and collaborative nature of methods allows the development of the client–therapist relationship in a positive and progressive manner. The strengths of the Socratic process and adaptations mentioned in this and in the previous chapter allow clients to generate their own material during therapy rather than being compliant with suggestions from therapists.

Homework and relapse prevention are particularly important. Although there may be difficulties with confidentiality and the possible intrusiveness of a significant other, research by Jahoda *et al.* (2008) and Rose *et al.* (2005) indicated the importance of engaging relatives and carers of the client during homework and relapse prevention exercises. By involving the client in choice and appropriateness of a carer or family member, treatment employs the use of the individual's social network and may be more systemic than treatment in mental illness settings. It is our view that once adaptations have been made, psychological therapy can be an even more powerful a therapeutic technique than that seen in mainstream therapy.

References

Beck, A.T., Epstein, N., Brown, G. & Steer, R.A. (1988). An inventory for measuring clinical anxiety: Psychometric properties. *Journal of Consulting and Clinical Psychology, 56,* 893–897.

Beck, A.T., Freeman, A. & Davis, D.D. (2003). *Cognitive therapy of personality disorders.* New York: The Guilford Press.

Beck, A.T., Rush, A.J., Shaw, B.F. & Emery, G. (1979). *Cognitive therapy of depression.* New York: The Guilford Press.

Beck, A.T., Steer, R.A. & Brown, G.K. (1996). *Beck Depression Inventory – 2nd edition manual.* San Antonio, TX: The Psychological Corporation.

Benson, B.A., Reiss, S., Smith, D.C. & Laman, D.S. (1985). Psychosocial correlates of depression in mentally retarded adults: II. Poor social skills. *American Journal of Mental Deficiency, 89,* 657–659.

Dagnan, D. & Sandhu, S. (1999). Social comparison, self-esteem and depression in people with intellectual disability. *Journal of Intellectual Disability Research, 43,* 372–379.

Dagnan, D. & Waring, M. (2004). Linking stigma to psychological distress: Testing a social-cognitive model of the experience of people with intellectual disabilities. *Clinical Psychology & Psychotherapy, 11*(4), 247–254.

Derogatis, L.R. (1993). *Brief Symptom Inventory: Administrative scoring and procedures manual* (3rd edn). Minneapolis, MN: National Computer Systems.

Jahoda, A., Selkirk, M., Trower, P., Pert, C., Srenfert-Kroese, B., Dagnan, D. *et al.* (2008). The balance of power in therapeutic interactions with individuals with intellectual disabilities. *The British Journal of Clinical Psychology, 48,* 63–78.

Keijsers, C.P., Schaap, C.P. & Hoogduin, C.A. (2000). The impact of interpersonal patient and therapist behavior on outcome in cognitive-behavior therapy. A review of empirical studies behaviour modification. *Behaviour Modification, 24,* 264–297.

Lindsay, W.R., Howells, L. & Pitcaithlie, D. (1993). Cognitive therapy for depression with individuals with intellectual disabilities. *The British Journal of Medical Psychology, 66,* 135–141.

Meichenbaum, D. (1977). *Cognitive behaviour modification: An integrative approach.* New York: Plenum.

Nagel, B. & Leiper, R. (1999). A national survey of psychotherapy with people with learning disabilities. *Clinical Psychology Forum, 129,* 14–18.

Palmer, E. (2003). An overview of the relationship between moral reasoning and offending. *Australian Psychologist, 38*, 165–174.

Payne, R. & Jahoda, A. (2004). The Glasgow Social Self-Efficacy Scale – A new scale for measuring social self-efficacy in people with intellectual disability. *Clinical Psychology & Psychotherapy, 11*(4), 265–274.

Power, M. (2009). *Emotion focused cognitive therapy.* Chichester: Wiley-Blackwell.

Richards, M., Maughan, B., Hardy, R., Hall, I., Strydom, A. & Wadsworth, M. (2001). Long term affective disorder in people with mild learning disability. *The British Journal of Psychiatry, 179*, 523–527.

Rose, J., Jenkins, R., O'Conner, C., Jones, C. & Felce, D. (2002). A group treatment for men with intellectual disabilities who sexually offend or abuse. *Journal of Applied Research in Intellectual Disabilities, 15*, 138–150.

Rose, J., Loftus, M., Flint, B. & Corey, L. (2005). Factors associated with the efficacy of a group intervention for anger in people with intellectual disabilities. *The British Journal of Clinical Psychology, 44*, 305–318.

Trower, P. & Chadwick, P. (1995). Pathways of the defence of self: A theory of two types of paranoia. *Clinical Psychology: Science and Practice, 2*, 263–277.

Young, J.E., Beck, A.T. & Weinberger, A. (1993). Depression. In D.H. Barlow (Ed.) *Clinical handbook of psychological disorders* (pp.240–277). New York: Guildford Press.

Chapter 7

Cognitive–Behavioral Therapy for Anxiety Disorders

William R. Lindsay
Paul Willner
Peter Sturmey

Introduction

There have been a number of studies investigating mental health disorders and their prevalence in people with intellectual disability (ID). Because many individuals with ID were housed in large hospitals through the middle decades of the twentieth century, much of the early research was conducted on these populations. Penrose (1938) reviewed 1280 people with ID living in an institution. He reported a prevalence rate for affective disorders of 1.9 percent. This is low compared with more recent studies, and Gardner (1967) noted that all early studies had severe methodological limitations being essentially anecdotal and impressionistic reviews of diagnosis.

In a large epidemiological study on developmental disability services in New York State, Jacobson (1982) reported on 30 578 service users. Several categories of problems including behavioral, cognitive, and affective were reviewed, and behavioral problems had by far the highest prevalence at 47.7 percent. Of those individuals, 17.1 percent had a coexisting psychiatric disorder. In this sample, 5.6 percent showed mood swings, 2.9 percent evidenced depression, 12.3 percent showed poor interpersonal responsiveness, 2.9 percent evidenced extreme irritability, and 13.7 percent reported crying and temper tantrums. Anxiety and agitation were not separated out in this study, but one might assume that they were present in all of those showing extreme irritability, and some of those categorized with mood swings, crying, and temper tantrums.

Contemporary research has been more discriminating in separating diagnoses. Deb *et al.* (2001) assessed 101 adults using structured psychiatric assessments. Depending on the assessment, they found that up to 7.8 percent of the participants showed anxiety disorder while a further 5.5 percent had affective disorder. They pointed out that there is considerable comorbidity with some individuals being recorded with

Psychological Therapies for Adults with Intellectual Disabilities, First Edition.
Edited by John L. Taylor, William R. Lindsay, Richard P. Hastings, and Chris Hatton.
© 2013 John Wiley & Sons, Ltd. Published 2013 by John Wiley & Sons, Ltd.

more than one mental health problem. At the same time, Cooper and Bailey (2001) reported on 207 individuals with ID and found a prevalence of 7.2 percent with anxiety disorder and 6 percent with affective disorder. These two studies are remarkably similar in their reporting of anxiety and affective disorders. Taylor *et al.* (2004), in a larger study on 1155 participants with ID, employed the mini Psychiatric Assessment Schedule for Adults with Developmental Disability (PAS-ADD) in order to screen for a number of mental health disorders. They found that 14 percent were reported to have affective disorders, a category that included all affective and neurotic disorders. In another large-scale study, Cooper *et al.* (2007) reported on 1023 participants. These authors found a point prevalence of 3.8 percent in anxiety disorders and 6.6 percent in affective disorders. Therefore, repeated studies have suggested that anxiety disorders in people with ID are at least consistent with those reported in the general population between 4 percent and 8 percent.

In a carefully controlled study, Richards *et al.* (2001) drew from the Medical Research Council's National Survey of Health and Development (NSHD). They selected only cases with nonmissing values on the relevant psychiatric symptoms and identified 41 cases with ID and 2119 comparison cases. They found that the ID group was four times more likely to be identified as having affective disorder. This was true both at age 36 years and at age 43 years. They then went on to consider a number of variables that might account for the increase in risk of affective disorder in the ID sample. They investigated four basic factors: medical, environmental neglect or inconsistency, an effect of the learning disability regardless of cause, and reverse causality (psychiatric disorder leading to impaired intellectual performance). Their data allowed them essentially to discard the first and last hypotheses. In considering the second and third hypotheses, they found some support although it was not strong. In this respect, they concluded that "Adverse circumstances in adulthood did not account for risk of affective disorder in learning disability in the present analysis, just as adverse circumstances in early life did not. However, there may be more subtle factors that are not taken into account, such as coping capacity and self worth" (p. 526).

Cognitive–Behavioral Therapy for Anxiety Disorders in the General Population

In the general population there have now been many published studies comparing cognitive–behavioral therapy (CBT) to a variety of control conditions, some of which have been conducted to extremely rigorous scientific standards. In an assessment of the effectiveness of CBT in generalized anxiety disorder (GAD), Linden *et al.* (2005) randomly assigned 72 outpatients to a 25-session CBT program and a contact control group. Treatment integrity was ensured by working with a CBT manual and rating taped sessions for the extent to which they adhered to the CBT process. Improvements were highly significant in the CBT treatment group with minimal changes in the control group. The differences between treatment and control groups were comparable with or even larger than those reported in other studies using pharmacological methods to alleviate anxiety. In a controlled study of generalized social anxiety, Clark *et al.* (2003) randomly assigned 60 patients to CBT, fluoxetine plus self-exposure, and placebo plus self-exposure conditions. All treatments improved clients' reports on social anxiety measures, but the CBT was superior to the two other conditions at posttreatment and 12 months' follow-up. On general mood measures (depression and anxiety), there were few differences between the treatments.

In relation to posttraumatic stress disorder (PTSD), Foa *et al.* (2005) conducted a careful trial comparing prolonged exposure to trauma-related memories and situations, with prolonged exposure plus CBT. As with the Clark *et al.* (2003) study, participants were randomly assigned to conditions, self-report measures were used, program integrity was maintained to its highest level, and outside assessors were blind to participant allocation. They found that prolonged exposure was an extremely effective treatment for PTSD with very large effect sizes that maintained to 12 months' follow-up. CBT procedures did not add to the effectiveness of prolonged exposure. These three examples demonstrate the extent to which controlled trials have developed in their scientific integrity for the assessment of the potency of CBT for anxiety disorders.

Meta-Analyses of CBT Studies for Anxiety Disorders in General Populations

Because there have been so many control group studies, there have emerged a number of meta-analyses reviewing the pooled effect sizes for CBT compared with the effect sizes for a range of placebo, drug treatment, and no treatment controls. Hofmann and Smits (2008) conducted a meta-analysis of randomized placebo control trials. They noted that there had been a number of previous meta-analyses but argued that some of the studies included in these analyses fell short of optimum standards since they had a variety of control procedures and had not confined themselves to randomization studies. These authors included only studies with placebo psychotherapy and a randomization design. Twenty-seven studies fulfilled their criteria (1165 studies were originally identified), 25 of which provided completer data for continuous measures of anxiety disorder severity with a total *n* of 1496 participants. They found large effect sizes with significant improvements in studies reporting the clinical utility of CBT for a range of anxiety disorders including obsessive–compulsive disorder (OCD) and GAD.

In a Cochrane Review of Psychological Therapies for GAD, conducted by Hunot *et al.* (2007), 22 studies (1060 participants) contributed to the meta-analysis. They found that those studies comparing CBT with a waiting list control or treatment as usual had a significant clinical response with a medium effect size while those studies comparing CBT with nondirective therapy or attention placebo conditions revealed a clinical response but no difference between treatment and control. They concluded that CBT was effective in reducing anxiety symptoms in GAD.

A meta-analysis of combined pharmacology and CBT for anxiety disorders was conducted by Hofmann *et al.* (2009). Eleven studies fulfilled their criteria (471 participants), and they found that CBT plus pharmacology was generally more effective that CBT plus a placebo with a medium effect size. They also noted that the enhanced effects of pharmacology were no longer evident at six months' follow-up. In an interesting meta-analysis, Haby *et al.* (2006) included 33 studies for depression and anxiety disorders to review factors that might predict outcome. As with other researchers, they reported that CBT was an effective treatment for depression and anxiety disorders with a moderate to large effect size. A number of variables emerged from the regression including duration of therapy, inclusion of patients with severe anxiety in the trial, era of study, country of the study, the type of control group, and number of dropouts from the control group. Only the inclusion of a waiting list control and the inclusion of severe patients were significant in predicting the effect size, with the former increasing the effect size and the latter reducing it.

Assessment of Anxiety and Emotion

Finlay and Lyons (2001) reviewed the methodological issues in the assessment of emotion for people with ID and concluded that there were encouraging results in the development of the instruments with sound psychometric properties (e.g., Lindsay *et al.*, 1994). They found ample evidence that suitably adapted assessments could be understood and used appropriately by the client group but a lesser amount of emerging evidence that these assessments retained their psychometric properties during these studies. In particular, they found that studies incorporating the use of a pictorial representation of the amount of emotion or frequency of the problem in combination with a Likert scale reported higher reliability. Examples of these pictorial representations can be seen throughout this book.

Since the publication of the Finlay and Lyons (2001) review, there has been additional work in the development of new assessments and revision of existing assessments. Two pieces of work are particularly useful for the clinician working with clients suffering from anxiety disorders. Kellet *et al.* (2004) conducted a factor analytic study of the Brief Symptom Inventory (BSI). The BSI screens for symptoms related to somatization, interpersonal sensitivity, anxiety, depression, phobia, paranoid ideation, hostility, psychoticism, and OCDs. They had previously established the usability and reliability of the BSI (Kellet *et al.*, 2003), and in this subsequent study, in addition to further evidence on reliability, they found that the factor structure when used with this client group was essentially similar to the original studies on mainstream populations. Mindham and Espie (2003) developed the Glasgow Anxiety Scale (GAS), standardizing it on a small sample of 19 people with ID suffering from anxiety, 16 nonanxious controls, and 19 individuals without ID who also suffered from anxiety. The GAS was also cross-validated with the Beck Anxiety Inventory (BAI), which is widely used, and assessment of anxiety in mainstream populations. They found that the GAS had good reliability and internal consistency, discriminated between anxious and nonanxious clients, and had a strong correlation with the BAI.

In another development in the assessment of anxiety and depression, Lindsay and Skene (2007) administered the BAI and the Beck Depression Inventory to a mixed group of 108 participants with ID. In a joint factor analysis of all the items, two main factors emerged representing anxiety and depression separately. They then analyzed each assessment separately and found that the emerging structures were similar to that of studies on mainstream participants. For the BAI, these factors emerged representing somatic complaints relating to balance, subjective anxiety, and finally, somatic aspects of feeling hot. Therefore, with a presentation assisted by visual analogue information recommended by Finlay and Lyons (2001), this assessment of anxiety could be used in a manner similar to the way it is used in mainstream populations. Therefore, there is some persuasive evidence that assessments of anxiety can be used reliably by people with ID in a way that reflects their emotion with validity.

Cognitive Processes and Anxiety Disorders

Given the prevalence of emotional disorders, it is unsurprising that a number of authors have reviewed the relationship between emotion and cognition in people with ID. Much of the work has been done in relation to depression and social comparison but still has relevance to anxiety and stress. Szivos-Bach (1993) found that people with ID rated people without ID higher on a self-esteem scale and others with ID slightly lower on a self-esteem scale. She found that positive self-esteem and social comparison to a socially attractive group were negatively related to mood disorders. Dagnan and Sandhu (1999) continued this work with 18 women and 25 men with mild ID. In addition to finding a negative relationship between depression and comparison to the socially attractive group, regression analysis indicated that social comparison to socially attractive groups significantly predicted mood disorder. Together with the finding that people with ID rate others with similar intellectual deficits as lower on a social attractiveness scale, this predictive relationship is particularly important for this client group.

Dagnan and Waring (2004) further developed this model in a study linking stigma to psychological distress in 39 participants. They found that stigma scales correlated with negative evaluative beliefs and concluded that core negative evaluative beliefs about self were fundamentally related to the experience of feeling different. They went on to hypothesize that the negative social constructions associated with ID might be a risk factor for emotional disorders. Support for this hypothesis comes from the previously reviewed study by Richards *et al.* (2001). They found that the ID group was four times more likely to be identified as having affective disorder. This was true both at 36 and 43 years of age.

In mainstream work on mental health, several studies have related negative social comparison and psychopathology (Allen & Gilbert, 1995; Cheng & Furnham, 2001; Thwaites & Dagnan, 2004). Dagnan and Sandhu (1999) adapted the social comparison scale of Allen and Gilbert (1995) and found that the three factors of group identification, social attractiveness, and social rank were significantly related to depression. In addition, group belonging and social attractiveness were independent predictors of depression in a regression analysis. This important study extended the findings on the relationship between psychopathology and the wider social context.

CBT for People with IDs and Anxiety Disorders

The elements of Beck's cognitive therapy (Beck & Emery, 1979) are fundamentally revised and simplified for use with this client group. Treatment retains the essential principles and components of CBT, and procedures are maintained as far as possible. It is essential that clients understand the process and can engage with the methods of CBT and, because of the intellectual limitations involved, clear basic processes will allow the individual to interact with the methods, internalize the various principles, and use them in target situations. Perhaps one of the major differences is the way in which CBT considers the wider social context for individuals. Given the potential importance, established earlier in this chapter, of social comparison and stigma related to psychopathology in the client group, it is clear that methods should be related from an early stage to address the wider social context.

Jahoda *et al.* (2008) have suggested that engaging the wider social context involves two main processes. The first is to use homework assignments extensively. This can be difficult for people with ID simply because, in order to engage the homework assignments, one is required to remember the details of the assignment. However, treatment progress will benefit from practice and rehearsal outside therapeutic sessions and, if possible, it can be supported by family members and carers. During treatment sessions, it is possible to rehearse straightforward strategies that might provide positive outcomes to particular target situations. The likelihood of these target situations arising during the subsequent days can then be identified and prompts given (drawings or diagrams) to help the person engage in the rehearsed adaptive scripts during the target situation.

The second method of influencing the wider social context is to enable carers or relatives to participate in sessions themselves either through actively supporting the client or simply by observing the therapist in the processes. In another context, during anger management sessions, Rose *et al.* (2005) found that having carers observe sessions improved treatment outcome for the client. Jahoda *et al.* (2008) noted that clients' achievements may not always be recognized outside the therapeutic setting, and having carers in sessions might disseminate more widely the knowledge of their achievements. In addition, it may be particularly useful to involve carers at key points in treatment when clients become aware that new ways of thinking or interacting with others may have a beneficial impact on their lives. Conversely, having carers in sessions can also give the therapist opportunities to observe the ways in which they interact. This may provide opportunities to suggest alterations in the way carers communicate with clients when supporting them. Carer or family inclusion can be beneficial in spreading any gains that are made during therapy into the client's wider social circumstances.

As CBT for people with ID has been tested and developed, the various methods have been evaluated for effectiveness. Unfortunately, this has not been done in an experimental manner but rather through clinical intuition and trial and error. Lindsay *et al.* (1997) wrote that they had thought that setting an agenda for each session (a basic method in CBT) might be too complex for clients to understand. They had thought originally that an agenda might confuse clients, interfering with the natural processes of therapy. The opposite happened and setting an agenda allowed clients to gain some control and predictability of the therapeutic session processes. In fact, an agenda clarified what might be considered a complex therapeutic process. The agenda is generally very straightforward and might include a review of homework, analyzing any significant incident that may have happened, reviewing the cognitions and behaviors associated with the incident, reflecting on the way in which cognitions and behavior might affect an underlying schema, projecting important lessons onto possible future interactions, developing homework assignments, and practicing possible future situations related to homework assignments. During a session, there may also be the opportunity to complete an interim assessment of the person's emotional state, either through a standardized assessment such as the GAS (Mindham & Espie, 2003) or with a simple Likert scale that will be described in the case study further on in this chapter.

Therefore, the following methods can be used during CBT for anxiety:

- Set an agenda.
- Develop an awareness of the role of underlying beliefs determining thinking.
- Establish the relationship between cognitions, the experience of anxiety, and the person's behavior.
- Monitor automatic thoughts.
- Relate automatic thoughts to underlying beliefs and schemas.
- Test the accuracy of cognitions and challenge any maladaptive beliefs. This is an important part of treatment and is one of the fundamental concepts in Beck's CBT methods. The client is encouraged to adopt the role of a scientist in analyzing the accuracy of cognitions and beliefs in relation to his or her own life. It is also known as collaborative empiricism indicating that the therapist and client will engage in this process together.
- Generate alternative cognitions and adaptive automatic thoughts. This can be done in a very straightforward fashion by simply adopting the opposite of the cognition reported by the client. Sometimes clients will approach situations with the simple self-statement "I can't do this" or "I'm hopeless at this." Clearly, this is a cognition that will undermine any attempts at adaptive, competent performance. Lindsay (1999) wrote that these simple thoughts may be all the more powerful because of their uncluttered simplicity. Where thoughts are direct and powerful, they may carry greater effectiveness because they are not conditional on personal circumstances or states of mind. A simple statement such as "I can't do this" or "They hate me" will act as a very powerful setting condition determining perceptions and expectancies of any situation. However, the simple opposite of the maladaptive cognition can act to alter the perception and expectancy of any given situation. Therefore, the thought "I can do this" may enable the client to engage with the situation in the first place. Of course, it should be remembered that any subsequent engagement accompanying the positive self-statement will have been rehearsed during treatment by the therapist and the client. Therefore, the likelihood of a reasonable outcome has been maximized. It will be further enhanced if it has been possible to include a supportive carer in sessions.
- As has been mentioned, it is a specific method to practice using these thoughts during therapy sessions, role plays, and real-life sessions. The therapist can role play the use of the thought by saying it out loud. It can be useful to ask the clients to say the thought out loud after I have said it. In this way, they get used to uttering what might be unusual words such as "I am good at this" or "they might like me." After the clients have uttered the adaptive cognitions out loud, they can then be encouraged to internalize them.
- Review the evidence to contradict maladaptive beliefs and begin to construct new underlying assumptions or schemas about the self. This can be done immediately during treatment. If the clients approach the situation by saying "I can't do this," they can first alter the maladaptive self-statement to a more supportive cognition and then role play the situation. The evidence from the role play will suggest that they have been at least reasonably successful in executing the task or piece of social interaction. If a carer is present, the way in which the therapist praises and supports the client will act as modeling for other situations between carer and client.

- Establish homework assignments. Employ any key situations that have been reported from the previous week or scheduled for the following week. The client and therapist can decide on and practice homework assignments in collaboration.

Case Study: Walter

Walter was a 21-year-old man who had had a very disrupted upbringing. He had spent a number of years with different sets of foster parents and, in his later teenage years, had spent time in residential special schools. His mother and father split up when he was four years of age, and his mother and grandfather were the most significant individuals in his life.

He had a measured Wechsler Adult Intelligence Scale (WAIS) IQ of 67, suggesting that he had the cognitive and linguistic capacity to engage with CBT procedures. He had responded well to service input when he was 19 and 20 years of age and had been set up with supported accommodation in one of a series of flats for people with ID. He was managing reasonably well with the community and domestic aspects of independent living. His shopping skills were good, although he preferred to have some support from one of the workers managing the eight-flat complex. He was also functioning independently, making meals and keeping his small flat reasonably tidy.

Unfortunately, despite managing with the demands of living in his flat, he was becoming increasingly unsettled with his circumstances. He began locking himself in his flat for long periods of time of up to two days. When he opened the door for support workers to come in, they found him disheveled and suspected that he had engaged in self-harm because of bruising and rubbing marks on his arms and legs. He was also going through periods of being argumentative and sullen with the staff, suggesting that they had no interest in him and did not want to support him. He was referred because of these increasing management difficulties and because of the concerns of the staff.

During the first session, Walter expressed a number of maladaptive thoughts related to staff rejection. It is a good habit in CBTid to write down the dialogue as it is emerging or, if consent has been given, tape some of the dialogue for later analysis. The analysis allows the therapist to reflect on any underlying meaning that might be in the self-statements and also it can be repeated back to the client in later sessions to illustrate the way in which he or she has changed over the weeks of treatment. The additional interviews with Walter went as follows:

THERAPIST: *When you argue with Jean (the carer) you keep telling her that she is not interested in you.*

WALTER: *Well that is what I think when I am talking to her. I think she doesn't care about me and she would rather work with some of the other guys. They get on much better than me.*

T: *So you think that she's not interested in you and you think the other guys are doing better than you?*

W: *Yes, well she would rather work with them and take them out shopping because that is what happens with people like me.*

T: *What do you mean "people like you"?*

W: *Well I have lived in a lot of different places and I have had a lot of different carers.*

T:	*Does that mean Jean isn't interested in you?*
W:	*Well it might because some of my foster parents weren't interested in me and maybe Jean is the same.*
T:	*Is that something to do with you locking yourself in your flat and not allowing anyone in?*
W:	*What do you mean? I just want to be on my own.*
T:	*Well, I am wondering if you don't want to see the support workers because you are worried that they don't like you. If you don't see them you don't have to worry.*
W:	*Well it's true. If I don't see them I'm not worried that they don't like me and I'm not worried that they won't support me.*

In some ways, working with people with ID is an uncluttered and transparent process. Walter was very open about his fears that his support workers would be unwilling to be with him or that they would rather be with other people in the supported flats. In fact, it became clear that his feelings of abandonment and isolation were deep rooted and extended to a recent concern about his mother going on holiday. She had booked a holiday to Spain for four weeks, and Walter had become convinced that she was emigrating to Spain. The various maladaptive cognitions such as "Jean is fed up with me," "they would rather work with the other guys and don't want to work with me," and "the other guys are doing better than me and they would rather work with them" were a manifestation of an underlying schema of fear of abandonment and concerns regarding isolation. Paradoxically, his behavior promoted and reinforced this schema because he locked himself, isolated in his flat, forcing his support workers to abandon him temporarily. Because they respected his wishes and his choice, they had not insisted on entering his flat until he had been there for two days on his own. Consequently, his dysfunctional thinking led him to the conclusion that they did indeed wish to stop working with him.

Treatment began by establishing these cognitive distortions along with the underlying schema of "worrying about being alone"/abandonment. It was possible to point out to Walter that his experience of different foster families and special school, together with periodic returns to his family home and the corresponding moves away from the family home, had built up an underlying concern about being away from his family and being cut off from others on a regular basis. He was quite open to the notion that he was now testing us out by finding out the extent to which his carers would tolerate him, pushing them away by locking them out of his flat.

By linking his developmental history of broken relationships, his schema of abandonment, and his maladaptive cognitions of thinking that others did not want to support him, it was then possible to link these to his behavior (locking support workers out of his flat and starting arguments), with his physiological arousal (worrying about his mother and engaging in self-harm). These can be seen in Figure 7.1.

Figure 7.1 shows Walter himself on the left expressing the maladaptive cognition "they do not want me" while telling his support workers to stay out. The figure shows the locked door while the support worker on the outside is saying "let us in." Walter was able to depict all of this information and understood, through collaborative empiricism, that support workers outside the door asking to be let in,

Figure 7.1   Walter's account of a critical incident related to his anxiety and agitation.

undermined his own schema that he was isolated with no one wanting to see him. We also role played Walter sitting in his flat with the therapist as staff outside the door asking to be let in.

He began to understand that his mother was simply going on holiday and that his grandfather would continue visiting him while his mother was on holiday in Spain. This increased the concept of continuity of relationships in his life.

Walter completed the Glasgow Anxiety and Depression Scales before, during, and after treatment and also made weekly ratings of his emotional well-being on a four-point rating scale.

Figure 7.2 shows part of the records of Walter's ratings of his weekly emotional well-being. The therapist has dated most of the ratings. He was able to recall all of his weeks and review them with some accuracy. Weeks were rated in the following way.

First, the therapist asked Walter how he was today. He would then rate his feelings at that time. The therapist would then ask him how he felt yesterday, and Walter would make the appropriate rating. Because they are slightly different days, weekends can usually be remembered quite accurately, and the therapist then asked Walter what he was doing at the weekend and how he felt at the weekend. He then made the appropriate ratings for the weekend. With these reference points, the weekend, yesterday, and today, Walter was then able to make a summary rating of how he had felt over the last week. If the week had altered sharply at some point, he made two ratings for that week. Figure 7.2 shows the weekly ratings made by Walter over the course of treatment. If two or more ratings varied significantly, an average was taken for the purposes of entering in the table. As can be seen, there was a steady

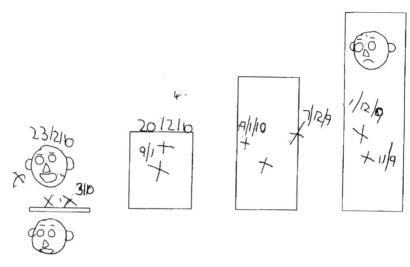

Figure 7.2 Walter's weekly ratings of anxiety.

improvement over the weeks of treatment from high emotional ratings to stably low emotional ratings in the last weeks.

The Glasgow Anxiety and Depression Scales were filled out by Walter prior to treatment, at the midpoint, at the end of treatment, and at two months' follow-up. The Glasgow Scales allow ratings to be made by the client and also by the carers. The carer ratings were filled out by Walter's support workers. They allow for some validity checks on his own ratings of anxiety and depression. They showed the same pattern with high scores prior to treatment falling quite quickly to fairly low scores at the midpoint that maintain to the end and the one month follow-up. In fact, both Walter and his support workers reported significant changes in him after only a few weeks of treatment. The support workers were able to sit in with sessions and were fascinated (this was the word they used themselves) about the way in which links were made between his current behavior and his developmental experiences. It also allowed them to reassure Walter that they had his interests in mind as they did all of the residents in the complex. Walter was encouraged to use the self-statement that "Staff are busy. They'll get round to me" to reassure himself that he was still supported. All of this proved to be a powerful intervention allowing him to be more comfortable with staff contact and relationships.

While this chapter has emphasized the applicability of the CBT toolkit for treating anxiety problems experienced by people with IDs, it is important to distinguish between the toolkit and the therapeutic principle underlying CBT: that psychological distress can be decreased by counteracting dysfunctional cognitions.

This objective can sometimes be achieved much more simply than by deploying the full CBT toolkit. For example, Willner (2006) described two cases where significant therapeutic improvements were achieved simply by correcting false beliefs (e.g., that breathing the air in a toilet causes illness). PTSD, and particularly, the nightmares associated with PTSD, is an area where a simpler approach to cognitive change has produced well-documented therapeutic benefits. Imagery Rehearsal Therapy (IRT) addresses the problem of recurrent nightmares by helping the client to change the nightmare story to a version that has a more acceptable ending, and then to rehearse the new story before going to sleep. The benefit of this approach has been demonstrated in a controlled trial in the general population (Krakow *et al.*, 2000, 2001), and there are four case studies reporting impressive effects in people with IDs (Bradshaw, 1991; Stenfert Kroese & Thomas, 2006; Willner, 2004). Here is another: Colin was a 30-year-old man who had suffered severe physical abuse as a child, leading to many years of heavy drug use, which he had recently more or less ceased. He had been troubled for two years by a recurrent nightmare in which he was chased by demons, waking up screaming just before they caught (and ate) him. A new story was suggested to him, in which he ran toward, and into, the sea, where he started fishing (his favorite hobby); meanwhile, the demons could not approach because they were frightened of the crowds on the beach. After six sessions, and rehearsal with a staff member, the nightmares ceased and had not returned at 12 and 24 months' follow-up. This case used almost none of the CBT tools but demonstrates the underlying principle: replacing a dysfunctional cognition with one that works better to promote psychological health.

CBT Anxiety Interventions for People IDs

Lindsay (1999) reported on a case series of 15 individuals all assessed on a revised version of the BAI or the Zung Anxiety Scale (ZAS). Both these scales have been used extensively to assess individuals presenting with anxiety symptoms. This series illustrated the catastrophic way in which people with ID can respond to their maladaptive cognitions. Lindsay (1999) transformed the BAI and ZAS scores into percentages of the total scale. Treatment lasted an average of 23 sessions with a range of 15–47 weeks. The total anxiety score fell from an average of 62 percent of the total score at baseline to 39 percent following treatment. It was reported that the improvement was statistically significant and maintained to six months' follow-up.

Lang *et al.* (2010, 2011) have reviewed the efficacy of CBT for anxiety disorders in people with autism spectrum disorders (ASDs). The main difficulty with this work is that it is not conducted on people with ID, but the suggestion is that for some studies, there is overlap in the two populations. Lang *et al.* (2010) conducted a systematic review of CBT for anxiety in people with ASDs and found nine studies that addressed symptoms of anxiety using CBT methods. These studies had 110 participants of whom 60 percent were male, and their ages ranged from 9 to 23 years. Sixty-seven percent were diagnosed with Asperger's syndrome; of the 20 (18 percent) who were diagnosed with autism, 9 were described as "high-functioning autism." Phobias included social phobias, OCD, and a range of other anxiety disorders. The participants were assessed using self- and other ratings and psychometric measures of psychopathology and adaptive behavior. They concluded that five studies were "suggestive" of treatment efficacy since they were nonexperimental. They classified three studies as providing evidence at the level of "preponderance level of certainty" since they were experiments but were either nonblind, did not randomize, or did not control for alternate explanations of change. Only one study was classified as providing "conclusive" evidence of treatment effects (Wood *et al.*, 2009) since it was an experiment with blinding, random assignment, treatment fidelity measures, interobserver agreement for the dependent variable and controlled for potential confounds. Based on these data, the authors concluded that "CBT is an effective treatment for anxiety in individuals with Aperger's. However, data involving other ASD sub-types is lacking" (p. 1).

Based on their descriptions of the participants, the relevance of this meta-analysis to people with IDs is limited. Some participants may have had some degree of intellectual impairment, but there was no direct evidence that CBT was an effective intervention for people with ID. Lang *et al.* (2011) conducted a similar updated systematic search and reached very similar conclusions. Their search identified four previous systematic reviews, no meta-analyses, and two randomized controlled trials, but all of the studies were conducted on people without IDs. This led Lang *et al.* to conclude that CBT seems an effective treatment for people with ASD and no ID, but where participants have an ID, much less evidence is available.

Conclusions

In this chapter, we have reviewed some of the information and research on CBT with anxiety problems in mainstream mental health populations. CBT has been shown to be successful for a range of difficulties including social anxiety, generalized anxiety disorder, and panic disorder both on its own and in combination with pharmacological approaches. Some authors have found that anxiety disorders are related to developmental experiences both in mainstream and ID populations. Attachment difficulties in childhood, experiences of stigma, and negative social comparisons all seem associated with psychopathology and may be involved in the genesis of anxiety disorders. The research is tentative, and all studies have been exploratory rather than definitive.

Nevertheless, these issues can be incorporated into CBT for anxiety disorders and there have been a number of case studies reported of successful treatment. Unfortunately, the state of the research is such that there are no comparison trials involving experimental and control conditions, and there are certainly not any randomized controlled trials. Even the case studies have not been particularly well controlled, usually comparing baseline measures with posttreatment and follow-up measures. In general, the form of treatment for people with learning disability has mirrored that of the mainstream population. The main aspects that have been changed have been the complexity of the language and simplification of the concepts of CBT. One important difference is that for this client group, it is possible to involve carers and family members from the person's wider social context. This has also been illustrated in the case of Walter. There is little doubt that CBT is being used for clinical populations. It appears a promising technique, but the field remains exploratory with only a series of case reports as evidence of effectiveness.

References

Allen, S. & Gilbert, P. (1995). A social comparison scale: Psychometric properties and relationship to psychopathology. *Personality and Individual Differences, 19*, 293–299.

Beck, A.T. & Emery, G. (1979). *Cognitive therapy of anxiety and phobic disorder.* Unpublished treatment manual. Philadelphia, PA: Centre of Cognitions.

Bradshaw, S.J. (1991). Successful cognitive manipulation of a stereotypic nightmare in a 40 year old male with Down's syndrome. *Behavioral Psychotherapy, 19*, 281–283.

Cheng, H. & Furnham, A. (2001). Attributional style and personality as predictors of happiness and mental health. *Journal of Happiness Studies, 2*, 307–327.

Clark, D.M., Ehlers, A., McManus, F., Hackman, A., Fennell, M., Campbell, H. *et al.* (2003). Cognitive therapy versus fluoxetine in generalised social phobia: A randomised placebo-controlled trial. *Journal of Consulting and Clinical Psychology, 71*, 1058–1067.

Cooper, S.-A. & Bailey, N.M. (2001). Psychiatric disorders amongst adults with learning disabilities: Prevalence and relationship to ability level. *Irish Journal of Psychological Medicine, 18*, 45–53.

Cooper, S.-A., Smiley, E., Morrison, J., Williamson, A. & Allan, L. (2007). Mental ill-health in adults with intellectual disabilities: Prevalence and associated factors. *The British Journal of Psychiatry, 190*, 27–35.

Dagnan, D. & Sandhu, S. (1999). Social comparison, self-esteem and depression in people with learning disabilities. *Journal of Intellectual Disability Research, 43*, 372–379.

Dagnan, D. & Waring, M. (2004). Linking stigma to psychological distress: Testing a social-cognitive model of the experience of people with intellectual disabilities. *Clinical Psychology & Psychotherapy, 11*, 247–254.

Deb, S., Thomas, M. & Bright, C. (2001). Mental disorder in adults with intellectual disability. I. Prevalence of functional psychiatric disorder among a community-based population aged between 16 and 64 years. *Journal of Intellectual Disability Research, 45*, 495–505.

Finlay, W.M. & Lyons, E. (2001). Methodological issues in interviewing and using self-report questionnaires with people with mental retardation. *Psychological Assessment, 13*, 319–335.

Foa, E., Hembree, E.A., Cahill, S.P., Rauch, S.A., Riggs, D., Feeny, N.C. *et al.* (2005). AA randomised trial of prolonged exposure to post dramatic stress disorder with and without cognitive restructuring: Outcome and academic and community clinics. *Journal of Consulting and Clinical Psychology, 73*, 953–964.

Gardner, J.E. (1967). Behavior therapy treatment approach to a psychogenic seizure case. *Journal of Consulting Psychology, 31*, 309–312.

Haby, M., Donnelly, M., Corry, J. & Vos, T. (2006). Cognitive behavioural therapy for depression, panic disorder and generalised anxiety disorder: A meta-regression of factors that may predict outcome. *The Australian and New Zealand Journal of Psychiatry, 40*, 9–19.

Hofmann, S.G., Sawyer, A.T., Korte, K. & Smits, J.A. (2009). Is it beneficial to hard pharmacotherapy to cognitive behaviour therapy when taking anxiety disorders? A meta analytic review. *International Journal of Cognitive Therapy, 1*, 160–175.

Hofmann, S.G. & Smits, J.A. (2008). Cognitive behavioural therapy for adult anxiety disorders: A meta-analysis of randomised placebo controlled trials. *The Journal of Clinical Psychiatry, 69*, 621–632.

Hunot, V., Churchill, R., Teixeira, V. & Silva de Lima, M. (2007). Psychological therapies for generalised anxiety disorder. *Cochrane Database of Systematic Reviews* (1), CD001848. DO1. The Cochrane collaboration, John Wiley & Sons, Ltd.

Jacobson, J. (1982). Problem behaviour and psychiatric impairment within a developmentally disabled population: I. Behaviour frequency. *Applied Research in Mental Retardation, 3*, 121–139.

Jahoda, A., Selkirk, M., Trower, P., Pert, C., Srenfert-Kroese, B., Dagnan, D. *et al.* (2008). The balance of power in therapeutic interactions with individuals with intellectual disabilities. *The British Journal of Clinical Psychology, 48*, 63–78.

Kellet, S., Beail, N., Newman, D.W. & Hawes, A. (2004). The factor structure of the Brief Symptom Inventory: Intellectual disability evidence. *Clinical Psychology & Psychotherapy*, *11*, 275–281.

Kellet, S.C., Beail, N., Newman, D.W. & Frankish, P. (2003). Utility of the Brief Symptom Inventory (BSI) in the assessment of psychological distress. *Journal of Applied Research in Intellectual Disabilities*, *16*, 127–135.

Krakow, B., Hollifield, M., Johnson, M.A., Koss, M., Shrader, R., Warner, T.D. *et al.* (2001). Imagery Rehearsal Therapy for chronic nightmares in sexual assault survivors with posttraumatic stress disorder. *Journal of the American Medical Association*, *286*, 537–545.

Krakow, B., Hollifield, M., Shrader, R., Koss, M., Tandberg, D., Lauriello, J. *et al.* (2000). A controlled study of imagery rehearsal for chronic nightmares in sexual assault survivors with PTSD: A preliminary report. *Journal of Traumatic Stress*, *13*, 589–610.

Lang, R., Mahonery, R., El Zein, F., Delaune, E. & Amidon, M. (2011). Evidence to practice: treatment of anxiety in individuals with autism spectrum disorders. *Neuropsychiatric Disease Treatment*, *7*, 27–30.

Lang, R., Regester, A., Lauderdale, S., Ashbaugh, K. & Haring, S. (2010). Treatment of anxiety in autism spectrum disorders using cognitive behaviour therapy: A systematic review. *Developmental Neurorehabilitation*, *13*(1), 53–63.

Linden, M., Zuandbraegel, D., Baer, T., Franke, U. & Schlattmann, P. (2005). Efficacy of cognitive behaviour therapy in generalised anxiety disorders: Results of a controlled clinical trial. *Psychotherapy and Psychosomatics*, *74*, 36–42.

Lindsay, W.R. (1999). Cognitive therapy. *The Psychologist*, *12*, 238–241.

Lindsay, W.R., Michie, A.M., Baty, F.J., Smith, A.H.W. & Miller, S. (1994). The consistency of reports about feelings and emotions from people with intellectual disability. *Journal of Intellectual Disability Research*, *38*, 61–66.

Lindsay W.R., Neilson C. & Lawrenson H. (1997). Cognitive behaviour therapy for anxiety in people with learning disabilities. In B.S. Kroese, D. Dagnan & K. Loumidis (Eds.) *Cognitive behaviour therapy for people with intellectual disabilities* (pp.124–140). London: Routledge.

Lindsay, W.R. & Skene, D.D. (2007). The Beck Depression Inventory II and the Beck Anxiety Inventory in people with intellectual disabilities: Factor analyses and group data. *Journal of Applied Research in Intellectual Disability*, *20*, 401–408.

Mindham, J. & Espie, C.A. (2003). Glasgow Anxiety Scale for People with an Intellectual Disability (GAS-ID): Development and psychometric properties of a new measure for use with people with mild intellectual disability. *Journal of Intellectual Disability Research*, *47*, 22–30.

Penrose, L.S. (1938). *A clinical and genetic study of 1280 cases of mental defect*. Special report series, Medical Research Council No. 229. London: HMSO.

Richards, M., Maughan, B., Hardy, R., Hall, I., Strydom, A. & Wadsworth, M. (2001). Long term affective disorder in people with mild learning disability. *The British Journal of Psychiatry*, *179*, 523–527.

Rose, J., Loftus, M., Flint, B. & Corey, L. (2005). Factors associated with the efficacy of a group intervention for anger in people with intellectual disabilities. *The British Journal of Clinical Psychology*, *44*, 305–318.

Stenfert Kroese, B. & Thomas, G. (2006). Treating chronic nightmares of sexual assault survivors with an intellectual disability – Two descriptive case studies. *Journal of Applied Research in Intellectual Disabilities*, *19*, 73–80.

Szivos-Bach, S.E. (1993). Social comparisons, stigma and mainstreaming: The self-esteem of young adults with mild mental handicap. *Mental Handicap Research*, *6*, 217–234.

Taylor, J.L., Hatton, C., Dixon, L. & Douglas, C. (2004). Screening for psychiatric symptoms: PAS-ADD Checklist norms for adults with intellectual disabilities. *Journal of Intellectual Disability Research, 48,* 37–41.

Thwaites, R. & Dagnan, D. (2004). Moderating variables in the relationship between social comparison and depression: An evolutionary perspective. *Psychology and Psychotherapy, 77*(3), 309–323.

Willner, P. (2004). Brief cognitive therapy of nightmares and post-traumatic ruminations in a man with a learning disability. *The British Journal of Clinical Psychology, 11,* 222–232.

Willner, P. (2006). Readiness for cognitive therapy in people with intellectual disabilities. *Journal of Applied Research in Intellectual Disabilities, 19,* 5–16.

Wood, J., Drahota, A., Sze, K., Har, K., Chiu, A. & Langer, D. (2009). Cognitive behavioral therapy for anxiety in children with autism spectrum disorders: A randomized, controlled trial. *Journal of Child Psychology and Psychiatry, and Allied Disciplines, 50,* 224–234.

Chapter 8

Cognitive–Behavioral Therapy for Mood Disorders

Anna J. Esbensen
Sigan L. Hartley

Introduction

It is well established that individuals with intellectual disabilities (IDs) suffer from mood disorders. Individuals with IDs present with a similar set of depressive behaviors, including dysfunctional cognitive deficits similar to individuals without IDs such as having a low self-concept, attending to negative features of an event, and making negative causal attributions for stressful events (Benson & Ivins, 1992; Esbensen & Benson, 2006; Hartley & MacLean, 2009). Standardized criteria for major depression episodes, manic episodes, dysthymia, and bipolar disorder among individuals with IDs are now available, with limited modifications needed from the criteria for the general population (Fletcher *et al.*, 2007). Although much is understood about the treatment of these disorders for the general population, less is known about their appropriateness among individuals with IDs. Cognitive–behavioral therapy (CBT) is one of the most common treatments, and one of the few established empirically supported treatments by the American Psychological Association (Chambless & Hollon, 1998) for depression in the general population. Preliminary studies suggest that CBT may also be beneficial for treating depression in individuals with IDs when training procedures and modifications are used (e.g., Lindsay *et al.*, 1997; McCabe *et al.*, 2006). This chapter will review the core features of CBT for treating depression, training procedures, and modifications to CBT appropriate for individuals with IDs, and the empirical support for these training procedures and modifications.

Review of CBT and Mood Disorders

The theoretical basis behind CBT is that depressive cognitive processes cause individuals to interpret experiences in such a way as to develop, maintain, or exacerbate

Psychological Therapies for Adults with Intellectual Disabilities, First Edition.
Edited by John L. Taylor, William R. Lindsay, Richard P. Hastings, and Chris Hatton.
© 2013 John Wiley & Sons, Ltd. Published 2013 by John Wiley & Sons, Ltd.

their depression. These dysfunctional cognitive processes are often acquired during childhood and adolescence and make the individual vulnerable to construing events in a negative way. Although there remains a debate about the development and nature of depressive cognitive processes (Esbensen & Rojahn, 2005), there is widespread agreement that therapies should be aimed at modifying these cognitive processes.

Depressed individuals are theorized to possess negative schemata for processing information as well as a negative view of themselves, the world, and their future. In the face of events the individual interprets as stressful, the negative schemata are activated and subsequent information is processed negatively, leading to the development of dysfunctional beliefs. The depressed individual automatically interprets situations in a negative manner and has limited ability to generate rational and obvious alternate explanations for the same event. For example, depressed individuals may consider themselves inadequate, believe that unpleasant experiences occur as a result of their own actions or characteristics, view the world as full of obstacles, interpret interactions with the environment in a negative manner, view the future as full of hardships, and view that current difficulties will continue endlessly. These dysfunctional beliefs predispose the individual to symptoms of depression. Thus, the focus of treatment is to identify negative thoughts that are associated with feelings of depression and encourage the individual to engage in more activities that are positive and rewarding in an effort to improve mood.

Current CBT packages for the general population focus on altering irrational and overly negative cognitions, identifying automatic thoughts and accurately labeling them as distorted or overly pessimistic, and challenging depressive thinking about the individual and his or her world. In addition, CBT packages educate the individual about depression, his or her depressive symptomatology, and the rationale behind CBT. Most CBT programs also include behavioral components of learning to monitor mood, identify feelings and emotions, and engage in effective problem-solving strategies.

There is a large body of research demonstrating the efficacy of CBT for depression in adults in the general population (e.g., Butler *et al.*, 2006; Westen & Morrison, 2001). CBT has also been shown to be an efficacious intervention for treating depression in children and adolescents in the general population (Brent *et al.*, 1997; Compton *et al.*, 2004; Ryan, 2005), although there are some discrepant findings (March *et al.*, 2004). When these CBT programs are implemented with children and adolescents, most programs share two core features. First, in addition to targeting affect regulation, social skills, and problem solving, these programs address the specific needs of the individual child or adolescent, such as any comorbid diagnoses, medical problems, and/or environmental stressors, in a more formal manner than is true of programs geared at adults. Second, parents and other family members often participate in sessions with the child/adolescent or attend separate sessions. The purpose of involving parents and other family members in the treatment is to educate them about depression, and teach them about CBT so that they can encourage and help the child/adolescent continue to monitor and modify his or her negative thoughts outside of the therapy sessions. In addition, by including parents or other family members in treatment, the therapist is able to better assess for and address any family environment (e.g., parent depression or recent change in the family) or relationship (e.g., problems with the parent–child relationship) problems that might be exacerbating the depressive symptomatology.

CBT programs for children and adolescents have other modifications from the CBT programs geared toward adults. CBT programs with children and adolescents tend to be more present oriented and focused on building skills. This comes from the assumption that skill deficits in problem solving and engaging socially are preventing the child or adolescent from interacting effectively with his or her world and contributing to or maintaining his or her depressive symptoms. Within a collaborative working relationship, the therapist helps the child or adolescent to learn new ways of thinking and behaving, which in turn is assumed to reduce the severity of the symptoms of depression.

There is empirical evidence that CBT will work better for some children and adolescents than others. Successful reduction of depressive symptomatology is more likely when the individual in therapy has fewer comorbid diagnoses or presenting problems (Hughes *et al.*, 1990). Having fewer comorbid diagnoses allows the therapy to focus more on the depressive symptoms and thoughts than on the other problems. Success is also more likely if the individual in therapy acknowledges that there is a problem and wants to get help, and more likely when family or important caregivers acknowledge that there is a problem and are willing to support the therapy. Finally, success is more likely for individuals with mild or moderate cases of depression as compared with individuals with severe depressive disorders (Brent *et al.*, 1999; Clarke *et al.*, 1992; Jayson *et al.*, 1998).

Thus, the efficacy of CBT for mood disorders is not altered by modifications to the intervention that take into account the developmental level and cognitive ability of children and adolescents, although there are a variety of factors that influence the success of the intervention. The presumption then is that CBT would also be efficacious among other populations with similar developmental levels and cognitive abilities including individuals with IDs, although this remains to be empirically tested. Clinicians have reported on the suitability of and several modifications to CBT for individuals with IDs and comorbid mood disorders, with encouraging support for the use of CBT for this disorder in this population.

Training and Modification of CBT for Individuals with IDs and Mood Disorders

CBT requires that the individual receiving treatment possess certain requisite skills. These skills include (1) adequate receptive and expressive communication skills, (2) the ability to identify emotions, (3) a cognitive capacity for the requirements of CBT (self-monitoring of emotions, memory skills for homework, conceptualization of temporal events, ability to self-reflect and self-evaluate), and (4) the ability to understand the CBT model (Hatton, 2002). Only a few studies have investigated the extent to which individuals with IDs have these skills. These studies indicate that individuals with IDs who have a well-developed receptive vocabulary are better equipped with these skills than individuals with lower IQs (Sams *et al.*, 2006). Thus, individuals with IDs who are higher functioning may be more suitable for CBT for depression than their lower-functioning peers. Researchers within the field of ID are beginning to design training procedures aimed at teaching these prerequisite skills to individuals with IDs as a precursor to conducting CBT (Dagnan *et al.*, 2000; Dagnan *et al.*, 2013, Chapter 4, of this book).

In addition to the individual with ID requiring certain skills, there are a variety of modifications that the therapist can implement to engage the individual in CBT for depression. Some modifications are global and apply to any form of CBT, and some are pertinent to the structure of CBT for depression. Within CBT for depression, there are several core components, including (1) psychoeducation of CBT and the relationship between thoughts, feelings, and behaviors; (2) setting an agenda; (3) identifying dysfunctional beliefs, maladaptive automatic thoughts, and their underlying assumptions; (4) reviewing the accuracy of these interpretations and testing alternate explanations; and (5) problem solving (Lindsay *et al.*, 1993). This chapter will review some general modifications to CBT for depression for individuals with IDs, then review modifications to the core components, and end with some additional techniques that may be complementary to CBT for individuals with IDs.

General modifications

Language is very important in CBT. It is imperative to ensure that not only does the individual with ID have adequate receptive and expressive language skills, but also that he or she understands the content of what is discussed in therapy. It is important to use words and sentences appropriate for the individual's cognitive level. It is also important to monitor the language of the individual with ID to ensure that the terms that he or she uses within therapy mean the same thing to him or her as to the therapist. "I feel bad" may have different meanings. It is helpful for the therapist to probe often to ensure that he or she is using the same language as the individual with ID. While these probes may need to be more direct, such as "are you feeling sick or sad?", it is also recommended that prior to probing, the therapist use open-ended questions to avoid acquiescence.

It is also important to simplify concepts discussed in therapy. Using concrete examples relevant to his or her life experiences (e.g., referencing a specific conflict that the individual had with his or her roommate, staff person, or job coach) and engaging in role plays or other hands-on exercises (e.g., drawing pictures, reading a story, and playing games) are preferable to discussing abstract concepts. This modification will be elaborated on more within the discussion of how to modify the core components of CBT. Also, it is helpful to underscore key information by stating it multiple times and in multiple ways throughout the session, and to have the individual with ID repeat and rephrase key concepts to ensure that he or she understands what is being discussed.

The structure of therapy and each session may also need to be tailored to the individual. It is often important for therapy to proceed at a slower pace, so that each concept can be adequately understood. Some individuals may require longer sessions to fully understand the concepts. Others may have a limited attention span and require numerous shorter sessions to complete the therapy. A good guideline is to limit the length of each therapy session to what would best suit the individual (Haddock & Jones, 2006).

During therapy, the therapist and the individual identify the cognitive distortions that underlie depressive thinking. Throughout the therapy sessions, it is also useful for the therapist to identify any deficits in the client's executive functioning (e.g., memory, attention, and motor skills), problem-solving, and reasoning skills, and to take these into account in the intervention. For instance, instructions for homework assignments could be audio recorded, and thus played back numerous times, for individuals with memory problems. Visual information, hands-on activities, and graphical rating scales (e.g., pictures of faces indicating various levels of sadness) could be used for individuals with poor verbal reasoning skills. Reminder cues may also be needed for individuals with short attention spans, such as giving them a watch that beeps every hour as a cue to record their thoughts or feelings or to engage in a pleasurable activity such as taking a walk or calling a friend.

For individuals with lower IQs and verbal skills, CBT may also need to be focused more on behavioral than cognitive components. The focus may need to be on teaching affective skills, coping skills for dealing with aversive events, activity scheduling, or problem-solving skills. The goal being that by changing behaviors, mood will improve.

The first sessions and psychoeducation

The goal of the first few sessions is to establish rapport with the individual with ID and to obtain a detailed description of the presenting problem. During this stage, it may be helpful to involve family or caregivers who work with the individual with ID, such as his or her day rehabilitation or group home staff, case manager, or job coach. Referrals often originate from family or caregivers, and thus, it may be valuable to include them in the information gathering stage to better understand the client's mood and affect difficulties and associated problems. The complaints presented by the individual with ID in the first session may be vague, and it is the therapist's role to use probes and simple language to generate a specific list of target problems for treatment. This process may be more difficult if the individual with ID did not self-refer and does not believe that he or she is depressed. If staff or family initiated the referral, more time may need to be spent in the first session to determine what the individual views as problematic and thus amenable to treatment.

The client's broader environmental (e.g., are there any signs of mistreatment, is the individual provided with an appropriate level of privacy and autonomy) and social context (relationships with family, friends, and staff) also needs to be assessed in the first couple of sessions to determine how this context may exacerbate the depressive symptoms and/or how it could be modified or used to reduce these symptoms. For example, a mismatch between an individual's functioning level and the degree of independence in his or her residential setting may be contributing to his or her depression, and moving the individual to a new residential setting may be an appropriate step in reducing his or her depressive symptoms. The therapist should also get an understanding of the nature of support for the individual, both social (e.g., do they have supportive people in their life) and functional (e.g., what services and assistance do they receive) and how this may contribute to depressive symptoms. For instance, an individual with ID may have many friends but not any transportation to visit these friends.

Prior to beginning the intervention, the individual with ID may benefit from knowing more about depression and CBT (McCabe *et al.*, 2006). Depending on the level of cognitive ability of the individual, this information could be verbally communicated, or presented through story examples. Stories are useful aids to describe various situations that could have several alternate interpretations or several different outcomes on how the individual in that situation may feel or think. For example, the scenario could be presented of getting into an argument with a friend. Then, various interpretations of the scenario (e.g., the friend did not like the individual vs. the friend was just in a bad mood vs. the friend liked the individual but did not agree about a specific topic) and outcomes (e.g., the individual feels sad vs. the individual understands that the friend is just having a bad day) could be examined.

To measure change during the intervention, the therapist may choose to use standardized baseline measures of the individual's behaviors and emotions during the first few sessions. However, little is known about how well some standardized instruments measure treatment change among individuals with IDs. In addition, the language and response options of instruments such as the Beck Depression Inventory (BDI) may be too complex for some individuals with IDs, and recalling events for a specific time period may be difficult (Lindsay & Lees, 2003). Still, standardized measures may be helpful in determining the presenting problems and symptoms, and providing tangible feedback to the individual with ID regarding how he or she has improved with therapy.

Setting an agenda

A set format for therapy is helpful to the individual with ID as it provides structure and predictability, which is often reassuring, and allows him or her to more quickly learn how therapy works and his or her role. It also allows the therapist to effectively manage time to ensure that target problems are adequately addressed within the allotted sessions. An example of the format for each session is (1) discuss current emotions and events, (2) review homework, (3) teach a specific skill, (4) assign homework, and (5) summarize the session. It is also beneficial to outline what topics will be addressed during each session so the individual has an understanding of what to expect. The format the therapist sets should also allow for flexibility. No format should be so rigid that it does not provide time to discuss new concerns that the individual with ID raises. This is particularly important for individuals with IDs who may contribute more during the course of therapy as they gradually become more comfortable with their treatment and aware of their thoughts and emotions.

Most importantly, the format, length, and frequency of therapy sessions should be tailored for the specific abilities and needs of the individual with ID. More sessions may be needed to account for the extra time spent repeating material within a session. The endurance, attention span, and motivation of the individual during each session will also dictate the length of each session. Additional sessions may be needed initially to establish rapport or to generate treatment targets. More support may be needed initially to guide the individual through the process of identifying the cognitive and behavioral factors that play a role in the initiating and maintaining of his or her problems and depressive symptoms. Additional sessions may also be needed to address topics or problems. Individuals with IDs often have comorbid diagnoses or conditions, and additional sessions targeting topics such as relaxation for anxiety or anger management for aggression or irritability may be beneficial.

Identifying dysfunctional beliefs

The therapist should take the time to establish a common language or vocabulary for describing mood and feelings. A common language helps the individual to identify his or her dysfunctional beliefs and maladaptive automatic thoughts. These skills can be learned by teaching the names for various emotions through emotion labeling programs, through games, or through helping the individual to recognize and identify various emotions that he or she is experiencing within the therapy session.

Once a common language is established for discussing mood and feelings, the therapist can work with the individual with ID to monitor his or her thoughts. Reviewing upsetting events from the past week, or couple days, is one way to generate a discussion of the thoughts and feelings the individual was experiencing at that particular point in time. Some individuals with IDs will have difficulty remembering events from the past week, or have difficulty remembering what they were thinking at that time. For these individuals, it may be preferable to identify thoughts that occur within a session. The therapist is then responsible for commenting when he or she observes the individual with ID becoming upset, and moving the discussion toward identifying the thoughts and feelings that the individual is currently experiencing.

Other techniques can be used within the session to help the individual with ID to identify his or her thoughts. Role playing a past event or novel situations is a useful way to aid the individual with ID in identifying his or her negative thoughts. These situations need to be as concrete as possible. For example, a role play session related to a scenario at work should reference the specific coworkers and supervisors or job coach at the client's job as well as the specific work-related issues that typically arise.

Reverse role playing, where the individual with ID plays a role other than himself or herself, can also be effective. Reverse role playing may help the individual identify new thoughts to be probed during therapy. In any role play situation, it is important to focus on the situations that make the individual feel sad, and to have the individual with ID identify the emotions that accompany those thoughts. Pictures of social situations may serve as a useful prop to generate a discussion of what the individuals in the pictures are thinking and feeling. Pictorial diagrams may also be helpful to some for drawing the link between thoughts and emotions (Lindsay *et al.*, 2005).

It is important for the therapist to be directive, in that he or she is leading the individual in identifying thoughts and emotions. But at the same time, the therapist needs to be aware of the cognitive abilities and deficits of the individual with ID. The techniques used to identify the dysfunctional beliefs need to match the ability and deficits of the individual with ID. For example, individuals with severe or moderate IDs may have particular difficulty understanding the thoughts or emotions of others, and require repeated practice on this skill using multiple formats such as pictures and role playing.

Once the individual with ID is able to identify emotions and negative thoughts within the therapy session, the therapist is encouraged to have the individual begin monitoring his or her mood and thoughts outside of the therapy session, generally termed "homework." However, it remains important for the therapist to continue to practice identifying mood and thoughts within therapy sessions as the validity and completion of homework cannot always be guaranteed. And depending on the individual with ID and his or her experiences with school, the therapist may choose to use a different term than "homework."

Homework may include a graphical monitoring of the emotions the individual feels throughout the day. Histograms measuring the valence of the emotion or pictures may be useful to aid the individual with ID to document his or her feelings throughout the day, or to communicate to the individual how to do the monitoring. More support may be needed initially to help the individual with ID to understand how to complete a homework, and depending on the individual with ID, it may also be useful to recruit a support person to aid the individual with ID in completing his or her homework (see section on "External Informants"; Hurley, 1989).

Testing dysfunctional beliefs

A core component of CBT is helping the individual to review the accuracy of his or her interpretations of events, to test his or her negative thoughts, and to generate more adaptive thoughts and positive statements about himself or herself. In CBT, the therapist and the individual determine the evidence for and against a specific belief, generate alternative ways of interpreting a situation, de-catastrophize the situation, and learn problem-solving strategies.

Some of these cognitive components are complex, and extra supports may be needed for each of these steps. The therapist of an individual with ID should take the simplest dysfunctional belief that was generated and focus on testing the accuracy of its underlying assumptions. It is useful to select a behavior or belief that is likely to occur during the therapy session in order for the therapist to model cognitive restructuring. The therapist is thus able to immediately reinforce the individual for accurately identifying a negative thought and for evaluating the accuracy of that thought. It is also beneficial to focus on behaviors and thoughts that occur during the therapy session as, due to cognitive limitations of concrete thinking and temporal fixedness, it may be difficult for the individual to recall and test thoughts that occurred outside of therapy.

Once the problematic thought is identified, the therapist should help the individual with ID generate as many potential solutions to the problem, choose the best solution, determine the steps to carrying out the solution, and try out that solution. As problem solving is not specific to CBT or alleviating symptoms of depression, the individual may benefit from learning the concepts of problem solving on more concrete tasks (difficulty completing household task or job), and then building this skill into therapy and applying it to his or her negative thoughts and beliefs (problems at work, problems with peers). Again, role playing and concrete examples or vignettes are helpful aids for guiding the individual with ID through testing his or her dysfunctional beliefs.

For individuals with ID for whom these cognitive components are too complex, the therapist is encouraged to apply more behavioral measures, such as increasing positive statements, directing attention to positive events, and encouraging the individual with ID to engage in social activities outside of therapy. For example, the individual with ID could be guided in identifying positive events that occurred throughout his or her day and developing a schedule of goal-directed and enjoyable activities. Breaking the cycle of negative thinking through engaging in positive statements and activities are helpful for reducing depressive symptoms. And engaging in social activities or projects can develop a sense of mastery and accomplishment for the individual with ID.

External informants

The involvement of parents, family members, and support staff within CBT may augment the therapy. Although individuals with IDs can reliably report on their depressive symptomatology (Esbensen & Benson, 2005), an external assessment of depressive symptoms can be useful when the individual with ID is initially less open about sharing his or her depressed thoughts with a clinician (Lagges & Dunn, 2003).

External informants can provide information about stressors or symptoms the individual with ID may be reluctant to talk about with a therapist. External informants can also serve as supports and be useful by (a) supporting treatment attendance, (b) supporting the individual to complete his or her homework (self-monitoring, engagement in social activities), (c) encouraging the use of problem-solving skills in the natural environment, and (d) changing environmental events that may exacerbate depressive thoughts and symptoms. In collaboration with the therapist, external informants can support the skills taught in therapy by coaching and modeling the skills throughout the day. They are also able to cue the individual with ID when they observe depressive behaviors, thus encouraging the individual to label thoughts and beliefs by himself or herself. External informants are a natural link between the acquisition of skills in therapy sessions and their application to the natural environment.

To enhance CBT, external informants can be brought in at the beginning and end of each therapy session to review progress and homework. Alternatively, they can be engaged in separate psychoeducation sessions about CBT and depression. Here, they are taught about the nature of the disorder, the components of CBT, and how to foster a more positive environment by using positive behavior management, praise, and reducing conflict. Key is flexibility, and making sure the involvement of the external informant maximally benefits the individual with ID. As part of the collaborative approach used in CBT, it is essential that the individual with ID dictates how involved the external informants are in his or her therapy.

It should be noted that although the use of external informants in CBT is theoretically enticing and supported by clinical practice, treatment outcome research has not been conducted for individuals with ID and mood disorders, nor has it been found to be efficacious for typically developing adolescents with depression (Birmaher *et al.*, 2000; Lewinsohn *et al.*, 1990).

Empirical Support for Modified CBT

To meet the criteria for an efficacious intervention, the selected treatment must be more effective than no treatment, a placebo, or an alternate treatment across multiple trials conducted by different investigative teams (Chambless & Hollon, 1998). A "possibly efficacious" intervention would meet the same criteria but has not been replicated or been replicated by independent investigative teams. There exist very few empirical studies examining the effectiveness of CBT among individuals with IDs (Beail, 2003; Dagnan, 2007; Willner, 2005), and even fewer empirical studies using control groups or treatment follow-ups. As such, the efficacy of the modifications described earlier may have support from clinical experiences but lack empirical support.

Nonetheless, the existing preliminary reports are encouraging. Case reports using CBT or its components with individuals with ID and depression have favorable outcomes (Dagnan & Chadwick, 1997; Lindsay, 1999; Lindsay & Olley, 1998; Lindsay *et al.*, 1993; Matson *et al.*, 1981). There is some evidence supporting the behavioral components of CBT with mood disorders (Carr *et al.*, 2003; Lindauer *et al.*, 1999). And there is empirical support for the use of parental involvement in CBT for anxiety in children with autism spectrum disorders (reviewed in Reaven & Hepburn, 2006).

The most encouraging support for the efficacy of CBT for mood disorders comes from a group in Australia (McCabe *et al.*, 2006). This group has examined the effectiveness of a group format of CBT for reducing depressive symptoms in adults with mild/moderate IDs. They targeted adults with sufficient language skills to participate in the intervention and with mild to severe depressive symptoms as reported on the BDI. The format of intervention was small groups of three to five individuals, for 2-hour sessions, over five weeks. Their group intervention contained the core components of CBT in that it identified negative cognitions, taught self-monitoring and adaptive behaviors, and reshaped cognitive distortions. Furthermore, the intervention used modeling, role play, and structured feedback to help apply CBT to adults with IDs. In addition, by adopting a group format, the intervention allowed for the practicing of skills with peers within a supportive social environment. This group intervention resulted in a significant improvement in depressive symptoms as compared with a wait-listed control group and the treatment effects were maintained three months posttreatment. The study of this application of CBT to individuals with depressive symptoms is not without its limitations. The study did not examine individuals suffering from clinical depression, individuals with limited language skills, nor did it examine relapse over longer periods of time. Nonetheless, this study is the most promising research to date examining CBT for individuals with IDs and depressive symptomatology.

Case Example

Jonathan is a 30-year-old white male of European decent. He has mild ID due to unknown etiology. Jonathan has lived in an apartment by himself for the past four years. Staff from Jon's disability service provider check in on Jonathan several times a week and take him to get groceries and run other errands. Jonathan does not have his driver's license and relies on transportation services through his disability service provider. Jonathan's parents live in the same city and spend time with Jonathan every Sunday. Jonathan has worked part-time as a dishwasher at a fast-food restaurant for the past six years.

Jonathan has a history of recurrent major depressive disorder. His most recent episode began four weeks ago, following a disagreement with his boss at work. Since this time, Jonathan feels sad most of the day, sleeps most of the day, goes for days without showering, has been late to work on several occasions, and avoids leaving his apartment. Jonathan was referred for therapy by his disability service case manager, Noah.

Sessions 1 and 2

Goals

- Establish rapport.
- Define presenting problem.
- Understand client's broader environment and social context.
- Identify ways of measuring change.

Prior to the first session, the therapist contacted Jonathan to ask if he would like to include a family member or staff person in some of the therapy sessions. Jonathan indicated that he would like to include his disability service case manager, Noah. Jonathan and Noah attended the first two sessions together. Jonathan initially stated that he was "depressed" and wanted therapy to "feel better." The therapist used a series of probing questions to guide Jonathan in identifying behaviors, thoughts, and emotions related to being "depressed" (e.g., "what do you do when you feel depressed?") and wanting to "feeling better" (e.g., "what would you be doing today if you felt better?"). Jonathan indicated that he felt "dark and stormy" when he is depressed and like "sunshine" when he feels good. These labels were then used by the therapist. Noah contributed to this discussion by commenting on changes in Jonathan's behaviors that he has noticed. Limited transportation and opportunity to socialize with others and lack of a job coach at work were identified as important environmental and social context variables contributing to Jonathan's depressed mood. The therapist created a picture of a ruler that went from "dark and stormy" to "sunshine," and asked Jonathan to rate his mood. Jonathan and Noah were then given several copies of the ruler and Jonathan was instructed to rate his mood once a day. By the end of session 2, a list of specific problem behaviors and the following list of positive desirable behaviors were identified: shower every day, spend time with friends, exercise, be on time to work, and do artwork. These desirable behaviors were written on a large poster board and taped to Jonathan's refrigerator. With the help of Noah, Jonathan was instructed to record if and how much time he spent engaged in each of these behaviors every day. For the remaining of the sessions, this homework was reviewed at the beginning of the session.

Sessions 3–5

Goals

- Learn to identify emotions and cognitions.
- Understand the connection between emotions and cognitions.
- Address social and environmental problems.

Several strategies were used to teach Jonathan about emotions and cognitions. Jonathan was told stories and guided in generating a list of what each character may be thinking and feeling. The therapist provided descriptions of emotions and Jonathan was asked to describe a time when he felt each emotion. Role playing was used to act out scenarios and Jonathan was guided in identifying his feelings and thoughts in each scenario. The therapist guided Jonathan in discussing how feelings and thoughts are connected. In all of these activities, the therapist highlighted how different interpretations of the same event are linked to different feelings. As a homework assignment during these weeks, Noah was asked to spontaneously ask Jonathan to identify his emotions and cognitions twice a day. This information was recorded. During these sessions, strategies for increasing access to transportation and opportunities for Jonathan to socialize with others were also identified. In addition, strategies for hiring a job coach to teach Jonathan ways to improve on his work and to help educate Jonathan's boss about Jonathan's disability were identified and implemented.

Session 6

Goal

• Learn muscle relaxation strategy.

Jonathan reported having difficulty dealing with feelings of frustration and anxiety. In order to help Jonathan learn how to manage these feelings, the therapist taught him a muscle relaxation strategy. This session was videotaped so that Jonathan could watch it at home and practice the strategy.

Sessions 7–10

Goal

• Identify and test dysfunctional beliefs.

Many of Jonathan's negative emotions and thoughts were focused on his interactions at work with coworkers and his new boss. Jonathan believed that his coworkers made fun of him and did not like him. He was also upset because he believed that his boss was mad at him because he did not work as fast as the other dishwashers. Jonathan also believed that he did not have any friends and would never have a girlfriend. The therapist guided Jonathan in reviewing the accuracy of his beliefs and thoughts. Jonathan's faulty logic was highlighted. Jonathan had a tendency to make issues "black and white" (i.e., he was either a good or a bad worker), to personalize situations (e.g., he was the cause of his boss's bad mood), and to jump to conclusions (his neighbor did not say hi to him because she didn't like him). Visual aids and role playing were used to challenging Jonathan to evaluate his beliefs. Noah attended two of these therapy sessions and continued to help Jonathan identify and evaluate his interpretations of events outside of therapy.

Sessions 11 and 12

Goal

- Learn problem-solving skills.

The therapist walked Jonathan through the steps of solving a problem: generate as many possible solutions as possible, choose the best solution, determine the steps to carry out that solution, and try the solution. A poster board with these steps and illustrative pictures was created, which Jonathan then took home. Jonathan was prompted to identify problems in his own life and the therapist guided him through the problem-solving steps. Noah was asked to attend one of these sessions so that he could also learn the problem-solving steps to use with Jonathan outside of therapy.

Session 13

Goals

- Review concepts and strategies learned.
- Identify obstacles to employing strategies once therapy is over.
- Create plan for booster sessions or additional support if needed.

The therapist reviewed the concepts learned in the therapy with Jonathan and Noah. The therapist also created a visual graph to show Jonathan how his mood had increasingly moved toward "sunshine" on the ruler scales and how Jonathan had increased the frequency and time spent engaging in his list of positive, desirable behaviors. A plan for a booster session in one month was created.

Conclusions

Individuals with IDs present with many of the same depressive behaviors as typical developing individuals, including dysfunctional cognitive processes. Preliminary research suggests that CBT may be a beneficial treatment for depression in individuals with IDs. In this chapter, we reviewed the core features of CBT and highlighted training procedures and modifications to CBT for use with individuals with IDs. The key to using CBT with individuals with IDs is to be flexible and tailor the intervention to match the cognitive and developmental abilities of the individual with ID. Recommended modifications include involving caregivers or supportive others in therapy, the use of games and activities to teach individuals how to label emotions and thoughts, careful consideration of language and checking in the individual with ID to ensure that words have a common meaning, using multiple learning formats including pictures and role playing and other active learning activities, and flexibility in terms of the length and number of sessions.

The development and maintenance of mood disorders is not solely cognitive, but rather is likely a combination of cognitive, behavioral, biological, social, and environmental factors interacting with each other (Stark *et al.*, 1991). Thus, the presentation of CBT here is not an indication that this method of treatment is superior to other interventions. Rather, CBT should be viewed as a complement to behavioral and pharmacological interventions. There is encouraging evidence that CBT is an appropriate and efficacious treatment for depression in individuals with IDs (e.g., Dagnan & Chadwick, 1997; McCabe *et al.*, 2006). However, additional research is needed to evaluate the effectiveness of CBT and better understand which components and modifications are best suited for individuals with IDs.

References

Beail, N. (2003). What works for people with mental retardation? Critical commentary on cognitive-behavioral and psychodynamic psychotherapy research. *Mental Retardation, 41,* 468–472.

Benson, B.A. & Ivins, J. (1992). Anger, depression and self-concept in adults with mental retardation. *Journal of Intellectual Disability Research, 36,* 169–175.

Birmaher, B., Brent, D.A., Kolko, D., Baugher, M., Bridge, J., Holder, D. *et al.* (2000). Clinical outcomes after short-term psychotherapy for adolescents with major depressive disorder. *Archives of General Psychiatry, 57,* 29–36.

Brent, D.A., Holder, D., Kolko, D., Birmaher, B., Baugher, M., Roth, C. *et al.* (1997). A clinical psychotherapy trial for adolescent depression comparing cognitive, family, and supported treatments. *Archives of General Psychiatry, 54,* 877–885.

Brent, D.A., Kolko, D.J., Birmaher, B., Baugher, M. & Bridge, J. (1999). A clinical trial for adolescent depression: Predictors of additional treatment in the acute and follow-up phases of the trial. *Journal of the American Academy of Child and Adolescent Psychiatry, 38,* 263–270.

Butler, A.C., Chapman, J.E., Forman, E.M. & Beck, A.T. (2006). The empirical status of cognitive-behavioral therapy: A review of meta-analyses. *Clinical Psychology Review, 26,* 17–31.

Carr, E.G., McLaughlin, D.M., Giacobbe-Grieco, T. & Smith, C.E. (2003). Using mood ratings and mood induction in assessment and intervention for severe problem behavior. *American Journal of Mental Retardation, 108,* 32–55.

Chambless, D.L. & Hollon, S.D. (1998). Defining empirically supported therapies. *Journal of Consulting and Clinical Psychology, 66,* 7–18.

Clarke, G.N., Hops, H., Lewinsohn, P.M., Andrews, J.A., Seeley, M.R. & Williams, J. (1992). Cognitive-behavioral group treatment of adolescent depression: Prediction of outcome. *Behavior Therapy, 23,* 341–354.

Compton, S.N., March, J.S., Brent, D., Albano, A.M., Weersing, R. & Curry, J. (2004). Cognitive-behavioral psychotherapy for anxiety and depressive disorders in children and adolescents: An evidence-based medicine review. *Journal of the American Academy of Child and Adolescent Psychiatry, 43,* 930–959.

Dagnan, D. (2007). Psychosocial interventions for people with intellectual disabilities and mental ill-health. *Current Opinion in Psychiatry, 20,* 456–460.

Dagnan, D. & Chadwick, P. (1997). Assessment and intervention. In B. Stenfert Kroese, D. Dagnan & K. Loumidis (Eds.) *Cognitive-behaviour therapy for people with learning disabilities* (pp.110–123). London: Routledge.

Dagnan, D., Chadwick, P. & Proudlove, J. (2000). Toward an assessment of suitability of people with mental retardation for cognitive therapy. *Cognitive Therapy and Research, 24,* 627–636.

Dagnan, D., Jahoda, A.J. & Kilbane, A. (2013). Preparing people with ID for psychological treatment approaches. In J.L. Taylor, W.R. Lindsay, R.P. Hastings & C. Hatton (Eds.) *Psychological therapies for adults with intellectual disabilities.* Chichester, UK: John Wiley & Sons, Ltd.

Esbensen, A.J. & Benson, B.A. (2005). Cognitive variables and depressed mood in adults with intellectual disability. *Journal of Intellectual Disability Research, 49,* 481–489.

Esbensen, A.J. & Benson, B.A. (2006). Diathesis-stress and depressed mood among adults with mental retardation. *American Journal of Mental Retardation, 111,* 100–112.

Esbensen, A.J. & Rojahn, J. (2005). Causes of mood disorders in people with mental retardation. In P. Sturmey (Ed.) *Mood disorders in individuals with mental retardation* (pp.67–88). Kingston, NY: NADD Press.

Fletcher, R., Loschen, E., Stavrakaki, C. & First, M. (Eds.) (2007). *Diagnostic Manual – Intellectual Disability (DM-ID): A textbook of diagnosis of mental disorders in persons with intellectual disability.* Kingston, NY: NADD Press.

Haddock, K. & Jones, R.S.P. (2006). Practitioner consensus in the use of cognitive behaviour therapy for individuals with a learning disability. *Journal of Intellectual Disabilities, 10,* 221–230.

Hartley, S.L. & MacLean, W.E. Jr. (2009). Stressful social interactions experienced by adults with mild intellectual disability. *American Journal on Intellectual and Developmental Disabilities, 114,* 71–84.

Hatton, C. (2002). Psychosocial interventions for adults with intellectual disabilities and mental health problems: A review. *Journal of Mental Health, 11,* 357–373.

Hughes, C.W., Preskorn, S.H., Weller, E., Weller, R., Hassanein, R. & Tucker, S. (1990). The effect of concomitant disorders in childhood depression on predicting treatment response. *Psychopharmacology Bulletin, 26,* 235–238.

Hurley, A.D. (1989). Individual psychotherapy with mentally retarded individuals: A review and call for research. *Research in Developmental Disabilities, 10,* 261–275.

Jayson, D., Wood, A., Kroll, L., Fraser, J. & Harrington, R. (1998). Which depressed patients respond to cognitive-behavioral treatment? *Journal of the American Academy of Child and Adolescent Psychiatry, 37,* 35–39.

Lagges, A.M. & Dunn, D.W. (2003). Depression in children and adolescents. *Neurologic Clinics, 21,* 953–960.

Lewinsohn, P.M., Clarke, G., Hops, H. & Andrews, J. (1990). Cognitive-behavioral treatment for depressed adolescents. *Behavior Therapy, 21,* 385–401.

Lindauer, S.E., DeLeon, I.G. & Fisher, W.W. (1999). Decreasing signs of negative affect and correlated self-injury in an individual with mental retardation and mood disturbances. *Journal of Applied Behavior Analysis, 32,* 103–106.

Lindsay, W., Neilson, C. & Lawrenson, H. (1997). Cognitive-behaviour therapy for anxiety in people with learning disabilities. In B. Stenfert Kroese, D. Dagnan & K. Loumidis (Eds.) *Cognitive-behaviour therapy for people with learning disabilities* (pp.128–144). London: Routledge.

Lindsay, W.R. (1999). Cognitive therapy. *The Psychologist, 12,* 238–241.

Lindsay, W.R., Howells, L. & Pitcaithly, D. (1993). Cognitive therapy for depression with individuals with intellectual disabilities. *The British Journal of Medical Psychology, 66,* 135–141.

Lindsay, W.R. & Lees, M.S. (2003). A comparison of anxiety and depression in sex offenders with intellectual disability and a control group with intellectual disability. *Sexual Abuse: A Journal of Research and Treatment, 15,* 339–345.

Lindsay, W.R. & Olley, S. (1998). Psychological treatment for anxiety and depression for people with learning disabilities. In W. Fraser, D. Sines & M. Kerr (Eds.) *Hallas' the care of people with intellectual disabilities* (pp.235–252). Oxford: Butterworth Heinemann.

Lindsay, W.R., Stenfert Kroese, B. & Drew, P. (2005). Cognitive-behavioral approaches to depression in people with learning disabilities. In P. Sturmey (Ed.) *Mood disorders in individuals with mental retardation* (pp. 241–271). Kingston, NY: NADD Press.

March, J., Silva, S., Petrycki, S., Curry, J., Wells, K., Fairbank, J. *et al.* (2004). Fluoxetine, cognitive-behavioural therapy, and their combination for adolescents with depression: Treatment for Adolescents with Depression Study (TADS) randomized controlled trial. *JAMA: the Journal of the American Medical Association, 292,* 807–820.

Matson, J.L., Dettling, J. & Senatore, V. (1981). Treating depression of a mentally retarded adult. *British Journal of Mental Subnormality, 26,* 86–88.

McCabe, M.P., McGillivray, J.A. & Newton, D.C. (2006). Effectiveness of treatment programmes for depression among adults with mild/moderate intellectual disability. *Journal of Intellectual Disability Research, 50,* 239–247.

Reaven, J. & Hepburn, S. (2006). The parent's role in the treatment of anxiety symptoms in children with high-functioning autism spectrum disorders. *Mental Health Aspects of Developmental Disabilities, 9,* 73–80.

Ryan, N.D. (2005). Treatment of depression in children and adolescents. *Lancet, 366,* 933–940.

Sams, K., Collins, S. & Reynolds, S. (2006). Cognitive therapy abilities in people with learning disabilities. *Journal of Applied Research in Intellectual Disabilities, 19,* 25–33.

Stark, K., Rouse, L. & Livingston, R. (1991). Treatment of depression during childhood and adolescence: Cognitive-behavioral procedures for the individual and family. In P.C. Kendall (Ed.) *Child and adolescent therapy* (pp. 165–206). New York: Guilford.

Westen, D. & Morrison, K. (2001). A multidimensional meta-analysis of treatments for depression, panic, and generalized anxiety disorder: An empirical examination of the status of empirically supported therapies. *Journal of Consulting and Clinical Psychology, 69,* 875–900.

Willner, P. (2005). The effectiveness of psychotherapeutic interventions for people with learning disabilities: A critical overview. *Journal of Intellectual Disability Research, 49,* 73–85.

Chapter 9

Anger Control Problems

John L. Taylor
Raymond W. Novaco

Introduction

Anger is a normal human emotion and is hardwired for survival. It has considerable adaptive value, although there are sociocultural variations in the manner in which it is expressed. Anger can help maintain one's self-esteem and dignity when confronted by provocation, insult or unjust treatment. In the face of danger, anger can help individuals to mobilize psychological resources and prime behaviors to deal with threat. It can communicate negative sentiment to others, potentiate the ability to face up to and redress grievances, and boost perseverance and determination to overcome obstacles to goal attainment. Thus, anger is an emotion with multiple functions (Novaco, 1976).

Recurrent and poorly controlled anger, however, adversely affects emotional and physical health and is disruptive of social relationships that sustain personal well-being. It is commonly observed in a range of mental health and emotional problems, including personality, psychosomatic, and conduct disorders; schizophrenia; and bipolar mood and organic disorders, and in conditions resulting from trauma (Novaco & Taylor, 2006). The central characteristic of anger in the context of mental health disorders is that it is *dysregulated* – that is, its activation, expression, and ongoing experience occur without appropriate controls.

The life experiences of many people with intellectual disabilities, from childhood onward, are conducive to the activation of anger. Moreover, the environmental settings and social circumstances in which many such people live and work are intrinsically constraining, potentially threatening, unrewarding, and limited in satisfaction. Recurrent thwarting of physical, emotional, and interpersonal needs can potentiate anger activation. Cognitive deficits can readily impair effective coping with frustrating or aversive events, and impoverished support systems limit problem-solving options.

Psychological Therapies for Adults with Intellectual Disabilities, First Edition.
Edited by John L. Taylor, William R. Lindsay, Richard P. Hastings, and Chris Hatton.
© 2013 John Wiley & Sons, Ltd. Published 2013 by John Wiley & Sons, Ltd.

Table 9.1   Studies of Prevalence of Aggression among People with Intellectual Disabilities

	N	Location	Prevalence (%)		
			Community	*Institution*	*Forensic*
Tyrer *et al.* (2008)	3065	England	16	—	—
Taylor *et al.* (2004)	782	England	12	—	—
Hill and Bruininks (1984)	2491	USA	16	37	—
Harris (1993)	1362	England	11	38	—
Sigafoos *et al.* (1994)	2412	Australia	10	35	—
Smith *et al.* (1996)	2202	England	—	40	—
Novaco and Taylor (2004)[a]	129	England	—	—	47
MacMillan *et al.* (2004)[a]	124	England	—	—	47

[a]These studies involved detained inpatients with offending histories. The prevalence concerns *physical* assaults postadmission.

While it is neither necessary nor sufficient for aggression to occur, anger has been found to predict physical aggression by psychiatric hospital patients prior to admission, in the hospital, and subsequently in the community following discharge (Novaco & Taylor, 2006). It has also been shown to be strongly associated with and predictive of violence in adults with intellectual disabilities and histories of aggression and offending (Novaco & Taylor, 2004).

In more general terms, large-scale surveys on several continents have found high rates of aggression among people with intellectual disabilities (see Table 9.1), with rates of aggression commonly found to be two to three times higher for those living in institutional settings than for those residing in community-based facilities. Rates of physical aggression are higher again for people with intellectual disabilities detained in secure settings. This is unsurprising as Lakin *et al.* (1983) found that aggression was the primary reason for people with intellectual disabilities to be admitted and readmitted to institutional settings.

Aggression was also the main reason for individuals in this client group to be prescribed antipsychotic and behavioral control drugs (Aman *et al.*, 1987; Robertson *et al.*, 2000), despite there being little evidence for their efficacy (e.g., Brylewski & Duggan, 2004; Deb & Unwin, 2007; Tyrer *et al.*, 2008). There has been some limited research suggesting that atypical antipsychotics – chiefly risperidone – can be effective in reducing aggression among adults with intellectual disabilities (Gagiano *et al.*, 2005; Ruedrich *et al.*, 2008). However, others have reviewed the effectiveness of these new generation compounds and have concluded that there is insufficient evidence for their use as anti-aggression agents in general clinical practice (Singh *et al.*, 2005; Tsiouris, 2010).

Aggression carries high costs for individuals with intellectual disabilities who may be exposed to ineffective treatments with potentially serious side effects. Detained patients are likely to experience prolonged periods of incarceration if they are physically violent. Aggressive behavior by people with intellectual disabilities also carries high costs for their direct carers and supporters (families and paid staff). Kiely and Pankhurst (1998) conducted a survey of aggression experienced by staff working in an intellectual disability service of an NHS Trust in the United Kingdom. They found that there were almost five times more incidents of patient violence than was recorded in the Trust's sister psychiatric service. As a result, carers can experience physical injury and consequent absence from work, and the services supporting them are exposed to increased costs through sick-leave payments, worker compensation, and high staff turnover (Singh *et al.*, 2008; Taylor *et al.*, 2005). Other studies have shown that as a consequence of service-user aggression, carers of people with intellectual disabilities feel annoyed, angry, and fearful (Bromley & Emerson, 1995), and there are high rates of staff turnover and "burnout" (Attwood & Joachim, 1994).

Assessment of Anger

Effective clinical interventions are based on sound formulations of anger problems. Both formulation and evaluation of treatment outcome require robust assessment methods. While anger is a normal human emotion and can be adaptive, intense anger and its expression have historically been semantically linked to being mad, wild, and out of control. Thus, angry clients may be, for these and other reasons, reticent about disclosing the extent of their anger problems during clinical assessment. As clinicians assessing client's anger control problems will inevitably be dependent on self-report to some extent, either through responses to structured measures or clinical interview, they need to be aware of this dynamic that may result in *reactivity bias* – that is, a client's tendency to report his or her anger experiences in anticipation of what his or her responses will mean to the observer.

In addition, assessors should be mindful of the potential for *proximity bias*. People generally describe (and ascribe) anger responses to events that are temporally close. However, chronically angry people have difficulties with self-monitoring and tend to look for immediate causes for their reactions. Clients and clinicians generally do not consider more distal events and setting conditions as having relevance to recent anger outbursts. Previous provoking events that did not result in an angry reaction at the time can leave (physiological and psychological) residues that linger and contribute to and intensify a person's response to more recent events. This phenomenon was referred by Zillmann (1971) as "excitation transfer" in his experimental research. When formulating a client's anger problems and treatment needs, clinicians need to bear in mind that the determinants of anger, anger experiences, and anger reactions are reciprocally influenced. Also, therapists will want to understand how often a client becomes angry, the degree of anger experienced, how long anger arousal lasts, and how it is expressed behaviorally. Thus, a range of assessments including self-reports, informant reports, and behavioral observations are required to formulate the client's anger treatment needs with regard to anger frequency, intensity, duration, and mode of expression.

The reliability of self-reports of emotions by people with intellectual disabilities, including anger, can be affected by factors such as cognitive aptitude, verbal comprehension, communication, and social interaction skills. These problems can lead to difficulties with the reliability of these measures including social desirability effects, response sets, and primacy and recency effects. However, by developing new instruments specifically for them, or by adapting measures developed for nondisabled populations, people with intellectual disabilities can identify their own emotions reliably and consistently (e.g., Lindsay *et al.*, 1994; Wigham *et al.*, 2011).

There has been some research concerning the reliability and validity of assessments of anger obtained from people with intellectual disabilities. Using a self-report, 35-item *Anger Inventory*, Benson and Ivins (1992) found that direct carers (mostly residential care staff) rated people with intellectual disabilities as angrier than the individuals did themselves. However, Rose and West (1999) used that Anger Inventory and found a significant association between self-reported anger scores and staff records of incidents of challenging behavior for five men with intellectual disabilities living in community settings. Walker and Cheseldine (1997) used a modified version of the *Provocation Inventory* (Novaco, 1988) to evaluate outcomes for clients with intellectual disabilities involved in a community anger management and assertiveness training group. Clients' verbal responses to provoking scenarios were rated according to the behavioral reactions they reported, for example, verbal aggression, physical aggression, and damage to property. Inter-rater reliability agreement reached 82 percent for the coding of responses on the Provocation Inventory into the seven categories used.

Novaco and Taylor (2004) evaluated the reliability and validity of self-report anger assessment measures in a study involving 129 detained patients with intellectual disabilities and forensic histories. Modified versions of the *State-Trait Anger Expression Inventory* (Spielberger, 1996), *Novaco Anger Scale*, and *Provocation Inventory* (Novaco, 2003) were used. High degrees of internal reliability, intermeasure consistency, and concurrent validity with staff ratings were found. Significant predictive validity of the self-report anger measures for physically assaultive behavior postadmission was also established. The Part B anger index of the staff-rated *Ward Anger Rating Scale* (Novaco, 1994) was also shown to have high internal consistency and to correlate significantly with patient-rated anger measures and postadmission hospital assaults.

Taylor *et al.* (2004) developed the *Imaginal Provocation Test* as an "idiographic" anger assessment procedure for people with intellectual disabilities that is easy to administer, has systematic measurement indices, taps key elements of the experience and expression of anger (emotional reaction, behavioral reactions, and anger control), and is sensitive to change associated with anger treatment. The imaginal provocation procedure has distinct value because it is easily adapted for use in a variety of settings and has minimal logistical requirements, and the content of the imaginal scenes can be tailored to a particular client group's or individual client's circumstances. The four parallel forms of the provocation test were found to successfully induce imagined anger in patients and to have good internal reliability and concurrent validity. Patients' scores on the test's behavioral reaction and anger control indices improved significantly following anger treatment.

Treatment of Anger Control Problems

Given its strong association with aggression and predictive relationship with violence, anger is a legitimate therapeutic target for people with intellectual disabilities who are aggressive and potentially violent. However, precisely because anger is a common precursor of aggression and violence, its treatment can be disconcerting for mental health practitioners. Engaging seriously angry people in therapy is difficult as they tend to be treatment avoidant. Attempts to achieve clinical change can be undermined by the adaptive functions of anger and by its embeddedness in the client's sense of self- and personal worth. Angry thinking and behavior that is strongly attached to a client's personal identity is not easily or readily relinquished. Deficits in cognitive functioning can add to the challenges of anger regulation from the standpoint of both clients and those who seek to help them therapeutically.

In reviewing the literature on the treatment of anger and aggression in people with intellectual disabilities, Taylor and Novaco (2005) suggested there were three distinct, if overlapping, areas of research. These were concerned with (a) psychopharmacological treatments, (b) behavioral treatments, and (c) cognitive behavioral therapies (CBTs). As indicated earlier, despite the apparently ubiquitous use of medications to reduce aggression in people with intellectual disabilities, there is no conclusive evidence to support their use as first-line treatments. Given their lack of specificity and variable effects, including significant dampening of adaptive behavior, routine use of these compounds to treat aggression is not thought to be justified (Matson *et al.*, 2000; Tsiouris, 2010).

The most significant literature concerning treatment of aggression in people with intellectual disabilities involves interventions based on applied behavioral analysis principles. Reviews by Lennox *et al.* (1988), Scotti *et al.* (1991), Whitaker (1993), and Carr *et al.* (2000) include studies of the effectiveness of behavioral interventions for aggression problems. The Lennox *et al.* and Scotti *et al.* reviews indicate that less intrusive and more constructive approaches can be more effective than more intrusive and restrictive techniques. The studies included in Whitaker's (1993) review suggest that contingency management techniques, which make up the bulk of the published studies available, are effective, mainly with more disabled client groups. Whitaker concluded that these approaches have been shown to be effective for clients with relatively high-frequency aggression in controlled environments with high staff ratios. Such conditions contrast with those in community and other services for people with intellectual disabilities who are relatively high functioning and display low frequency, yet serious aggression and violence. A further potential limitation of behavioral approaches to the treatment of aggression is that they tend not to be presented as "self-actualizing" in nature. That is, they do not actively promote self-regulation in emotional and behavior control.

Cognitive–behavioral approaches

Promoting internalized control over behavior to facilitate maintenance over time and generalization across settings is intrinsic to CBT-based interventions. For this and for other reasons, there has been increasing interest in CBT approaches for anger problems experienced by people with intellectual disabilities. Whitaker (2001), Taylor (2002), Taylor and Novaco (2005), and Willner (2007) have reviewed studies of cognitively based anger treatments specifically for people with intellectual disabilities. Table 9.2 sets out an up-to-date list of 34 studies of CBT interventions for anger problems in people with intellectual disabilities published post-1985.

Table 9.2 Studies (Post-1985) Involving Cognitive–Behavioral Interventions for Anger in People with Intellectual Disabilities (Ordered Chronologically then Alphabetically by Author)

Study	Design	Participants	Setting (I/C)	Treatment format/components	Duration
Benson et al. (1986)	Group study RCT	37 men 17 women Mild–moderate ID	C	Group therapy format: Self-instruction versus relaxation versus problem solving versus combined condition	12-week, 90-minute sessions (total = 18 hours)
Murphy and Clare (1991)	Case study	1 male Mild ID	I	Multiple, staged individual and group therapy interventions: Self-monitoring, social skills training, coping skills training, relaxation training, token economy	Unclear/varied over a 49-week period
Black and Novaco (1993)	Case study	1 male Mild ID	I	Individual therapy format: Self-monitoring, psychoeducation, arousal reduction, coping skills training	28 sessions, 40 minutes each (total = 18.7 hours)
Cullen (1993)	Case series	12 Mild–moderate ID	C = 2 I = 10	Group therapy format: Self-monitoring, education, relaxation training, behavioral skills training	Up to 100 hours – twice a week sessions over 1 year
Rose (1996)	Case series	3 men 2 women Moderate–severe ID	C	Group therapy format: Relaxation training, self-monitoring, identification of triggers, emotional recognition, coping skills training, self-instruction, thought stopping	16 sessions of 90 minutes over 19 weeks (total = 24 hours)
Moore et al. (1997)	Group study A-B	2 men 4 women Mild–moderate ID	C	Group therapy format: Emotional recognition, self-monitoring, relaxation training, role play, problem-solving skills	8-week, 90-minute sessions (total = 12 hours)
Walker and Cheseldine (1997)	Case series	4 men ID level unclear	C	Group therapy format: Psychoeducation, social skills training, relaxation training, self-instruction	8-week, 90-minute sessions (total = 12 hours)

Study	Study type	Participants		Format and content	Duration
Lawrenson and Lindsay (1998)	Case study	1 male Mild ID	C	Group therapy format: Psychoeducation, relaxation training, problem-solving skills, distraction techniques, self-instruction, role play	26-week, 50-minute sessions (total = 21.7 hours)
Lindsay et al. (1998)	Case series	3 men 2 mild ID 1 severe ID	C = 1 I = 2	Individual therapy format – differed for each subject: Self-monitoring, relaxation training, emotional recognition, psychoeducation, role play	Varied between 50 daily sessions over 10 weeks – weekly sessions for 6 months
Rossiter et al. (1998)	Case series	4 men 2 women Moderate–severe ID	C = 2 I = 4	Group therapy format: Psychoeducation, self-monitoring, relaxation training, self-instruction, role play	8-week, 90-minute sessions (total = 12 hours)
King et al. (1999)	Group study A-B-A	7 men 4 women Mild ID	C	Group therapy format: Education, relaxation training, self-instruction, problem-solving skills	15-week, 90-minute sessions (total = 22.5 hours)
Rose and West (1999)[b]	Case series	5 men Mild–moderate ID	C	Group therapy format: Relaxation training, self-monitoring, identification of triggers, emotional recognition, coping skills training, self-instruction, thought stopping (in four cases augmented by individual, staff, or behavioral interventions)	16-weekly, 2-hour sessions (total = 32 hours)
Howells et al. (2000)	Case series	3 men 2 women Mild ID	C	Group therapy format: Emotional recognition, self-monitoring, identification of physical and cognitive triggers, coping skills training, problem-solving skills, role play with video feedback	12-week, 2-hour sessions (total = 24 hours over 18 weeks due to break)

(Continued)

Table 9.2 (*Continued*)

Study	Design	Participants	Setting (I/C)	Treatment format/components	Duration
Rose et al. (2000)[b]	Group study CT	23 men 2 women Mild–moderate ID	C	Group therapy format: Relaxation training, self-monitoring, identification of triggers, emotional recognition, coping skills training, self-instruction, thought stopping, role play with video feedback	16-week, 2-hour sessions (total = 32 hours)
Allan et al. (2001)	Case series	5 women Mild–borderline ID	C	Group therapy format: Psychoeducation, arousal reduction through relaxation exercises, identification of angry thoughts, role played problem solving	Approximately forty 1-hour sessions over 9 months (total = 40 hours)
Taylor et al. (2002)[a]	Group study CT	20 men Mild–borderline ID	I	Individual therapy format: Psychoeducation, self-monitoring, cognitive restructuring, relaxation training, self-instruction, stress inoculation, role play problem solving	18 twice weekly, 60-minute sessions (total = 18 hours)
Willner et al. (2002)	Group study CT	9 men 5 women Mild ID	C	Group therapy format: Relaxation training, identification of triggers, behavioral and cognitive coping strategies, assertiveness training, "brainstorming," homework tasks, use of anger diaries	9-week, 2-hour sessions (total = 18 hours)
Lindsay et al. (2003)	Case series	6 men Mild ID	C	Group therapy format: Psychoeducation, arousal reduction through relaxation exercises and imagery, identification of angry thoughts, role played problem solving	Approximately forty 1-hour sessions over 9 months (total = 40 hours)

Study	Design	Sample		Intervention	Dosage
Singh et al. (2003)	Case study	1 man Mild ID	I	Individual therapy format: Mindfulness-based approach; training to use a simple meditation procedure termed *Soles of the Feet*; recognition of triggers of aggression; role played practice of meditation technique to adopt natural posture, control breathing, and calm mind, and to withdraw from provocation	2 daily, 30-minute sessions over 5 days (total = 5 hours)
Burns et al. (2003)	Case series	3 men Mild–borderline ID	I	Group therapy format: Cognitive–behavioral approach, awareness of the nature and functions of anger, exploration of beliefs about anger, control of thoughts, physiological aspects of anger, understanding situational components of anger and lifestyle choices, development of risk prevention plans	12-week, 2-hour, 30-minute sessions – each session with a break (total = 30 hours)
Lindsay et al. (2004)	Group study CT	33 men 14 women Mild ID	C	Group therapy format: Psychoeducation, arousal reduction through relaxation exercises, identification of angry thoughts, stress inoculation, role played problem solving	Approximately forty 1-hour sessions over 9 months (total = 40 hours)
Taylor et al. (2004)[a]	Group study CT	17 men Mild–borderline ID	I	Individual therapy format: Psychoeducation, self-monitoring, cognitive restructuring, relaxation training, self-instruction, stress inoculation, role play problem solving	18 twice weekly, 60-minute sessions (total = 18 hours)

(*Continued*)

Table 9.2 (*Continued*)

Study	Design	Participants	Setting (I/C)	Treatment format/components	Duration
Hagiliassis *et al.* (2005)	Group study CT	29 5 borderline ID 1 mild ID 4 moderate ID 4 severe ID	C	Group therapy format: Psychoeducation, relaxation training, self-instruction, cognitive restructuring, problem solving, assertiveness skills training, role play	Twelve 2-hour sessions (total = 24 hours)
Rose *et al.* (2005)[b]	Group study CT	86	C	Group therapy format: Relaxation training, self-monitoring, identification of triggers, emotional recognition, coping skills training, self-instruction, thought stopping, role play with video feedback	16 week, 2-hour sessions (total = 32 hours)
Taylor *et al.* (2005)[a]	Group study CT	40 men Mild–borderline ID	I	Individual therapy format: Psychoeducation, self-monitoring, cognitive restructuring, relaxation training, self-instruction, stress inoculation, role play problem solving	18 twice weekly, 60-minute sessions (total = 18 hours)
Willner *et al.* (2005)	Group study CT	17	C	Group therapy format: Relaxation training, identification of triggers, behavioral and cognitive coping strategies, assertiveness training, "brainstorming," homework tasks, use of anger diaries	Twelve 2-hour sessions (total = 24 hours)
Novaco and Taylor (2006)	Case study	1 man Borderline ID	I	Individual therapy format: Psychoeducation, self-monitoring, cognitive restructuring, relaxation training, self-instruction, stress inoculation, role play problem solving	18 twice weekly, 60-minute sessions (total = 18 hours)

Study	Design	Participants	Rating	Intervention	Sessions
Singh et al. (2007)	Case series – multiple-baseline design	3 men Moderate ID	C	Individual therapy format: Modified mindfulness-based approach termed *Soles of the Feet*; recognition of triggers of aggression; role played practice of meditation technique involving posture, controlled breathing, clearing mind, and withdrawal from provocation	Unclear
Willner and Tomlinson (2007)	Group study A-B-A	6 men 5 women Mild–moderate ID	C	Group therapy format: Relaxation training, identification of triggers, behavioral and cognitive coping strategies, assertiveness training, "brainstorming," homework tasks, use of anger diaries	Twelve 2-hour sessions (total = 24 hours)
Singh et al. (2008)	Case series – multiple-baseline design	6 men Mild ID	I	Individual therapy format: Modified mindfulness-based approach termed *Soles of the Feet*; recognition of triggers of aggression; role played practice of meditation technique involving posture, controlled breathing, clearing mind, and withdrawal from provocation	Unclear
Rose et al. (2008)[c]	Group study CT	29 men 12 women Level of ID unclear	C	Individual therapy format: Psychoeducation, self-monitoring, relaxation training, development of coping and preventative strategies using a problem-solving framework	Between fourteen and eighteen 30- to 60-minute sessions (total = ~7–18 hours)

(*Continued*)

Table 9.2 (*Continued*)

Study	Design	Participants	Setting (I/C)	Treatment format/components	Duration
Taylor et al. (2009)	Group study A-B-A	67 men 16 women Mild–borderline ID	I	Individual therapy format: Psychoeducation, self-monitoring, cognitive restructuring, relaxation training, self-instruction, stress inoculation, role play problem solving	18 twice weekly, 60-minute sessions (total = 18 hours)
Rose et al. (2009)[c]	Group study CT	43 men 21 women	C	Group *and* individual therapy formats: See Rose et al. (2000) for an outline description of the content of the group therapy. See Rose et al. (2008) for an outline description of the content of the individual intervention	Group: 16-week, 2-hour sessions (total = 32 hours) Individual: Between fourteen and eighteen 30- to 60-minute sessions
Taylor (2009)	Group Study A-B-A	44 men 6 women	I	Individual therapy format: Psychoeducation, self-monitoring, cognitive restructuring, relaxation training, self-instruction, stress inoculation, role play problem solving	18 twice weekly, 60-minute sessions (total = 18 hours)
Chilvers et al. (2011)	Group study A-B	15 women 11 mild ID 4 moderate ID	I	Group therapy format: Each session involved an introduction phase, a participation exercise, an observation exercise, a description exercise, and a reflection period	Twice weekly, 30-minute sessions over a 5-month period (total = ~20 hours)

[a]The Taylor et al. (2005) study includes some participants from the 2002 and 2004 studies.
[b]The Rose et al. (2005) study includes some participants from the Rose and West (1999) and Rose et al. (2000) studies.
[c]The Rose et al. (2009) study includes some participants from the 2008 study.
RCT, randomized controlled trial; CT, controlled trial (without randomization); A-B, pre-post intervention evaluation (without randomization or comparison group); A-B-A, pre-post follow-up intervention evaluation (without randomization or comparison group); I, institutional setting; C, community setting.

There have been numerous case studies and case series reports of group-based anger management treatments using cognitive behavioral approaches for people with mild to severe levels of intellectual disability. These have had promising outcomes in spite of substantial flaws and weaknesses in study methods and designs, including lack of adequate baseline measures, comparison groups, and robust outcome measures (e.g., Howells *et al.*, 2000; Rossiter *et al.*, 1998; Walker & Cheseldine, 1997). In addition, group studies using cognitive–behavioral approaches have resulted in significant pre-post treatment reductions in anger in clients with mild–moderate intellectual disabilities living in the community (King *et al.*, 1999; Moore *et al.*, 1997). There has been a small number of pre-post treatment group studies of cognitive behavioral treatment incorporating follow-up phases that have found improvements in anger following cognitive–behavioral interventions that were maintained at three to six months' follow-up in community settings (King *et al.*, 1999; Willner & Tomlinson, 2007) and 12 months' follow-up in an inpatient setting (Taylor *et al.*, 2009).

Somewhat unusually for the intellectual disability treatment outcome literature, there have been a significant number of studies (12) concerning psychological interventions for anger problems that have incorporated control conditions. In the earliest study of this kind, Benson *et al.* found significant posttreatment changes across four treatment conditions (self-instruction, relaxation training, problem solving, and a combined condition), but there were no significant differences between conditions following treatment. A number of studies have compared group-based CBT anger management interventions for community clients with wait-list control groups (Hagiliassis *et al.*, 2005; Lindsay *et al.*, 2004; Rose *et al.*, 2000, 2005, 2009; Willner *et al.*, 2002, 2005). These studies have utilized mainly psychoeducational approaches that focus on behavioral skills training and have yielded significant improvements on anger measures over wait-list control groups that were maintained between 3 and 12 months' follow-up.

Rose *et al.* (2008) found that individual delivery of an anger management intervention with community service clients resulted in significant gains on an anger measure compared with wait-list control participants that were maintained at three to six months' follow-up. Taylor *et al.* (2002, 2004, 2005) developed an intensive individual anger treatment for use with patients in forensic settings with significant histories of aggression and violence. These controlled studies, which incorporated arousal reduction, cognitive restructuring, and behavioral skills training elements within a stress inoculation paradigm, found that treatment group participants achieved significant improvements on a number of anger indices compared with wait-list control patients. These gains were maintained at up to four months' follow-up. Rose *et al.* (2009) found no pre-post treatment differences between outcomes for community clients who received group-based and individually delivered versions of their anger management intervention.

It is possible to conclude from this body of research that group and individual cognitive–behavioral anger treatment for people with mild, moderate, and borderline intellectual disabilities living in community and inpatient settings can result in significant improvements in self- and informant-rated anger. Furthermore, gains on these outcome measures are maintained at up to 12 months' follow-up. At this stage, we know less about the transfer of these treatment gains across settings. A notable exception is a study by Willner and Tomlinson (2007), which found, that following a group-based CBT intervention community, clients showed significant improvements in a number of observer-rated anger-coping skills (e.g., relaxation, walking away, distraction, help seeking, thinking differently) that carried over from the day service context to clients' residential home settings.

Another key issue in considering the effectiveness of anger treatment interventions is the impact they have on aggressive and violent behavior. The majority of psychological treatment outcome studies conducted in the intellectual disability field to date have focused on reductions in self- and informant-rated measures of anger. However, a smaller number of studies have also demonstrated a relationship between these improvements and reductions in the levels of observed aggression and violence – in community treatment settings (Allan *et al.*, 2001; Lindsay *et al.*, 2003, 2004; Moore *et al.*, 1997; Rose, 1996; Taylor, 2008) and inpatient settings with offender patients (Chilvers *et al.*, 2011; Taylor, 2009).

A recent development in the anger treatment literature is the work of Nirbay Singh and his colleagues (see Chapter 16 in this book). Using a mindfulness-based procedure (*Meditation of the Soles of the Feet*) within a cognitive–behavioral framework, Singh *et al.* (2003, 2007, 2008) have demonstrated the effectiveness of this individually delivered intervention in reducing aggressive behavior in a careful case study and two multiple-baseline case series studies. Singh *et al.* (2003, 2007) reported significant reductions in physical aggression following intervention with community clients that were maintained at 24 months' follow-up for three case series participants (Singh *et al.*, 2007). In a multiple-baseline study involving six male forensic inpatients with mild intellectual disabilities, significant postintervention reductions were reported in verbal and physical aggression, and use of medication and restraint, along with significant reductions in associated staff injuries, staff sick-leave days, and financial costs (Singh *et al.*, 2008).

A Model CBT Anger Treatment for People with Intellectual Disabilities

In this section, a cognitive behavioral treatment protocol is described that involves the delivery of the intervention to individual patients over 18 sessions. The primary clinical focus of the sessions making up the protocol is described in Table 9.3. Detailed session-by-session guidance on the delivery of the protocol is provided by Taylor and Novaco (2005). Many published studies have utilized group-based interventions that have some potential advantages. However, practitioners in routine service settings are often referred individuals with anger and aggression problems, and it may not be possible for ethical or practical reasons to wait for other referrals to be received so that a group can be formed. As indicated above, preliminary research findings suggest that group and individual anger treatment can achieve similar outcomes (Rose *et al.*, 2009).

It is recommended that whenever possible, treatment is delivered at the rate of two sessions each week, with a minimum of one session per week. More intensive treatment schedule can reduce clients' resistance to change by maintaining

Table 9.3 Primary Focus of Preparatory and Treatment Phase Sessions of Anger Treatment

Preparatory phase – session focus		*Treatment phase – session focus*	
Session 1	Explaining the purpose of anger treatment	Session 7	Introduction to the treatment phase sessions
Session 2	Feeling angry is OK – anger as a normal emotion	Session 8	Building an anger hierarchy
Session 3	Understanding our own and other peoples' feelings	Session 9	Introduction to stress inoculation
Session 4	How to control the physical feelings of anger – physiological arousal	Session 10	Beginning cognitive restructuring
Session 5	Reasons for changing the way we cope with angry feelings	Session 11	Developing cognitive restructuring
Session 6	Review of the preparatory phase and preview of treatment phase	Session 12	Perspective taking and role playing
		Session 13	Using self-instructions effectively
		Session 14	Problem solving through effective communication
		Session 15	Development of problem solving through effective communication
		Session 16	Dealing with rumination and escalation
		Session 17	Integration of skills and dealing with repeated provocation
		Session 18	Review and evaluation of anger treatment phase

Note: All sessions are guided by a detailed manual, delivered by qualified therapists to individual patients. Each session is of approximately one-hour duration. Feedback is provided routinely to direct care staff at the end of each session concerning the patient's presentation and progress within the session, and any homework that is to be completed between sessions.

momentum and preventing therapy drift. Also, a higher therapeutic dosage can offset some of the cognitive limitations of this client group, which can result in problems with assimilation and recall of information from session to session.

Although treatment sessions routinely involve the therapist and client, a carer or supporter is involved whenever possible at the end of each session to discuss the client's progress and any "homework" to be completed between sessions. For example, from the second session onward, clients are encouraged to complete daily anger logs (diaries) to record the nature, frequency, and intensity of any angry incidents. Where possible, anger logs are completed with the assistance of a carer in order to promote a collaborative approach to treatment through open discussion, shared problem solving, and mutual reflection concerning anger-provoking incidents.

Case study: Richie

Richie[1] is a 28-year-old man with mild–borderline intellectual disabilities who lives in a supported residential placement with two other male clients with similar levels of disability and case histories. Richie has a long history of impulsive and aggressive behavior. He had been arrested by the police on two occasions following alleged assaults on others (family members and carers); however, no further action was taken on both occasions. Previous placements had broken down due to Richie's aggressive and occasionally violent behavior. Staff supporting Richie reported a recent increase in the frequency of verbally aggressive behavior toward his housemates and support team, and the intensity of some of these outbursts had led to concerns about the increased risk for violent behavior. This situation was putting Richie's current placement at risk. He was referred to the community learning disability service for assessment and intervention concerning his anger control problems. Richie's case will be used to illustrate two important components of cognitive–behavioral anger treatment: engagement and motivation, and cognitive reappraisal.

Engagement and motivation

Like many offenders with intellectual disabilities, Richie has a personal history that has created barriers to his engagement in trusting therapeutic relationships. Over the years, he has experienced physical and emotional abuse, deprivation, and repeated failures in support service setting. Thus, perceived rejection by important others has been a frequent experience for him. For these and other reasons, Richie was offered and completed a six-session *preparatory phase* of treatment aimed at desensitizing him to any fears that he had about embarking on intensive psychological therapy and engaging him in the therapy process. The goals of this preparatory phase are (a) to give the patient information on the nature and purpose of anger treatment; (b) to emphasize the collaborative nature of the treatment that is aimed primarily at helping the patient achieve better self-control; (c) to develop some basic skills needed for successful treatment including self-disclosure, emotional awareness, self-monitoring and recording, and basic relaxation techniques; (d) to foster trust and confidence in the therapist and the therapeutic process; and (e) to encourage motivation to change current unhelpful anger-coping responses by identifying the costs of this behavior.

Encouraging Richie's motivation to change was important because of the positive functions of his anger and the rewarding aspects of his aggressive behavior. In session 5 of the preparatory phase of anger treatment, the therapist explored with Richie the costs and benefits of his anger and aggression, both in the short and longer term. This was to help him understand that the benefits of developing self-control over anger and aggression can outweigh those gained by continuing to be angry and aggressive. A "decision matrix" was used to facilitate this exercise. Richie was to think about immediate benefits when he becomes angry and aggressive. He explained that

---

[1] Richie is a pseudonym. All personal and descriptive details have been altered to ensure client confidentiality.

It gets the stress and anger out of my system and I feel more relaxed, chilled. After I've blown my top I feel better for a while. People keep out of my way – they don't bother me about stuff.

Despite the immediate benefits of becoming aggressive when he is angry, Richie could not readily identify any longer-term advantages of responding in this way. He was, however, able to explain a number of short- and long-term disadvantages of behaving in this way. The short-term costs identified by Richie included getting into trouble with his support staff, key worker, and family; being restrained; getting hurt; and others getting hurt. When thinking about the longer-term problems of being angry and aggressive, Richie said,

Everybody gets upset with me and the whole thing in the end. I hurt my support staffs' feelings and my relationship with them gets worse. Everyone avoids me and doesn't want to know me. I can end up losing my house with nowhere to go.

At the end of this exercise, Richie felt more motivated to go onto the next stage of treatment so that he could learn how to manage his angry feelings in a calmer and more constructive way. On the successful completion of the preparatory phase, Richie chose to go on to the 12-session *treatment phase*, the core components of which are arousal reduction, cognitive restructuring, and behavioral skills training. These elements map onto the key domains of the model of anger proposed by Novaco (1994).

Cognitive reappraisal

A distinctive characteristic of the anger treatment described here is the modification of perceptual schemas and entrenched beliefs that can maintain anger problems. A basic premise of many cognitive behavioral therapeutic approaches is that psychological distress is associated with distortions in processing information about oneself and environmental demands. This assumptive framework has been articulated with regard to anger (Novaco & Welsh, 1989). Intrinsic to problems of anger and aggression are attentional biases and cognitive processing distortions associated with threat perception, as well as memory biases for distressing experiences. This treatment approach aims to shift attentional focus, modify appraisals of events, and question belief systems and self-defeating schemas.

In session 10, cognitive restructuring (or "thinking differently" about things) was introduced to Richie. The therapist and Richie selected a salient incident from his anger logs in which he had described his thoughts at the time of an anger incident. Together, they explored what he selectively perceived in the situation that led to him feel angry ("perceived intentionality"). Specific situations recorded in anger logs provide material for cognitive restructuring exercises that encourage patients to think differently about anger situations, to work through what actually happened from the patient's perspective, and then to explore possible alternative explanations and perspectives.

In session 11, Richie was encouraged to think about anger situations in terms of attentional focus, expectations, and appraisals that can cue angry feelings. He was also introduced to "perspective taking" as a means of identifying and modifying his judgments. After the review of his most recent anger logs, Richie was asked to notice his selective attention to particular aspects of others' behavior that he judges to be deliberately provocative or threatening, as well as the associated "self-talk":

THERAPIST: *Richie, let's have a look at what happened in this situation you wrote about in your anger log. Tell me what happened here.*

RICHIE: *Alright. I was in the sitting room watching the telly and Tom was shouting and bawling – going on and on and on . . . doing my head in!*

T: *I see. What was going through your mind when this happened? What were you thinking?*

R: *I was thinking "I wish he's shut up. He always does this when I'm trying to watch something. He'd better shut up or I'll punch his lights out. That'll shut him up."*

T: *And how were you feeling when this happened?*

R: *Well, I'm raging by this time.*

T: *How angry were you – out of ten?*

R: *Oh, nine out of ten, easy.*

T: *What did you do?*

R: *In the end I said to him "If you don't shut up I'll effing shut you up, you useless ****."*

T: *How well do you think you handled this situation, looking back on it?*

R: *A bit of a mess really – not very well.*

At this point, the therapist talks to Richie about how he might think differently about this situation and whether this can help him to modulate his emotional, physical, and behavioral responses. Richie was prompted to shift his attentional focus and alter his expectations by encouraging him to view the situation from his housemate's perspective, to put himself "in his shoes," or "see things through his eyes":

THERAPIST: *Right, Ritchie. Let's think about how you might have handled this differently. Let's say you're in exactly the same situation. OK?*

RICHIE: *OK.*

T: *So straight away you're thinking these angry thoughts, "He always does this to me. Shut up or I'll punch your lights out."*

R: *That's it.*

T: *Instead of thinking those angry thoughts can you come up with some other ideas about why Tom was behaving like that?*

R: *I'm not sure. . .*

T: *Well, try to put yourself in Tom's shoes, see the situation from his point of view.*

R: *Umm. Yeah well, Tom's got some mental problems. Maybe he's feeling crap – having bad thoughts like.*

T: *OK, that might be right. So why would he be shouting and bawling?*

R: *Cos he's not coping very well – he wants some help?*

T: *Right. So, if you are thinking like that how would you be feeling do you think?*

R: *I'd be feeling sad for him.*

T: *Would you still be feeling angry?*

R: *Not as much.*

T: *How much?*

R: *Err, say three out of ten.*

T:	*And do you think you might have behaved in a different way?*
R:	*Maybe, yes I would have maybe talked to him to ask him if he wanted some help. I could have asked one of the support workers to come and talk to him.*

During this discussion, the therapist and Richie were using a worksheet with illustrations to record two lines: first what actually happened (situation/thoughts/feelings/actions), then what could have happened (alternative thoughts/feelings/actions).

Cognitive reappraisal work is a component part of each session from this point on in treatment. Thinking about situations differently becomes integrated in to the behavioral skills training using the stress inoculation imaginal practice procedure and role play. From session 12 onward, clients are asked to do the cognitive reappraisal exercise for themselves, between sessions, each time they record an incident in their anger log so that "thinking differently" moves temporally closer to actual incidents and is less abstract. In this way, work on cognitions that might maintain a client's anger and shape his or her emotional and behavioral responses to provocation is instilled in this treatment approach and has equal weight and is given the same amount of attention as arousal reduction and behavioral skills training procedures.

Conclusions

Anger is a normal human emotion that can become a problem for individuals and others if it is uncontrolled (happens too often, is too intense, and persists for too long). Anger is neither necessary nor sufficient for the activation of aggression, but it is strongly associated with and is predictive of aggression in a number of clinical populations, including people with intellectual disabilities. Due to its association with aggression, anger is an important clinical target for people with intellectual disabilities who may be detained and prescribed behavior control drugs more frequently than others. Thus, the development of effective interventions for this vulnerable group is a priority. In this chapter, we have set out the available literature to guide the assessment of anger problems and the evidence to support psychological interventions with people with intellectual disabilities. The evidence base is relatively well developed in this area, with a number of controlled study demonstrating the effectiveness of cognitive–behavioral interventions in reducing self- and informant-rated anger and observed aggression and violence. More research is required to examine the sustainability and generalizability of these effects and further elucidation of the active ingredients of treatment. Case material is provided to demonstrate key aspects of treatment including engagement and motivation of angry clients, and cognitive reappraisal as core component of treatment.

References

Allan, R., Lindsay, W.R., MacLeod, F. & Smith, A.H.W. (2001). Treatment of women with intellectual disabilities who have been involved with the criminal justice system for reasons of aggression. *Journal of Applied Research in Intellectual Disabilities, 14,* 340–347.

Aman, M.G., Richmond, G., Stewart, A.W., Bell, J.C. & Kissell, R. (1987). The Aberrant Behavior Checklist: Factor structure and the effect of subject variables in American and New Zealand facilities. *American Journal of Mental Deficiency, 91,* 570–578.

Attwood, T. & Joachim, R. (1994). The prevention and management of seriously disruptive behavior in Australia. In N. Bouras (Ed.) *Mental health in mental retardation: Recent advances and practice* (pp. 365–374). Cambridge, UK: Cambridge University Press.

Benson, B.A. & Ivins, J. (1992). Anger, depression and self-concept in adults with mental retardation. *Journal of Intellectual Disability Research, 36,* 169–175.

Benson, B.A., Johnson Rice, C. & Miranti, S.V. (1986). Effects of anger management training with mentally retarded adults in group treatment. *Journal of Consulting and Clinical Psychology, 54,* 728–729.

Black, L. & Novaco, R.W. (1993). Treatment of anger with a developmentally disabled man. In R.A. Wells & V.J. Giannetti (Eds.) *Casebook of the brief psychotherapies.* New York: Plenum Press.

Bromley, J. & Emerson, E. (1995). Beliefs and emotional reactions of care staff working with people with challenging behavior. *Journal of Intellectual Disability Research, 39,* 341–352.

Brylewski, J. & Duggan, L. (2004). Antipsychotic medication for challenging behaviour in people with learning disability. *Cochrane Database Systematic Review* (3), CD000377.

Burns, M., Bird, D., Leach, C. & Higgins, K. (2003). Anger management training: The effects of a structured programme on the self-reported anger experience of forensic inpatients with learning disability. *Journal of Psychiatric and Mental Health Nursing, 10,* 569–577.

Carr, J.E., Coriaty, S., Wilder, D.A., Gaunt, B.T., Dozier, C.L., Britton, L.N. *et al.* (2000). A review of "noncontingent" reinforcement as treatment for the aberrant behavior of individuals with developmental disabilities. *Research in Developmental Disabilities, 21,* 377–391.

Chilvers, J., Thomas, C. & Stanbury, A. (2011). The impact of a ward-based mindfulness programme on recorded aggression in a medium secure facility for women with learning disabilities. *Journal of Learning Disabilities and Offending Behaviour, 2,* 27–41.

Cullen, C. (1993). The treatment of people with learning disabilities who offend. In K. Howells & C. Hollin (Eds.) *Clinical approaches to the mentally disordered offender.* Chichester: Wiley.

Deb, S. & Unwin, G.L. (2007). Psychotropic medication for behaviour problems in people with intellectual disability: A review of the current literature. *Current Opinion in Psychiatry, 20,* 461–466.

Gagiano, C., Read, S., Thorpe, L., Eerdekens, M., & Van Hove, I. (2005). Short and long-term efficacy and safety of risperidone in adults with disruptive behaviour disorders. *Psychopharmacology, 179,* 629–636.

Hagiliassis, N., Gulbenkoglu, H., Di Marco, M., Young, S. & Hudson, A. (2005). The Anger Management Project: A group intervention for anger in people with physical and multiple handicaps. *Journal of Intellectual and Developmental Disability, 30,* 86–90.

Harris, P. (1993). The nature and extent of aggressive behaviour amongst people with learning difficulties (mental handicap) in a single health district. *Journal of Intellectual Disability Research, 37,* 221–242.

Hill, B.K. & Bruininks, R.H. (1984). Maladaptive behavior of mentally retarded individuals in residential facilities. *American Journal of Mental Deficiency, 88,* 380–387.

Howells, P.M., Rogers, C. & Wilcock, S. (2000). Evaluating a cognitive/behavioural approach to anger management skills in adults with learning disabilities. *British Journal of Learning Disabilities, 28,* 137–142.

Kiely, J. & Pankhurst, H. (1998). Violence faced by staff in a learning disability service. *Disability and Rehabilitation, 20,* 81–89.

King, N., Lancaster, N., Wynne, G., Nettleton, N. & Davis, R. (1999). Cognitive behavioural anger management training for adults with mild intellectual disability. *Scandinavian Journal of Behaviour Therapy, 28,* 19–22.

Lakin, K.C., Hill, B.K., Hauber, F.A., Bruininks, R.H. & Heal, L.W. (1983). New admissions to a national sample of public residential facilities. *American Journal of Mental Deficiency*, *88*, 13–20.

Lawrenson, H. & Lindsay, W.R. (1998). The treatment of anger in individuals with learning disabilities. In W. Fraser, D. Sines & M. Kerr (Eds.) *Hallas' the care of people with intellectual disabilities* (9th edn). Oxford: Butterworth Heinemann.

Lennox, D.B., Miltenberger, R.G., Spengler, P. & Erfanian, N. (1988). Decelerative treatment practices with persons who have mental retardation: A review of five years of the literature. *American Journal of Mental Retardation*, *92*, 492–501.

Lindsay, W.R., Allan, R., MacLeod, F., Smart, N. & Smith, A.H.W. (2003). Long-term treatment and management of violent tendencies in men with intellectual disabilities convicted of assault. *Mental Retardation*, *41*, 47–56.

Lindsay, W.R., Allan, R., Parry, C., Macleod, F., Cottrell, J., Overend, H. *et al.* (2004). Anger and aggression in people with intellectual disabilities: Treatment and follow-up of consecutive referrals and a waiting list comparison. *Clinical Psychology and Psychotherapy*, *11*, 255–264.

Lindsay, W.R., Michie, A., Baty, F., Smith, A. & Miller, S. (1994). The consistency of reports about feelings and emotions from people with intellectual disability. *Journal of Intellectual Disability Research*, *38*, 61–66.

Lindsay, W.R., Overend, H., Allan, R., Williams, C. & Black, L. (1998). Using specific approaches for individual problems in the management of anger and aggression. *British Journal of Learning Disabilities*, *26*, 44–50.

MacMillan, D., Hastings, R. & Coldwell, J. (2004). Clinical and actuarial prediction of physical violence in a forensic intellectual disability hospital: A longitudinal study. *Journal of Applied Research in Intellectual Disabilities*, *17*, 255–266.

Matson, J.L., Bamburg, J.W., Mayville, E.A., Pinkston, J., Bielecki, J., Kuhn, D. *et al.* (2000). Psychopharmacology and mental retardation: A 10 year review (1990–1999). *Research in Developmental Disabilities*, *21*, 263–296.

Moore, E., Adams, R., Elsworth, J. & Lewis, J. (1997). An anger management group for people with a learning disability. *British Journal of Learning Disabilities*, *25*, 53–57.

Murphy, G. & Clare, I. (1991). MIETS: A service option for people with mild mental handicap and challenging behaviour or psychiatric problems. 2. Assessment, treatment, and outcome for service users and service effectiveness. *Mental Handicap Research*, *4*, 180–206.

Novaco, R.W. (1976). The function and regulation of the arousal of anger. *The American Journal of Psychiatry*, *133*, 1124–1128.

Novaco, R.W. (1988). Novaco Provocation Inventory. In M. Hersen & A.S. Bellack (Eds.) *Dictionary of behavioral assessment techniques*. New York: Pergamon.

Novaco, R.W. (1994). Anger as a risk factor for violence among the mentally disordered. In J. Monahan & H. Steadman (Eds.) *Violence and mental disorder: Developments in risk assessment* (pp.21–59). Chicago, IL: University of Chicago Press.

Novaco, R.W. (2003). *The Novaco Anger Scale and Provocation Inventory (NAS-PI)*. Los Angeles, CA: Western Psychological Services.

Novaco, R.W. & Taylor, J.L. (2004). Assessment of anger and aggression in male offenders with developmental disabilities. *Psychological Assessment*, *16*, 42–50.

Novaco, R.W. & Taylor, J.L. (2006). Cognitive-behavioural anger treatment. In M. McNulty & A. Carr (Eds.) *Handbook of adult clinical psychology: An evidence based practice approach* (pp.978–1009). London: Routledge.

Novaco, R.W. & Welsh, W.N. (1989). Anger disturbances: Cognitive mediation and clinical prescriptions. In K. Howells & C.R. Hollin (Eds.) *Clinical approaches to violence*. Chichester: John Wiley & Sons.

Robertson, J., Emerson, E., Gregory, N., Hatton, C., Kessissoglou, S. & Hallam, A. (2000). Receipt of psychotropic medication by people with intellectual disability in residential settings. *Journal of Intellectual Disability Research, 44,* 666–676.

Rose, J. (1996). Anger management: A group treatment program for people with mental retardation. *Journal of Developmental and Physical Disabilities, 8,* 133–149.

Rose, J., Loftus, M., Flint, B. & Carey, L. (2005). Factors associated with the efficacy of a group intervention for anger in people with intellectual disabilities. *The British Journal of Clinical Psychology, 44,* 305–317.

Rose, J., O'Brien, A. & Rose, D. (2009). Group and individual cognitive behavioural interventions for anger. *Advances in Mental Health and Learning Disabilities, 3,* 45–50.

Rose, J. & West, C. (1999). Assessment of anger in people with intellectual disabilities. *Journal of Applied Research in Intellectual Disabilities, 12,* 211–224.

Rose, J., West, C. & Clifford, D. (2000). Group interventions for anger in people with intellectual disabilities. *Research in Developmental Disabilities, 21,* 171–181.

Rose, J.L., Dodd, L. & Rose, N. (2008). Individual cognitive behavioural intervention for anger. *Journal of Mental Health Research in Intellectual Disabilities, 1,* 97–108.

Rossiter, R., Hunniset, E. & Pulsford, M. (1998). Anger management training and people with moderate learning disabilities. *British Journal of Learning Disabilities, 26,* 67–74.

Ruedrich, S.L., Swales, T.P., Rossvanes, C., Diana, L., Arkadiev, V. & Lim, K. (2008). Atypical antipsychotic medication improves aggression, but not self-injurious behaviour, in adults with intellectual disabilities. *Journal of Intellectual Disability Research, 52,* 132–140.

Scotti, J.R., Evans, I.M., Meyer, L.H. & Walker, P. (1991). A meta-analysis of intervention research with problem behavior: Treatment validity and standards of practice. *American Journal of Mental Retardation, 96,* 233–256.

Sigafoos, J., Elkins, J., Kerr, M. & Attwood, T. (1994). A survey of aggressive behavior among a population of persons with intellectual disability in Queensland. *Journal of Intellectual Disability Research, 38,* 369–381.

Singh, A.N., Matson, J.L., Cooper, C.L., Dixon, D., & Sturmey, P. (2005). The use of risperidone among individuals with mental retardation: Clinically supported or not? *Research in Developmental Disabilities, 26,* 203–210.

Singh, N.N., Lancioni, G.E., Winton, A.S.W., Adkins, A.D., Singh, J. & Singh, A.N. (2007). Mindfulness training assists individuals with moderate mental retardation to maintain their community placements. *Behavior Modification, 31,* 800–814.

Singh, N.N., Lancioni, G.E., Winton, A.S.W., Singh, A.N., Adkins, A.D. & Singh, J. (2008). Clinical and benefit-cost outcomes of teaching a mindfulness-based procedure to adult offenders with intellectual disabilities. *Behavior Modification, 32,* 622–637.

Singh, N.N., Wahler, R.G., Adkins, A.D., Myers, R.E. & The Mindfulness Research Group (2003). Soles of the Feet: A mindfulness-based self-control intervention for aggression by and individual with mild mental retardation and mental illness. *Research in Developmental Disabilities, 24,* 158–169.

Smith, S., Branford, D., Collacott, R.A., Cooper, S.-A. & McGrother, C. (1996). Prevalence and cluster typology of maladaptive behaviours in a geographically defined population of adults with learning disabilities. *The British Journal of Psychiatry, 169,* 219–227.

Spielberger, C.D. (1996). *State–Trait Anger Expression Inventory Professional Manual.* Odessa, FL: Psychological Assessment Resources, Inc.

Taylor, J.L. (2002). A review of assessment and treatment of anger and aggression in offenders with intellectual disability. *Journal of Intellectual Disability Research, 46*(Suppl. 1), 57–73.

Taylor, J.L. (2009). Treatment of anger and aggression for offenders with intellectual disabilities in secure settings. In R. Didden & X. Moonen (Eds.) *Met het oog op behandeling 2* (pp. 9–14). Amersfoort, The Netherlands: Bergdrukkerij.

Taylor, J.L., Lindsay, W.R. & Willner, P. (2008). CBT for people with intellectual disabilities: Emerging evidence, cognitive ability and IQ effects. *Behavioural and Cognitive Psychotherapy, 36*, 723–733.

Taylor, J.L. & Novaco, R.W. (2005). *Anger treatment for people with developmental disabilities: A theory, evidence and manual based approach.* Chichester: Wiley.

Taylor, J.L., Novaco, R.W., Gillmer, B.T., Robertson, A. & Thorne, I. (2005). Individual cognitive-behavioural anger treatment for people with mild-borderline intellectual disabilities and histories of aggression: A controlled trial. *The British Journal of Clinical Psychology, 44*, 367–382.

Taylor, J.L., Novaco, R.W., Gillmer, B. & Thorne, I. (2002). Cognitive-behavioural treatment of anger intensity among offenders with intellectual disabilities. *Journal of Applied Research in Intellectual Disabilities, 15*, 151–165.

Taylor, J.L., Novaco, R.W., Guinan, C. & Street, N. (2004). Development of an imaginal provocation test to evaluate treatment for anger problems in people with intellectual disabilities. *Clinical Psychology and Psychotherapy, 11*, 233–246.

Taylor, J.L., Novaco, R.W. & Johnson, L. (2009). Effects of intellectual functioning on cognitive behavioural anger treatment for adults with intellectual disabilities in secure settings. *Advances in Mental Health and Learning Disabilities, 3*, 51–56.

Tsiouris, J.A. (2010). Pharmacotherapy for aggressive behaviours in persons with intellectual disabilities: Treatment or mistreatment? *Journal of Intellectual Disability Research, 54*, 1–16.

Tyrer, P., Oliver-Africano, P.C., Ahmed, Z., Bouras, N., Cooray, S., Deb, S. *et al.* (2008). Risperidone, haloperidol, and placebo in the treatment of aggressive challenging behaviour in patients with intellectual disabilities: A randomised controlled trial. *Lancet, 371*, 57–63.

Walker, T. & Cheseldine, S. (1997). Towards outcome measurements: Monitoring effectiveness of anger management and assertiveness training in a group setting. *British Journal of Learning Disabilities, 25*, 134–137.

Whitaker, S. (1993). The reduction of aggression in people with learning difficulties: A review of psychological methods. *The British Journal of Clinical Psychology, 32*, 1–37.

Whitaker, S. (2001). Anger control for people with learning disabilities: A critical review. *Behavioural and Cognitive Psychotherapy, 29*, 277–293.

Wigham, S., Hatton, C. & Taylor, J.L. (2011). The Lancaster and Northgate Trauma Scales (LANTS): The development and psychometric properties of measures of trauma for people with mild to moderate intellectual disabilities. *Research in Developmental Disabilities, 32*, 2651–2659.

Willner, P. (2007). Cognitive behaviour therapy for people with learning disabilities: Focus on anger. *Advances in Mental Health and Learning Disabilities, 1*(2), 14–21.

Willner, P., Brace, N. & Phillips, J. (2005). Assessment of anger coping skills in individuals with intellectual disabilities. *Journal of Intellectual Disability Research, 49*, 329–339.

Willner, P., Jones, J., Tams, R. & Green, G. (2002). A randomised controlled trial of the efficacy of a cognitive-behavioural anger management group for clients with learning disabilities. *Journal of Applied Research in Intellectual Disabilities, 15*, 224–235.

Willner, P. & Tomlinson, S. (2007). Generalization of anger coping skills from day-service to residential settings. *Journal of Applied Research in Intellectual Disabilities, 20*, 553–562.

Zillmann, D. (1971). Excitation transfer in communication-mediated aggressive behavior. *Journal of Experimental Social Psychology, 7*, 419–434.

Chapter 10

Cognitive–Behavioral Therapy for People with Intellectual Disabilities and Psychosis

Stephen C. Oathamshaw
Alastair L. Barrowcliff
Gillian Haddock

Introduction

The prevalence of psychosis in people with intellectual disabilities (IDs) has been generally recognized as higher than the general population, where a prevalence of 1 percent has been established (Fraser & Nolan, 1994), with a point prevalence of 3 percent for schizophrenia suggested (Eaton & Menolascino, 1982; Turner, 1989). More recent research (Cooper *et al.*, 2007) suggests a figure of 2.6 percent for psychotic disorder using the International Classification of Disease, 10th Revision, Diagnostic Criteria for Research (ICD-10-DCR) criteria, but 3.4 percent for the same sample using the Diagnostic and Statistical Manual of Mental Disorders, Fourth Edition Text Revision (DSM-IV-TR) diagnostic criteria. The stress vulnerability model provides a possible explanation for a higher prevalence of psychosis in this population as neurological impairments caused by genetic factors or trauma are common in people with IDs (Robertson & Murphy, 1999) and have been identified as risk factors for developing psychosis, although a causal relationship has not been established. Stressors suggested as likely to increase the chances of a vulnerable individual developing psychosis, including the effects of limited life opportunities and low self-esteem, are also more common for people with IDs (Clarke, 1999).

Despite these research findings, other researchers question the reliability of diagnosing schizophrenia and other psychotic disorders in people with IDs (Hare, 2002; Hurley, 1996; Stenfert Kroese *et al.*, 2001). Diagnosis in the general population is usually heavily reliant on clinical interview, a method that has been criticized as unreliable (Bentall, 1990), and may be even less reliable when conducted with someone who has limited verbal skills (Hare, 2002). Auditory hallucinations are the most common psychotic symptoms described by the general population (Slade & Bentall, 1988). These symptoms may be particularly challenging to diagnose in

Psychological Therapies for Adults with Intellectual Disabilities, First Edition.
Edited by John L. Taylor, William R. Lindsay, Richard P. Hastings, and Chris Hatton.
© 2013 John Wiley & Sons, Ltd. Published 2013 by John Wiley & Sons, Ltd.

people with IDs due to factors such as interviewees with IDs having difficulties in differentiating between internal and external events, or misattributing events such as dreams to an external source (Stenfert Kroese *et al.*, 1998). Negative symptoms of schizophrenia can also be difficult to diagnose as behaviors such as social withdrawal and apparent apathy or lack of motivation can be part of the characteristic profile of some people with IDs (Turner, 1989).

While these factors may, as some researchers have suggested, create a risk of over-diagnosis of psychosis in people with IDs, there are also a number of factors that may result in underdiagnosis. These include diagnostic overshadowing (symptoms of psychosis being inappropriately attributed to an individual's ID) and the difficulty in using standard diagnostic classification systems for diagnosing psychosis or any other mental health problem in people with more severe and profound IDs, due to their limited behavioral and communicative repertoire (Sturmey & Bertman, 1994). These difficulties have been alleviated to some extent in recent years by the development of assessment schedules for mental health problems, including psychosis, for people with IDs and the validation of schedules originally designed for other populations.

Standardized Assessments of Psychosis in People with IDs

The Psychiatric Assessment Schedule for Adults with Developmental Disability (PAS-ADD) schedules developed by Moss and colleagues at the Hester Adrian Research Centre are the most widely used standardized schedules developed specifically for people with IDs and include subscales for the assessment of psychosis (Moss, 2002; Moss, Goldberg *et al.*, 1996; Moss, Prosser *et al.*, 1996). The Brief Symptom Inventory (BSI; Derogatis, 1993) is a schedule originally developed for the general population but has been validated for people with mild IDs including community, clinical, and forensic groups (Kellett *et al.*, 2003). The BSI includes subscales for assessing paranoid ideation and psychoticism, including positive and negative symptoms of schizophrenia.

There are no standardized scales developed specifically for use with people with IDs that are designed to assess the component dimensions of psychotic illness and assist in identifying areas for psychological intervention, although two scales developed for the general population have been validated with this group. The Positive and Negative Syndrome Scale (PANSS; Kay *et al.*, 1989) and the Psychotic Symptom Rating Scales (PSYRATS; Haddock *et al.*, 1999) have been shown to have adequate psychometric properties (Hatton *et al.*, 2005), with the exception of the PANSS negative syndrome scale. The PSYRATS is useful when PANSS assessment identifies positive symptoms, as it assesses delusions and hallucinations in greater depth.

The original version of the Beliefs About Voices Questionnaire (BAVQ; Chadwick & Birchwood, 1995) has not been validated for people with IDs, but two of the authors (S.C.O. and A.L.B.) have used it successfully in clinical practice and one has described its use in the literature (Barrowcliff, 2007). The BAVQ is a 30-item questionnaire asking for "yes/no" responses to items regarding five dimensions of an individual's beliefs about a voice: malevolence, benevolence, resistance, engagement, and omnipotence.

Use of these assessments in combination with individual clinical assessment can produce a comprehensive picture of a client's psychotic symptoms and identify priority areas for collaborative intervention.

Psychological treatment for psychosis in people with IDs is a new and recent innovation. Outside this population, there is a significantly greater body of evidence.

Psychological Therapies for Psychosis in the Nonintellectual Disability Population

Psychological treatments for psychotic disorders in the general population have been supported for many years. In 1911, Bleuler (1911, 1950) specifically advocated the use of psychotherapy in the treatment of schizophrenia, and this has been further endorsed over subsequent years (e.g., Beck, 1952; Sullivan, 1962). Beck, well known for his development of cognitive therapy, published a case study in 1952 describing a successful treatment of a young man with a delusional disorder using psychological approaches. Since then, there have been many published reports of psychological treatments for psychosis. Initially, these were mainly case studies or case series rather than controlled trials. However, more recently, there has been an increase in controlled research describing and evaluating psychological treatments for psychosis. This work has led to recent government legislation in the United Kingdom endorsing the use of psychological approaches in the management of psychosis. The National Institute of Clinical Effectiveness (NICE, 2009) makes the following recommendations:

1.3.4.1. (Services should) offer cognitive behavioural therapy (CBT) to all people with schizophrenia. This can be started either during the acute phase or later, including in inpatient settings.
1.3.4.2. Offer family intervention to all families of people with schizophrenia who live with or are in close contact with the service user. This can be started either during the acute phase or later, including in inpatient settings.

The psychological interventions used in psychosis have been influenced by a range of theoretical schools such as the psychoanalytic field, the literature on psychopathological processes in schizophrenia, and the behavioral school and learning theory. Psychoanalytical approaches for the treatment of psychosis have not been evaluated widely or systematically, and hence the evidence base in relation to these approaches in psychosis is weak (Tarrier *et al.*, 2002).

The areas that have been most studied and evaluated for psychosis in the nonintellectual disability field have tended to be in the cognitive and behavioral domain. These have varied from individual one-to-one cognitive–behavioral therapy (CBT) interventions, CBT-oriented family interventions, neuropsychological and cognitive remediation approaches, social and other skills training approaches, and contingency management approaches.

Behavioral approaches

Early approaches were influenced more by the strictly behavioral psychology school, such as the use of contingency or reward approaches for reducing the occurrence of particular target behaviors (Haynes & Geddy, 1973; Nydegger, 1972), distraction procedures (Margo *et al.*, 1981; Nelson *et al.*, 1991), and thought stopping (Allen *et al.*, 1983; Samaan, 1975), and the use of aversion therapy (Alford & Turner, 1976; Turner *et al.*, 1977). While successful reduction in the occurrence of target behaviors were frequently reported using these approaches, there was little evaluation in larger controlled trials and little evidence that the approaches generalized across situations or people (see Dickerson *et al.*, 2005 for a review of some of these approaches).

Behavioral approaches highlighted an emphasis on the removal of psychotic symptoms and the notion that symptoms of psychosis were "ununderstandable" phenomena, suggesting that they were unlikely to respond to reason or discussion (Jaspers, 1963). However, the "ununderstandability" of psychotic symptoms has been much disputed by both psychopathology researchers and service users in more recent years. For example, the application of effective techniques to help individuals test out the reality of delusional beliefs (e.g., Chadwick & Lowe, 1990) has demonstrated that, contrary to Jaspers' earlier assertion, these beliefs do indeed respond to reason and are often understandable when considered in relation to the individual's beliefs and life goals (Garety & Hemsley, 1997; Pitt *et al.*, 2007).

Cognitive–behavioral therapy

The growing interest in "talking" therapies for the treatment of other disorders (e.g., cognitive therapy for anxiety and depression), as well as the greater interest in understanding the nature of particular psychotic symptoms, led to the development of psychological approaches that involved exploring and treating psychotic phenomena in one-to-one talking therapies where a partnership between service user and clinician guides treatment. This heralded the development of cognitive–behavioral treatments for psychotic disorders, which lent themselves well to evaluation in larger controlled trials of their effectiveness.

CBT has been applied to all phases of the disorder (i.e., acute and recent onset psychosis) with good results (Garety *et al.*, 2007; Lewis *et al.*, 2002) and chronic and treatment-resistant psychosis (Sensky *et al.*, 2000; Tarrier *et al.*, 1998). In addition, CBT has also been shown to be effective at reducing the transition to full-blown psychosis in those people experiencing prepsychotic or high risk for psychosis states (Morrison *et al.*, 2004), and has been used with people who are experiencing comorbid or dual disorders (Barrowclough *et al.*, 2001; Haddock *et al.*, 2009) and to increase adherence to antipsychotic medication (Kemp *et al.*, 1996).

The cognitive–behavioral approach to psychosis adopts a multicomponent approach to therapy with aims of intervention potentially including strategies to reduce distress associated with symptoms, reduce emotional disturbance, increase the individual's ability to prevent relapse, and limit the social disability associated with psychotic illness (Fowler *et al.*, 1995).

CBT for positive symptoms may adopt an ABC perspective (Chadwick & Birchwood, 1994) where voices are seen as activating events rather than thoughts. Cognitive theory would suggest if therapy were successful in modifying the thoughts (the "B" in the ABC perspective) relating to the activating event (A), distress associated with the person's experience of psychosis (C) would be reduced, even if the voice itself does not disappear. Evidence to support this hypothesis is provided by research that indicates beliefs held about a voice, particularly if the voice is perceived as malevolent or omnipotent, are associated with resistance and negative affect (Chadwick & Birchwood, 1995; Chadwick *et al.*, 2000).

Family interventions

In addition to the developments in individual psychological interventions, a substantial amount of research has been carried out on whether providing family interventions (often aimed at increasing family communication, improving problem solving, and reducing conflict and stress) could improve outcomes (particularly reduce relapse rates) for people with psychosis (Pfammatter *et al.*, 2006; Pharoah *et al.*, 2006). This followed evidence demonstrating that stressful family environments that were high in "expressed emotion" (Brown *et al.*, 1962) could result in significantly higher relapse rates (Vaughn & Leff, 1976). Although these interventions may differ in techniques used, they tend to use cognitive–behavioral models and approaches (see Pharoah *et al.*, 2006 for review).

The application of these therapeutic principles, in addition to the adaptations required to make them accessible to people with IDs, will be described in the next section.

Psychological Interventions for Psychosis with People Who Have IDs

It is only recently that any literature describing the efficacy of psychological treatment for psychosis in people with IDs has been published. A single case study was published in the 1990s (Leggett *et al.*, 1997) describing the effects of a 10-session group treatment program in a secure hospital, which included one woman with mild ID. Following the group, the assessment demonstrated she had experienced a reduced duration of auditory hallucinations, reduced depressive symptoms, lower use of pro re nata (PRN; "as needed") medication, and increases on a self-esteem measure. A case series including five participants (Haddock *et al.*, 2004) used an intervention based on therapy previously developed for people who had treatment-resistant psychosis (Haddock *et al.*, 1998) including strategies to manage positive and negative symptoms, other nonpsychotic mental health problems, and poor social functioning. Two of the cases described also included family interventions for participants who lived with family carers. Reductions in positive symptoms were reported, although there appeared to be relatively little impact on social functioning.

Kirkland (2005) reported work with three participants with mild IDs with interventions focusing on using simplified formulations to enhance collaborative working designed to increase the clients' understanding of their difficulties and ability to address them. Barrowcliff (2007) described a single case study reporting the use of adapted CBT specifically designed to address command hallucinations. Following a course of 20 sessions, reductions in positive symptoms measured by the PANSS and PSYRATS were demonstrated and maintained at three and six months' follow-up. Crowley *et al.* (2008) described a psychoeducational group, using cognitive–behavioral techniques, for eight participants, five of whom had a diagnosis of schizophrenia. Results indicated a significant increase in knowledge on a questionnaire designed for the group, but no significant increases in self-esteem.

Engagement in therapy

In common with other people with IDs, the assessment of cognitive skills related to CBT can be used for an individual with psychosis to identify his or her understanding of the links between activating events, thoughts, feelings, and behavior, and to increase socialization to the cognitive model. Measures developed by Reed and Clements (1989), Dagnan and Chadwick (1997), and Oathamshaw and Haddock (2006) to assess these skills can also be used in clinical practice to supplement idiosyncratic clinical assessment. Motivation to engage in therapy, alliance potential, and ability to recognize and differentiate emotions have also been recognized as important factors to consider, and with people who have ID support available can also be of crucial importance (Willner, 2006).

Interpersonal and environmental factors can be important in increasing motivation to engage in therapy as people with IDs may value their relationship with their therapist highly (Willner, 2006) and regard a valued environment for therapy sessions as an extra incentive to engage in therapy (Oathamshaw, 2007). Failure to consider these factors sufficiently can lead to the interruption or failure of therapy. Oathamshaw (2007) described an example where a woman who was experiencing persecutory auditory hallucinations stopped attending therapy after sessions were moved to an environment that provoked memories of previous negative experiences, instead of the therapist's office she would rather have used.

People with IDs and psychosis may have had previous negative and aversive experiences of services and this may necessitate a longer engagement phase of therapy. The use of humor during therapy sessions should also be carefully considered when a client's overall communication ability and understanding of more subtle communication is not fully assessed, or elevated levels of paranoia or suspiciousness are present.

Adaptations to therapy

Many of the adaptations described in research studies with people who have IDs and psychosis are similar to those described in the literature reporting CBT for other mental health problems including simplified language and visual representation of abstract concepts (see Whitehouse *et al.*, 2006 for a review). Involvement of family members and caregivers is described in studies with the nonintellectually disabled psychosis population (Sellwood *et al.*, 2001) and those with IDs (Haddock *et al.*, 2004).

The case study described in the next section illustrates the use of many of the adaptations described by Whitehouse *et al.* (2006), though a family intervention was not necessary. Some of the engagement and therapy issues described earlier are also discussed, and consideration of these issues and need for adaptations are combined idiosyncratically to make cognitive therapy designed for the general psychosis population accessible to a woman with mild ID.

Case Study: Joan

Joan,[1] a lady in her late fifties, had been in receipt of numerous diagnoses and labels within adult mental health services over the past 20 years, including "diagnosis complex and psychotic in nature," "schizophrenia," and "personality disorder." Contact with the Adults with Learning Disability Service (AwLDS) during this period had been purely on a community nursing level, with support for a number of physical health complaints including heart problems, diabetes, and chronic obesity. The Community Mental Health Team (CMHT) had to this point retained responsibility for the management of her mental health presentation, which comprised medication and monitoring only: no psychotherapeutic intervention had been made available to her in regard to psychotic features of her presentation. Formal assessment had indicated a level of intellectual and adaptive functioning within the mild ID range, with a supporting historical and developmental history.

At the time of referral to AwLDS psychology services, Joan had been experiencing an acute psychotic episode for which she had been detained under a treatment section on an inpatient psychiatric ward for several months. At this time, Joan reported frequent and highly distressing command hallucinations to self-harm, with which she complied on a daily basis with severe lacerations to her chest and arms, and setting fire to her body with lighter fuel. Additional beliefs included perceptions that the ward staff wanted to prostitute her, that CMHT staff had planted bugs in her home, and that other people were talking about her in a negative way.

Preliminary assessment

Due to the nature of her presentation, preliminary assessment focused on psychotic features, utilizing the PANSS (Kay *et al.*, 1989), the PSYRATS (Haddock *et al.*, 1999), the Command Hallucination Interview (Barrowcliff & Haddock, unpublished data), and the adapted Social Comparison Scale (Barrowcliff, 2007). Idiographic assessment of her understanding of those components contained within a CBT-directed intervention was also completed and developed over the course of intervention. Concurrent with this period of initial assessment was the early development of a basic formulation with a focus on harm-reduction methods, and the recommendation of behavioral management strategies to facilitate a period of stability prior to engagement in CBT. It is noted that Joan would not engage therapeutically on a one-to-one basis for CBT in an inpatient setting, only following discharge home. Although she was considered to be more stable (hence the discharge), command hallucinations to self-harm and continued engagement with self-harm behavior, low mood, and paranoid ideation remained core themes in her presentation. We detail here the delivery of CBT in regard to these long-standing and distressing features of her presentation.[2]

---

[1] Identifying details have been changed. Joan consented to have details of her case shared here.
[2] Note that we do not present here details of specific theoretical issues in working with elements of command hallucinations in adults with learning disability and psychosis (for this, see Barrowcliff, 2007), but with broader elements of psychosis within this clinical population.

Inner speech and internal cognitive processes

Joan had no conceptual understanding of inner speech at the outset of sessions and attributed her experiences of auditory hallucinations to established frames of reference, specifically external sources. Thus, she had always believed that voices could only come from outside, not inside a person's head. The primary content of the dominant female voice experienced was commanding and directing self-harm. As a consequence of their abusive relationship, Joan attributed this voice to her dead mother: it seemed to her a natural continuation of the psychological abuse that she had experienced from her mother until her death 20 years previously. The link with her mother also fitted with other elements of her reported experiences, including reference to commands to set fire to herself ("she is in hell") and a self-deprecating style of self-reference (internalized blame), maintaining the belief that she deserved to be punished for being an evil person ("cut yourself").[3] Once causal explanations as to the perceived origin of her hallucinations had been recorded and it was considered that an external source was the only opinion currently held, it was necessary to enter an episode of "suspended disbelief" for Joan to consider alternative explanations within a shared framework. This required the conceptual development of internal thought (the "cognitive" component) for Joan. A number of approaches were utilized, as follows.

Seeking a shared experience of internal speech and thought. Through discussion, it was established that we could each hear our own speech/voices when talking aloud. Similarly, we could each hear ourselves as we lowered the vocal output, all-be-it quieter and quieter. With repeated practice and critically, directed attention, Joan was able to recognize that she too had an inner voice that was evident in the absence of generating sounds. While a common response to such experiences initially can be "yes, but it isn't the sound of the [hallucinatory] voice," it is an axiomatic stage in developing such conceptual understanding of internally driven stimuli. Mapping of the direct association between self-generated sounds and thoughts using line-drawn images served as a useful representation and summary, with blank homework sheets made available to reinforce the message. Comparable exercises were completed with visual and tactile stimuli where applicable, with directed attention being the key to generating such experiences. Once Joan had established that she had internal speech, she was able to engage in "detached mindfulness" exercises to observe her own inner thought processes. It should be noted that this did at times introduce a level of added distress for Joan at this initial stage, as it heightened her awareness of an underlying stream of distressing material (e.g., thoughts, images, and memories) that she was hitherto less able to directly access, such that employment of distraction techniques was an important adjunct at this stage.

---

[3] It is interesting to note that self-harm in this case was not just attributed to compliance with command hallucinations, but had a secondary component of managing negative affective states, which required a different level of intervention to that described here for the management of psychotic features. It was important to differentiate these components within the formulation, although we deal with issues specific to the psychosis presented here.

Seeking to normalize internal experiences. Joan was initially skeptical of inner cognitive events being a universally held experience, and so we embarked on an exercise to test such a belief. The standard Prepare–Expose–Test–Summarize (PETS) protocol (Wells, 1997) was applied in this context, noting that issues of comprehension and retention of alternative hypotheses require enhanced attention prior to the test and summary components to limit any alternative rationalization of unexpected outcomes (e.g., Barrowcliff, 2007). The PETS mnemonic represents the sequence for a typical behavioral experiment, although applied in this context at a targeted belief rather than specific behavior, the PETS protocol remained a useful heuristic process to follow.

Following the PETS protocol, we embarked on a survey of others to establish the veracity of such an opinion ("Do you think it is normal to experience thoughts/ images/ideas in your head?"). Questionnaires were given out with a dichotomous response option of "yes" or "no." Joan had a relatively good concept of numbers and was able to reflect, for example, that 3 was more than 1, and 6 less than 9, such that tallying up survey responses was a meaningful activity. Other more concrete forms of representation, such as stacked boxes representing "more" and "less," can be applied where concept of number is lacking. A summary sheet was completed with the different possible outcomes detailed, importantly stating that if respondents did believe this was a normal experience that Joan should also accept that it was a normal experience (Prepare). Following Exposure (the survey), Joan was surprised to learn that all respondents gave a "yes" response (Test). However, it was of interest to note that while she was able to adapt her belief that internal cognition was actually normal (Summarize), she was keen to point out that command hallucinations were not normal.

Normalization of negative content. Negative or highly ego-dystonic content of voices or thoughts is a common theme within this clinical population. For Joan, her primary hallucinatory voice was extremely negative in content, being demeaning, critical, and directing self-harm. As indicated, this voice was initially attributed to her abusive mother. Once it was recognized that such stimuli could be generated internally, a context for understanding such derogatory content needed to be established (i.e., how else could Joan account for such abusive content of what we had now established may be an internally generated event?). Here, it was critical to understand the under-lying features of experience and memory, and in the recognition that the generation of ego-dystonic thoughts is a relatively normal experience. For example, Joan believed that having any negative thoughts about others was evidence that she was "evil like her mother" and thus that she deserved to "burn in hell" and suffer in life (as repeat-edly reinforced by the content of her auditory hallucinations). Survey techniques were again applied to develop an understanding of the normality of negative thoughts regarding others without self-labeling as "evil."

Working with dichotomous thinking and ego-dystonic beliefs

Dichotomies in conceptualizing the world are not uncommon and present a simpli-fied way to classify events, experiences, and people. Often, observed dichotomies in clinical settings include voices being either "good" or "bad," relating to instructions from God or the devil, although more generally, this is observed as people being happy or sad, or tangibles in life being loved or hated. Considering the limited emotional language observed in adults with learning disabilities (e.g., Dagnan *et al.*, 2000) and, for example, generalized difficulties in abstract and conceptual understanding, it is unsurprising that Joan also conceptualized many of her experiences within the confines of such dichotomies. Joan believed that as a consequence of her repeated thoughts of self-harm and attentional bias toward news reports of female killers that she "must be evil." She did not believe that "good" people would focus their attention toward such awful and personally repulsive content. This also related to her attribution of justification in regard to the content of her command hallucinations to self-harm (i.e., it was further evidence that she deserved to be punished). Core therapeutic issues here concerned the introduction of a spectrum from each dichotomized anchor point, personal reflection on events along this spectrum, and the reframing of negative personal attributions regarding her attentional biases. Furthermore, working within dichotomies, it was necessary to bring Joan to a point of understanding of the distinction between thoughts and behavior within the basic CBT model.

Attentional biases and ego-dystonic thoughts. Joan initially struggled to understand the concept of attentional biases and why she noticed the "bad" internal stimuli more than other people. A specific focus was directed toward ego-dystonic material. A concrete example was required to augment understanding at this point. Here, we used pictures of a head with an exit point for certain shaped "thoughts." Other shaped thoughts were unable to exit through this hole and thus were stuck within Joan's head and hence awareness. Those "escaping thoughts" were referred to as "not upsetting" type thoughts that pass unnoticed, while those stuck within were considered to be the "upsetting" thoughts that were attended to. Putting certain descriptions of internal cognitive events, occurring as images, ideas, thoughts, or other experiences, as either written descriptions or meaningful pictures onto shaped pieces of paper that would stay in or go out of the head, provided a concrete representation of this process. This process also augmented Joan's ability to focus on and identify different types of cognitive experiences and represent them using pictures when she struggled with verbal language.

Reframing of negative attentional biases. It became clear that Joan classified her attentional bias to news reports of female child abusers and murderers as reflecting her evil nature, such that just thinking about these women's actions became manifest as an internal belief that she must be like them to think about such details so frequently and consistently. First, we sought to establish the baseline emotion that people had toward the material presented utilizing the two main dichotomies presented by Joan, namely how "good" people and how "evil" people would respond. Joan was clear in her belief that "good" people would be distressed by such material and "evil" people would not. This information was produced on a piece of paper, and Joan was encouraged to place cutouts of "good" and "evil" people within the camps of "not distressed by the material" or "distressed by the material." Once it was established that Joan was able to differentiate, she was asked to place a representation of herself in the respective camp. The visual impact of placing herself with all the "good" people in the "distressed camp" was a powerful message for her that thinking about such material was not a sign of her being evil.

Reflections on memory activation and frequency of distressing thoughts. It was necessary to provide Joan with a rational as to why these distressing thoughts occurred with such frequency, as they were not indicative of her "being evil" but, rather, "good." An initial attempt to demonstrate the "Wegner effect" utilizing the "white bear" imagery technique (Wegner *et al.*, 1987) was too abstract and thus unsuccessful. Therefore, a concrete representation of memory activation was required. An analogy of pathways between two points, with point A being a memory and point B awareness, was used. Joan was asked to imagine a field of tall grass, which she was able to do. She was then asked if walking through the field once was likely to leave a clear path, to which she replied it would not. We also agreed that it would likely take some time to walk though the thick and high field of grass as there was no established path. We then agreed that walking along the same route over and over again would result in a pathway being established and that it would be far quicker and more likely that people would travel between those two points. This was represented visually, with people traveling between these two points. We then replaced the people with memories and thoughts, concluding that once a pathway is established, that those types of thought are more likely to be recognized as they are more likely to appear at point B.

Linking antecedents, thoughts, and feelings

Details given to this point indicate a core focus on the cognitive features of Joan's presentation. These clearly needed to be placed within an overall basic sequence linking thoughts to antecedents and subsequent emotional/physiological experiences. Consistent symbolization and recording of these components was introduced from the outset, such that recorded reference to each step of the ABC process was established early in the process.

Summary

Described here are some core areas of work completed with Joan and methods of intervention as adapted and applied in the main from the established intervention literature for psychosis. This case illustrates a number of intervention methods applied by the authors across a range of clients with features of psychosis. Issues of introspection, conceptual understanding, poor recognition of internal processes, dichotomous thinking, and alternative hypothesis generation all represent core themes explored across adults with IDs and psychosis, with differing levels of ability and understanding presented by respective clients. Adaptation, creativity, and establishing a meaningful dialogue and shared frames of reference with your client remain the keys to successful intervention; after all, cognitive processing (e.g., Bentall, 2003) remains at the core of their presentation, irrespective of their ID classification.

Conclusions

Chadwick *et al.* (1996) described how psychosis in the nonintellectually disabled population was viewed for many years as a condition so complex and daunting that many clinicians did not view the likelihood of successful psychological intervention with any degree of optimism. Despite this pessimism, there is now a significant body of evidence that psychological therapy can be effective for people with psychosis (Rector & Beck, 2001), and it is recommended by government guidelines in the United Kingdom and United States.

In the field of ID, psychosis has also been an area that has, until recently, not been the focus of therapy interventions or research endeavor. There is now evidence available that people with ID and psychosis can do as well as other people with IDs on assessments of skills necessary for CBT (Oathamshaw & Haddock, 2006) and can benefit from CBT approaches adapted from the general population (Barrowcliff, 2007; Haddock *et al.*, 2004; Kirkland, 2005) and applied in nonresearch settings. Given the complex psychological and social problems experienced by this group, we hope the work described in this chapter and recommendations therein will encourage therapists to consider using psychological therapy with people who have IDs and psychosis.

References

Alford, G.S. & Turner, S.M. (1976). Stimulus interference and conditioned inhibition of auditory hallucinations. *Journal of Behavior Therapy and Experimental Psychiatry, 7,* 155–160.

Allen, H.A., Halperin, J. & Friend, R. (1983). Removal and diversion tactics and the control of auditory hallucinations. *Behaviour Research and Therapy, 23,* 601–605.

Barrowcliff, A.L. (2007). Cognitive-behavioural therapy for command hallucinations and intellectual disability: A case study. *Journal of Applied Research in Intellectual Disabilities, 21,* 236–245.

Barrowclough, C., Haddock, G., Tarrier, N., Lewis, S.W., Moring, J., O'Brien, R. *et al.* (2001). Randomized controlled trial of motivational interviewing, cognitive behaviour therapy, and family intervention for patients with comorbid schizophrenia and substance use disorders. *The American Journal of Psychiatry, 158,* 1706–1713.

Beck, A.T. (1952). Successful outpatient psychotherapy with a schizophrenic with a delusion based on borrowed guilt. *Psychiatry, 15,* 305–312.

Bentall, R.P. (1990). *Reconstructing schizophrenia.* London: Routledge.

Bentall, R.P. (2003). *Madness explained: Psychosis and human nature.* London: Penguin.

Bleuler, E. (1911, 1950). *Dementia praecox or the group of schizophrenias.* New York: International Universities Press.

Brown, G.W., Monck, E.M., Carstairs, G.M. & Wing, J.K. (1962). Influence of family life on the course of schizophrenic illness. *British Journal of Preventive & Social Medicine, 16,* 55–68.

Chadwick, P. & Birchwood, M. (1994). The omnipotence of voices: A cognitive approach to auditory hallucinations. *The British Journal of Psychiatry, 164,* 190–201.

Chadwick, P. & Birchwood, M. (1995). The omnipotence of voices II: The Beliefs About Voices Questionnaire (BAVQ). *The British Journal of Psychiatry, 166,* 773–776.

Chadwick, P., Birchwood, M. & Trower, P. (1996). *Cognitive therapy for delusions and paranoia*. Chichester: John Wiley & Sons.

Chadwick, P., Lees, S. & Birchwood, M. (2000). The revised Beliefs About Voices Questionnaire (BAVQ-R). *The British Journal of Psychiatry, 177*, 229–232.

Chadwick, P.D. & Lowe, C.F. (1990). Measurement and modification of delusional beliefs. *Psychological Assessment, 58*(2), 225–232.

Clarke, D. (1999). Functional psychoses in people with mental retardation. In N. Bouras (Ed.) *Psychiatric and behavioural disorders in developmental disabilities and mental retardation*. Cambridge, UK: Cambridge University Press.

Cooper, S.A., Smiley, E., Morrison, J., Williamson, A. & Allan, L. (2007). Mental ill-health in adults with intellectual disabilities: Prevalence and associated factors. *The British Journal of Psychiatry, 190*, 27–35.

Crowley, V., Rose, J., Smith, J., Hobster, K. & Ansell, E. (2008). Psycho-educational groups for people with a dual diagnosis of psychosis and mild intellectual disability. *Journal of Intellectual Disabilities, 12*(1), 25–39.

Dagnan, D. & Chadwick, P. (1997). Cognitive-behaviour therapy for people with learning disabilities: assessment and intervention. In B. Stenfert Kroese, D. Dagnan & K. Loumidis (Eds.) *Cognitive-behaviour therapy for people with learning disabilities*. London: Routledge.

Dagnan, D., Chadwick, P. & Proudfoot, J. (2000). Toward and assessment of suitability of people with mental retardation for cognitive therapy. *Cognitive Therapy and Research, 24*, 627–636.

Derogatis, L.R. (1993). *Brief Symptom Inventory: Administration scoring and procedure manual* (3rd edn). Minneapolis, MN: National Computer Systems.

Dickerson, F.B., Tenhula, W.N. & Green-Paden, L.D. (2005). The token economy for schizophrenia: Review of the literature and recommendations for future research. *Schizophrenia Research, 75*(2–3), 405–416.

Eaton, L.F. & Menolascino, F.M. (1982). Psychiatric disorders in the mentally retarded: Types, problems and challenges. *The American Journal of Psychiatry, 139*, 1297–1303.

Fowler, D., Garety, P. & Kuipers, E. (1995). *Cognitive behaviour therapy for psychosis: Theory and practice*. Chichester: John Wiley & Sons.

Fraser, W. & Nolan, M. (1994). Psychiatric disorders in mental retardation. In N. Bouras (Ed.) *Mental health in mental retardation: Recent advances and practices*. Cambridge, UK: Cambridge University Press.

Garety, P.A., Bebbington, P., Fowler, D., Freeman, D. & Kuipers, E. (2007). Implications for neurobiological research of cognitive models of psychosis: A theoretical paper. *Psychological Medicine, 37*(10), 1377–1391.

Garety, P.A. & Hemsley, D.R. (1997). *Delusions. Investigations into the psychology of delusional reasoning*. Hove: Psychology Press Ltd.

Haddock, G., Barrowclough, C., Shaw, J.J., Dunn, G., Novaco, R.W. & Tarrier, N. (2009). Cognitive-behavioural therapy v. social activity therapy for people with psychosis and a history of violence: Randomised controlled trial. *The British Journal of Psychiatry, 194*(2), 152–157.

Haddock, G., Lobban, F., Hatton, C. & Carson, R. (2004). Cognitive behaviour therapy for psychosis and mild learning disability: A case series. *Clinical Psychology and Psychotherapy, 11*, 282–298.

Haddock, G., McCarron, J., Tarrier, N. & Farragher, E. (1999). Scales to measure dimensions of hallucinations and delusions: The Psychotic Symptom Rating Scales (PSYRATS). *Psychological Medicine, 29*, 879–889.

Haddock, G., Tarrier, N., Spaulding, W., Yusupoff, L., Kinney, C. & McCarthy, E. (1998). Individual cognitive-behaviour therapy in the treatment of hallucinations and delusions: A review. *Clinical Psychology Review, 18*, 821–838.

Hare, D.J. (2002). Psychotic symptoms in people with learning disabilities. Paper presented at the CBT with People with Learning Disabilities and Mental Health Problems National Network Seminar 2, Lancaster.

Hatton, C., Haddock, G., Taylor, J., Coldwell, J., Crossley, R. & Peckham, N. (2005). The reliability and validity of general psychotic rating scales with people with mild and moderate intellectual disabilities: An empirical investigation. *Journal of Intellectual Disability Research, 49,* 490–500.

Haynes, S.N. & Geddy, P. (1973). Suppression of psychotic hallucinations through time-out. *Behavior Therapy, 4*(1), 123–127.

Hurley, A.D. (1996). The misdiagnosis of hallucinations and delusions in persons with mental retardation: A neurodevelopmental perspective. *Seminars in Clinical Neuropsychiatry, 1,* 122–133.

Jaspers, K. (1963). *General psychopathology* (translated from German by J. Hoenig & M.W. Hamilton). Manchester: Manchester University Press.

Kay, S.R., Fiszbein, A. & Opler, L.A. (1989). The Positive and Negative Syndrome Scale (PANSS) for schizophrenia. *Schizophrenia Bulletin, 13,* 261–276.

Kellett, S., Beail, N., Newman, D.W. & Frankish, P. (2003). Utility of the Brief Symptom Inventory in the assessment of psychological distress. *Journal of Applied Research in Intellectual Disabilities, 16,* 127–134.

Kemp, R., Hayward, P., Applewhaite, G., Everitt, B. & David, A. (1996). Compliance therapy in psychotic patients: Randomised controlled trial. *British Medical Journal, 312,* 345–349.

Kirkland, J. (2005). Cognitive-behaviour therapy for three men with learning disabilities who experience psychosis: How do we make it make sense? *British Journal of Learning Disabilities, 33,* 160–165.

Leggett, J., Hurn, C. & Goodman, W. (1997). Teaching psychological strategies for managing auditory hallucinations. *British Journal of Learning Disabilities, 25,* 158–163.

Lewis, S., Tarrier, N., Haddock, G., Bentall, R., Kinderman, P., Kingdon, D. *et al.* (2002). Randomised controlled trial of cognitive-behavioural therapy in early schizophrenia: Acute-phase outcomes. *The British Journal of Psychiatry. Supplement, 18,* s91–s97.

Margo, A., Hemsley, D.R. & Slade, P.D. (1981). The effects of varying auditory input on schizophrenic hallucinations. *The British Journal of Psychiatry, 139,* 122–127.

Morrison, A., French, P., Walford, L., Lewis, S.W., Kilcommons, A., Green, J. *et al.* (2004). Cognitive therapy for the prevention of psychosis in people at ultra-high risk. *The British Journal of Psychiatry, 185,* 291–297.

Moss, S. (2002). *The mini PAS-ADD interview pack.* Brighton: Pavilion Publishing Ltd in association with the Estia Centre.

Moss, S.C., Goldberg, D., Patel, P., Prosser, H., Ibbotson, B., Simpson, N. *et al.* (1996). The Psychiatric Assessment Schedule for Adults with a Developmental Disability (PAS-ADD). Manchester: Hester Adrian Research Centre, University of Manchester and The Institute of Psychiatry.

Moss, S.C., Prosser, H., Costello, H., Simpson, N. & Patel, P. (1996). PAS-ADD Checklist. Manchester: Hester Adrian Research Centre, University of Manchester and The Institute of Psychiatry.

National Institute for Health and Clinical Excellence (NICE) (2009). Schizophrenia. Core interventions in the treatment and management of schizophrenia in adults in primary and secondary care. NICE clinical guideline 82. National Collaborating Centre for Mental Health. London, UK.

Nelson, H.E., Thrasher, S. & Barnes, T.R.E. (1991). Practical ways of alleviating auditory hallucinations. *British Medical Journal, 302,* 327.

Nydegger, R.V. (1972). The elimination of hallucinatory and delusional behavior by verbal conditioning and assertive training: A case study. *Journal of Behavior Therapy and Experimental Psychiatry, 3*(3), 225–227.

Oathamshaw, S.C. (2007). Delivering cognitive behavioural therapy in community services for people with learning disabilities: Difficulties, dilemmas, confounds. *Advances in Mental Health and Learning Disabilities, 1*(2), 22–25.

Oathamshaw, S.C. & Haddock, G. (2006). Do people with intellectual disabilities and psychosis have the cognitive skills required to undertake cognitive behavioural therapy? *Journal of Applied Research in Intellectual Disabilities, 19*, 35–46.

Pfammatter, M., Junghan, U.M. & Brenner, H.D. (2006). Efficacy of psychological therapy in schizophrenia: Conclusions from meta-analyses. *Schizophrenia Bulletin, 32*, S64–S80.

Pharoah, F.M., Rathbone, J. & Wong, W. (2006). Family intervention for schizophrenia. *Cochrane Database of Systematic Reviews* (4), CD000088.

Pitt, L., Kilbride, M., Nothard, S., Welford, M. & Morrison, T. (2007). Researching recovery form psychosis: A user-led project. *Psychiatric Bulletin, 31*, 55–60.

Rector, N.A. & Beck, A.T. (2001). Cognitive behavioural therapy for schizophrenia: An empirical review. *The Journal of Nervous and Mental Disease, 185*, 278–287.

Reed, J. & Clements, J. (1989). Assessing the understanding of emotional states in a population of adolescents and young adults with mental handicaps. *Journal of Mental Deficiency Research, 33*, 229–233.

Robertson, D. & Murphy, D. (1999). Brain imaging and behaviour. In N. Bouras (Ed.) *Psychiatric and behavioural disorders in developmental disabilities and mental retardation.* Cambridge, UK: Cambridge University Press.

Samaan, M. (1975). Thought-stopping and flooding in a case of hallucinations, obsessions, and homicidal-suicidal behavior. *Journal of Behavior Therapy and Experimental Psychiatry, 6*, 65–67.

Sellwood, W., Barrowclough, C., Tarrier, N., Quinn, J., Mainwaring, J. & Lewis, S. (2001). Needs-based cognitive-behavioural family intervention for carers of patients suffering from schizophrenia: A 12-month follow-up. *Acta Psychiatrica Scandinavica, 104*, 346–355.

Sensky, T., Turkington, D., Kingdon, D., Scott, J.L., Scott, J., Siddle, R. *et al.* (2000). A randomised controlled trial of cognitive-behavioral therapy for persistent symptoms in schizophrenia resistant to medication. *Archives of General Psychiatry, 57*(2), 165–172.

Slade, P.D. & Bentall, R.P. (1988). *Sensory deception: A scientific analysis of hallucinations.* London: Croom Helm.

Stenfert Kroese, B., Cushway, D. & Hubbard, C. (1998). The conceptualisation of dreams by people with intellectual disabilities. *Journal of Applied Research in Intellectual Disabilities, 11*, 146–155.

Stenfert Kroese, B., Dewhurst, D. & Holmes, G. (2001). Diagnosis and drugs: Help or hindrance when people with learning disabilities have psychological problems. *British Journal of Learning Disabilities, 29*, 26–33.

Sturmey, P. & Bertman, J.L. (1994). Validity of the Reiss screen for maladaptive behaviour. *American Journal of Mental Retardation, 99*, 201–206.

Sullivan, H.S. (1962). *Schizophrenia as a human process.* New York: W.W. Norton and Company, Inc.

Tarrier, N., Haddock, G., Barrowclough, C. & Wykes, T. (2002). Are all psychological treatments for psychosis equal? The need for CBT in the treatment of psychosis and not for psychodynamic psychotherapy. *Psychology and Psychotherapy, 75*(4), 365–373.

Tarrier, N., Yusupoff, L., Kinney, C., McCarthy, E., Gledhill, A., Haddock, G. *et al.* (1998). Randomised controlled trial of intensive cognitive behaviour therapy for patients with chronic schizophrenia. *British Medical Journal, 317*, 303–307.

Turner, S.M., Hersen, M. & Bellack, A.S. (1977). Effects of social disruption, stimulus inter-ference, and aversive conditioning on auditory hallucinations. *Behavior Modification, 1*(2), 249–258.

Turner, T.H. (1989). Schizophrenia and mental handicap: An historical review, with implica-tions for further research. *Psychological Medicine, 19*, 301–314.

Vaughn, C.E. & Leff, J.P. (1976). The measurement of expressed emotion in the families of psychiatric patients. *The British Journal of Social and Clinical Psychology, 15*, 157–165.

Wegner, D.M., Schneider, D.J., Carter, S.R. & White, T.L. (1987). Paradoxical effects of thought suppression. *Journal of Personality and Social Psychology, 53*, 5–13.

Wells, A. (1997). *Cognitive therapy of anxiety disorders.* Chichester: John Wiley & Sons.

Whitehouse, R.M., Tudway, J.A., Look, R. & Kroese, B.S. (2006). Adapting individual psychotherapy for adults with intellectual disabilities: A comparative review of the cognitive-behavioural and psychodynamic literature. *Journal of Applied Research in Intel-lectual Disabilities, 19*, 55–65.

Willner, P. (2006). Readiness for cognitive therapy in people with intellectual disabilities. *Journal of Applied Research in Intellectual Disabilities, 19*(1), 5–16.

Chapter 11

Cognitive–Behavioral Treatment for Inappropriate Sexual Behavior in Men with Intellectual Disabilities

Introduction

Several authors have suggested that the prevalence of sex offenders among offenders with intellectual disability (ID) is higher than that in the general criminal population (Cooper, 1995; Day, 1994; Hawk *et al.*, 1993; Walker & McCabe, 1973). In recent review of the literature, Craig and Lindsay (2010) reported on a number of studies suggesting that these findings reporting higher prevalence rates may be an artifact of several study and population biases. People with ID are generally under greater scrutiny from relatives and carers than those in the general population. Men with ID who behave inappropriately, sexually, are more likely to be supervised and detected by significant others than men without ID in ordinary circumstances. As a result, inappropriate sexual behavior in men with ID may be more likely to be reported. Another factor is that inappropriate sexual behavior in men with ID may be the result of lack of knowledge and lack of understanding of the laws of society rather than deviant sexual interest (Hingsburger *et al.*, 1991). Craig and Hutchinson (2005) have also pointed out that when men with ID commit a sexual offense, it is often less sophisticated than similar offenses in mainstream populations, and this correspondingly increases the possibility of detection.

Information on recidivism is similarly difficult to evaluate. Several studies since the early 1960s have reported reoffending rates of around 50 percent in mixed groups of offenders (not exclusively sexual) with ID (e.g., Gibbens & Robertson, 1983; Lund, 1990; Wildenskov, 1962). In one recent study, Gray *et al.* (2007) conducted a two-year follow-up of 145 offenders with ID and 996 offenders without ID, all discharged from independent sector hospitals in the United Kingdom. The ID group had a lower rate of reconviction for violent offenses after two years (4.8 percent) than the non-ID group (11.2 percent). This trend also held true for general offenses (9.7 percent for the ID group vs. 18.7 percent for the non-ID group). While this latter

Psychological Therapies for Adults with Intellectual Disabilities, First Edition.
Edited by John L. Taylor, William R. Lindsay, Richard P. Hastings, and Chris Hatton.
© 2013 John Wiley & Sons, Ltd. Published 2013 by John Wiley & Sons, Ltd.

study is not specifically restricted to sexual offenders, its well-controlled design casts doubt on the hypothesis that offenders with ID have a higher reconviction rate than mainstream offenders. However, all of the research studies agree that there is a significant proportion of men with ID in the sex offender population and that these individuals require treatment and service provision if we are to deal with their risk for future reoffending. Therefore, there is a need to develop and establish effective treatments for inappropriate sexual behavior in men with ID.

Types of Sexual Offending and Inappropriate Sexual Behavior

There have been a small number of reports surveying offenders with ID and suggesting the proportion of this population carrying out different types of sexual offenses. Day (1994) carried out a survey of 47 sex offenders with ID committing a total of 191 sexual offenses. Of these offenses, 55 percent were heterosexual, 26 percent were indecent exposure, and 12 percent were homosexual. He argued that the evidence suggested that sex offenders with ID showed far less specificity in relation to offense type and victim characteristics than their counterparts without ID. Lindsay *et al.* (2006) reviewed 247 offenders with ID referred to a forensic assessment and treatment service. In this cohort, there were 121 sexual offenders of whom 34.8 percent had committed offenses against children, 20.4 percent had committed offenses of indecent exposure, and 57.8 percent had committed offenses against adults including sexual assault, sexual harassment, rape, and attempted rape.

In another fairly large study ($n = 103$), McGrath *et al.* (2007) reported that just over half (53.4 percent) of their sample had a history of committing more than one type of sexual offense. For example, of 10 who had sexually assaulted an adult male, 4 had also assaulted an adult female and 1 had assaulted a male child. In total, 27.2 percent had committed assaults against adult victims, 44.7 percent against child victims, 11.7 percent were incest offenders, and 16.5 percent were noncontact offenders. In a further reasonably large-scale study, Murphy *et al.* (2010) reported on 46 sexual offenders with ID following a one-year treatment program. For 71 percent of these men, the victim was female, and in 60 percent, the victim was a child. Therefore, in these three more recent studies, there is contrasting information on the types of offenses and types of victims with Lindsay *et al.* (2006) reporting a majority of adult victims and McGrath *et al.* (2007) and Murphy *et al.* (2010) reporting a majority of child victims. However, in all studies, there are significant proportions of both types of offense and a significant percentage committing noncontact offenses. Therefore, there is ample research indicating the importance of establishing treatment procedures for men with ID who commit a range of inappropriate sexual behavior.

The Development of Treatment Procedures

Through the 1970s, a number of clinicians presented a series of case studies using behavioral methods to reduce sexual arousal or reorientate sexual preference in men with ID. This followed mainstream work where around 78 percent of studies at the time employed aversion therapy in an attempt to change deviant sexual preference, especially in those interventions for offenders against children (Kelly, 1982). As an example, Rosenthal (1973) described the treatment of a 21-year-old man with mild ID who had committed offenses against children. He was referred for aversion therapy following his third arrest and prior to treatment; the painful nature of the therapy was explained to the client who subsequently discussed it with his lawyer and probation officer. The description of treatment is disturbing with electric shocks being administered after the presentation of images of girls. The duration and intensity of the shocks increased over the treatment period and did result in rapid increases in response latencies until the client spontaneously reported an inability to obtain deviant sexual images or sexual impulses while being presented with the stimulus items. Periodic follow-ups over 32 months suggested that treatment effects maintained with the absence of pedophilic images and sexual arousal to children. While this case study suggested that it is indeed possible to suppress pedophilic images and sexual arousal to them, the disturbing nature of the treatment would, rightly, preclude any consideration in contemporary programs.

Luiselli *et al.* (1977) used a very different approach to eliminate the persistent in-class masturbation of an eight-year-old male with ID. His teachers had noted a high rate of masturbatory behavior that prevented him from engaging in educational activities. Sessions were conducted during schooltime and by his usual teachers. During the first phase of treatment, he was provided with tokens, social praise, and positive feedback for on-task (educational) behavior. However, this failed to reduce the frequency, and an overcorrection procedure (Foxx & Azrin, 1973) was added. This consisted of instructing him to follow each incidence of masturbation by moving his arms to one of four positions (over his head, latterly extended to the front, latterly extended to the side, and folded across his chest). Each position was held for three seconds. Masturbation was completely suppressed after nine days, and this was maintained over a 12-month follow-up period. Cook *et al.* (1978) demonstrated the effectiveness of a milder punishment (lemon juice) for the suppression of public masturbation in a boy with ID. Again, improvements were reasonably quick and behavior was maintained. However, early case studies had a number of obvious drawbacks. On at least one occasion, the aversion therapy was extremely noxious, and although the participant's lawyer and probation officer were made fully aware of treatment procedures (as well as the individual himself), the ethics of such treatments are unacceptable. Additionally, the treatment objectives in these early studies were largely restrictive rather than rehabilitative with no consideration whatever that individuals with ID who have inappropriate sexual behavior may not know how to express sexuality in an appropriate manner.

In contrast to these early reports, and indeed in contrast to reports on most treatment procedures with mainstream sexual offenders, the first significant and influential development in the field of sex offenders with ID was a comprehensive treatment program aimed at improving social functioning, improving sexual awareness and sexual knowledge, extending relationships, improving coping skills, and reducing inappropriate sexuality (Griffiths *et al.*, 1989). These authors took as a starting point the fact that individuals may have restricted social and sexual opportunities that caused them to develop inappropriate choices. They wrote "clearly, the (*previous*) treatment objectives for developmentally delayed individuals who display sexually inappropriate behaviour have been restrictive rather than rehabilitative. Considering that many of the individuals who have displayed inappropriate sexual behaviour may not know how to express sexuality in an appropriate manner, the punishment for inappropriate sexual expression places the individual in a sexual void" (p. 11).

With each client, Griffiths *et al.* developed a multifactorial treatment plan, which was designed to review risky aspects of their environment, increase personal and social skills, and address the issues of sexuality. Specific aspects of training included sex education, social competency training, training in relationships, training in coping skills and personal responsibility, and, where appropriate, intervention for inappropriate sexual preference, which included aversion in imagination and measures to promote appropriate masturbation. Even at this early stage in the development of treatment for offenders with ID, they included protective relapse prevention procedures in their methods. These authors also reported on a series of 30 case studies in which they recorded no reoffending and described a number of successful cases to illustrate their methods.

The Development of Behavioral Methods

Plaud *et al.* (2000) reviewed aversion therapy techniques in masturbatory recondition techniques in some detail. With reference to deviant sexual arousal, aversion therapy links thoughts and behavior with an aversive image or event. This then results in a negative reaction to the deviant sexual stimulus. The aversive stimulus or event may be tactile, olfactory, behavioral, or imagined. The aim is to link the aversive consequence with the offense cycle in order to promote self-regulation and self-restraint skills in a real setting, through the employment of the aversive connotation. Such aversive conditioning in imagination has been termed "covert sensitization" (Cautela, 1970) and was considered one of the first cognitive treatments in that it involved thoughts and covert images rather than behavior.

These exercises can be incorporated into individual or group treatment in a fairly straightforward fashion. Previously (Lindsay, 2004, 2009), I have described case examples that involve the successful use of these techniques. I had thought originally that they might be best used in individual treatment, but latterly, it has been eminently feasible to use them in small group settings as long as the individual being targeted is comfortable with other group members.

Case study: Bill

One example is of a group member who had been convicted of three counts of indecent exposure and public masturbation to adult women and one count of sexual assault. In fact, the latter charge was similar to the three former charges in that he followed the women to a park, sat beside her on a park bench, and, in the process of attempting to expose himself and masturbate, touched her. The contact, which he maintained had been inadvertent, resulted in the sexual assault charge. During one session, the man (we shall call him Bill) reported that he had seen a female while on a bus into town. The female had been passing a public park, and Bill had an urge to alight from the bus and follow her into the park. During a group session with three other men, we constructed the following session in imagination.

Bill was asked to imagine himself getting off the bus rather than staying on it. He imagined getting off at the next stop and going back to where the woman had been. He imagined following behind her as she made her way through the park. By his account during the session, he was able to imagine the path, the grass, and the bushes around him. Surprisingly, he described a small outbuilding as he passed it while following the woman. He then was able to describe features of the woman as he was walking behind her. As he became more comfortable in his description of the scene, he was then told to imagine a park gardener noticing him and remembering him from another incident. Even though the other incident had happened in another park, the gardener worked across different parks and remembered both what he looked like and his name. At that point, other members of the group began to add details that were far more dramatic than I as the therapist could have added. They began to suggest that this gardener had young apprentices who ran over and confronted Bill about his behavior.

At that point, we stopped the covert sensitization exercise and began a role play exercise whereby Bill was in the park following a woman and he was confronted by two other group members who took the roles of the gardening apprentices. This role played exercise resulted in the apprentices deciding they were going to telephone the police. Bill himself became extremely agitated during both the exercise in imagination and the role play scenario. It then occurred to me that his agitation was a result of the fact that he had indeed imagined this previously but when he had thought about the possibility of the incident, he had not inserted any aversive consequences.

We therefore continued the exercise by going back to the point where he was following the woman and the gardener noticed him. Other group members then suggested that the gardener phoned the police who came promptly and began to chase Bill through the park. He was encouraged to imagine himself panicking and running for an exit while police ran after and eventually caught him. Group members then went on to complete the sequence by describing ways in which he would be put into the police car, taken to the police cells, interrogated, and charged with an offense of stalking and sexual harassment. In this way, aversion and imagination of covert sensitization can be inserted easily into an ongoing treatment session while employing group processes to increase the pressure on the individual and increase the realism of the imagined, sensitizing situation. For Bill, this proved a highly effective sensitizing scenario to which we were able to return on future occasions during "booster sessions." Therefore, the procedures of early behavioral interventions have been updated so that they are more suitable for contemporary interventions. Currently, they could never constitute the sole means of progressing a sex offender treatment program, but they can make a useful contribution at specific points.

The Development of Cognitive Treatments

Even from the time of the early comprehensive programs described previously, some cognitive elements were incorporated into treatment processes. Griffiths *et al.* (1989)

employed covert sensitization using images of adverse consequences contingent on sequences of problematic behavior. Haaven *et al.* (1990) employed a more explicit intervention to disrupt the sequence of cognitions that they termed "high-risk thinking." If, for example, a participant were to see children and have thoughts of playing with them, a disruptive thought such as "the police will come" or "kids mean jail" was introduced. Thoughts were labeled according to whether they were maladaptive under the heading "old me" or adaptive, under the heading "new me." Therefore, Haaven *et al.* (1990) were making some early attempts to disrupt cognitive distortions, replacing them with more adaptive thinking that was inconsistent with inappropriate sexual behavior.

In a meta-analysis of sex offender treatments, Hanson *et al.* (2002) reported that "current treatments (any treatment currently offered and cognitive behavioural treatments offered since 1980) were associated with significant reductions in both sexual and general recidivism whereas the older treatments were not" (p. 187). Older treatments were predominantly behavioral, employing techniques already reviewed such as aversion therapy, reorientation of sexual preferences through masturbatory reconditioning, and the promotion of social competence.

Taking into account these previous developments, O'Conner (1996) developed a problem-solving approach for the treatment of sex offenders with ID. Her approach included identifying high-risk thinking and substituting adaptive sequences of cognitions, reviewing the sequence of individual sex offenses and promoting skills to disrupt the chain of events; using simplified covert sensitization, employing consequence training linked to covert sensitization, and developing relapse prevention programs involving continued supervision. Sessions were conducted individually and held weekly. The intervention was continued until each participant achieved his individual intervention goals (the number of sessions was not stated in the report). Thirteen men participated in this problem-solving approach, and the reports of outcomes were somewhat anecdotal. Two participants were charged with a further sexual offense during the intervention and a third made admissions of offending behavior. Four participants required less supervision, nine increased their community access, and five increased their level of community and residential living. Two were living independently in the community. O'Connor concluded that "although some participants were supervised so closely it was difficult for them to offend, others showed a reduction in high risk behaviour and offending while moving freely in the community" (p. 230). This was one of the first reports suggesting that cognitive–behavioral treatment for sex offenders with ID might produce positive outcomes for both the individual and the community.

Lambrick and Glaser (2004) developed the model of Haaven *et al.* (1990) by incorporating a number of social, cognitive, and behavioral aspects into the "old me, new me" approach. Their treatment lasted up to two years and involved the construction of a personal developmental map incorporating behavior, risk factors, cognitions, and emotions in "old me" that might lead to the perpetration of a sexual offense and, by contrast, protective factors in the same personal areas of emotion, cognition, behavior, and risk in a "new me" construction that would lead to a socialized offense free life. Each life map was personalized and developed with the client so that he could have a constant reminder prompting socialized routines. Unfortunately, these authors did not report any outcome results.

Identifying underlying schemas and challenging cognitive distortions

In a series of reports, Lindsay and colleagues (Lindsay, 2009; Lindsay, Marshall *et al.*, 1998; Lindsay, Neilson *et al.*, 1998) reported on a comprehensive treatment involving a program of sessions designed to address the cycle of offending and related cognitive distortions. In these reports, various forms of denial and mitigation of the offense were challenged over treatment periods of up to three years. These authors noted several aspects of treatment that adapted basic principles from mainstream treatment to work with offenders with ID. The first procedure was simplifying the rules of the group and the induction. Most agencies that have programs for sex offenders with ID have a number of rules. Because of the intellectual limitations of the individuals involved, the information given to group members should be as simple as possible. Therefore, induction and group rules were confined to the important aspects of attendance and confidentiality (see Lindsay 2009 for descriptions).

Motivational issues. For sex offenders with ID, it will be the case that very few referrals will show any motivation to address the issues of offending or to change their behavior. Rather, most seek to deny that the problem has occurred at all and avoid discussing or addressing the important issues. Therefore, motivation will be a crucial and constant issue for treatment in any community sex offender treatment service. Lindsay (2009) has described several methods to increase levels of motivation. These include attempts to ensure that legal processes would take their course so that the offender realizes that his behavior was totally unacceptable to society; discussion of news on television and radio about inappropriate sexual behavior and sex offenders with emphasis on the need for group members to change in order to avoid the consequences reported in the newspapers for individual sex offenders; using periods of time that are extremely enjoyable and reinforcing such as taking group members out to lunch after the formal session; and employing group pressure that can be used as a highly motivating factor during sessions. Since motivation is such an important aspect of treatment, facilitators should always be aware of any possible motivating opportunity during the session.

Dealing with cognitive distortions. As has been mentioned, treatments incorporating cognitive–behavioral therapy (CBT) techniques appear more successful in terms of lower recidivism rates than those that do not employ CBT. In fact, there is a long history of sociological research in which investigators have considered the development of denial by various groups of offenders. In an early theory of delinquency, Sykes and Matza (1957) mentioned several types of denial as techniques that "neutralize" the offending act for the offender. Other writers have classified such accounts into excuses and justifications. For example, Kennedy and Grubin (1992) outlined several types of denial exhibited by offenders. They identified four categories – denial that any harm was done to the victim; shifting blame onto the victim; invoking significant others such as spouses as the reason that they behaved in a manner that resulted in a sexual offense; and attributing the action to a temporary aberration in behavior or an aberration in mental state, out of keeping with their normal character. In subsequent years, such cognitive distortions have become central to considerations regarding the cycle of abuse and pathways to sexual offending. Ward *et al.* (1997) reviewed the importance of cognitive distortions, the nature of cognitive distortions, and the way in which they support the sex offending process. Ward and Hudson (1998) made hypotheses about the way in which cognitive distortions might change depending on the pathway to sex offending pursued by each individual offender. Because cognitive distortions and attitudes toward sexuality have become so central both in the consideration of ways in which the offense is perpetrated and in the relapse prevention process, they required to be examined in more detail as part of the treatment process.

Denial of offenses. It is not unusual for sex offenders with ID to deny the fact that an offense took place, even when they have been tried and convicted. For this reason, it is important to document for each offender that the incident has occurred. At the initial stages of treatment, group members should be encouraged to describe the incident, reviewing in detail the various actions that took place. Several weeks of treatment may be necessary to get over these initial aspects of denial. The initial sessions are likely to be typified by evasion, lack of engagement, and lack of acknowledgment of any reason for being in group sessions. In an open group where there are members who have been engaged for two or three years, this process is considerably shortened. Group members who have been through these procedures will be both confrontational and supportive with statements such as "we have all been through and it is better when it is over with" and "you will have to speak about it anyway so you might as well get it over with." Despite the fact that group members will continue to be reluctant, embarrassed, and angry about engaging with the process, it is important to establish the disclosure accounts as an acceptance that an offense has taken place warranting group membership and treatment.

Denial of intent to offend. In some cases, the offender will accept that an incident has taken place but continue to maintain that his intent was misunderstood as a sexual offense. As an example, one sex offender against children used to make minor repairs on their bikes. He accepted that he touched the children inappropriately but maintained that this was when his hand slipped as he was repairing the bicycles. He then maintained that his actions had been misunderstood as sexually motivated.

Mitigation of responsibility. It is fairly common for sex offenders to deny the extent of their own responsibility for the offense. They are likely to assert that the victims encouraged them, that the victims are lying about the extent of the behavior, and that the victims are to blame because they did not need to respond to the perpetrator's behavior in the way they did. The same is true for offenders with ID, and this is one of the most important issues during treatment. Any substantive work on this set of cognitions can only take place once the participant has accepted that the focus of the session is on the sex offense or inappropriate sexual behavior that has taken place. Many of the men seen for sex offender treatment will argue that there are mitigating circumstances and many will invoke the victim's behavior as being responsible for the incident. Group members may further argue that because the victim responded to the incident in a certain way, they were encouraged to repeat the behavior. These cognitions indicate complicity on the part of the victims in that they enjoyed the incident, that they pretended to be shocked in cases of indecent exposure, that they are sexually stimulated by the incident, or that it afforded them a degree of comfort or even nurturance. All of these cognitions move some of the responsibility onto the behavior of the victim and require to be challenged repeatedly throughout treatment.

Minimization of harm caused. Related to denial of responsibility is a degree of denial that any harm was done to the victim. If the offender argues that the victim's behavior was, to some extent, responsible for the incident, then it follows that in some instances, the victim was expecting or encouraging the sexual behavior and so would not be subsequently surprised or harmed. The offender may accept that the incident took place and that he was to some extent responsible but deny that any harm was done to the victim. In these cases, group members may argue that the lack of protest from the victim is an indication of both mutuality of the sexual contact and the lack of harm done.

Denial of normal state. In a review of denial, Kennedy and Grubin (1992) stated that one of the most common forms of denial was that the man accepted the offense occurred but said he had a temporary aberration of mental state. On this basis, he argued that this behavior was not typical because he had been in a state of depression, anxiety, or inebriation. In the case of sex offenders with ID, a minority have mentioned intoxication through alcohol or drugs. The individual may then go on to argue that there is no requirement for treatment or group attendance because he will never use alcohol or substances to that degree again.

Example of a group session which challenges cognitions

In this book, there have been a number of chapters in which the Socratic process has been described. This example illustrates the way in which the process can be used in a group setting in order to challenge cognitive distortions regarding individual victims. In this case, the targeted group member is a man who has been convicted of sexual assault against an 11-year-old girl. The exercise is designed to elicit his cognitions regarding the sexuality of 11-year-old girls and subsequently, if necessary, to challenge any distortions he may hold about their thoughts and attitudes toward sex. In this extract, the therapist is T, the targeted group member A, and the other group members are B, C, and D.

The group is looking at a picture of a man walking into a park with a young teenage girl:

T: *What's happening in this picture?*
D: *That's a Dad taking a girl into a park, maybe they are going for a walk.*
T: *Anybody got any other ideas?*
A: *No, he is not old enough to be her dad, he is only about 25 and she's too old.*
T: *How old is she?*
A: *I think she is about 12.*
B: *Yes she is 11 or 12 or maybe 10.*
T: *Ok, so we have had three suggestions that she is 10, 11 or 12. Why don't we just take the middle one? Let's say she is 11.*

B: *I think she is probably 11 and he's 25.*
T: *So why is he taking her into the park?*
D: *I think he is going to try and have sex with her.*
B: *Yes, he is going to have sex with her.*

This conclusion may seem astonishing to those individuals not familiar with sex offender treatment groups. It should be remembered that the demand characteristics of a group are that we talk about sexual offenses. The context of the group is that each man is attending because he has committed a sexual offense. During every group session, sexual offenses are discussed and analyzed, and conclusions are drawn. Therefore, it is quite usual for men to make a suggestion about a completely neutral picture that would suggest some sexual contact between the characters in the picture:

T: *Ok, so what is she thinking when she goes into the park with him?*
A: *An 11 year old would want to find out about sex, their school teacher tells them at school.*
T: *So is this 11 year old thinking about sex and wants to find out about it?*
A: *Probably.*
T: *Do you think she is leading him on then?*
A: *Older girls can sometimes lead men on and if she's getting sex education she would be wanting to find out.*
T: *So if girls get sex education at 11, do they want to find out about sex and find men to find out?*
A: *Well if she gets sex education at school she will.*
T: *So they lead men to find out about sex what do they want men to do?*
A: *Men touch the wee girls and that.*
T: *What do the wee girls do?*
A: *Well they're frightened to tell their parents but they'd be too scared.*
B: *She wouldn't understand, she's too young.*
C: *He will get her in a quiet place and grab her and then push her.*
T: *This is what you did isn't it A? You took the girls into the park and had sex with them so were these girls leading you on?*
A: *Yes.*

As can be seen, the therapist has moved from a hypothetical vignette to employing it as an example of a similar incident to that perpetrated by A. This is a common technique – to draw parallels between cognitions elicited to the vignette and personal cognitions held by group members:

T: *And this girl is leading this man on?*
A: *Yes, because she wants to find out about sex education.*
C: *No she's not, 11 year -old girls are not going to want to have sex with an old man.*
T: *What do you think A?*
A: *I think I'm getting confused.*
T: *What you said to me was, 11 year old girls get sex education at school, and they want to find out about sex so they lead men on to find out about sex, is that right?*
A: *Yes. That's right, that's what they do.*
T: *Are you confused about that or is it ok?*
A: *It's ok. I'm not confused.*

Here, the therapist is clarifying once again the cognitions expressed by A. It should be noted that throughout all of these examples, the therapist uses a supportive, even tone of voice. This is especially so if group members become agitated or annoyed by the process:

T:	*So the man takes her into the park and touches her. What was it you said C? He pushes her and grabs her?*
C:	*Yes that's what I said he does; that is what he is going to do.*
T:	*So the man touched her and who's to blame then? Do you think the girl is partly to blame or do you think the man is to blame?*
A:	*It could be. But the man is partly to blame.*
T:	*Why?*
A:	*Because he touched her.*
T:	*So if the girl is thinking about sex because of sex education, what's the man thinking about?*
C:	*He's thinking about raping her.*
T:	*What does rape mean?*
GROUP:	*Forcing someone to have sex.*
T:	*What does rape mean A?*
A:	*Forcing them to have sex.*
T:	*What would the man do if he was doing that?*
A:	*You hold them down and the girl will be frightened, or the woman will be frightened.*
T:	*Right, she'll be scared. So what do you think he's thinking about?*
C:	*I don't know, he'll get on top of her.*
B:	*Men are stronger than women.*
T:	*Surely the woman can shake the man off if she shouts and struggles?*

Here, the therapist is provoking group members into expressing a cognitive distortion that if women do not struggle, they are complicit in a sexual assault:

C:	*No, men have got strong muscles and they can hold the women.*
T:	*Could this man hold this girl?*
A:	*Yes he could definitely hold this girl. No problem.*
T:	*So if the man is thinking about forcing her to have sex, how is he feeling inside himself?*
C:	*Sexy.*
T:	*How do you think he is feeling inside, A?*
A:	*Sexy feelings.*
T:	*How strong does that sexy feeling get?*
A:	*It comes and goes.*
T:	*Think back to when you were in the park A. How strong was your sexy feeling?*
A:	*I don't know.*

Again, the therapist is relating the general principle that offenders act illegally on sexual feelings to one specific case:

T:	*Try and think, how strong was that feeling?*
C:	*Strong enough to attack her.*
T:	*What do you think about what C says? Was it strong enough to attack her? That's quite strong.*
A:	*Well I was stronger than her.*

A is clearly deflecting the question to an issue of general strength rather than the strength of sexual feeling. The therapist will focus the exchange on sexual feelings:

T: *So could this girl get away if she wanted to? (Pointing to the picture).*
A: *No she couldn't get away coz he's far too strong. And then he would rape her.*
T: *So that's a really strong feeling isn't it? Do you think an 11 year old girl knows how strong a man feels when he gets sexy?*
B: *No she wouldn't understand. She wouldn't have a clue.*
T: *What do you think A? Do you think she knows how strong this man feels?*
A: *No because she's just young.*
C: *She wouldn't know, she wouldn't know a thing about it.*
T: *You said she wouldn't understand, what do you mean by that?*
C: *She wouldn't understand what's going on coz she's only 11.*
T: *What wouldn't she understand? I think you're right in what you say just explain it a bit more.*

Notice that the therapist has made it clear that the Socratic method is, in this case, supportive rather than challenging. He has noted that the group member has expressed a socialized cognition while asking for further information:

C: *What you want to do, what he wants to do to her, like doing sexy things. She wouldn't understand.*
T: *Now what do you think A?*
A: *What?*
T: *Say it again C.*
C: *She won't understand what he is doing cause she's only 11.*
T: *What do you think A?*

Here, the therapist is using information from one participant to challenge another, thus invoking group pressure rather than expressing an opinion of his or her own:

A: *No she doesn't understand.*
T: *Does she understand that a man would feel strong enough to push her to the ground or not?*
A: *No she wouldn't understand that. Not if she's only 11.*
C: *She'll only be in primary seven.*
T: *So you said an 11 year old can't understand how strong a man can feel and doesn't know what sex is. Does she know how strong this man is?*
C: *She'll know a wee bit, from sex education, she'll not know about a man going to attack her.*
T: *Does that tell you how strong a man feels and how he can attack you when you get sex education?*
A: *No it doesn't.*
T: *So would an 11 year old girl understand any of that?*
A: *No.*
T: *So, if a man thinks an 11 year old girl is leading him on is the 11 year old wanting a man to attack her?*
A: *No, just to be friends, she just wants to be friends.*

Here A has expressed a more socialized cognition in response to the extended Socratic process. The therapist now emphasizes this socialized cognition:

T: *So if an 11 year old went into a park with a man what will she be wanting?*
A: *I've just told you, she's just wanting to be friends.*
T: *But you said at the beginning that an 11 year old wants to find out about sex and so she wants to lead the man on.*

The therapist attempts to set up a degree of cognitive dissonance between the two cognitions as expressed by A. He now uses the socialized cognition to challenge the cognitive distortion expressed previously by the same group member:

A: *You're twisting it.*
T: *No, I'm not twisting it I'm just trying to find out what you think about 11 year old girls.*
B: *He's just trying to find out about your ideas.*
A: *I'm not focussing much, you're getting me confused and I'm getting tired.*

A has indicated that he wishes, understandably, to disengage from this challenging process and the cognitive dissonance that the therapist has fashioned:

T: *What is it you were charged with?*
A: *Sexual assault.*
T: *And what age was the person you assaulted?*
A: *11.*
T: *So do you think it's important to find out about what you think about 11 year old girls?*
A: *(getting annoyed) It's not going to help me to get me all confused is it? It's not going to help me when I don't understand you.*
T: *You said an 11 year old girl doesn't understand what a man feels. Is that right?*
A: *I think the school teachers can speak about sex and they want to try it. I think that's what it could be.*
T: *So you think it might be the school's fault?*
A: *Yes. The school's fault and the girl's. Teaching them about sexual.*
B & C: *They're not teaching them about sexual they are teaching them about babies. How babies grow. They don't speak about that at school, it's not that sex thing, it's just about babies.*
A: *Well I don't know about that, I think it could be the school and I think that girl doesn't know about sex but that girl who took me to the park knew about sex.*

It can be seen here that A is not going to change his cognitions easily. However, the purpose of the exercise is to undermine the certainty with which certain cognitive distortions are held. It is highly unlikely that a set cognitive belief system underpinning self-image and self-concept is going to be changed in a single session or even a series of sessions. Rather, this particular extract illustrates the way in which cognitive distortions can begin to be questioned through the Socratic process and through the group members own logic. This logic is clearly supported by other group members who both challenge the antisocial attitudes supporting inappropriate sexual behavior and support the socialized attitudes that would prevent further sexual assault. In this case, A is beginning to question his own attitudes. The fact that he becomes annoyed, irritated, or feigns tiredness and disengagement from the group is, again, quite understandable.

It is only to be expected that when one's self-concept and beliefs are being undermined that one begins to defend them in a fairly straightforward manner. It is likely that we all use a range of fundamental beliefs to sustain self-concept in the face of our less desirable characteristics. If, for any of us, these were to be questioned or challenged, it is likely that we would become disturbed or disengaged in some manner. Therefore, it is to be expected that when a therapist begins to challenge a sex offender's world view, a view that maintains his self-image and self-concept, then he is likely to become distressed. This may take the form of aggression or disengagement and, paradoxically, should be viewed as an indication of treatment progress. It is likely that other group members will support the individual with understanding remarks such as "I got angry when I had to talk about my offenses" or "everybody gets upset when they talk about what they did." In this way, group members not only assist in challenging cognitions and underlying assumptions that an individual may have, they also subsequently support the individual when they become distressed and when, in fact, these challenges begin to take effect.

Outcomes for Treatment of Sex Offenders with IDs

There have been a number of case studies and uncontrolled small group studies evaluating treatment of sex offenders with ID. Rose *et al.* (2002) reported on the outcome of a six-month treatment program with six individuals who had committed inappropriate sexual behavior. The treatment program was cognitive–behavioral in nature, and they recorded improvements in cognitive distortions with no reoffending after one year. However, they also noted that all participants were under supervision during the follow-up period, and this is a practical difficulty that has beset such evaluations of sex offender treatment. Craig *et al.* (2006) conducted a similar evaluation with six sex offenders with ID. They conducted a seven-month treatment program incorporating sex education and CBT, reviewing the offense cycle, and promoting relapse prevention but found no significant improvements on any measures including the assessment of sexual knowledge. In a follow-up period of 12 months, they reported no further incident of sexual offending but also noted that all participants received 24-hour supervision. Where individuals are continually supervised in the community, they presumably have little opportunity to engage in any inappropriate sexual behavior including sexual offending. Therefore, the value of outcome data in these studies is limited.

In a series of case studies by Lindsay and colleagues (Lindsay, Marshall *et al.*, 1998; Lindsay, Neilson *et al.*, 1998), treatment was developed on the basis of interventions for cognitive distortions and skills teaching. They assessed improvements in cognitions using an early version of the Questionnaire on Attitudes Consistent with Sexual Offences (QACSO; Lindsay *et al.*, 2007). They also reported follow-up periods of four to seven years, which at the time, was an extensive follow-up period. Taken together, the studies by Lindsay and colleagues reported on 17 sex offenders with ID all of whom had free access to the community during the follow-up period. They reported one documented incident of reoffending and one case in which they suspected that inappropriate sexual behavior had once again taken place, although there was no documented evidence of it.

There have been a number of comparison studies where the researchers have taken advantage of already existing groupings. In these comparisons of convenience, the control condition is always less than the optimum. One of the first was by Lindsay and Smith (1998) when they compared seven individuals who had been in treatment for two or more years with another group of seven who had been in treatment for less than one year. The comparison was predicated on probation sentences delivered by the court. Those individuals who had been in treatment for less than a year showed significantly poorer progress and were more likely to reoffend than those treated for two years. These authors concluded that shorter treatment periods may be of limited value for this client group. Keeling *et al.* (2006) compared 11 "special needs" offenders and 11 mainstream offenders matched on level of risk, victim sex, offense type, and age. All participants were treated in prison; all were released from prison into the community, and the average time since release was 16 months. There were no further recorded convictions for sex offending for any of the "special needs" participants. The authors noted a number of limitations including the fact that "special needs" was not synonymous with ID, and as a result, they were unable to verify the intellectual differences between mainstream and special needs populations. Special needs of participants included significant numeracy and literacy deficits and one individual with brain damage.

Two uncontrolled treatment studies demonstrated the important effects of prolonged CBT, at least 12 months' treatment, on cognitive distortions supporting inappropriate sexual behavior. Both assessed victim empathy and cognitive distortions, and both found very significant treatment gains. Craig *et al.* (2012) found that of 14 participants, none had reoffended after 6–12 months' follow-up, while in Rose *et al.* (2012), of 12 participants followed up for 18 months, only one reoffended. One important point in both studies was that participants were living relatively unsupervised in the community and so could have committed an incident at any time. A further study on the effects of treatment on sex offender's progress was conducted by Michie and Lindsay (2012) when they evaluated a module to promote victim empathy in a treatment and control group. The module lasted for six sessions and the treatment group showed significant improvements over the control group, and these gains lasted at three months' follow-up.

Lindsay *et al.* (2011) conducted a comparison between 15 men who had committed sexual offenses against adults and another 15 who had committed sexual offenses against children. All were treated for 36 months, repeated measures were taken on the QACSO, and records on reoffending were kept for all individuals. Differences in cognitive distortions between the two groups at baseline reflected their offenses (against children and adults), and these ceased to exist as treatment progressed. By the end of the process, both groups endorsed cognitive distortions on the QACSO at a rate consistent with nonoffending and nonsexually offending males. The trends, although showing some variations, were close to linear with large effect sizes suggesting that treatment effects continued throughout the 36-month period, reinforcing the need for lengthy periods of sex offender treatment. The follow-up data for offending again showed no differences between the groups. All individuals were followed up for at least six years, and of the 30 participants, 7 committed another incident with 3 reoffenders in one group and 4 in the other. Taken together, this represented a reoffending rate of 23.3 percent, which was consistent with rates reported in other studies.

There have been three fairly large-scale reports on the outcome of treatment and management systems for sex offenders with ID. Following a program of total deinstitutionalization in Vermont, USA, McGrath *et al.* (2007) reviewed the treatment and management regimes for 103 adult sex offenders with ID. Social and daily living skills were taught to participants, they were encouraged to interact in the community, and there were treatments to promote skills managing risk. In an 11-year follow-up period, with an average of 5.8 years' follow-up, they reported 10.7 percent reoffending. The 11 individuals who reoffended committed 20 new sexual offenses. As a comparison, they reported 195 treated and untreated adult male sexual offenders without ID who had been followed up for an average period of 5.72 years. These individuals had had prison sentences, and 23.1 percent were charged with a new sexual offense at some point in the follow-up period. In a further comparison, they reported 122 treated and untreated male sex offenders who had received probation orders and in a follow-up of 5.24 years, 6.5 percent were charged with a new sexual offense. They also reported a considerable amount of harm reduction in that 83 percent of the participants were classified as contact sexual offenders while only 45 percent of the reoffenses were contact offenses. The rest were typified by exhibitionism and public masturbation. As with other studies, one of the difficulties in the sex offenders with ID cohort was that 62.1 percent had received 24-hour supervision, which presumably limited their access to potential victims.

Murphy *et al.* (2010) conducted a treatment study on 46 sex offenders with ID who were living in community settings. Treatment groups ran over a period of one year and assessments included several attitudinal measures. They found that sexual knowledge, victim empathy, and cognitive distortions improved significantly following treatment but that only improvements in sexual knowledge and reduced cognitive distortions maintained at six months' follow-up. They also reported that 8.7 percent of their sample reoffended after a one-year treatment program. Lindsay *et al.* (2006) published a similarly comprehensive report. The sample in their community forensic ID service consisted of 247 consecutive referrals, of whom 121 were referred for sexual offending or inappropriate sexual behavior, 105 were referred for other types of offending such as assault or alcohol-related offenses, and 21 were women, of whom 5 were referred for sexual offenses. Perhaps because the follow-up period was 13 years, reoffending rates were higher at 23.9 percent for the sex offender cohort in comparison with the 10.7 percent reoffending reported by McGrath *et al.* (2007). However, it should be noted that in the Lindsay *et al.* (2006) study, most participants had full access to the community and were not supervised. The authors also reported that the sex offender cohort had a lower reoffending rate than the 59 percent reoffending recorded in other types of male offenders. These authors also recorded the number of incidents perpetrated by the participants over the follow-up period. This was possible because the study was conducted in a circumscribed region were incidents were gathered routinely. Six monthly case reviews were held on each client for as long as any agent dealing with the client wished them to continue.

They found that, for reoffenders only, there was a significant reduction in the number of offenses committed when comparing figures from two years prior to referral up to 12 years after referral. For the sex offender cohort, 23.9 percent of the individuals who had recidivated committed 235 sexual offenses prior to referral and 68 after referral. This represented around 70 percent reduction in the number of incidents and a significant amount of harm reduction in those individuals who did commit further offenses.

Conclusions

This chapter has reviewed in detail the way in which CBT has been revised and adapted to meet the needs of sex offenders with ID. These methods have been specifically tuned to address cognitive distortions held by sex offenders. These attitudes support denial of an offense, denial of harm to victims, mitigation of responsibility, denial of a normal state, and denial of any intent to offend. A number of methods have been developed including problem-solving activities, sex education, and specific CBT techniques. The chapter illustrates the way in which these techniques can be employed with examples of the way in which group processes can be brought to bear in order to challenge and ultimately alter cognitive distortions and underlying assumptions about sexuality and victims.

A number of studies have been published, suggesting the effectiveness of these approaches. There are several reports of case illustrations in which treatment has been successful and follow-up periods have been significant up to seven years. There have also been a number of comparisons of convenience including comparisons on length of treatment, comparisons between special needs offenders and mainstream sexual offenders, comparisons of offenders with ID and mainstream sex offenders, and comparisons of different types of sexual offender (offenders against women and offenders against children). In all cases, the comparisons have demonstrated the effectiveness of treatment and have also shown that treatment is at least as effective on sex offenders with ID as it is with other client groups. Longer periods of treatment also appeared to be more effective than shorter periods. Three large cohort studies have found that effective treatment and management both reduced offending and produced significant amounts of harm reduction over follow-up periods of up to 13 years.

References

Cautela, J.R. (1970). Covert reinforcement. *Behavior Therapy, 1,* 33–50.

Cook, J.W., Altman, K., Shaw, J. & Blaylock, M. (1978). Use of contingent lemon juice to eliminate public masturbation by a severely retarded boy. *Behaviour Research and Therapy, 18,* 131–134.

Cooper, A.J. (1995). Review of the role of two anti-libidinal drugs in the treatment of sex offenders with mental retardation. *Mental Retardation, 33,* 42–48.

Craig, L.A. & Hutchinson, R. (2005). Sexual offenders with learning disabilities: Risk, recidivism and treatment. *Journal of Sexual Aggression, 11*(3), 289–304.

Craig, L.A. & Lindsay, W.R. (2010). Sexual offenders with intellectual disabilities: Characteristics and prevalence. In L.A. Craig, W.R. Lindsay & K.D. Browne (Eds.) *Assessment and treatment of sex offenders with intellectual disabilities: A handbook* (Chapter 2, pp.13–36). Chichester: Wiley-Blackwell.

Craig, L.A., Stringer, I. & Moss, T. (2006). Treating sexual offenders with learning disabilities in the community. *International Journal of Offender Therapy and Comparative Criminology*, *50*, 111–122.

Craig, L.A., Stringer, I. & Sanders, C.E. (2012). Treating sexual offenders with intellectual limitations in the community. *The British Journal of Forensic Practice*, *14*(1), 5–20.

Day, K. (1994). Male mentally handicapped sex offenders. *The British Journal of Psychiatry*, *165*, 630–639.

Foxx, R.M. & Azrin, N.H. (1973). The elimination of autistic self stimulatory behaviour by overcorrection. *Journal of Applied Behavior Analysis*, *6*, 1–14.

Gibbens, T.C. & Robertson, G. (1983). A survey of the criminal careers of restriction order patients. *The British Journal of Psychiatry*, *143*, 370–375.

Gray, N.S., Fitzgerald, S., Taylor, J., MacCulloch, M.J. & Snowden, R.J. (2007). Predicting future reconviction in offenders with intellectual disabilities: The predictive efficacy of VRAG, PCL-SV and the HCR-20. *Psychological Assessment*, *19*, 474–479.

Griffiths, D.M., Quinsey, V.L. & Hingsburger, D. (1989). *Changing inappropriate sexual behaviour: A community based approach for persons with developmental disabilities*. Baltimore, MD: Paul Brooks Publishing.

Haaven, J., Little, R. & Petre-Miller, D. (1990). *Treating intellectually disabled sex offenders: A model residential programme*. Orwell, VT: Safer Society Press.

Hanson, R.K., Gordon, A., Harris, A.J.R., Marques, J.K., Murphy, W., Quinsey, V.L. *et al.* (2002). First report of the collaborative outcome data project on the effectiveness of psychological treatment for sex offenders. *Sexual Abuse: A Journal of Research and Treatment*, *14*, 169–194.

Hawk, G.L., Rosenfeld, B.D. & Warren, J.I. (1993). Prevalence of sex offences among mentally retarded criminal offenders. *Hospital and Community Psychiatry*, *44*, 784–786.

Hingsburger, D., Griffiths, D. & Quinsey, V. (1991). Detecting counterfeit deviance: Differentiating sexual deviance from sexual inappropriateness. *Habilitative Mental Health Newsletter*, *10*, 51–54.

Keeling, J.A., Rose, J.L. & Beech, A.R. (2006). A comparison of the application of the self-regulation model of the relapse process for mainstream and special needs offenders. *Sexual Abuse: A Journal of Research and Treatment*, *18*, 373–382.

Kelly, R.J. (1982). Behavioral reorientation of pedophiliacs: Can it be done? *Clinical Psychology Review*, *2*, 387–408.

Kennedy, H.G. & Grubin, D.H. (1992). Patterns of denial in sex offenders. *Psychological Medicine*, *22*, 191–196.

Lambrick, F. & Glaser, W. (2004). Sex offenders with an intellectual disability. *Sexual Abuse: A Journal of Research and Treatment*, *16*, 381–392.

Lindsay, W.R. (2004). Sex offenders: Conceptualisation of the issues, services, treatment and management. In W.R. Lindsay, J.L. Taylor & P. Sturmey (Eds.) *Offenders with developmental disabilities* (pp.163–186). Chichester: John Wiley.

Lindsay, W.R. (2009). *The treatment of sex offenders with developmental disabilities: A practice workbook*. Chichester: Wiley-Blackwell.

Lindsay, W.R., Marshall, I., Neilson, C.Q., Quinn, K. & Smith, A.H.W. (1998). The treatment of men with a learning disability convicted of exhibitionism. *Research in Developmental Disabilities*, *19*, 295–316.

Lindsay, W.R., Michie, A.M., Steptoe, L., Moore, F. & Haut, F. (2011). Comparing offenders against women and offenders against children on treatment outcome in offenders with intellectual disability. *Journal of Applied Research in Intellectual Disabilities, 24*(4), 361–369.

Lindsay, W.R., Neilson, C.Q., Morrison, F. & Smith, A.H.W. (1998). The treatment of six men with a learning disability convicted of sex offences with children. *The British Journal of Clinical Psychology, 37,* 83–98.

Lindsay, W.R. & Smith, A.H.W. (1998). Responses to treatment for sex offenders with intellectual disability: A comparison of men with 1 and 2 year probation sentences. *Journal of Intellectual Disability Research, 42,* 346–353.

Lindsay, W.R., Steele, L., Smith, A.H.W., Quinn, K. & Allan, R. (2006). A community forensic intellectual disability service: Twelve year follow-up of referrals, analysis of referral patterns and assessment of harm reduction. *Legal and Criminological Psychology, 11,* 113–130.

Lindsay, W.R., Whitefield, E. & Carson, D. (2007). An assessment for attitudes consistent with sexual offending for use with offenders with intellectual disability. *Legal and Criminological Psychology, 12,* 55–68.

Luiselli, J.H., Helfen, C.S., Pemberton, B. & Reisman, J. (1977). The elimination of a child's in-class masturbation by overcorrection and reinforcement. *Journal of Behavior Therapy and Experimental Psychiatry, 8,* 201–204.

Lund, J. (1990). Mentally retarded criminal offenders in Denmark. *The British Journal of Psychiatry, 156,* 726–731.

McGrath, R.J., Livingston, J.A. & Falk, G. (2007). Community management of sex offenders with intellectual disability: Characteristics, services and outcome of a statewide programme. *Journal of Intellectual & Developmental Disability, 45,* 391–398.

Michie, A.M. & Lindsay, W.R. (2012). A treatment component designed to enhance empathy in sex offenders with an intellectual disability. *British Journal of Forensic Practice, 14*(1), 40–48.

Murphy, G.H., Sinclair, N., Hays, S.J., Heaton, K., Powell, S., Langdon, P. *et al.* (2010). Effectiveness of group cognitive-behavioural treatment for men with intellectual disabilities at risk of sexual offending. *Journal of Applied Research in Intellectual Disabilities, 6,* 537–551.

O'Conner, W. (1996). A problem solving intervention for sex offenders with intellectual disability. *Journal of Intellectual & Developmental Disability, 21,* 219–235.

Plaud, J.J., Plaud, D.M., Colstoe, P.D. & Orvedal, L. (2000). Behavioural treatment of sexually offending behaviour. *Mental Health Aspects of Developmental Disabilities, 3,* 54–61.

Rose, J., Jenkins, R., O'Conner, C., Jones, C. & Felce, D. (2002). A group treatment for men with intellectual disabilities who sexually offend or abuse. *Journal of Applied Research in Intellectual Disabilities, 15,* 138–150.

Rose, J., Rose, D., Hawkins, C. & Anderson, C. (2012). A sex offender treatment group for men with intellectual disabilities in a community setting. *British Journal of Forensic Practice, 14*(1), 21–28.

Rosenthal, T.H. (1973). Response contingent versus fixed punishment in aversion conditioning of pedophilia: A case study. *The Journal of Nervous and Mental Disease, 156,* 440–443.

Sykes, G.M. & Matza, D. (1957). Techniques of neutralisation: A theory of delinquency. *American Sociological Review, 22,* 67–69.

Walker, N. & McCabe, S. (1973). *Crime and insanity in England.* Edinburgh: University Press.

Ward, T. & Hudson, S.M. (1998). A model of the relapse process in sexual offenders. *Journal of Interpersonal Violence, 13,* 700–725.

Ward, T., Hudson, S.M., Johnston, L. & Marshall, W.L. (1997). Cognitive distortions in sex offenders: An integrative review. *Clinical Psychology Review, 17,* 479–507.

Wildenskov, H.O.T. (1962). A long term follow-up of subnormals originally exhibiting severe behaviour disorders or criminality. *Proceedings of the London Conference on the Scientific Study of Mental Deficiency* (pp. 217–222). London: May & Baker.

Chapter 12

Developing Psychotherapeutic Interventions for People with Autism Spectrum Disorders

Dougal Julian Hare

Introduction

The inclusion of a chapter on autism spectrum disorder (ASD) in a book examining psychotherapeutic work with people with intellectual disabilities may at first sight seem rather out of place, given that ASD is not necessarily synonymous with intellectual disabilities, and some people with ASD, those diagnosed with Asperger's syndrome or so-called high-functioning autism, are by definition not intellectually disabled in the generally understood sense (i.e., globally impaired cognitive functioning as indicated by an IQ score of less than 70). However, people with the forms of developmental disorders that are encompassed by what is now termed the autism spectrum (Wing, 1996) share many characteristics with other developmental disorders that involve intellectual disability, and, on a practical level, the clinical skills necessary for working with people with ASD, including Asperger's syndrome are more akin to those required when working with people with intellectual disabilities. Moreover, adults with ASD can fall between intellectual disability services on the one hand and mental health services on the other, with their psychological and emotional needs going unmet and unrecognized, often with serious consequences (Barnard *et al.*, 2001). Thus, the provision of appropriate individual therapeutic work is but one part of the appropriate response to meeting these needs, but it is an important one that presents many specific challenges for therapists. It is not the author's intention to provide an account of cognitive–behavioral therapy (CBT) per se nor to present any form of manualized therapy for people with ASD, but rather to discuss some of the issues that frequently arise in therapeutic work with people with ASD, including those who are not intellectually disabled. In order to do this, it is first necessary to understand both the nature of the condition itself and the difficulties associated with it.

Psychological Therapies for Adults with Intellectual Disabilities, First Edition.
Edited by John L. Taylor, William R. Lindsay, Richard P. Hastings, and Chris Hatton.
© 2013 John Wiley & Sons, Ltd. Published 2013 by John Wiley & Sons, Ltd.

Definition of ASDs

Autism was first defined as a developmental disorder, as opposed to the description of a psychological state, in the mid-1940s, with the term *Asperger's syndrome* being later used to describe people with ASD who are not intellectually disabled (Wing, 1981). It is important to note that both *semantic–pragmatic disorder*, as characterized by poor conversational skills and inappropriate language usage (e.g., endless questioning and stereotypical utterances) but normal articulation and syntax, and *nonverbal learning disability*, as characterized by deficits in social functioning, communication, and interaction are probably but partial descriptions of Asperger's syndrome (Volkmar & Klin, 1998). Differentiation of subgroups within the broad *autism spectrum* is still ongoing, with the recent emergence of multiple and complex developmental disorder (Sturm *et al.*, 2004), a syndrome characterized by distinct affective problems in childhood with apparently psychotic features in adulthood. Empirical and clinical studies of multiple and complex developmental disorder are limited at the time of writing, and no specifically psychological interventions have been developed.

Case example 1: Eileen

Eileen is a young woman aged 22 with a diagnosis of autism who previously attended a special school and who is now enrolled on a local college course for young adults with intellectual disabilities. She lives at home and has abiding interests in UFOs, reading television listings magazines, and collecting pens and pencils. For several weeks, she has been refusing to attend college and has stayed in her room engaging in sorting her vast collection of pens. She says that she is scared of going into town and college, but she regularly goes out at night to look for UFOs from a nearby park.

As illustrated by the cited example, therapists need to be cognizant of the defining characteristics of the ASDs, even if they themselves are not directly involved in assessment and diagnosis, as the various features of the condition have implications for both the development and the remediation of emotional and psychological distress. All forms of ASD are characterized by the "triad of impairments," comprising impairments in communication, social interaction, and imagination, together with the presence of routine and repetitive actions and interests. Although autism is increasingly being recognized, with a concomitant rise in estimated prevalence of all forms of ASD and current estimated prevalence between 8.4 and 27.1 per 10 000 (Baird *et al.*, 2001), it can still go unrecognized in clinical settings with undiagnosed adults continuing to be regarded as having treatment-resistant mental illnesses (Dossetor, 2007), the so-called revolving door clients (Tantam, 2000).

The Cognitive Basis of ASD

The nature of the underlying cognitive and neurological basis of ASD is complex and much remains unclear despite extensive research (Bowler, 2007). However, social cognition difficulties are central to how people with ASD understand, or perhaps more appositely, fail to understand, the world. Specifically, problems with "theory of mind" or mentalization ability (Happé, 1994a) are manifest in ASD as a central difficulty in understanding and relating to other people, due to an inability to infer the mental state of another person through their speech, actions, and nonverbal communication, in particular due to specific impairments in reading the mind in the eyes (Baron-Cohen *et al.*, 2001). Unfortunately, specific training in using mentalization techniques has shown but limited success in developing generalizable skills (Howlin *et al.*, 1999). Although impaired mentalization is an important factor in disorders such as psychosis, such a direct linkage has not been demonstrated in Asperger's syndrome (e.g., Abell & Hare, 2005) and remains to be investigated in the case of people with intellectual disabilities and ASD. Executive functioning has been identified as impaired in ASD (Bowler, 2007), in particular, the ability to generate novel responses (Ruble & Scott, 2002) together with other impairments in planning and shifting attention. However, there is often still a tendency to perseverate and as with other aspects of cognitive functioning, people with ASD perform better when provided with an external framework, as demonstrated by the success of the Treatment and Education of Autistic and Related Communication Handicapped Children (TEACHH) approach (e.g., Keel *et al.*, 1997). At the interpersonal level, provision of structure has been consistently demonstrated to facilitate processing social and emotional information in people with ASD (Loveland *et al.*, 1997), leading to the proposal of the *task support hypothesis* (Bowler *et al.*, 2004), namely that people with ASD will always perform better on a given task when given support. In the case of memory functioning, people with ASD seem to have normal abilities with regard to semantic and procedural memory functioning but often have difficulties in autobiographical memory functioning, manifesting as an impairment in the spontaneous recall of self-experienced information regardless of whether they are intellectually disabled or not (Bowler *et al.*, 2004; Hare *et al.*, 2007).

In addition, many people with ASD experience sensory problems that significantly impact on their social and psychological functioning. A frequently reported difficulty is hypersensitivity to sound, especially high-pitched frequencies, such as those made by babies and young children, sirens and audible reversing indications on vehicles, and explosions and banging, especially of doors. Such auditory hyperacusis appears to be a "hardwired" sensory dysfunction that is not readily amenable, if at all, to desensitization through graded exposure. Clinical experience to date indicates that attempts to desensitize people with ASD to such sounds may result in a severe abreaction and is not recommended.

When undertaking therapeutic work with people with ASD, it is important to be aware of the wider context in which the person is experiencing his or her psychological and emotional difficulties. In particular, there may be an absence of protective factors, such as relationships, social support, or meaningful activities, even in the case of people with Asperger's syndrome, very few of whom are gainfully employed in adulthood with a significant disparity between level of employment and educational attainment. At an individual level, there is accumulating evidence of disturbances in circadian rhythm function (Hare *et al.*, 2006), meaning that people with ASD may literally be out of synchronization with the world around them, and clinical observation indicates that a fair number of such people seem to have adopted a strategy of day–night reversal, with all this implies in terms of increasing social isolation.

Summary points

- People with ASD have specific difficulties in understanding other people's thinking and may have problems thinking about their own mental state.
- People with ASD have difficulties in recalling and reporting their own experiences and role in events.
- People with ASD perform cognitive tasks much better when provided with structure.

Psychological and Emotional Distress in ASD

In a national study of the needs of people with ASD in the United Kingdom, up to 32 percent of parents reported their son or daughter with ASD to have experienced significant psychological and emotional distress, which increased to 50 percent if they had not been diagnosed until after the age of 30 (Barnard *et al.*, 2001), with the development of such psychological problems being associated with poor long-term outcome (Ballaban-Gil *et al.*, 1996). While systematic large-scale research is limited, there appears to be a higher prevalence of emotional and psychological problems in this group compared with both the general population and age peers with intellectual disabilities (Brereton *et al.*, 2006). With regard to specific disorders, both bipolar disorder (Bradley & Bolton, 2006) and depression have been identified as serious problems for people with ASD with prevalence of the latter estimated at around 15–37 percent of this population (Gillberg & Billstedt, 2000). Thoughts of self-harm without any active plans for carrying this out are frequently reported in clinical assessment as well as an increased risk of suicide in people with Asperger's syndrome (Wolff & McGuire, 1995), with two prominent people with Asperger's syndrome well known in the United Kingdom for their lecturing and writing having taken their own lives in recent years. Clinical anxiety is a very frequent problem in ASD (Gillberg & Billstedt, 2000; Gillott *et al.*, 2001), and some studies suggest it to be an almost universal experience (Abell & Hare, 2005; Wood *et al.*, 2008). Of particular interest is emerging data on the specific nature of anxiety associated with Asperger's syndrome, which indicates that myriad everyday events have very rapid impact on feelings of anxiety with the cognitive component of such anxious experiences being absent or hard to identify (Wood *et al.*, 2008).

Although people with ASD are often diagnosed with obsessive–compulsive disorder (OCD), the actual prevalence of this remains contentious and it is not always clear as to whether OCD is a discrete form of psychological disorder in people with ASD distinct from the obsessional interests that form part of the diagnostic criteria for ASD. This hinges on whether the obsessions and compulsions are ego-dystonic, as in OCD, or ego-syntonic, as in the case for the preoccupations and all-encompassing interests that characterize ASDs (Baron-Cohen, 1989). Given this caveat, OCD has been identified in conjunction with autism, with the consistent finding of the prevalence of less sophisticated compulsions (Zandt *et al.*, 2007), and has been successfully treated in Asperger's syndrome using cognitive–behavioral methods (Reaven & Hepburn, 2003).

Questions of comorbidity raise the question of whether characteristics of ASD may be seen in isolation and regarded as separate mental illnesses. For example, aloofness and social withdrawal coupled with seemingly bizarre behavior can be regarded, albeit inappropriately, as indicative of schizophrenia (Dossetor, 2007), emphasizing the need for careful differential assessment. Similarly, it is established that delusional cognitions per se, particularly paranoid ideation and grandiosity, are very prevalent in Asperger's syndrome and are linked to everyday worries, hassles, and anxiety (Abell & Hare, 2005). Thus, the psychological and emotional problems of people with ASD are not necessarily discrete mental illnesses but often arise from their interactions with and within a social world for which they are cognitively ill-equipped.

Summary points

- People with ASD are frequently very anxious about everyday events.
- Increased anxiety seems to be related to delusional thoughts in people with ASD.
- OCD should be distinguished from the repetitive behavior and interests inherent in ASD.
- Identify the nature and impact of any sensory difficulties.

Psychotherapeutic Interventions for People with ASD

Case study 2: Eric

Eric is a young man with Asperger's syndrome who's repetitive questioning, rumination, and ritualistic behavior take up much of his time. As a result, he usually fails to complete any other activities resulting in increasing low self-esteem and low mood. Much of Eric's repetitive questioning and rumination concern his need to know exactly how autistic he is. This obsessive interest in his own autism has displaced his previous all-abiding interest in collecting and lining up Star Wars action figures.

Existing evidence base for CBT for people with ASD

On the basis of the available research and clinical evidence, particularly the inherent difficulties in interpersonal relationships and insight, when individual psychotherapeutic work is required, it is proposed that this should be based in the first instance on CBT. To date, there is a small but growing literature demonstrating the effectiveness of such approaches through case studies (e.g., Bauminger, 2002; Hare, 1997; Reaven & Hepburn, 2003; Sze & Wood, 2007, 2008) and more recently randomized controlled trials (RCTs) (Sofronoff *et al.*, 2005, 2007). Hare (1997) described the process of basic CBT with a young man with Asperger's syndrome presenting with severe depression, excessive solitary drinking, and self-harm who was seen for 15 therapy sessions in conjunction with his key worker. The sessions were structured around written work using a retrospective diary and formal measures such as the Beck Depression Inventory (BDI), as the client found sustained 1:1 interaction very difficult. The effective parts of the therapeutic work were found to be recording of his feelings and using long walks as distraction. At the end of therapy, there were reductions in measured depressive symptoms and a cessation of solitary drinking and self-harm, together with the client achieving his therapy goals of making up his mind and expressing himself. The imposition of structure through appointments and diary keeping led to "the expectation that he would be asked for accounts of his actions" being suggested as a central factor in the outcome of the intervention, alongside increasing his activity level, both factors being important in mainstream CBT practice.

Although their work describes the use of CBT to treat OCD in a young girl with Asperger's syndrome, Reaven and Hepburn (2003) similarly utilized writing and a preagreed schedule, together with a third party (in this case, the parents), to facilitate the delivery of the therapeutic intervention. An interesting feature of this intervention was the application of "social stories," a comic strip form of communication developed for children with ASD (Gray, 1993) to set out explanations and coping strategies with regard to the OCD symptoms. Both formal assessment and idiosyncratic ratings indicated the remission of the original symptoms at the end of 14 weeks of therapy. More recently, Sze and Wood (2007, 2008) have described work with children with ASD who present with anxiety, OCD, and separation difficulties. In these cases, modified manualized CBT was used with an emphasis on self-monitoring, remediating deficits in social and communication skills, and again, structured interventions involving third-party input and the visual presentation of information, as well as the incorporation of the particular special interests.

To date, only two RCTs of psychotherapeutic interventions with people with ASD have been reported using essentially the same manualized CBT-based intervention for both anxiety (Sofronoff et al., 2005) and for anger problems (Sofronoff et al., 2007), both RCTs involving older children aged 10–14 years. With regard to the delivery of the therapeutic interventions, key factors in both RCTs were the high level of structure and the involvement of peers, parents, and therapist in therapeutic "unit." Important elements of the interventions were the use of a metaphor of exploration (Sofronoff et al., 2007) and a therapeutic "toolbox" including emotional recognition, relaxation, and basic CBT techniques to examine the link between thoughts and feelings and to test out the actual probability of feared outcomes occurring. The primary outcome measures in both of these studies were increased alternative response generation by the children and third-party assessment of the children's behavior together with parental confidence in supporting them.

From the limited evidence base, it can be seen that the importance of providing structured interventions is paramount, which is synergistic with the research findings that people with ASD syndrome always perform better on cognitive tasks when provided with appropriate cues and structure. This need for structure also supports a role for carer input to the therapeutic process in addition to the traditional 1:1 therapeutic relationship (Hare, 1997; Reaven & Hepburn, 2003; Sofronoff et al., 2005, 2007). In at least 50 percent of the author's individual therapeutic work, the person with ASD has been supported either by a family member or a carer, and this need should generally be accommodated rather than automatically be seen as an issue to be addressed in the course of the therapeutic work. However, as with young adults with psychosis, issues around individuation and interdependence may need to be addressed in the medium to longer term (cf. Harrop & Trower, 2003).

From the outset, it is important that there should be no attempt to treat or re-mediate the core aspects of a person's ASD per se and that any therapeutic work undertaken should focus on those discrete difficulties that are amenable to change. However, such a focus on the disorder itself may well be brought up by the person with ASD syndrome and can manifest in an obsessive interest in Asperger's syndrome per se, a point noted by Wing (1996) who has suggested that in some people with ASD, such an interest might even constitute the necessary obsessional interest in terms of diagnosis.

In some cases, the person with ASD may make continual reference to a system of rigid self-knowledge that is used to discount the validity of any therapeutic work and/or the possibility of change ("If you can't fix my autism then there is no point in talking to you") while seeking validation of his or her difficulties. It perhaps goes without saying that this "help me – you can't help me – help me" cycle can make the process of therapeutic engagement very difficult, and therapists should not expect that the person with ASD to automatically be able to engage in a collaborative thera-peutic relationship. Thus, at this stage and subsequently throughout therapy, it is often necessary and appropriate for the therapist to take the lead and to work in a much more directive and indeed didactic manner than is usual in CBT, even to the point of being pedantic (Reaven & Hepburn, 2003). Although possibly uncomfort-able for the therapist, this should be seen in the light of the inherent need for both structure and cues in people with ASD. In other circumstances, the person themselves may feel more comfortable undertaking therapeutic work outside of the actual therapy sessions and the necessary support and material should be provided.

Assessment

When undertaking the assessment of specific clinical symptoms, it is feasible to utilize the same range of formal measures as are used in the general adult population, with the *Hospital Anxiety and Depression Scales* (Zigmund & Snaith, 1983), *BDI, Beck Anxiety Inventory* (Beck *et al.*, 1961), *Peters Delusional Inventory* (Peters *et al.*, 1999), and *Yale–Brown Obsessions and Compulsions Scale* (Goodman *et al.*, 1989) having all been successfully used in clinical and research work with people with ASD. One issue that can arise given the thinking styles and tendency to grandiosity noted previously is the tendency of the person with ASD to argue over the wording of individual items on standard measures and to question the validity of using any form of normative assessment. Thus, the idiosyncratic nature of the cognitive–behavioral assessment and formulation process should be emphasized from the outset, and idiographic assessment techniques such as those derived from personal construct psychology may be useful (Hare *et al.*, 1999).

Given the nature of the psychological impairments in ASD, both specific *cognitive deficits* and *cognitive distortions* will need to be assessed and taken into consideration when developing individual clinical formulations. With regard to the former, the person's ability to mentalize should be assessed at the start of any therapeutic work. This can be facilitated through the use of formal assessments such as *Strange Stories* (Happé, 1994b), the *Mind in the Eyes Task* (Baron-Cohen *et al.*, 2001), the *Projective Imagination Test* (Blackshaw *et al.*, 2001), and the *PET Metaphors* tasks (Corcoran,

2003). It should be borne in mind that such tasks, which involve explicit and structured questioning, may *overestimate* mentalization ability in real-world, real-time situations (Ponnet *et al.*, 2004) and may be measuring different aspects of mentalization ability (Coffait, 2008). However, such specificity may be of utility to clinicians as it permits a more fine grain assessment of a person's mentalization difficulties. Another factor of particular relevance to the use of cognitive–behavioral approaches is the degree to which people with ASD can accurately and effectively associate mood, cognition, and behavior in making social judgments (Begeer *et al.*, 2007). A further cognitive deficit that is less obvious but one that can have serious implications for assessment and intervention relates to the autobiographical memory difficulties associated with ASD, which can mean that the person will find it difficult to spontaneously recall emotions and thoughts associated with past actions and events, even though they can readily recall the situation and other people's actions. Therefore, it may be necessary to focus on "here and now" feelings and to work *in situ*, rather than presume that the person with ASD will be able to recall experiences in detail. It is important to remember that these difficulties in autobiographical memory may also affect recall of therapy sessions, and the presence of a third-party can be of practical benefit in helping the person with ASD both during and between therapy sessions.

Another way in which this can influence assessment and intervention is that emotions and experience may be very context specific, such that the person may find it very difficult to link his or her current experience with past events and experiences or to link experiences across different contexts. Therefore, assessment of the degree to which spontaneous autobiographical memory is impaired may be called for during the initial stages of assessment and formulation. Finally, given that reciprocal social interaction is a fundamental problem for people with ASD syndrome, the usual question and answer approach to assessment may need to be replaced by a more monologue-based approach in which the person "downloads" the information to the therapist. For example, a young man with Asperger's syndrome found it very difficult to engage in reciprocal discussion, and so time was allocated in the initial stage of therapeutic work for a monologue about his life and difficulties. Thus, a sequence of alternate monologues by the therapist and the person with ASD may be more productive.

Socialization to CBT and formulation

Having undertaken an assessment, it may be that some people with ASD do not wish to proceed to therapeutic work, having seen being referred to a clinical psychologist or similar professional as an opportunity to gain information about their condition, the more so given that diagnosis may have occurred later in life (Punshon *et al.*, 2009). Such "informational interventions" can in themselves be very powerful, and there should not necessarily be a push toward engaging the person in further therapeutic work. More problematic is the "help me – you can't help me – help me" conundrum mentioned previously, which can be the major sticking points in engaging people with ASD, and conventional approaches to socializing clients to CBT may be ineffective. In this and other circumstances, it is vitally important that the therapist does not engage in long discussions about the merits of CBT, but emphasizes the practical goals of adapting to and coping with the world around them. A frank "take it or leave it" approach, while somewhat out of character and possibly uncomfortable for the therapist, is often appreciated given the tendency to either/or thinking in people with ASD! Other problematic issues that may be encountered include the person with ASD taking previous psychiatric assessments in a wholly literal fashion (e.g., "I have been told that I have faulty chemicals in my brain and therefore need to have them flushed out and replaced"), a fixation on the therapist understanding the extent of his or her difficulties and taking them seriously that may be related to the tendency to grandiosity, and seeing therapy as an opportunity to acquire a detailed set of rules and heuristics to cover every conceivable social interaction. Again, all such issues should be explicitly addressed prior to the onset of work on more specific difficulties. The setting of clear rules and boundaries may also be required in order to progress therapeutic work. In the work with "Eric," it was agreed that he could ask his questions at set intervals throughout the session, and this was gradually reduced to writing out a stock answer on a card that was placed between himself and the therapist.

As with all forms of CBT, the development of a shared idiosyncratic formulation is central. When working with people with ASD, the ability to work visually using a diagrammatic formulation can be of particular utility given the often observed tendency of people with ASD to think in terms of imagery and also the need to make concrete links across time and place. This can be further developed through the concept of "social stories" (Gray, 1998) involving drawings, speech bubbles, and comic strips. Although primarily developed for use with children with ASD (see Reaven & Hepburn, 2003), these can be adapted for working with adults. Technical and scientific images and analogies are often favored and may be highly idiosyncratic, for example, using different waveforms (sine/square/sawtooth) to represent specific emotions. A particularly useful analogy that can be introduced by the therapist to help socialization to the therapeutic process is that of prosthesis; that is, just as a person with impaired eyesight can function perfectly well with the correct lenses, someone with impaired social understanding could use a *prosthetic mind* to help them understand, a metaphor suggested to the author by a man with Asperger's syndrome.

Summary points

- Accept the need for support for person from third parties.
- Focus on very specific "here and now" issues.
- Avoid getting into logical arguments.
- Provision of structure is essential.
- Do not expect a person with ASD to reciprocate and allow for monologues and "downloads."
- Use visual descriptions and mechanical analogies as appropriate.

CBT interventions

Given that people with ASD often define themselves more in terms of what they do and what they have done rather than as agents in the world (Jackson *et al.*, 2012), it is important to avoid using cognitive challenges that may be construed by the person as an attack on who they are. For example, suggesting even in a spirit of therapeutic collaboration that a particular action or interpretation is wrong may be perceived by person with ASD more as a value judgment rather than a suggestion for change in the way the person understands events. Moreover, given the tendency to very black-and-white thinking, the person with Asperger's syndrome may have a tendency to see the concept alternative explanations and interpretations as morally flawed. For example, when a verbally able but very autistic young man was being introduced to the basic CBT notion of alternative interpretations of a given event, he became very agitated and said "If there are two explanations, one must be wrong and therefore how will I know in advance which is the correct one to choose to avoid telling myself and other people lies?" The result was a breakdown in the therapeutic relationship as he regarded the therapist as morally untrustworthy.

Therefore, a more explicit emphasis on the behavioral elements of therapy may be needed when working with people with ASD. One useful approach drawn from personal construct work with this population (Hare *et al.*, 1999) is to introduce the idea of "fixed-role" therapy at an early stage of the therapeutic process. An example of this involved asking a person with ASD who was very anxious not to change the way in which he interpreted events or even to interpret them at all, but to act like a nonanxious person would act in those situations that result in anxiety. This he was able to do and reported that his anxiety when "in role" was markedly reduced. Overall, an emphasis on the factual and procedural should take emphasis over the purely cognitive as in line with behaviorist accounts of attitude formation (cf. Bem, 1967); people with ASD often seem to base their thoughts on their actions in a post hoc manner, rather than the "common sense" supposition implicit in CBT that thinking precedes action and emotion. By taking this approach in therapeutic work with people with ASD, the emphasis can be on behavior and an external focus, rather than on introspection and rumination. A good example of this was when an impasse in therapeutic work with "Eric" was resolved very simply by his key worker, making a sign that proclaimed "Less thinking, more action." In this regard, the importance of embedding any such individual therapeutic work in a wider program encompassing appropriate social, vocational, and educational support cannot be overemphasized and also that such a program may well be based on the formulation derived from the therapeutic assessment.

Summary points

- Accept the need for support for person from third parties.
- Use highly structured approaches.
- Behavioral emphasis on trying new roles and new ways of acting.
- Do not attempt to bring about cognitive change as primary goal.
- Avoid direct cognitive challenges that might be construed as attacking.
- Accept that therapeutic work may be very long or very quick.

Conclusions

The social and interpersonal difficulties that follow from ASD are pervasive, sometimes very evident and sometimes very subtle, yet always disabling. However, they are understandable particularly when the generic techniques of CBT are combined with insights from developmental and cognitive psychology. Such an understanding often indicates a need for broad ongoing support rather than treatment per se. Thus, the individual therapeutic work with people with ASD may be but a small part of a broader psychosocial support package (Powell, 2002), encompassing social services, education, and housing. Such work tends to be a very idiosyncratic form of CBT, with a particular emphasis on the behavioral, and may need to be longer than usual even for apparently straightforward issues such as anxiety – work with "Eric" took over two years! It is hoped that through even the relatively brief overview of the issues involved in such as can be presented here, more therapists will realize that they already have the necessary skills to engage with and support people with ASD when they seek such help, be it in intellectual disability or mental health services. In order to facilitate this, there should be less of an emphasis on fitting people with ASD into predetermined diagnostic categories and more on obtaining accounts of the nature and function of psychological distress. The primary emphasis should be on helping the person cope with everyday life, with therapeutic work emphasizing overcoming, or perhaps more accurately working around inherent cognitive deficits, though not ignoring the need to carefully correct acquired and dysfunctional cognitive distortions.

References

Abell, F. & Hare, D.J. (2005). An experimental investigation of the phenomenology of delusional beliefs in people with Asperger's syndrome. *Autism, 9*, 515–531.

Baird, G., Charman, T., Cox, A., Baron-Cohen, S., Swettenham, J., Wheelwright, S. *et al.* (2001). Screening and surveillance for autism and pervasive developmental disorders. *Archives of Disease in Childhood, 84*, 468–475.

Ballaban-Gil, K., Rapin, I., Tuchman, T. & Shinnar, S. (1996). Longitudinal examination of the behavioral, language, and social changes in a population of adolescent and young adults with autistic disorder. *Pediatric Neurology, 15*(3), 217–223.

Barnard, J., Harvard, V., Potter, D. & Prior, A. (2001). *Ignored or ineligible? The reality for adults with autism spectrum disorders.* London: National Autistic Society.

Baron-Cohen, S. (1989). Do autistic children have obsessions and compulsions? *The British Journal of Clinical Psychology, 28*, 193–200.

Baron-Cohen, S., Wheelwright, S., Hill, J., Raste, Y. & Plumb, I. (2001). The "Reading the Mind in the Eyes" test revised version: A study with normal adults and adults with Asperger's syndrome or high functioning autism. *Journal of Child Psychology and Psychiatry, 42*, 241–251.

Bauminger, N. (2002). The facilitation of social-emotional understanding and social interaction in high-functioning children with autism: Intervention outcomes. *Journal of Autism and Developmental Disorders, 32*, 283–298.

Beck, A.T., Ward, C.H., Mendelson, M., Mock, J. & Erbaugh, J. (1961). An inventory for measuring depression. *Archives of General Psychiatry, 4*, 561–571.

Begeer, S., Meerum Terwogt, M., Rieffe, C., Stegge, H. & Koot, H.M. (2007). Do children with autism acknowledge the influence of mood in behaviour? *Autism, 11*, 503–521.

Bem, D.J. (1967). Self-perception: An alternative interpretation of cognitive dissonance phenomena. *Psychological Review, 74*, 183–200.

Blackshaw, A., Kinderman, P., Hare, D.J. & Hatton, C. (2001). Theory of mind, causal attribution and paranoia in Asperger syndrome. *Autism, 5,* 147–165.

Bowler, D.M. (2007). *Autism spectrum disorders; psychological theory and research.* London: Wiley.

Bowler, D.M., Gardiner, J.M. & Berthollier, N. (2004). Source memory in Asperger's syndrome. *Journal of Autism and Developmental Disorders, 34,* 533–542.

Bradley, E.A. & Bolton, P. (2006). Episodic psychiatric disorders in teenagers with learning disabilities with and without autism. *The British Journal of Psychiatry, 189,* 362–366.

Brereton, A.V., Tonge, B.J. & Einfeld, S.L. (2006). Psychopathology in children and adolescents with autism compared to young people with intellectual disability. *Journal of Autism and Developmental Disorders, 36,* 863–870.

Coffait, F.-M. (2008). *Concurrent validity of social cognition measures for adults with Asperger syndrome and high-functioning autism.* Unpublished MPhil dissertation, University of Manchester.

Corcoran, R. (2003). Inductive reasoning and the understanding of intention in schizophrenia. *Cognitive Neuropsychiatry, 8,* 223–235.

Dossetor, D.R. (2007). All that glitters is not gold: Misdiagnosis of psychosis in pervasive developmental disorders – A case series. *Clinical Child Psychology and Psychiatry, 12,* 537–548.

Gillberg, C. & Billstedt, E. (2000). Autism and Asperger syndrome: Coexistence with other clinical disorders. *Acta Psychiatrica Scandinavica, 102,* 321–330.

Gillott, A., Furniss, F. & Walter, A. (2001). Anxiety in high-functioning children with autism. *Autism, 5,* 277–286.

Goodman, W.K., Price, L.H., Rasmussen, S.A., Mazure, C., Fleischman, R.L., Hill, C.L. *et al.* (1989). The Yale-Brown Obsessive Compulsive Scale. *Archives of General Psychiatry, 46,* 1006–1011.

Gray, C. (1993) Social stories: Improving responses of children with autism with accurate social information. *Focus on Autistic Behaviour, 8,* 1–10.

Gray, C. (1998). Social stories and comic strip conversations with students with Asperger's syndrome or high-functioning autism. In E. Schopler, G.B. Mesibov & L.J. Kunce (Eds.) *Asperger's syndrome or high-functioning autism.* New York: Plenum Press.

Happé, F. (1994a). *Autism: An introduction to psychological theory.* London: UCL Press.

Happé, F.G. (1994b). An advanced test of theory of mind: Understanding of story characters' thoughts and feelings by able autistic, mentally handicapped and normal children and adults. *Journal of Autism and Developmental Disorders, 24,* 129–154.

Hare, D.J. (1997). The use of cognitive-behavioural therapy with people with Asperger syndrome: A case study. *Autism, 1,* 215–225.

Hare, D.J., Jones, J. & Payne, C. (1999). Approaching reality: The use of personal construct techniques in working with people with Asperger's syndrome. *Autism, 3,* 165–176.

Hare, D.J., Jones, S.H. & Evershed, K. (2006). Objective investigation of the sleep-wake cycle in adults with intellectual disabilities and autistic spectrum disorders. *Journal of Intellectual Disability Research, 50,* 701–710.

Hare, D.J., Mellor, C. & Azmi, S. (2007). Episodic memory in adults with autistic spectrum disorders: Recall for self- versus other-experienced events. *Research in Developmental Disabilities, 28,* 311–329.

Harrop, C.E. & Trower, P. (2003). *Why does schizophrenia develop at late adolescence?* Chichester: Wiley.

Howlin, P., Baron-Cohen, S., Hadwin, J. & Swettenham, J. (1999). *Teaching children with autism to mind-read.* London: Wiley.

Jackson, P., Skirrow, P. & Hare, D.J. (2012) Asperger through the looking glass: An exploratory study of self-understanding in people with Asperger's Syndrome. *Journal of Autism and Developmental Disorders, 42,* 697–706.

Keel, J.H., Mesibov, G.B. & Woods, A.V. (1997). TEACHH-supported employment programme. *Journal of Autism and Developmental Disorders, 27,* 3–9.

Loveland, K.A., Tunali-Kotoski, B., Chen, Y.R., Ortegon, J., Pearson, D.A., Brelsford, K.A. *et al.* (1997). Emotional recognition in autism: Verbal and non-verbal information. *Development and Psychopathology, 9,* 579–593.

Peters, R., Joseph, S.A. & Garety, P.A. (1999). Measurement of delusional ideation in the normal population: Introducing the PDI (Peters Delusion Inventory). *Schizophrenia Bulletin, 25,* 553–576.

Ponnet, K.S., Roeyers, H., Buysse, A., De Clercq, A. & Van Der Hayden, E. (2004). Advanced mind-reading in adults with Asperger syndrome. *Autism, 8,* 249–266.

Powell, A. (2002). *Taking responsibility: Good practice guidelines for services – Adults with Asperger syndrome.* London: The National Autistic Society.

Punshon, C., Skirrow, P. & Murphy, G. (2009). The "not guilty verdict": Psychological reactions to a diagnosis of Asperger syndrome in adulthood. *Autism, 13,* 265–283.

Reaven, J. & Hepburn, S. (2003). Cognitive-behavorial treatment of obsessive-compulsive disorder in a child with Asperger syndrome. *Autism, 7,* 145–164.

Ruble, L.A. & Scott, M. (2002). Executive functions and natural habitat behaviors of children with autism. *Autism, 6,* 365–382.

Sofronoff, K., Attwood, T. & Hinton, S. (2005). A randomized controlled trial of a cognitive behavioural intervention for anxiety in children with Asperger syndrome. *Journal of Psychology and Psychiatry and Allied Disciplines, 46,* 1152–1160.

Sofronoff, K., Attwood, T., Hinton, S. & Levin, I. (2007). A randomized controlled trial of a cognitive behavioural intervention for anger management in children diagnosed with Asperger syndrome. *Journal of Autism and Developmental Disorders, 37,* 1203–1214.

Sturm, H., Fernell, E. & Gillberg, C. (2004). Autism spectrum disorders in children with normal intellectual levels: Associated impairments and subgroups. *Developmental Medicine and Child Neurology, 46,* 444–447.

Sze, K.M. & Wood, J.J. (2007). Cognitive behavioral treatment of co-morbid anxiety disorders and social difficulties in children with high-functioning autism: A case report. *Journal of Contemporary Psychotherapy, 37,* 133–143.

Sze, K.M. & Wood, J.J. (2008). Enhancing CBT for the treatment of autism spectrum disorders and concurrent anxiety. *Behavioural and Cognitive Psychotherapy, 36,* 403–409.

Tantam, D. (2000). Psychological disorder in adolescents and adults with Asperger syndrome. *Autism, 4,* 47–62.

Volkmar, F.R. & Klin, A. (1998). Asperger syndrome and nonverbal learning disabilities. In E. Schopler, G.B. Mesibov & L.J. Kunce (Eds.) *Asperger syndrome or high functioning autism?* (pp.107–122). New York: Plenum Press.

Wing, L. (1981). Asperger's syndrome: A clinical account. *Psychological Medicine, 11,* 115–129.

Wing, L. (1996). *The autistic spectrum: A guide for parents and professionals.* London: Constable.

Wolff, S. & McGuire, R.J. (1995). Schizoid personality in girls: A follow-up study – What are the links with Asperger's syndrome? *Journal for Child Psychology and Psychiatry, 36,* 793–817.

Wood, C., Skirrow, P. & Hare, D.J. (2008). Real time experience and everyday anxiety in people with Asperger's syndrome. Paper presented at 36th Annual Conference of the

British Association for Behavioural and Cognitive Psychotherapy 17th–19th July 2008, University of Edinburgh.

Zandt, F., Prior, M. & Kyrios, M. (2007). Repetitive behavior in children with high-functioning autism and obsessive-compulsive disorder. *Journal of Autism and Developmental Disorders*, *37*, 251–259.

Zigmund, A.S. & Snaith, R.P. (1983). The hospital anxiety and depression scale. *Acta Psychiatrica Scandinavica*, *67*, 361–370.

Chapter 13

Supporting Care Staff Using Mindfulness- and Acceptance-Based Approaches

Stephen J. Noone

A Key Challenge Facing Care Staff

Challenging behavior can be a daily occurrence in the working environment of care staff. Some behaviors have a direct physical effect (e.g., being hit, pulled, kicked, spat on), while others are psychological (witnessing clients inflicting pain on themselves), but all affecting them emotionally. The challenging behaviors of individuals with an intellectual disability (ID) are one of the factors implicated in the decreased well-being of care staff.

Although work stress levels may not exceed those in other human service settings (Skirrow & Hatton, 2007), studies show that care staff find challenging behaviors aversive (Hall & Oliver, 1992; Hartley & MacLean, 2007; Oliver, 1995). Direct experience of challenging behaviors has been shown to lead to negative emotional reactions (Bailey *et al.*, 2006; Hawkins *et al.*, 2005; Raczka 2005), and such experiences are linked with poor psychological well-being such as burnout (Hastings & Brown, 2002; Rose *et al.*, 2004). Although meta-analysis has not found sufficient empirical evidence to suggest a direct link between challenging behavior and staff burnout, high levels of emotional exhaustion and depersonalization are consistently reported across studies (Skirrow & Hatton, 2007). However, qualitative longitudinal studies on the consequences of exposure to challenging behaviors have emphasized that care staff report experiencing stress (Razcka, 2005). Surveys of general ID services have also found between 32.5 percent (Hatton, Emerson *et al.*, 1999) and 25 percent (Robertson *et al.*, 2005) of staff experienced significant levels of stress. These adverse consequences underline the need to address stress and negative emotional reactions in care staff.

Psychological Therapies for Adults with Intellectual Disabilities, First Edition.
Edited by John L. Taylor, William R. Lindsay, Richard P. Hastings, and Chris Hatton.
© 2013 John Wiley & Sons, Ltd. Published 2013 by John Wiley & Sons, Ltd.

Theoretical Perspectives on Care Staff Stress

Another consistent finding is that staff behavior is implicated in the development and maintenance of challenging behavior (Hall *et al.*, 2001). Research on staff behavior suggests that care staff are likely to provide counter-habilitative antecedents and consequences for challenging behaviors (Hastings & Remington, 1994) through either positive or negative reinforcement (Hall & Oliver, 1992; Oliver, 1995; Watts *et al.*, 1997).

Hastings and colleagues (2003) have suggested that staffs' negative emotional experiences associated with dealing with client behavior might directly interfere with interventions to reduce client challenging behavior. Staff at particularly high risk may include those in contact with severe challenging behaviors (Hastings, 2002), those lacking support from colleagues and supervisors (Dyer & Quine, 1998; Ito *et al.*, 1999), and those who report significant problems with managers and other aspects of the organization (Hatton, Emerson *et al.*, 1999; Hatton, Rivers, Mason, Mason, Emerson *et al.*, 1999). In addition to the impact on care staff themselves and service users, service organizations are affected negatively by worker stress. Work stress predicts staff turnover in ID services (Hatton & Emerson, 1998), and staff reporting high levels of stress have been observed to engage in fewer positive interactions with service users (Lawson & O'Brien, 1994; Rose *et al.*, 1998a, 1998b).

A recent review of carer stress in ID research (Devereux *et al.*, 2009) identified five distinct theories used in the literature:

1. The *emotional overload model* (Maslach, 1982, 1999) proposes that the interpersonal demands in human services deplete emotional resources to create stress and eventual burnout. Burnout is defined in terms of emotional exhaustion, that is, being drained of one's emotional resources; depersonalization (which refers to deterioration in the quality of interpersonal relations); and finally, personal accomplishment, which is a measure of self-evaluation (Maslach, 1993).

2. The assumption within *equity theory* is that distress may be caused by a perception of inequity in a care relationship (Adams, 1965). This perception can be a motivation to alter one's contribution to the relationship or by cognitively distorting the perception of inputs and outputs. Furthermore, in cases of extreme inequity, the ultimate strategy is to withdraw entirely from the relationship.

   When equity theory has been applied to ID services, there is evidence that where staff experience inequity, in either direction, in their relationships with clients, there is an association with burnout (Van Dierendonck *et al.*, 1996; Van Yperen, 1995).

3. *Person–environment theory* (Caplan *et al.*, 1975) focuses on the interaction between the person and the work environment. A mismatch between the person and the work environment through role overload, role ambiguity, and role conflict can lead to stress. Role conflict may occur when there is a divergence between what the care staff are asked to do and their norms and values. Role ambiguity refers to a state of confusion about what is expected within the role. Only one study has broadened the perspective to include the relationship between an individual and the organization within ID (Hatton, Rivers, Mason, Mason, Kiernan *et al.*, 1999).

4. The *demand–support–constraints model* (Payne, 1979) suggests that occupational stress is the interaction between job demands, support, and constraints at work, where

certain combinations influence whether an individual becomes stressed. It proposes that as demands and constraints increase, stress is likely to increase but can be reduced by increasing support. Demands are defined as any aspect of the environment that requires the individual to respond, and support is defined as the degree to which the environment may assist the individual in meeting the demands. Constraints are anything that impedes the individual from meeting the demands. The typical predictor of occupational stress within this model would therefore be a job that is high in demands, low in support, and high in constraints. However, any job that is low in demands, low in support, and high in constraints can also lead to psychological stress. A number of authors have found support for the model (Rose, 1993; Rose *et al.*, 1998b).

5. Finally, the *cognitive appraisals model* suggested by Lazarus and Folkman (1984) has come to dominate the stress literature (Cooper & Dewe, 2004; Flaxman & Bond, 2006) and can be found in several studies within ID research (Cottle *et al.*, 1995; Hastings & Brown, 2002; Hatton, Emerson *et al.*, 1999; Mitchell & Hastings, 2001). Its central tenant is that stress is inherent in neither the environment nor the person but results from the relationship between them, which is called a transaction. Therefore, nothing by itself is considered a stressor. Something can only become a stressor if it is perceived as such (Lazarus, 1995). That is why people can vary in their stress response when exposed to the same situations. Coping is defined as the "cognitive and behavioral efforts a person makes to manage demands that tax . . . personal resources" (Lazarus, 1995, p. 6) and fall within two types. Problem-focused coping, involving information seeking, is used to change either the person's behavior or the environment to ameliorate psychological threat. While emotion-focused coping involves strategies aimed at reducing emotional distress. This may involve avoidance, denial, or even positive thinking. Lazarus (1995) proposed that stress occurs when people's appraisal of external or internal demands placed on them exceed their resources to cope.

Implications for Intervention

Ultimately, there are only two different levels of intervention to promote stress reduction (Flaxman & Bond, 2006). The first typically involves the redesign of work and management processes to reduce workers' exposure to sources of stress. The second aims to bring about change within individual staff.

Resources may not always allow work at both levels, and some researchers have suggested that there are a number of features of the stress process that support the use of individual-focused worksite interventions (Flaxman & Bond, 2006). First, some work-related stressors (e.g., caring for clients who can be unpredictable and aggressive) cannot easily be removed or reduced. Second, several models of stress emphasize the importance of an individual's coping resources while inappropriate coping efforts (e.g., avoidance) have the potential to exacerbate sources of stress at work (e.g., Lazarus & Folkman, 1984).

A small number of studies have evaluated stress reduction programs for staff working with people with IDs with some success (e.g., Gardner *et al.*, 2005; Innstrand *et al.*, 2004) and more importantly have improved the quality and frequency of interactions with service users (Rose *et al.*, 1998b). These interventions have included promoting increased worker control (Innstrand *et al.*, 2004), increasing levels of personal support (Rose *et al.*, 1998b), and using a cognitive–behavioral intervention (Gardner *et al.*, 2005).

Recent developments in psychological therapy more broadly have shifted the focus from attempting to remove aversive psychological experiences to one that builds resilience to stressful life situations and events. Rather than simply challenging cognitions or thoughts, approaches based on mindfulness and acceptance have been gathering a strong evidence base to ameliorate occupational stress (Bond & Bunce, 2000; Bond & Flaxman, 2006; Bond *et al.*, 2008). Thus, there is the suggestion that workers can develop psychological resilience through acceptance that will enable them to cope over time with work-related stressors. Although perceptions of work demands may not decrease, workers' psychological well-being can improve.

Mindfulness and acceptance bring several different assumptions to understanding psychopathology compared with traditional cognitive–behavior therapy techniques (Hayes *et al.*, 2004). In the new behavior therapies, including Acceptance and Commitment Therapy (ACT), much of human psychological distress is conceptualized as an unhealthy effort to control private experiences such as emotions, thoughts, and memories (Hayes *et al.*, 2006). Put simply, people spend too much time engaged in thinking, regretting, and worrying about things that have happened or might happen and too little time focused on their actual experience. The extra mental effort used in these endeavors ultimately fails to resolve problems, and actually contributes to greater feelings of distress. Mindfulness and acceptance approaches help to emphasize that psychopathology is related to a lack of psychological flexibility to aversive experiences. Rather than seeing psychopathology as a disease that needs to be eradicated, ACT attempts to promote greater flexibility of responses and to help clarify an individual's core values and the practical ways of living in accordance with these values. Acceptance and the commitment to behave in accord with one's personal values are core features of ACT.

A series of studies have successfully shown ACT-based interventions to be effective in reducing occupational stress within brief interventions of three 3-hour workshops (Bond & Bunce, 2000; Bond & Flaxman, 2006; Bond *et al.*, 2008). These have been able to use mindfulness exercises as a central part of the intervention. Mindfulness has become an exciting development of a host of other psychological therapies (Dielectical Behaviour Therapy, Linehan, 1993; Mindfulness-Based Cognitive Therapy, Segal *et al.*, 2002; Mindfulness-Based Stress Reduction, Kabat-Zinn, 1990). Yet still no consensus on the definition of mindfulness exists (Singh *et al.*, 2008). In its clinical application, the most common definition is "Paying attention in a particular way, on purpose in the present moment, non-judgementally" (Kabat-Zinn, 1994, p. 4).

Mindfulness- and Acceptance-Based Intervention with Care Staff

Some of the most innovative use of mindfulness in the field of IDs with care staff has been undertaken by Singh and his colleagues. One multiple baseline study across group homes delivered training in behavior management followed by a mindfulness intervention. It showed that service user aggressive behavior reduced more dramatically and learning improved more steeply once mindfulness had been added to the training staff received (Singh *et al.*, 2006). Another study showed that directly train-ing care staff in mindfulness reduced the use of physical restraints in ID services settings (Singh *et al.*, 2009). Mindfulness in combination with other interventions helped staff to better integrate behavioral and psychopharmacological treatment approaches (Singh *et al.*, 2002).

Singh's work suggests that mindfulness intervention with care staff has important benefits for service users, but his studies to date have not addressed benefits for the well-being of care staff. Work that has been successful in demonstrating positive outcomes for care staff working with people with IDs has built on the ideas first proposed by Bond and Bunce (2000) that placed mindfulness as a central ingredient in staff support (Noone & Hastings, 2009). The Promotion of Acceptance in Carers and Teachers (PACT) (Noone & Hastings, 2009) is a protocol designed to help care staff gain an understanding of the processes involved in developing stress with three areas of self-help based on acceptance, mindfulness, and values clarification.

Using a waiting list control design, the PACT was delivered to a group of care staff working in a typical community service for people with IDs (Noone & Hastings, 2009). Two main measures were taken pre- and posttraining: the General Health Questionnaire-12 (GHQ-12) (Goldberg & Williams, 1988) as a measure of well-being and the Staff Stressor Questionnaire (SSQ) (Hatton, Rivers, Mason, Mason, Kiernan *et al.*, 1999) that records the range of stressors in the work environment. The nine hours of intervention (see following section for details) showed significant positive improvement on the GHQ-12 compared with the control, while the SSQ remained the same. This suggests that staff had improved in their well-being scores while still experiencing the same levels of environmental stress. Further exploration of the data, after increasing participant recruitment, suggests that the intervention was most effective with the staff with least qualifications and the highest baseline stress scores (Noone & Hastings, 2010).

Promotion of Acceptance in Carers and Teachers

In this section, the content of PACT will be summarized. A number of the exercises have been taken from the first ACT book (Hayes *et al.*, 1999), and to save space, these have been referenced rather than described in detail. The workshops are meant to be practical interventions for staff working with challenging clients and should have enough flexibility to respond to discussion points from members of the group. PACT is typically delivered as a one-day workshop, followed by a half-day booster session 8–12 weeks later.

PACT Session 1: Developing a rationale for the work

After a short introduction, the first exercise acts both as an icebreaker and sets the context for later work. People are asked to work in pairs and to describe what per-sonally they bring to their job. Once each pair has completed the task, feedback is recorded on a flip chart. After this, everyone is invited to call out any difficult behaviors they have experienced within their job. Everything is recorded on a separate flip chart.

> **Box 13.1   Example of a job advert generated from initial PACT exercises**
>
> Job advert
>
> *Wanted*:
> A patient, calm, understanding, empathic, energetic, enthusiastic person who is able to keep to care plan, protect the rights of a vulnerable person, ensure the safety of clients and members of the public, will protect the dignity of stigmatized people, and be a keen advocate.
>
> *To work with people who will*:
> Bite, throw objects, scratch, attack you with objects, head bang with fist, withdraw, bang head against wall, spit, bite their own hand, run away, break furniture, attack other clients, kick, eye gouge, scream, ask continuous questions, pick own wounds, swallow air.
>
> A good sense of humor and a clean driving license are desirable.
> The organization is committed to promoting a work–life balance.

Once the list is exhausted both exercises are brought together in the following way. Ask the group members to imagine they are looking for a job in the local paper when they come across the following: *Wanted*. . . and then read back all the positive attributes that the group members have listed that they bring to their work. After this is done, add: *To work with*. . . and then list all the difficult client behaviors that the group members have experienced. A typical range of responses can be seen in Box 13.1.

The reaction of most staff teams is to laugh at the idea of the challenge of their work. Yet it can be the starting point to highlight that, although service users may not be the source of stress in their job, the fact that they set standards of delivering such highly sophisticated behaviors in their work, it may be reasonable to suggest that, from time to time, these will be compromised by the personal impact of fatigue and stress.

With that as a backdrop, it is time to investigate the group's experience of the phenomena of stress. To do this, the group members are broken up into small groups and asked to list how they respond when they are stressed and to list their response into four columns: their physical reactions, how they respond emotionally, how they behave differently, and how they think.

Feedback again is recorded from all the groups on flip chart paper. This exercise helps to normalize everyone's response. People often comment on how extreme some of the examples are (e.g., examples of feeling paranoid, crying, locking oneself away) and yet how similar they are. This allows the concept of stress to be seen as inevitable in most people's lives. There is typically a range of examples that reflect different mood, ranging from heightened arousal and anxiety-based feelings to feeling sad and depressed. Finally, any examples of stress-based thinking are highlighted to show that such thinking may serve a function and the function can often be about avoiding.

The next section is to help understand experiential avoidance. Following from the discussion of flight and fight, the model is expanded to consider how these instinctive responses result in the narrowing of behavioral options. When stressed we do less and what we do can be motivated by reducing harmful experiences that accompany the "stress response." The problem is exacerbated by the influence of the verbal mind that has evolved to predict and prevent potential harm and to offer problem solving. Therefore, the dilemma that most of us experience is that we have a mind that antici-pates negative emotional responses by proposing some form of avoidant strategy. Enormous time and effort can be lost in simply trying to avoid or stop experiencing ordinary emotional reactions. To help illustrate this, another exercise is used to try and chart how we think when we are stressed.

Working in pairs, group members are asked to think of a stressful incident (prefer-ably recent and at work) and describe it to their partner. The description should have enough information to provide an overview of the event. Then the partner should ask questions to drill down to get more detailed information about any stress reactions that may have occurred before, during, and after the incident, with special emphasis on how thinking may have changed immediately after the event and later on when the person got home. After completing the task, they swap roles.

The aim of the discussion is to highlight the function of thoughts when we are stressed, drawing attention to similarities among the group. In particular, the way the mind attempts to offer control and provide solutions to our experience. It is helpful to explore the attempts that people make in trying to resolve their problems. A common experience is ruminating over an event. During rumination, our mind will attend and reattend to the same event, considering it from every conceivable angle without providing an effective solution. What can we do if there is no effective solution?

From such an example we can begin to consider an alternative response; instead of seeking control of our situations by removing the "problem," what would it be like if we chose willingness to experience physical sensation or discomfort? Such a position would also lead to a different relationship with our thoughts.

To help in both these tasks, mindfulness exercises are undertaken. The first is a short body scan (see Williams *et al.*, 2007 for a description). This short exercise helps to illustrate how attention always has multiple options but tends to become domi-nated by the activity of the mind. It also helps to show how much of our attention can be closed off to us until prompted.

Mindfulness provides an alternative to trying to control and remove any physical sensation. It provides a way of simply observing and accepting experience as it is, without defense. A number of metaphors can be used at this stage to further illustrate these points.

For example, Chinese handcuffs operate by tightening the more a person attempts to pull his or her fingers apart. It is only by taking a counterintuitive approach and pushing your fingers together that the handcuffs release their hold. The more we attempt to escape from our negative experiences, the more likely these experiences will take a greater hold of us. It is by facing our experiences fully that we can begin to break free.

Following the mindfulness exercise, everyone is encouraged to share their experiences. They are asked to consider in what ways might an exercise like this help to change our relationship with our thoughts. This introduces the concept of defusion, which is an attempt to establish a distance between oneself and one's thoughts, to lessen the control and domination of thinking. It attempts to establish an understanding that there is an "I" that looks out onto the world that can attend to different sensory experiences and attend and observe the stream of thoughts that accompany our experiences. The session finishes with the suggestion that in some way, our thoughts independently occur to us and we always have the choice of whether to become an observer of our thinking.

There is central idea to this approach that is significantly different from many other approaches to occupational stress. Other approaches attempt to alleviate distress and unpleasant sensations. This approach advocates that we should become more present to our feelings of distress. We are actively seeking to become observers of our negative and destructive thoughts. Yet why would anyone want to do such a thing? The answer to this question is this. While we waste time trying to avoid the things we are actually not able to avoid, we become more and more restricted in what we do. By applying an ineffective strategy, we have less time and less of an inclination to get on with our lives and invest in things that really matter. Therefore, the second part of the day is to try and help participants to be clearer about what is most important to them. This section involves a series of exercises that help each participant articulate his or her personal values.

The first step is to discriminate between life values and life goals. Values are general principles that act as guiding lights in our lives that can never be fully achieved. For example, I may have a value to invest in my personal growth. There will never be a point that I achieve this because there will always be more growth and more development that I could pursue. On the other hand, a goal is something tangible that can be achieved. So if my goals are to get a qualification and run a marathon, these will have points in time when they are achieved.

Values exercise 1: Coat of arms. The aim of this first exercise is to start to identify core life values and life goals. Invite the group to work in pairs to construct a coat of arms that is split into four sections. Everyone is asked to complete two drawings that symbolize one goal and one value in their lives. Then each pair constructs a motto that captures the themes from the drawings. Each couple then takes it in turn to present their drawings. The group members are then asked to reflect on what they have heard. A general comment is how similar the values are and how they express a general compassion and humanity.

When introducing the *values assessment exercise*, it is suggested that a great deal of vitality and life satisfaction can be obtained by consistently engaging in actions that move us in valued directions. All participants are encouraged to see that a life dedicated to controlling unwanted internal events is unlikely to be infused with vitality, because living a valued (and hence, vital) life will inevitably, and often, expose people to undesirable psychological events.

Values exercise 2: Writing a eulogy. The focus of this exercise is to help participants connect with their values. Sitting mindfully with their eyes closed, they are asked to imagine the following scenario:

> Like Scrooge, you have miraculously been able to show up, in spirit form, at your own funeral. Imagine the event attended by family and friends. Choosing someone to say your eulogy, consider what they might say about you if between now and then you don't really get round to doing some of the things that really matter to you. Imagine how they would speak about you if it was tinged with the sense that your life had not been fully lived.

The group is asked to ponder this thought for a few minutes. Remaining in the same mindfulness position, the group participants are asked to consider the following:

> Now keeping everything the same in your mind's eye: the person saying the eulogy, the venue, the invited people, try to imagine what would be said if between now and this event you are able to suck the marrow out of life and the eulogy is one almighty celebration of a life lived to the full.

The group is again asked to consider what things come to mind. The general theme of the discussion is "what do you want your life to stand for?"

The Valued Living Questionnaire (VLQ; Wilson *et al.*, 2010) is then given out. This provides a range of possible values and covers common areas such as personal relationships, friendships, romantic relationship, family networks, and personal development. The VLQ is only meant as a starting point for reflecting about what is important and requires a judgment around a score of 1–10 with 10 being highly important. After this is completed, a second version of the questionnaire is given. This has the same scoring system but asks for how much time has been given over to the value in the last two weeks. This not only allows the identification of a key value, but also checks whether one is consistent in investing time to it.

The final part of this session is given over to two tasks: the Values Assessment Rating Form and the Goals, Actions and Barriers Form (see Bond, 2004, pp. 288–290). These provide individuals an opportunity to reflect on the barriers that may impede the development of key goals in pursuit of values. Toward the end of the session, the *passengers on the bus* metaphor is introduced to draw the mindfulness and values components together (Hayes *et al.*, 1999, p. 157). This metaphor is accompanied by a cartoonlike drawing of "scary" passengers on a bus. Participants are asked to imagine that they are the driver of a bus that is full of passengers (some of whom are scary looking). These passengers represent the driver's thoughts, emotions, memories, urges, and so on. The idea is that the scary-looking passengers will often try to commandeer the bus and demand that the driver takes the bus in directions that may not serve the driver's valued directions. Our attempts to struggle with or placate these passengers tend to be counterproductive, in that to do so, we must either hand over control of the bus to the passengers or stop the bus to struggle with them. Participants are encouraged to view the direction of the bus as representing their chosen values, and the "unhelpful" passengers as the psychological barriers that may be encountered along the way.

At the end of the session, participants are reminded that the next half-day session does not occur for three months, and they are encouraged to use that time to continue developing their mindfulness skills. They are also strongly encouraged to finish the values assessment exercise at home, and, over the next three months, to begin taking steps, however small, that are consistent with their chosen life directions.

PACT Session 2 (approximately three months later)

The aims of session 2 are (1) to provide a booster session for mindfulness skills, (2) to discuss any barriers to valued action, and (3) to further highlight the link between mindfulness and valued action. The session begins with a short mindfulness exercise and a discussion of any issues related to the training that may have arisen over the last three months. Following this discussion, a link is made between mindfulness and acceptance and values, using the *bubble in the road* metaphor (Hayes et al., 1999, p. 229).

The purpose of the discussion following the use of this metaphor is to try and identify the nature of the barriers (or "bubbles") that interfere with movement in valued directions. Examples of values, goals, actions, and barriers are listed on a whiteboard in an attempt to highlight those barriers that are internal events (e.g., worry, low self-confidence, doubts). The general theme of this dialogue is that when these internal events are observed mindfully (i.e., seen for what they are, not for what they say they are), their potential to be barriers is greatly reduced. This discussion of psychological barriers to valued action is then related to the *passengers on the bus* metaphor.

The final exercise is to invite each member of the group, if they so choose, to make a statement of commitment to a goal that is in the service of a core value. This is a way of asking what they have personally got out of the workshops and to create an opportunity to make a public commitment.

Processes within PACT

Why might an acceptance- and mindfulness-based intervention be helpful for care staff working within the field of IDs? At present, there is not sufficient data to answer this question with great confidence, but it may be possible to speculate.

The workshop itself had three aims. The first is to promote a willingness in care staff to experience the full range of emotional responses, even aversive or unpleasant ones. Second is to help to create a broader context to judge "personal progress" in relation to how successfully one is living in accordance to ones values. Third, it uses mindfulness exercises to lessen the control of thoughts so that they are not automatically accepted.

How would teaching the principles of acceptance and mindfulness to care staff help people with an ID? If the teaching is successful in stopping care staff from dwelling on any negative thoughts and from shutting down to a client after experiencing a negative emotional response, it is feasible that that the care staff may remain more available to potential positives in their interaction. These positives may be sufficient to reinforce the staff to interact in the future. Therefore, a willingness by care staff to stay longer with personal discomfort may help to salvage both the frequency and quality of social interaction for the person with ID.

Yet how would this benefit the well-being of the care staff? The model developed in mindfulness-based cognitive therapy (MBCT) (Segal *et al.*, 2002) suggests that reducing the dominance of thoughts through mindfulness prevents the avalanche of further negative thinking that often occurs and the associated negative emotional response that can co-occur. Therefore, one payoff for staff may be to have fewer negative consequences. At the same time, if the training is capable of increasing access to available reinforcement, then there is the chance that the experience at work may be more positive. If staff are also able to clarify their own personal values and make a commitment to investing time in activities that have a real purpose for them, then again, they will have greater chance for improving the quality of their lives.

In such an explanation, an acceptance and mindfulness intervention may help in stopping care staff from succumbing to the aversive control around natural but often toxic consequences of caring. Such a conclusion would have important implications on how we prepare staff to work in this field. It argues for a greater commitment to developing a resilience that is driven by developing positive attributes rather than ones that focus entirely on limiting pathology.

Conclusions

All the stress models discussed predict potential fault lines that may lead to personal distress. Any attempt to invest in staff support may choose to integrate some of the principles from the models. It would appear sensible to promote insight in care staff about the impact of caring, whether they occur by feeling overwhelmed (as suggested by Maslach) or as a consequence of experiencing a sense of inequality (as equity theory proposes) or because it leads to avoidant coping as explained by the transactional and ACT model. The response for any effective service should be to minimize unnecessary deterioration in its workforce. This may involve preparing staff not only through induction but also through regular supervision. Whether there is a need for detailed assessment and allocation to a specific intervention remains to be supported by further research. But any of the interventions that suggest they can limit avoidance in care staff and lower their distress need to be more integrated into our services.

It would be foolish to pose interventions at the intrapersonal staff level when there is a failure to provide adequate resources for the job or adequate basic training. This would result in stress management workshops being used to prop up inept services.

A final point is that acceptance- and mindfulness-based interventions should not be seen in competition with other stress models. If a noxious event occurs that can be removed, then it should be removed and an appropriate adaptation should be made. Acceptance- and mindfulness-based interventions may have an especially important role to play in situations that do not lend themselves to easy solutions.

What is essential is that the needs of care staff are taken seriously and that research continues to investigate the best ways of offering support that will be beneficial for helping care staff maintain high levels of quality care within a mutually rewarding relationship.

References

Adams, J.S. (1965). Inequity in social exchange. *Advances in Experimental Social Psychology,* *2*, 267–299.

Bailey, B.A., Hare, D.J., Hatton, C. & Limb, K. (2006). The response to challenging behaviour by care staff: Emotional responses, attributions of cause and observations of practice. *Journal of Intellectual Disability Research, 50,* 199–211.

Bond, F.W. (2004). Acceptance and Commitment Therapy for stress. In S.C. Hayes & K.D. Strosahl (Eds.) *A clinician's guide to Acceptance and Commitment Therapy.* New York: KA/PP.

Bond, F.W. & Bunce, D. (2000). Mediators of change in emotion-focused and problem-focused worksite stress management interventions. *Journal of Occupational Health Psychology, 5,* 156–163.

Bond, F.W. & Flaxman, P.E. (2006). The ability of psychological flexibility and job control to predict learning, job performance, and mental health. *Journal of Organizational Behavior Management, 26,* 113–130.

Bond, F.W., Flaxman, P.E. & Bunce, D. (2008). The influence of psychological flexibility on work redesign: Mediated moderation of a work reorganization intervention. *The Journal of Applied Psychology, 93,* 645–654.

Caplan, R.D., Cobb, S., French, J.R.P., Van Harrison, R. & Pinneau, S.R. (1975). *Job demands and worker health.* Cincinnati, OH: National Institute for Occupational Safety and Health (Publication No. 75-168).

Cooper, C.L. & Dewe, P.J. (2004). *Stress: A brief history.* Oxford: Blackwell.

Cottle, M., Kuipers, L., Murphy, G. & Oakes, P. (1995). Expressed emotion, attributions and coping in staff who have been victims of violent incidents. *Mental Handicap Research, 8,* 168–183.

Devereux, J., Hastings, R.P. & Noone, S.J. (2009). Staff stress and burnout in intellectual disability services: Work stress theory and its application. *Journal of Applied Research in intellectual Disabilities, 22,* 561–573.

Dyer, S. & Quine, L. (1998). Predictors of job satisfaction and burnout among the direct care staff of a community learning disability service. *Journal of Applied Research in Intellectual Disabilities, 11*(4), 320–332.

Flaxman, P.E. & Bond, F.W. (2006). Acceptance and Commitment Therapy in the workplace. In R.A. Baer (Ed.) *Mindfulness-based treatment approaches.* San Diego, CA: Elsevier.

Gardner, B., Rose, J., Mason, O., Tyler, P. & Cushway, D. (2005). Cognitive therapy and behavioural coping in the management of work-related stress: An intervention study. *Work and Stress, 19,* 137–152.

Goldberg, D.P. & Williams, P. (1988). *A user's guide to the General Health Questionnaire.* Windsor: NFER-Nelson.

Hall, S. & Oliver, C. (1992). Differential effects of severe self-injurious behaviour on the behaviour of others. *Behavioural Psychotherapy, 20,* 355–365.

Hall, S., Oliver, C. & Murphy, G. (2001). Early development of self-injurious behavior: An empirical study. *American Journal on Mental Retardation, 106,* 189–199.

Hartley, S.L. & MacLean, W.E. (2007). Staff-averse challenging behaviour in older adults with intellectual disabilities. *Journal of Applied Research in Intellectual Disabilities, 20,* 519–528.

Hastings, R.P. (2002). Do challenging behaviours affect staff psychological well-being? Issues of causality and mechanism. *American Journal on Mental Retardation, 107,* 455–467.

Hastings, R.P. & Brown, T. (2002). Behavioural knowledge, causal beliefs and self-efficacy as predictors of special educators' emotional reactions to challenging behaviours. *Journal of Intellectual Disability Research, 46,* 144–150.

Hastings, R.P. & Remington, B. (1994). Staff behaviour and its implications for people with learning disabilities and challenging behaviours. *The British Journal of Clinical Psychology, 33,* 423–438.

Hastings, R.P., Tombs, A.K.H., Monzani, L.C. & Boulton, H.V.N. (2003). Determinants of negative emotional reactions and causal beliefs about self-injurious behaviour: An experimental study. *Journal of Intellectual Disability Research, 47,* 59–67.

Hatton, C. & Emerson, E. (1998). Organisational predictors of actual staff turnover in a service for people with multiple disabilities. *Journal of Applied Research in Intellectual Disabilities, 11,* 166–171.

Hatton, C., Emerson, E., Rivers, M., Mason, L., Swarbrick, R., Kiernan, C. *et al.* (1999). Factors associated with staff stress and work satisfaction in services for people with intellectual disability. *Journal of Intellectual Disability Research, 43,* 253–267.

Hatton, C., Rivers, M., Mason, H., Mason, L., Emerson, E., Kiernan, C. *et al.* (1999). Organisational culture and staff outcomes in services for people with intellectual disabilities. *Journal of Intellectual Disability Research, 43,* 206–218.

Hatton, C., Rivers, M., Mason, H., Mason, L., Kiernan, C., Emerson, E. *et al.* (1999). Staff stressors and staff outcomes in services for adults with intellectual disabilities: The Staff Stressor Questionnaire. *Research in Developmental Disabilities, 20,* 269–285.

Hawkins, S., Allen, D. & Jenkins, R. (2005). The use of physical interventions with people with intellectual disabilities and challenging behaviours – The experience of service users and staff members. *Journal of Applied Research in Intellectual Disabilities, 18,* 19–34.

Hayes, S.C., Luoma, J., Bond, F., Masuda, A. & Lillis, J. (2006). Acceptance and Commitment Therapy: Model, processes, and outcomes. *Behaviour Research and Therapy, 44,* 1–25.

Hayes, S.C., Strosahl, K.D. & Wilson, K.G. (1999). *Acceptance and Commitment Therapy: An experiential approach to behavior change.* New York: Guilford Press.

Hayes, S.C., Strosahl, K.D., Wilson, K.G., Bissett, R.T., Pistorello, J., Toarmino, D. *et al.* (2004). Measuring experiential avoidance: A preliminary test of a working model. *The Psychological Record, 54,* 553–578.

Innstrand, S.T., Espnes, G.A. & Mykletun, R. (2004). Job stress, burnout and job satisfaction: An intervention study for staff working with people with intellectual disabilities. *Journal of Applied Research in Intellectual Disabilities, 17,* 119–126.

Ito, H., Kurita, H. & Shiiya, J. (1999). Burnout among direct-care staff members of facilities for persons with mental retardation in Japan. *Mental Retardation, 37,* 477–481.

Kabat-Zinn, J. (1994). *Wherever you go, there you are: Mindfulness meditation in everyday life.* New York: Hyperion.

Kabat-Zinn, J. (1990). *Full catastrophe living: Using the wisdom of your body and mind to face stress, pain and illness.* New York: Delacorte Press.

Lawson, D.A. & O'Brien, R.M. (1994). Behavioural and self-report measures of burnout in developmental disabilities. *Journal of Organizational Behavior Management, 14,* 37–54.

Lazarus, R.S. (1995). Psychological stress in the workplace. In R. Crandall & P.L. Perrewe (Eds.) *Occupational stress: A handbook* (pp.3–15). Washington, DC: Taylor and Francis.

Lazarus, R.S. & Folkman, S. (1984). *Stress, coping and adaptation.* New York: Springer.

Linehan, M.M. (1993). *Cognitive behavioral treatment of borderline personality disorder.* New York: Guilford Press.

Maslach, C. (1982). *Burnout. The cost of caring.* Englewood Cliffs, NJ: Prentice Hall.

Maslach, C. (1993). Burnout: A multidimensional perspective. In W.B. Schaufeli, C. Maslach & T. Marek (Eds.) *Professional burnout: Recent developments in theory and research* (pp.19–32). Washington, DC: Taylor and Francis.

Maslach, C. (1999). A multidimensional theory of burnout. In C.L. Cooper (Ed.) *Theories of organisational stress* (pp.68–85). Oxford: Oxford University Press.

Mitchell, G. & Hastings, R.P. (2001). Coping, burnout, and emotion in staff working in community services for people with a learning disability. *American Journal on Mental Retardation, 106,* 448–459.

Noone, S.J. & Hastings, R.P. (2009). Building psychological resilience in support staff caring for people with intellectual disabilities: Pilot evaluation of an acceptance-based intervention. *Journal of Intellectual Disabilities, 13,* 43–53.

Noone, S.J. & Hastings, R.P. (2010). Using acceptance and mindfulness-based workshops with support staff caring for adults with intellectual disabilities. *Mindfulness, 1,* 67–73.

Oliver, C. (1995). Self-injurious behaviour in children with learning disabilities: Recent advances in assessment and intervention. *Journal of Child Psychology and Psychiatry, 36,* 909–927.

Payne, R. (1979). Job demands, supports and constraints. In C. Mackay & T. Cox (Eds.) *Responses to stress: Occupational aspects.* London: International Publishing Corporation.

Raczka, R. (2005). A focus group enquiry into stress experienced by staff working with people with challenging behaviours. *Journal of Intellectual Disabilities, 9,* 167–177.

Robertson, J., Hatton, C., Felce, D., Meek, A., Carr, D., Knapp, M. *et al.* (2005). Staff stress and morale in community-based settings for people with intellectual disabilities and challenging behaviour: A brief report. *Journal of Applied Research in Intellectual Disabilities, 18,* 271–277.

Rose, D., Horne, S., Rose, J.L. & Hastings, R.P. (2004). Negative emotional reactions to challenging behaviour and staff burnout: Two replication studies. *Journal of Applied Research in Intellectual Disabilities, 17,* 219–223.

Rose, J. (1993). Stress and staff in residential settings: The move from hospital to the community. *Mental Handicap Research, 6,* 312–332.

Rose, J., Jones, F. & Fletcher, B. (1998a). Investigating the relationship between stress and worker behaviour. *Journal of Intellectual Disability Research, 42,* 163–172.

Rose, J., Jones, F. & Fletcher, B. (1998b). The impact of a stress management programme on staff well-being and performance at work. *Work and Stress, 12,* 112–124.

Segal, Z.V., Williams, J.M.G. & Teasdale, J.D. (2002). *Mindfulness-based cognitive therapy for depression: A new approach to preventing relapse.* New York: Guildford.

Singh, N.N., Lancioni, G.E., Wahler, R.G., Winton, A.S.W. & Singh, J. (2008). Mindfulness approaches in cognitive behavior therapy. *Behavioural and Cognitive Psychotherapy, 36,* 659–666.

Singh, N.N., Lancioni, G.E., Winton, A.S.W., Curtis, W.J., Wahler, R.G., Sabaawi, M. *et al.* (2006). Mindful staff increase learning and reduce aggression in adults with developmental disabilities. *Research in Developmental Disabilities, 27,* 545–558.

Singh, N.N., Lancioni, G.E., Winton, A.S.W., Singh, A.N., Adkins, A.D. & Singh, J. (2009). Mindful staff can reduce the use of physical restraints when providing care to individuals with intellectual disabilities. *Journal of Applied Research in Intellectual Disabilities, 22,* 194–202.

Singh, N.N., Wahler, R.G., Sabaawi, M., Goza, A.B., Singh, S.D. & Molina, E.J. (2002). Mentoring treatment teams to integrate behavioral and psychopharmacological treatments in developmental disabilities. *Research in Developmental Disabilities, 23,* 379–389.

Skirrow, P. & Hatton, C. (2007). Burnout amongst direct care workers in services for adults with intellectual disabilities: A systematic review of research findings and initial normative data. *Journal of Applied Research in Intellectual Disabilities, 20,* 131–144.

Van Dierendonck, D., Schaufeli, W.B. & Buunk, B.P. (1996). Inequity among human service professionals: Measurement and relation to burnout. *Basic and Applied Social Psychology, 18,* 429–451.

Van Yperen, N.W. (1995). Communal orientation and the burnout syndrome among nurses: A replication and extension. *The Journal of Applied Psychology, 26,* 338–354.

Watts, M.J., Reed, T.S. & Hastings, R.P. (1997). Staff strategies and explanations for intervening with challenging behaviours: A replication in a community sample. *Journal of Intellectual Disability Research, 41,* 258–263.

Williams, M.G., Teasdale, J., Segal, Z. & Kabat-Zinn, J. (2007). *The mindful way through depression: Freeing yourself from chronic unhappiness.* New York: Guilford Press.

Wilson, K.G., Sandoz, E.K., Kitchens, J. & Roberts, M.E. (2010). The Valued Living Questionnaire: Defining and measuring valued action within a behavioral framework. *The Psychological Record, 60,* 249–272.

Chapter 14

Behavioral Approaches to Working with Mental Health Problems

Robert S.P. Jones
Alan Dowey

Introduction

The following chapter is perhaps unusual in the context of this book as a whole. Unlike other chapters, the present authors do not wish to introduce the reader to a novel skill set or series of techniques that can be used or adapted with people with intellectual disability (ID) who may be presenting with mental health difficulties. In writing this chapter, the authors are conscious that the central role of the book is to assist in providing effective psychological therapies to people with ID who experience mental health and emotional problems. We are particularly aware that clinicians working in routine clinical services are likely to see clients with such problems relatively infrequently and therefore need to be able to use their existing therapeutic skills in a new way and perhaps from a new perspective. In presenting the behavioral approach to mental health problems, our main aim is to encourage therapists to look at this population with fresh eyes and to challenge the reader to adopt a more systemic and advocacy-based role than is typically found in routine clinical services. As such, the behavioral perspective is presented, not as a series of discrete skills, but as an overarching conceptual framework designed to equip the clinician to think beyond the boundaries that typically regard a mental health problem as something that exists inside the heads of our clients and that needs to be fixed or cured through one-to-one talking therapy.

In adopting this perspective, we will draw particularly on an awareness of the issues previously discussed in Chapter 2 where the relative contributions of deprivation and social factors in the development of mental health problems were discussed. We are also aware that a significant section of this book discusses adaptations of the cognitive–behavioral approach as a default treatment for mental health problems.

It is important from the outset, therefore, for the authors of this chapter to "nail their colors to the mast" and state that they do not share this perspective on the

Psychological Therapies for Adults with Intellectual Disabilities, First Edition.
Edited by John L. Taylor, William R. Lindsay, Richard P. Hastings, and Chris Hatton.
© 2013 John Wiley & Sons, Ltd. Published 2013 by John Wiley & Sons, Ltd.

central importance of cognitive therapy. Although there is little doubt that there is a strong evidence base supporting the efficacy of cognitive–behavioral therapy (CBT) interventions, we will argue that a more detailed analysis of this literature supports the centrality of behavioral, rather than cognitive variables. Indeed, we believe that a radical behavioral perspective on this literature presents the best philosophical perspective from which to understand this large body of evidence.

In the first section of this chapter, we will outline the central defining aspects of radical behaviorism. We will then present evidence to support our contention that it is behavioral analysis, rather than cognitive analysis, that holds the greatest potential to provide a theoretical basis for the treatment of mental health problems in people with ID.

We will then illustrate the behavioral approach to working with individuals with ID and mental health problems through a discussion of the importance of ordinary life experiences for people with ID. This is then illustrated by a brief outline of active support (AS) as it relates to the prevention of the circumstances that foster the development of mental health problems. The chapter ends with a list of recommendations for working with this client group that draws from behavior analysis but which is relevant to any theoretical approach.

The Nature of Behaviorism

Within the mainstream psychological literature, behaviorism is criticized on many fronts. In particular, it is often regarded as mechanistic, simplistic, and essentially incapable of providing a plausible explanation for much human behavior. Perhaps not surprisingly, behavior analysts refute such claims. In this section, we address these criticisms with the aim of demonstrating to the reader that the approach is both philosophically and theoretically sophisticated, and is of direct relevance to therapists working with people with ID (and indeed those without ID).

For the present purposes, we will focus on two common criticisms of behaviorism. First, it is often argued that the approach can only deal with observable behavior and consequently ignores thoughts and feelings that happen inside the body. This is often reflected in "black box" accounts where the focus is on the stimulus applied to the organism and the associated response – with no reference to what the organism does with (i.e., processes) the stimulus. Second, it is suggested that behaviorism views the organism as entering the world as a "blank slate" and consequently that it is only important to examine what happens to the organism during its lifetime. Critics of behaviorism reasonably suggest that such a stance ignores important individual differences.

Before addressing these criticisms, it is first important for the reader to understand that "behaviorism" refers to a *family* of views and that there are important differences between types or variations of behavioral accounts (Miles, 1993). The cited criticisms reflect quite accurately J.B. Watson's *Methodological Behaviorism*, where, for example, it was argued that psychology had to limit itself to the study of observable behavior if it was going to be a science. What appears less widely acknowledged is that B.F. Skinner developed another variation of behaviorism – *Radical Behaviorism* (e.g., Skinner, 1974) – in a direct attempt to address these shortcomings (see, e.g.,

Lowe, 1983). According to Lowe, Skinner's efforts successfully "disavowed the taboo on private events and introspection" (p. 72).

We now turn our attention to how radical behaviorism deals with the cited criticisms.

Criticism 1: "The black box"

Skinner's primary aim was to develop a philosophy of science that could account for human behavior – he was not just interested in rats in Skinner boxes. He acknowledged that in trying to achieve this, it would be necessary to explain core aspects of human behavior such as our self-awareness or self-consciousness. Skinner described these phenomena as "exclusively human" (Skinner, 1945, 1974), noting that while animals see, humans see that they see. In doing this, Skinner clearly acknowledges that what happens inside an organism *is* important.

This leads us to ask, how did Skinner propose to address this? Like other behaviorists, Skinner rejected dualism, the philosophical stance that argued that the world can be divided into physical entities and mental entities that originate from the mind. In a radical behavioral account, mental entities such as thoughts and cognitions are deemed to play a central role in determining human behavior. Rather than reject such notions as thoughts and cognitions as Watson would have done, Skinner instead argued that such "mental entities" while important have been incorrectly labeled or conceptualized. Rather than being mystical in origin and originating in a mind or as the result of free will, Skinner viewed these as *types of behavior* and as such are governed by the laws that govern other, usually overt behaviors.

What this means is that core behavioral processes such as reinforcement, punishment, and extinction, which are usually evoked to explain our overt behavior, are also proposed to be at work in shaping our beliefs, views, thoughts, and indeed our emotions. Thus, when radical behaviorists emphasize the importance of the environment in selecting different behavior, this applies as much to behavior *inside* our bodies as it does to the behavior we do with our bodies and that others can observe. People's thoughts come from their experiences, and because of this, they are similar to any other behavior – they can be strengthened, weakened, changed, shaped, and extinguished using exactly the same behavioral approaches that are successful with more overt behaviors.

When trying to understand a person's behavior at any one time, it is necessary to look at what is going on around that person in his or her environment and also how he or she thinks and feels about this. Conceptualizing behavior in this way means that behavior analysts need to maintain a "healthy skepticism" about explanations that rely too heavily on internal factors as *causes* of behavior. If thoughts and feelings are essentially the same as other behaviors, then it is necessary to account for how these have developed, and this leads us back to the environment and the things that have happened to us. Compared with therapists from other theoretical perspectives, behaviorists remain very skeptical about the assumption that cognitions always cause behaviors. They are more likely to argue from the opposite perspective – that behaviors themselves cause cognitions (see Jones *et al.*, 1997 for a detailed discussion of "causal primacy" in this regard). We will now examine the second criticism outlined earlier.

Criticism 2: "The blank slate"

From a radical behavioral perspective, there is no doubt that learning during one's lifetime (via contingencies of reinforcement, punishment, extinction) plays a central role in determining behavior. However, Skinner argued that focusing exclusively on this level misses important influences on behavior.

Skinner did not reject the idea that individuals are different, and he acknowledged the importance of genetic selection, or learning at the level of the species. He referred to this in his writings on phylogenetic contingencies (see, e.g., Skinner, 1981). There is no question that we all enter the world differently. However, exactly how this "difference" impacts on us will depend, at least to some extent, on what happens to us during our lifetime. The opportunities provided to us may allow us to realize our full potential. Conversely, a lack of such opportunities may result in such potential remaining largely untapped. From a radical behavioral perspective, therefore, we are a product of a combination of our genes and our environment and ignoring either influence does not allow a full picture to emerge.

We can extrapolate this line of argument further and apply it to people with ID – a population that Skinner did not consider at any length in his writings. Recent research on behavioral phenotypes (e.g., Basile *et al.*, 2007) suggests that individuals with particular genetic syndromes have a tendency to display specific behavioral topographies (e.g., self-injury). In such cases, we cannot account for the frequency and intensity of such behaviors by reference to learning processes alone, and consequently, it is appropriate to attribute at least some aspects of behavior in these cases to genetic/biological underpinnings. Lack of appropriate acknowledgment of the importance of genetic influences on behavior has been a clear weakness of behavioral approaches in the past.

In terms of understanding the role of mental health difficulties in people with ID, it is clear that such influences are relevant. For example, an abundance of research informs us that people with ID cannot process information at the same rate, or at the same level of complexity as those deemed to be of typical development. We also know, for example, that individuals on the autism spectrum (autism spectrum disorder (ASD)) have difficulty understanding aspects of communication and social interaction. Once again, to account for these difficulties, we have to evoke genetic/biological causes, as attempts to account for the presence of these difficulties through learning theory alone have proven insufficient. Put simply, it is not the case that individuals with ASD *learn* their social and communicative difficulties, or that these arise from trauma or adversity. Rather, their presentation is a combination of their genetic and learning history, and the relative contribution of each will be different in each individual.

If we think about biological/genetic difficulties in context, we can see, for example, that the child with ID will have a very different experience of the education system when compared with his or her typically developing peers. Placing too high expectations on such individuals simply sets them up to fail. Conversely, an assumption that the person cannot learn or be educated will mean that potential skills are not nurtured, and this will lead to a reduced level of development.

Skinner also talked about learning at another level – *cultural contingencies* (e.g., Skinner, 1956, 1974, 1981) – and this adds another level of sophistication to his account. He noted that groups of individuals pass practices and modes of behavior across the generations. For example, it has been noted that any given culture will utilize only a small amount of edible substances as food (e.g., Rozin, 1982). Consequently, items in one culture (e.g., certain insects) may be deemed as food, while rejected as items of disgust in another. The members of the community will gradually shape a child's behavior to ensure that customs and cultural practices are followed.

Skinner argued that language was the key mechanism via which cultural information is passed across the generations. Consequently, verbal rules develop that are used to guide behavior, and social reinforcement is used as a means of ensuring compliance. The child is instructed to do something, or not to do something, and the controlling consequences often do not relate to the action directly (e.g., the actual consequences of putting something in your mouth). Rather, the contingency that does the work is a social one whereby the adult praises or chastises the child accordingly.

We argue that cultural contingencies are very important to consider in our work with individuals with ID. The explanation for this importance lies in the central role played by language in determining our behavior (and ultimately our thoughts and feelings).

Skinner proposed that as a result of living in a culture, one learns language by first talking to and with others. Once acquired, however, individuals are capable of talking to themselves and formulating their own rules. Individuals can carry rules around – usually deemed to be "in their head" – which can guide behavior. This means that although human behavior can be "contingency shaped," that is, shaped directly by the consequences of a particular action, verbally able humans can also engage in what is referred to as "rule-governed" behavior. Importantly, the main controlling element then becomes not the environment itself, but how the individual describes the environment using internal verbal rules.

When following a rule, it is thought that social reinforcement is often of central importance (Zettle & Hayes, 1982). A familiar example will illustrate. It is common for teenagers in our culture to begin experimenting with alcohol. Prior to taking any alcohol, it is likely that the individual will have been exposed to all sorts of rules and language extolling the virtues of excessive consumption. Usually, however, the initial immediate consequences of drinking alcohol are aversive (i.e., beer and wine do not taste nice and are usually considered to be an "acquired taste"). If behavior was just contingency shaped, then the aversive taste should function to punish drinking behavior. With language-based social rules, however, the immediate effects of the environmental contingency are often overridden by social reinforcement processes.

Having considered language, we return to the question of the relevance of this to working with people with ID. Because of the ubiquitous nature of language, cultural practices apply to virtually all aspects of life, including how groups of individuals are viewed and how they are treated in society. We do not need to look too far back in our history to see that people with ID were often viewed as idiots, criminals, and dangerous individuals, to the extent to which they were locked up in order to keep the rest of society safe. Even today, they are frequently viewed as individuals deserving of our pity, but not perhaps individuals with whom we would like to forge strong relations. This being the case, think how people with ID experience culture. How often are they listened to or taken seriously? How often are adults with learning disability ridiculed and laughed at in the street by others? How often are they asked to do things with insufficient support, only to have subsequent opportunity removed from them because they are not capable? It is perhaps not surprising that an individual with ID presents as being reluctant to leave the house, frightened of social interaction with strangers, having low energy levels, and having personal feelings of worthlessness. It is likely that such a presentation would lead to a diagnosis of depression on presentation to a clinic. While we are not suggesting that a diagnosis of depression is inappropriate, we are suggesting that a therapeutic "stance" that locates the problem inside the person's head and attributes it to a faulty thinking mechanism is perhaps ignoring very valuable sources of information about the causes of the presenting problem.

Questioning the Evidence for the Efficacy of CBT

There has been intense debate over the last decade about the relationship between "cognitive" and "behavioral" variables in the treatment of people with intellectual disabilities. For example, Sturmey (2006) has questioned the assertion that there is a sufficient evidence base to justify the widespread use of cognitive therapy with people with intellectual disabilities. He pointed out that in making the case for cognitive therapy with this population, there have been a number of inappropriate assertions and errors made in the literature concerning behavior analysis. Such errors include misrepresenting behavioral analysis as an approach that is limited to high-frequency problems in people with severe intellectual disabilities in institutional settings, mislabeling behavioral interventions as cognitive therapy, and "attributing the alleged efficacy of treatment packages to cognitive therapy, when it is more parsimonious to attribute it to behavioural elements of the package of known efficacy" (Sturmey, 2006, p. 110).

A particularly informative exchange of opinion took place in 2005 in the *Journal of Applied Research in Intellectual Disabilities* (see Emerson, 2006 and Sturmey, 2006 for further reading in this regard).

The present authors do not wish to join the ownership battles concerning which camp has more legitimate right to the efficacy findings regarding particular interventions in the ID literature. Rather, we wish to widen our focus to examine research in the general literature as a means to better understand the respective roles of behavioral and cognitive variables and their relevance to people with IDs and mental health problems.

The term "second wave" therapies have been used to describe the emergence of cognitive-based therapies such as CBT and rational emotive therapy in the 1970s and 1980s. This label has been adopted to distinguish these therapies from the first wave behavioral therapies that dominated the field in the 1950s and 1960s. Despite the apparent dominance of cognitive therapies since that time (to the extent that the term "cognitive revolution" has been used), authors such as Hayes (2004) and Longmore and Worrell (2007) have pointed to weaknesses in the evidence base supporting the effectiveness of second wave therapies. In relation to CBT, for example, Hayes (2004) pointed out three such weaknesses. First, studies that deconstruct cognitive interventions into their respective components, consistently fail to show that cognitive interventions provide significant added value to the therapy over and above the effects of the behavioral components (e.g., behavioral activation) that are included in the CBT "package."

Second, CBT interventions have been shown to lead to rapid reductions in symptoms and, indeed, such rapid symptom improvement has been hailed as one of the major sources of support for the intervention. More careful analysis, however, has revealed that in many cases, the rapid improvement occurred *before* the introduction of specific cognitive interventions (i.e., as a consequence of the behavioral experiments used at the beginning of the interventions). Finally, there is very little evidence that symptom changes directly follow changes in the thoughts and beliefs thought to mediate and underpin the disorders being treated.

In discussing the work of Hayes (2004) outlined earlier, Longmore and Worrell (2007) have questioned the basic theoretical underpinnings of CBT. In an article provocatively entitled "Do we need to challenge thoughts in CBT," they provided a compelling accumulation of evidence that behavioral aspects of many treatments for anxiety and depression may explain the observed symptomatic improvements.

We think this is an important finding in relation to people with intellectual disabilities. Specifically, we are not making a case that because of some assumed cognitive deficit, behavioral interventions are more relevant than cognitive interventions to people with IDs. We are, rather, making a much more explicit point that, *irrespective of levels of assumed cognitive abilities*, behavioral interventions are centrally relevant to the treatment of mental health problems per se. More specifically, it is our position that much of the apparent evidence base for the efficacy of "cognitive" interventions is, in fact, evidence for the importance of behavioral interventions.

Understanding the Development of Mental Health Problems

There is a widely cited correlation between a diagnosis of ID and the presence of mental health problems (e.g., Bouras & Holt, 2007). This is a complex relationship and, as we have seen in Chapter 2, an analysis of vulnerability factors for the development of mental health difficulties in the wider population suggests that we need to look beyond a diagnosis of ID alone to explain this correlation. In particular, it is clear that many characteristics of the environment that typically surrounds people with ID have a significant influence on the subsequent development of mental health problems. Put more simply, chronic poverty, loneliness, boredom, and continued lack of opportunities to exert influence or control over one's life, friendships, and future are characteristics both of the ID population and causal influences underlying the development of mental health problems in any population. This leads to two interrelated conclusions. First, that we must be careful not to suggest that it is the *diagnosis* (as opposed to the enforced lifestyle) of ID that leads to the higher incidence of mental health problems. Second, we need to move beyond a view that locates mental health problems inside the heads of people with ID, to a view that sees the immediate environment of people with ID as a legitimate target for the prevention and treatment of such problems. The next section of this chapter examines the behavioral emphasis on developing and supporting ordinary life environments for people with ID and, using the example of AS, shows how this emphasis is relevant to the prevention of mental health problems.

Behavior analysis and ordinary life

There is a long and valued tradition within behavior analysis of adopting a functional approach to assessment and intervention for people with ID. Central to this has been the development of procedures to understand the function of a behavior and, once established, teaching the person a more adaptive alternative behavior that has the same function (i.e., functional communication training; Carr & Durand, 1985). Work has also focused on modifying environments to reduce reliance on inappropriate or challenging behavior (Ringdahl *et al.*, 1997). It is perhaps no surprise that in addition to emphasizing risk, definitions of challenging behavior have also highlighted the risk of denial of access to "ordinary community facilities" (e.g., Emerson, 1995).

Particularly in the United Kingdom, behavior analysts adopted a values-based approach to their work, drawing on, for example, nonbehavioral schools of thought such as the normalization movement (Wolfensberger, 1983). This resulted in a key aim of intervention focusing on facilitating individuals to access an "ordinary life." It was proposed that cultural contingencies meant that people with ID lived marginalized lives in which they could exercise little control, had little social contact, and had little meaningful engagement in activity, and that this was exacerbated by an often understandable challenging response on the part of the person.

It is perhaps easy to overlook the importance of the concept of "ordinary life." This may reflect in part a likely common fantasy that many of us hold to escape the routine chores and activities that make up an ordinary life by winning the lottery, or achieving fame and fortune through some other means. Many of us, with hectic, busy lives would welcome having someone else who was willing to complete the onerous and boring chores that fill our spare time and get in the way of us having more fun.

The picture for people with ID is perhaps a little different, as illustrated in the following discussion. Clearly, the differences do not concern the fantasies concerning fame and fortune – we can see no reason why such aspirations should not be attributed to people with ID as such desires reflect our humanity as opposed to our intellect. The crucial difference lies in the extent to which we are able to exercise independent control over our daily lives. People without ID have likely developed the skills necessary to take full advantage of the escape from "ordinary life" and could replace the boring chores of everyday existence with engaging and stimulating alternatives. Contrast this with people with ID who typically have lower levels of adaptive skills that promote independence and are usually reliant on others in many aspects of daily living. Quite simply, for most people with ID, enforced denial of access to the minutiae of an "ordinary life" have significantly reduced their skills, learning opportunities, and important opportunities to extract reinforcement from the environment. This leaves people with little option but to be "busy doing nothing." This is a long way from a positive life of pleasure – enforced disengagement leads to reduced rather than enhanced quality of life and yet this is a daily reality for the majority of people with ID (Mansell *et al.*, 2002). This enforced disengagement and disempowerment can, in turn, supply the perfect condition for the development of mental health problems.

When considering the broader category of mental health difficulties and, in particular, the issue of protective factors, we argue that much of the work carried out by behavior analysts over the last 20 years is of central relevance. Essentially, it is proposed that what are viewed as traditional behavioral interventions may be particularly important in mental health prevention, given the emphasis on

- making environments more sensitive to individual needs
- increasing social contact and engagement
- increasing engagement in meaningful activity
- increasing an individual's repertoire of functional skills
- generally improving an individual's quality of life.

It is in these areas where, we believe, behaviorism has made its greatest contribution to the mental welfare of people with ID. We believe that increasing access to psychological therapy for this population cannot, and should not, be restricted to the activities that take place in a quiet room, on a one-to-one basis between a therapist and a client. Rather, an understanding of the genesis of mental health problems and the role of clinical advocacy and systemic awareness must be part and parcel of a therapist's role with this population. We will return to the implications of this perspective toward the end of the chapter. At this point, however, we outline one behavioral intervention that directly aims to reduce the chronic disengagement that characterizes the lives of many people with ID. This intervention is known as AS.

Active support

AS emerged in the United Kingdom in the 1980s, and its development was linked to the deinstitutionalization program of the 1990s, which saw the relocation of individuals with ID from large-scale institutional care to small-scale community-based living projects (Totsika, Toogood & Hastings, 2008).

Although a number of different AS procedures have been developed over time, a number of key principles or central themes have been responsible for the development of the various approaches (Totsika, Toogood, Hastings & Nash, 2008). We argue that these core principles, although not conceived within such a framework, are fundamental in relation to the prevention and intervention with respect to issues concerning mental health.

Totsika, Toogood and Hastings (2008) noted that a key concept in the development of AS was the idea of "engagement as a major determinant of quality of life" (p. 207). According to Koritsas *et al.* (2008), AS involves two distinct stages, the first of which centers on working with support staff to seek out and create opportunities for resident involvement. In doing so, the aim is to identify situations that are meaningful and therefore more likely to provide natural reinforcement and emphasize functional skills. This may, for example, focus on teaching clients to wash up, operate a washing machine, or engage in a valued leisure activity. Contrast this with teaching a nonfunctional skill that does not generalize beyond a day center setting and fails to extract any reinforcement from the environment within which the client operates. Obviously, opportunity creation is a dynamic and constantly evolving process that needs to be sensitive to the client's ongoing skill acquisition, needs, and preferences, in a way that reflects a process that probably happens in a somewhat less contrived way with people who do not have ID.

Once opportunity has been identified, a trainer then works with the staff on how best to effectively support resident involvement. Obviously, it is at this point that the client's strengths and weaknesses are considered, and this allows tailor-made support to be implemented. Consequently, the emphasis is shifted from "doing for" to "doing with."

Totsika, Toogood and Hastings (2008) reviewed the AS literature since its development in the 1980s and concluded that

1. it increases client participation in daily activity,
2. it increases staff/client interaction, and
3. it positively impacts on challenging behavior.

Measures relating directly to mental health issues have been included in a number of very recent studies examining AS, with encouraging results. For example, Koritsas *et al.* (2008) reported a study examining the utility of AS with 12 adults with ID living in supported community-based group homes. Consistent with the cited review, they reported that AS resulted in increased client engagement in domestic tasks. In discussing a positive impact on challenging behavior levels, as reported by staff using the Developmental Behaviour Checklist for Adults (Einfeld *et al.*, 2003), they noted significant decreases in subscale scores measuring anxiety and "self-absorbed" behavior.

Similarly, Stancliffe *et al.* (2010) reported work with 41 adult residents and staff from across nine community-based group homes. Significant positive increases in "domestic participation" and other adaptive behavior were mirrored by positive effects on overall challenging behavior, "internalized" challenging behavior (e.g., self-injury), and staff ratings of depression using the Depression Scale (Evans *et al.*, 1999).

Although AS certainly appears to have great potential with respect to mental health difficulties, data are only beginning to emerge that confirms this prediction. If we hypothesize that low levels of activity increase the risk of depression, it is perhaps not surprising that positive impacts are recorded with an intervention designed to increase participant activity and engagement (e.g., Stancliffe *et al.*, 2010). Nonetheless, the fact that increasing activity levels do indeed seem to reduce levels of depression is a very significant finding in relation to both our understanding of depression and ability to treat it. There are, perhaps, also implications in this research for interventions with non-ID populations who might also exist in conditions of enforced disempowerment.

Implications for Clinical Practice

The contents of this chapter attest to the relevance of behavior analysis to the Improving Access to Psychological Therapies (IAPT) therapist working with people with ID. We would suggest that behavioral analysis offers a great deal not only in terms of direct intervention work with the individual and considering wider systemic aspects of the client's life, but perhaps most importantly, by providing a framework for structuring clinical thinking when formulating a client's difficulties.

Based on other chapters in this book, the therapist can draw on a range of clinical interventions designed to target specific symptoms and behaviors. We would also suggest, however, that it would be prudent to keep in mind Skinner's writings on how contingencies operate at different levels. We have already highlighted the importance of not losing sight of learning at the ontogenetic level – how have the experiences of this individual impacted on his or her learning and the development of any difficulties. We have also shown the relevance of the difficulties that the person may have entered the world with – phylogenetic contingencies. As a consequence of these genetic contingencies, we are more likely to see particular behaviors when demands are placed on individuals or when they are trying to communicate with other people around them. Finally, we must consider cultural contingencies – we need to examine the expectations of those charged with supporting our clients, how this client group is viewed in society, and what expectations are placed on them. And this in turn leads us to consider important systemic variables as highlighted in the work on AS. Formulation at this level may lead us to intervene less with the client directly, but instead with the client's best interests targeting the contexts or systems within which the client operates.

Behavioral analysts have a long tradition of intervention at the individual, environmental, and even societal level, and the authors of this chapter inevitably bring this wider perspective to our understanding of the nature of the therapist's role.

We have deliberately taken a broad perspective on what constitutes increasing access to psychological therapy for this client group. As practicing clinical psychologists, we have frequently intervened in the systems and environments that surround our clients in an effort to effect changes in their daily lives. Sometimes, it is only by changing the behaviors of others (i.e., family members, carers, staff) that we can truly effect positive changes in the lives of the individuals who are referred to us. Indeed, it is very often the institutions and organizations that we work for who are the main stumbling blocks in improving the quality of life of the individuals with ID who come to see us. The tradition of clinical advocacy that emerges from a tradition of seeing the therapist's role as someone who needs to fight for the rights of the clients has inevitably colored our perspective not only on the treatment of mental health problems, but also on the very nature and definition of these problems.

We are very aware that such a perspective will not necessarily be shared by the readership of this book, and there may or may not be opportunities to intervene in the wider system within which the client lives or works. But we argue that it is sometimes essential to adopt this wider perspective, and we further believe that clinical advocacy is a neglected but essential role for any therapist. For example, if a client complains of being bullied, is it always sufficient only to work on the impact of this bullying on the client's self-perceptions, thoughts, and feeling? Or are there times when attempts to intervene in the system that is causing the bullying should be seen as a legitimate part of the therapeutic process itself?

In conclusion, we are making a case for widening the definition of what we understand when we use the phrase "increasing access to psychological therapy." A comprehensive intervention for mental health problems includes increasing access to the factors that we know are protective against the development of mental health problems in vulnerable populations. For example, we argue that a legitimate focus for psychological therapy is to increase access to activities and environments that encourage well-being, social contact, and meaningful friendships. If we continue to restrict the conceptualization of psychological therapy to one-to-one talking interventions that aim to fix faulty thinking inside our clients' heads, then we do a disservice not only to our individual clients but also to the very nature of therapy itself.

References

Basile, E., Villa, L., Selicorni, A. & Molteni, M. (2007). The behavioural phenotype of Cornelia de Lange Syndrome: A study of 56 individuals. *Journal of Intellectual Disability Research, 51,* 671–681.

Bouras, N. & Holt, G. (2007). *Psychiatric and behavioural disorders in intellectual and developmental disabilities.* Cambridge, UK: Cambridge University Press.

Carr, E.G. & Durand, V.M. (1985). Reducing behaviour problems through functional communication training. *Journal of Applied Behavior Analysis, 18,* 111–126.

Einfeld, S.L., Tonge, B.J. & Mohr, C. (2003). *Developmental Behavior Checklist for Adults (DBC-A).* Melbourne: Monash University.

Emerson, E. (1995). *Challenging behaviour: Analysis and intervention in people with learning difficulties.* Cambridge, UK: Cambridge University Press.

Emerson, E. (2006). The need for credible evidence: Comments on "some recent claims for the efficacy of cognitive therapy for people with intellectual disabilities". *Journal of Applied Research in Intellectual Disabilities, 19,* 121–123.

Evans, K., Cotton, M., Einfeld, S. & Florio, T. (1999). Assessment of depression in adults with severe or profound intellectual disability. *Journal of Intellectual & Developmental Disability, 42,* 147–160.

Hayes, S.C. (2004). Acceptance and commitment therapy and the new behavior therapies. In S.C. Hayes, V.M. Follette & M.M. Linehan (Eds.) *Mindfulness and acceptance: Expanding the cognitive behavioral tradition* (pp.1–29). New York: Guilford.

Jones, R.S.P., Miller, B.Y., Williams, W.H. & Goldthorp, J. (1997). Theoretical and practical issues in cognitive behavioural approaches for people with learning disabilities: A radical behavioural perspective. In B. Kroese, D. Dagnan & K.S. Loumidis (Eds.) *Cognitive therapy in people with learning disability.* London: Routledge.

Koritsas, S., Iacono, T., Hamilton, D. & Leighton, D. (2008). The effect of active support training on engagement opportunities for choice, challenging behaviour and support needs. *Journal of Intellectual & Developmental Disability, 33,* 247–256.

Longmore, R.J. & Worrell, M. (2007). Do we need to challenge thoughts in cognitive behavior therapy? *Clinical Psychology Review, 27,* 173–187.

Lowe, C.F. (1983). Radical Behaviourism and human psychology. In G.C.L. Davey (Ed.) *Animal models of human behaviour* (pp.72–93). Chichester, UK: Wiley.

Mansell, J., Elliott, T., Beadle-Brown, J., Ashman, B. & Macdonald, S. (2002). Engagement in meaningful activity and "active support" of people with intellectual disabilities in residential care. *Research in Developmental Disabilities, 23,* 342–352.

Miles, T.R. (1993). Cognitive processes: A critique. *Mexican Journal of Behavior Analysis, 19,* 163–176.

Ringdahl, J.E., Vollmer, T.R., Marcus, B.A. & Roane, H.S. (1997). An analogue evaluation of environmental enrichment: The role of stimulus preference. *Journal of Applied Behavior Analysis, 30,* 203–216.

Rozin, P. (1982). Human food selection: The interaction of biology, culture, and individual experience. In L.M. Baker (Ed.) *The psychology of human food selection* (pp.225–253). Chichester: Wiley.

Skinner, B.F. (1945). An operational analysis of psychological terms. *Psychological Review, 52,* 270–277.

Skinner, B.F. (1956). Freedom and the control of men. *The American Scholar, 25,* 47–65.

Skinner, B.F. (1974). *About behaviorism.* London: Jonathan Cape.

Skinner, B.F. (1981). Selection by consequences. *Science, 213,* 501–504.

Stancliffe, R.J., McVilly, K.R., Radler, G., Mountford, L. & Tomaszewski, P. (2010). Active support, participation and depression. *Journal of Applied Research in Intellectual Disabilities, 23,* 312–321.

Sturmey, P. (2006). On some recent claims for the efficacy of cognitive therapy for people with intellectual disabilities. *Journal of Applied Research in Intellectual Disabilities, 19,* 109–117.

Totsika, V., Toogood, S. & Hastings, R.P. (2008). Active support: Development, evidence base, and future directions. *International Review of Research in Mental Retardation, 35,* 205–249.

Totsika, V., Toogood, S., Hastings, R.P. & Nash, S. (2008). Interactive training for active support: Perspectives from staff. *Journal of Intellectual and Developmental Disability, 33,* 225–238.

Wolfensberger, W. (1983). Social role valorization: A proposed new term for the principle of normalization. *Mental Retardation, 21,* 234–239.

Zettle, R.D. & Hayes, S.C. (1982). Rule governed behavior: A potential theoretical framework for cognitive behavior therapy. In P.C. Kendall (Ed.) *Advances in cognitive behavioral research and therapy* (pp.73–118). New York: Academic.

Chapter 15

Psychodynamic Psychotherapy and People with Intellectual Disabilities

Nigel Beail
Tom Jackson

Introduction

People who have intellectual disabilities (IDs) are at risk of suffering from psychological problems like anyone else. Thus, they need access to a range of psychological therapies like anyone else. In this chapter, the provision of psychodynamic psychotherapy for people who have IDs will be discussed. Psychodynamic psychotherapy developed from psychoanalysis, but should not be confused with it. Psychoanalysis has only had a limited application with people who have IDs. Psychoanalysis was developed as a treatment by Sigmund Freud and is undertaken for 50 minutes, five times a week. It is not widely available outside major cities and is mostly provided in private practice. Thus, it is outside of the means of most people and certainly the means of people who have IDs. Psychodynamic psychotherapy has developed from psychoanalysis and is usually undertaken once a week in an outpatient setting. It may be time limited or open ended. Psychodynamic psychotherapy has been provided in some state-funded services and supported charities in the United Kingdom and in some European states. Little is known about provision in other parts of the world, and reports of provision in, for example, the United States, are few.

People who have IDs have only been in receipt of psychodynamic psychotherapy since about 1980, and then provision is not widespread. Prior to 1980, there was some limited, but poorly documented, provision. One of the barriers to access has been the various selection criteria concerning suitability for psychodynamic psychotherapy. These include factors such as ability to enter an intensive treatment relationship, emphasizing the importance of possessing psychological mindedness, motivation, and adequate ego strength. However, these concepts are not readily defined. For example, Freud (1940) described a psychical apparatus of three parts: the id, the ego, and the superego. The id contains everything that is inherited and in particular the life and death drives. The ego develops in early childhood as an intermediary between

Psychological Therapies for Adults with Intellectual Disabilities, First Edition.
Edited by John L. Taylor, William R. Lindsay, Richard P. Hastings, and Chris Hatton.
© 2013 John Wiley & Sons, Ltd. Published 2013 by John Wiley & Sons, Ltd.

the id and the real world. The ego has the task of self-preservation and performs such tasks as becoming aware of stimuli and building memories. The ego also takes action in the service of self-preservation in the form of helping people to avoid or adapt to situations or, through activity, bring about changes to their advantage. The ego simultaneously gains control over the internal drives and decides whether to allow, deny, or postpone satisfaction. Thus, the ego is the location of feelings of tension. When tension is raised, displeasure is felt, and any subsequent displeasure that is expected and foreseen gives rise to what we call anxiety. Also, as we develop, the ego takes into itself representations of the parents, and through this agency, which Freud called the superego, the parental influence is prolonged. Thus, the ego has to manage the tensions that arise between the internal world of the id, reality, and the superego. So, if we consider here what poor ego strength may mean, then it suggests that the capacity to manage the tensions is poor. However, how this should make someone unsuitable for psychotherapy is not clear. One hypothesis might be that it makes them more in need. The definition of the ego has also changed over time, and there has been a major dispute as to its origin and development. Freud's followers in the Ego Psychology School have described the ego as containing the functions of thought, perception, language, learning, memory, and rational planning (Hartmann, 1964). Thus, the ego has many of the features that make up the construct of intelligence. Thus, it is not surprising to find that some even suggest that the person should be of at least average intelligence to undertake psychodynamic psychotherapy (Brown & Pedder, 1991). Clearly, the application of such criteria would exclude people with IDs from treatment. However, the application of psychodynamic therapy with adults who have IDs has shown that these factors may not be as relevant as claimed. Psychodynamic therapy has been adapted and developed for use with children. If it can be used with children, how can it be argued that adults who are developmentally delayed and could be age matched with a child are not suitable? Thus, the work of Anna Freud and Melanie Klein, along with the ideas of John Bowlby and Donald Winnicott, among others, has influenced the development of an adapted age-appropriate treatment approach for people who have intellectual and developmental disabilities.

Psychodynamic psychotherapy may be implicated for some people who have IDs who present with psychological problems, including behavioral difficulties. Prescriptive therapies such as cognitive–behavioral therapy (CBT) tend to work from the basis that the client has an awareness of his or her problem and is able to make a problem statement in response to questions about his or her difficulties. This is also the case for people who have IDs (Willner, 2005). However, some clients with IDs frequently present for treatment without such understanding. Stiles *et al.* (1990) developed a pan-theoretical model of the way people assimilate their problematic experience. They found that for people in the general population, most started psychotherapy at what they called the "problem statement" level. Thus, the clients could articulate what they thought was their problem. Research by Newman and Beail (2005), using this model with people with IDs, found that they present for treatment at the lower levels of assimilation – such as "warded off," experiencing "unwanted thoughts," or having some "vague awareness" of the problem. This lack of understanding found in adults who have IDs may be due to a variety of reasons. It may be that the problem, as seen by others, is not discussed with the person and so he or she is not part of any discussions about it. Often, the therapist has to draw the client's attention to what others are having a problem with. Psychological factors may also play a role. Central to psychodynamic theory is the concept of the defense mechanism. Defense mechanisms are mental operations that remove thoughts and feelings from conscious awareness. Basically, individuals deal with emotional conflicts, or internal or external stressors, by keeping something out of conscious thought or altering how events are perceived. These defenses or defensive behaviors are observable in therapy sessions and identified, and the person's attention is drawn to them. This is a key function of the therapist in psychodynamic psychotherapy. Thus, the psychodynamic approach can help the clients identify what they are doing unaware and help them come to terms with the reasons why they are doing it. Newman and Beail (2010) have shown that adults who have IDs use a wide range of defense mechanisms. They used the Defence Mechanisms Rating Scale (Perry, 1996) that comprises of detailed descriptions of 28 defenses and also guidance on how to differentiate between them. The scale is used to identify defenses used from recordings of therapy sessions and to monitor changes in their use across sessions. Newman and Beail (2010) found that the participants in their study used 24 of the 28 defenses described, but they did not observe any change in use across eight sessions. They also observed that individuals in the study tended to have particular defensive styles. Newman and Beail (2002, 2005) have also demonstrated that psychodynamic psychotherapy can enable clients with IDs to move toward and beyond the level of problem statement in a few sessions. It may also be that when offered a choice, people with IDs may choose psychodynamic therapy rather than CBT or other approaches.

Distinctive Features of the Psychodynamic Technique

Blagys and Hilsenroth (2000) identified seven features of psychodynamic therapy that distinguish it from other therapies. These are (1) a focus on the relationship between client and therapist, (2) a focus on interpersonal relations, (3) a focus on affect and expression of emotions, and (4) the exploration of fantasy life. The therapist (5) explores attempts to avoid distressing thoughts and feelings, (6) identifies recurring themes and patterns, and (7) recognizes that past experience affects our relation to and experience of the present.

The first stage is similar to all models of therapy in that the therapist would assess the client's problem and his or her circumstances and history. The therapist needs to also gauge the client's developmental level and cognitive abilities to make adaptations to the treatment so that it meets his or her needs. Thus, the therapist needs to pay attention to the clients' communication skills, what words they use, and how they express themselves. The therapist then needs to work within the client's vocabulary, or provide opportunities for vocabulary development to assist and improve communication and understanding. This is an adaptation of technique as such educational interventions would not normally occur in psychodynamic psychotherapy.

When working with a client who had been the victim of a sexual assault, the therapist had to help the client to learn words for some parts of his or her body and for sexual acts to enable better communication between them. This problem often occurs in therapy as clients may not have the level of vocabulary needed to communicate what they have experienced. Bruner identified the development of the cognitive ability of representation. Initially, experiences are represented through actions then through visual images and then through the development of vocabulary. People with ID develop in the same way but at a slower rate. Thus, the ability to represent visual images (iconic representation) in words (symbolic representation) is delayed. However, the therapist needs to bear in mind that his or her client may be recalling past events iconically but prevented from effectively communicating due to delayed language development. In simple terms, the client has not developed a vocabulary that covers all the things he or she can recall visually. The therapist's act of empathic engagement with the client builds trust and a safe place to explore past events that may be troubling him or her. The client may then be thinking about the event through visual representation and reexperiencing the event and being distressed by this but struggling to communicate his or her recollections verbally. This may lead to the client communicating through other means such as acting out what has happened. Alternatively, therapists may assist their clients to communicate by the provision of materials such as paper and pens or figures.

In psychodynamic psychotherapy, the intention is to allow the client–therapist relationship to be therapeutic. Central to this approach is close observation of the client's verbal and nonverbal behavior, his or her attitudes, mannerisms, and so on. These are developed though relationships with parents, siblings, friends, and so on, and result in the developing personality. These are then transferred into the relationship with the therapist. Thus, difficulties in relationships outside of therapy will show themselves in the relationship with the therapist. For example, if the clients spend most of their time when with people talking about their pet dog, they are highly likely to do the same with the therapist. The therapist allows the client to do this and focuses on what it is like to be with this person. The therapist may try and explore the reasons why the person has been referred, but the client quickly returns to telling the therapist about his or her dog. The therapist observes that the client is being avoidant (some form of defense mechanism is being used) but at the same time starts to feel what it is like for others to be with this client, which, in psychodynamic psychotherapy, we call the countertransference. So whatever happens between them, they seek to understand in terms that will serve the underlying aim of therapy.

In psychodynamic work, therapists maintain certain boundaries in the relationship with the client. They communicate to the client that this is a safe place to talk and that the relationship is confidential. The therapists refrain from revealing anything personal about themselves, which can be quite difficult. Clients may ask personal questions that have to be dealt with in a positive way. So when asked if you are married, you need to find out why. The question needs to be dealt with without the client feeling rejected. So you can simply say "that's an interesting question, I'm wondering why you asked." The referral may also provide information that will inform the therapist about other boundaries that may need to be put in place, or boundaries that may be challenged. For example, a client referred with a history of anger management difficulties may express this or act it out in the session. However, the therapist can at the beginning draw the client's attention to the possibility of this and make clear what is acceptable (i.e., saying how angry they feel) and what would be unacceptable (being aggressive).

The safe setting, the clear boundaries, and the therapeutic relationship are all designed to facilitate the clients in exploring and clarifying the reason why they are there. We advise that therapists focus on the client's problem rather than take the traditional psychoanalytic "free association" approach. Free association involves asking the client to talk about whatever is in the mind and then seek associations to the material that follows. Clients with IDs may not understand what you are asking, and the question would need to be simplified. Then, if you ask them to say what is in their head, they may have a different conceptualization of that than you. Thus, to work this way would need some education and development work. In our experience, working this way only leads to why they are there, and so why not start at that point in the first place. The reason why the client is there is most likely to be because of some psychological distress or behavioral excesses. Thus, the therapist helps contain the client in a manner whereby past intolerable feelings such as anger can become held within the session, clarified, and, where possible, resolved and reintegrated in a tolerable form by the client. In psychodynamic psychotherapy, the therapist is concerned with the patient's representation of himself or herself within the world and seeks to identify the origin, meaning, and resolution of difficult feelings and inappropriate behaviors. The work entails making links between how they are in the therapy room with their current life and earlier life experiences, in order to show how these past experiences influence unconscious and conscious expectations of relationships in the present day.

Most people who have IDs do not refer themselves for treatment. The referral is usually triggered by a family member, carer, professional, or other agency. The therapists will have their concerns in the form of a written referral, which can then be shared with the client. The client's response need to be observed as it may be evidence of defensiveness or acceptance. However, the behavior will inform the therapist of the client's responsive style to others when presented with a view about them.

Psychodynamic psychotherapy is an exploratory method, and the therapist uses a number of ways to help the client to tell his or her story. The therapist will listen carefully to and observe the client's verbal and nonverbal communications. In psychodynamic psychotherapy with people who have IDs, the therapist needs to pay particular attention to what the clients do in the session. For example, how they sit, do they get up and down, do they pick at skin, and so on. Clients may bring things to the session with them. This may not be relevant, but it may have some communicative function.

The therapist observes the clients' mood, as communicated through what they say, the way they say it, but also how they behave. The client may talk about a range of things, and the therapist does not interrupt. The therapist attends to the factual content of what the person says, the words used, and also what is not said. Some topics the clients may not talk about may include among others their disability, feelings of dependency, sex and sexuality, pain and loss, and feelings of annihilation. These topics have been called the five mutative themes by Hollins and Sinason (2000). The psychodynamic psychotherapist would ask questions about the person's childhood, parental relationships, and about other relationships.

Developing a Formulation

The therapist makes information- and exploratory-seeking responses in order to draw out more information from the client. Information-seeking responses are aimed at clarification, which helps sort out what is happening by questioning and rephrasing. Exploratory responses are generated from hypotheses about what the client might not be saying in words but could be hinting at through behavior or tone of voice. For example, clients may not talk about their disability but distinguish themselves from other people who have disabilities. They may not mention their parents or one parent. These are two areas a psychodynamic psychotherapist would seek more information on and wish to explore further. Others may then follow. So the therapist may draw attention to the clients not mentioning that they have a disability and then progress to explore their fantasies regarding the origin of their disability. Then, seeking information about the parents may lead to exploration of fantasies about say an absent parent or lost parent. If parents are absent or lost, the therapist would want to explore how this may have impacted on attachments or their internal representation of parents and other people in their lives and their emotional development. Initially, these are hypotheses that a psychodynamic psychotherapist may silently hold and wishes to obtain more information on. As part of the therapeutic process, the psychodynamic therapists may begin by reflecting back, paraphrase, or précis what the clients have been telling them or acting out before seeking more information or exploring the issue further.

Psychodynamic therapists seek to help clients understand the unconscious meaning of their communications. The therapist uses a number of processes to recontextualize the manifest content of the communications. The first of these is transference (Smith, 1987). Freud (1912) described transference as occurring when psychological experiences are revived and, instead of being located in the past, are applied to dealings with a person in the present. In psychodynamic psychotherapy, the establishment, modalities, interpretation, and resolution of the transference are, in fact, what define the cure (Laplanche & Pontalis, 1988). Transference allows the therapist to identify interpersonal issues and deal with them as empirical data in the here and now. For example, this process allows early traumatic experiences and empathic failures on the part of parents and other caregivers to be relived and corrected. Thus, in the session, the therapist would explore the client's account of his or her problem, but also explore those issues that are unsaid in an attempt to develop a fuller history of the role of the problem in his or her life. The model guides the therapist to explore all relationships, especially those with carers.

Second, the therapist seeks to understand unconscious communications through models of the internal world. Most significantly, we all have an ego, which is the location of the anxiety caused by the tensions between the internal world of drives and the real world and the people we internalize. It is the ego that employs a range of defenses to ward off anxiety. People with IDs have delayed ego development and therefore may tolerate anxiety less well and, consequently, are more prone to poor anxiety management, anger, and aggression. The therapists will be monitoring the defenses their clients use to ward off their anxiety. Published case studies of psychodynamic psychotherapy with adults who have IDs suggest that the defenses used by clients are more primitive than those used by the general population (Sinason, 1992). However, Newman and Beail (2010) found that people who have IDs use a wide range of defenses from primitive, such as acting out and denial, to mature ones, such as repression and affiliation. People who have ID may have negative feelings about being disabled and may deal with this by denial. However, they may also be engaging in behaviors that might help them pass as being like everyone else. Thus, they may be unable to read but carry a book or newspaper. They may copy the behavior of nondisabled relatives and carers. Alternatively, they may distinguish themselves from other disabled people or refer to other disabled people in derogatory terms. When faced with failure, they may make poor rationalizations that the task was rubbish, or if they find they cannot do a job and are asked to leave, they may say it was the poor pay rather than their lack of ability that caused them to leave.

Many of Freud's followers have developed the view that the personality evolves through the internalization and integration of the people into the self or ego. These internal people or objects are those who have cared for us and, over time, those we have relationships with. However, we may also encounter some people who cause distress or create traumatic feelings. Therapists' explore the clients' internal representations of past and current relationships whether good or bad. The aim of therapy is to link experiences in the past with problems in the present. The client's way of being in the world has developed through experiences in these relationships. Past relationships may also become distorted through revisions and modifications through defenses such as repression or splitting off and disowning negative or traumatic experiences in relationships. Past relationships may also become distorted through cognitive processes such as fantasy. Past negative relationships may, through fantasy, become idealized so that the anger the client feels toward them cannot be expressed. However, the presenting problem may be aggressive behavior toward current substitute carers or acquaintances. Only through discovery of the source of the anger and allowing that anger to be felt can such difficulties be resolved.

Third, there are a range of psychodynamic theories of development that the therapist may employ to understand the origins or development of difficulties and conflicts, as well as coping styles. Some clients who have ID may experience poor parenting, or poor or inconsistent substitute care. This is often identified through the client refusing to leave a carer to join the therapist, the client referring all questions to a carer, or through coy behavior toward the therapist. Thus, for some, their earliest developmental needs such as having an attachment to a carer have not been met. In such situations, Clarkson (1993) highlighted the reparative/developmentally needed relationship and defined this as the internal provision by the therapist of a corrective/reparative or replenishing parental relationship (or action) where the original parenting was deficient, abusive, or overprotective. Such a relationship modality is a further facet of the therapist's intervention and style. Only through exploration of the internal representation of the parents and other people can the therapist help with any difficulties that may be located in his or her past but impacting on behavior now. People who have ID are to varying degrees in dependent relationships with carers or supporters. Thus, threats to withdrawal of support may give rise to the type of depressive anxiety identified by Klein (1975) in young children, that is, fear of loss and associated anxieties as to causes and consequences of the feared loss.

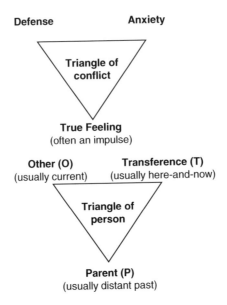

Figure 15.1   Malan's two triangles.

The Formulation

There are several ways in which psychodynamic psychotherapists depict their formulation. Malan (2001) depicted the aim of psychotherapy in the form of the "two triangles" (see Figure 15.1) that describe the process of psychodynamic psychotherapy. Each triangle stands on its apex. The aim of the psychodynamic psychotherapy is to reach beneath the defense and anxiety to the true feeling. At this point, the true feeling can be traced back from the present transference location – in the therapy room toward the therapist – to its current expression in relationships outside the therapy room, to its origin in the past – usually to the relationship with parents or significant carers. For Malan (1979), "The importance of these two triangles is that between them they can be used to represent almost every intervention that a therapist makes; and that much of the therapist's skill consists of knowing which parts of which triangle to include in his interpretation at any given moment" (p. 91). For an illustration of this process with a client who has IDs, see also Beail and Newman (2005) and Beail and Jackson (2009). However, when working with adults who have ID, the clients' relationship with their parents may still be one of dependency, and thus, the past and the current will have features of dependency of differing degrees.

We would advise that therapists work from the assumption that people with IDs develop the same psychic structures as everyone else, but at a slower rate. Thus, their psychic structures can be understood better through theories of early development such as Bowlby's attachment theory and Klein's positions. Kleinian theory is useful in our work, as it provides a framework for understanding most common problems – anxiety, depression, and anger. Klein identified psychological processes at earlier stages of development including defense mechanisms that are used in childhood.

These include *projection, introjections, idealization, denial, related identifications, omnipotence*, and *splitting*, which serve to protect against anxieties. Kleinian theory guides us to look at the utility in defending the self against feelings of dependency, inadequacy, fear of rejection or annihilation, and envy. These primitive defenses operate by fragmenting and keeping apart those conflicting parts or by denying their existence. The defense of "splitting" is considered to be central to this process and describes the unconscious separating of conflicting aspects of other people and the self (ego), so that they are perceived as either entirely good (loved) or entirely bad (hated). "Projection" is the processes in which people get rid of parts of themselves and then locate them in other people (projects). The projected parts are aspects of themselves that do not assimilate with their existing understanding of themselves, or take into themselves (introjection) aspects of other people that do not assimilate with their existing perception of them. "Denial" and "idealization" are the defensive process that we deny the existence of negative aspects of people and the self and may also result in the idealization of others. People who have IDs may also defend themselves against the anxiety associated with disability and associated dependency by the defense *omnipotence*. They may say they do not need the therapist and can sort their own problems out, or say they do not need support and can manage alone.

Another relevant issue for people who have IDs is what Winnicott identified as the dysynchrony between their physical, cognitive, and emotional development. This may also be a source of anger and frustration and needs to be explored and understood.

In therapy, the therapist needs to explore as much about past relationships as possible and how they are integrated or not into the client's internal world. People in the past who have caused the person to feel guilt, fear, and shame may not readily be mentioned until the client has full trust in the therapeutic relationship. The therapist may find that the client keeps such feared people split off from the others. If the feared person is someone usually found in the family such as a parent, sibling, or uncle, then it is likely he or she would not be mentioned, and thus, the therapist would initially raise his or her absence by making this observation. Unfortunately, strangers are more difficult to identify. However, the behavior of the client in the session may give clues. For example, James who we discovered was abused by a complete stranger showed a major fear reaction in the session. The therapist does not see this as a fear reaction to them but the transference of fear from another person to them. The therapist gently explores whom this was in relation to their past. By a process of elimination of the people known, we arrive at the stranger. However, the therapist will start by making a comment on their observations in the session and then may have to make a statement to the client that they have been frightened by someone outside the family and that it may be helpful to talk about this.

It is the experience that we have people (objects) inside ourselves that give us a sense of existence and identity. The struggle to attain a secure and stable good internal world inside ourselves is seen as the core of a stable personality that can weather emotional disturbance. To achieve this, the self (ego) has to form an integration of the various part objects and of the parts of the self. It is the psychodynamic hypothesis that people who need psychological help may have had significant difficulties in this integration.

The Treatment Process

Basically in psychodynamic psychotherapy, the therapists would continuously listen and observe. At appropriate times, they would reflect back, seek further information, and ask exploratory questions. They would draw attention to (reflect back) or gently confront aspects of the clients' defensiveness and try to help them locate the feelings they are trying to avoid. At the same time, they would be monitoring their countertransference. The therapist would see the client's behavior and communication through the concept of transference and consider the material in terms of the client's internal world and the development of that internal world. These facilitate the formulation of hypotheses about aspects of the client that are hidden and disowned. The therapist thinks carefully how to communicate these to the client. Is the client ready and able to be made aware of unconscious aspects of his or her thinking and life? Exploration may result in further resistance. This would need to be drawn to the client's attention by the therapist. This then would be linked to his or her anxiety and then to the hidden parts. In this process, the here-and-now issues of the therapy session are gradually linked to problems in current relationships and then those that are the basis of the problems from the past (usually with the parents). The therapist needs to consider whether or not the client could retain the interpretation in full or does it need to be delivered in parts. Freudian therapists prefer to wait until the client is in a state of positive transference. However, Klein recommends making interpretations when people are at their maximal level of anxiety. As people who have IDs have more difficulties in life with their memory and are also more prone to primitive defenses such as splitting, we would argue from a pragmatic point of view that the Kleinian approach is more likely to be effective.

Case study: George

George was transferred to adult ID services because he had reached the age of 18 years and needed help with an ongoing problem of self-strangulation. George was small for his age and his sexual development was delayed. However, there was concern that the behavior was autoerotic and that he was at risk of serious harm or death. George attended an assessment session with his parents. At the session, his father did all the talking; George did not respond to the therapist's attempt to involve him and his mother said very little. His father said that George had been strangling himself with clothes, cables and so on since he was about six years old. He had been an inpatient in a children's behavioral treatment service but this had no effect. It was observed at the assessment session that George's father talked about him in very derogatory terms and blamed George's mother for his disability. George was offered one-to-one psychotherapy to explore his difficulties and he accepted.

At his first appointment, the session started by the therapist restating the reason for referral, thus starting with a focus on the problem. George presented as more able than expected from the first session. He said he felt something inside him telling him to do it and if he says no to it, it gets angry and forces him to do it. The therapist then explored when this behavior happens. He was quite clear he did it when he felt stressed and identified other people that bullied him as the source of stress. He described others at his college as the bullies and that he engaged in strangulation more often at college. At this time, he was engaging in this behavior several times a day at college and his parent said he was doing this at home. During his first session with the therapist, George said that he had watched a pornographic film and tried to communicate that his penis enlarged. He then said that the bullies at college talk about his delayed sexual development. George had a limited sexual vocabulary, and if sexual matters were going to be a theme, some educational work on this would be needed to help him talk about this. However, it was observed by the therapist that George's accounts continued, and the content became more fantastic and unbeliev able. He continued to talk about the bullies; in his account, these young men were suspended from college, then arrested and given lie detector tests, and then sent to prison. Also, all the evidence about what they had said about George was recorded on mobile telephones. At this point, the therapist made an intervention in the form of a confrontation. That is, the story of what occurred in a week was not credible. The therapist's hypothesis was that George was defending himself by forming fanta sies in his mind that brought about a result that he would wish for. The fantasies also inhibited the expression of true feeling. After the confrontation by the therapist, George stated to modify the account, but then changed the subject and started to strangle himself. This lasted a few seconds and then he dropped his hands. He then started to talk and talk about football and telephones and computers leaving no space for any intervention from the therapist.

At the next session, the therapist began by trying to focus on the problem behavior. George changed the subject and talked about his parents; his mother was severely depressed and his father was stressed about it. He then stopped and said we are not here to talk about them but about me. He then went into a monologue about events in college. When possible, the therapist intervened to ask about the problem behavior. George said he was not doing it so often but felt relief when he did. He then talked in a dissociated way about the "it" that told him to strangle himself. Now, the "it" liked him and was making him feel happy. He said it felt as if someone else was strangling him; but, he said he knew it was him.

By the next session, his parents had separated and George blamed his mother. He said he would leave home and live with his mates. He did not mention his problem behavior and when asked about it, he attributed it to stress at home, but then changed this to problems at college and gave a detailed account of a fight he had with another student. Further attempts to focus on the problem behavior were avoided. Thus, George had for the first time attributed his behavior to problems at home and had expressed some anger toward his mother. But when he did this, he quickly reverted to defensive behavior. Thus, George's avoidance taken with the history of the problem led the therapist to hypothesize that the problem behavior was more likely linked to problems at home and that George could not accept this and so he defended himself from experiencing true feelings (most likely anger) toward his parents. A number of themes were now emerging across sessions; George defends himself against the true feelings through turning against the self (strangulation), splitting off any thoughts of anger toward his parents (by changing the subject), projecting those thoughts into others (bullies at college), and resolving problems through fantasies that have an underlying wish (the bullies are punished).

As sessions continued, a theme of a strong identification with his father emerged; in fact, George idealized this man. However, the focus on the problem behavior and the confrontation of the fantasies led to George blaming himself for his difficulties, but confirming this by saying what his father called him; this was very demeaning and undermining of George's confidence. Over time, the true extent of his father's bullying became evident.

As sessions progressed, the strangulation was reported to be less frequent, but George was developing very quickly secondary sexual characteristics. He started to tell the therapist about how he masturbated and then this became so violent that medical attention was needed. The therapist made some space in the session to develop George's sexual vocabulary and knowledge. As this improved, his technique improved, and the injuries ceased. The concern that the strangulation was linked to sexual acts was not confirmed.

The content of sessions varied from short periods focusing on the problem behavior to longer periods of talking without pause about computers and telephones or accounts of situations in which he was victimized and the perpetrator was dealt with. Confrontation was the main mode of intervention, and self-strangulation in the session was a frequent response. However, this brought George back to the focus of the therapy. Over time, there were increasing references to his parents' behavior (violent rows or not speaking) and his father's bullying. This enabled the therapist to focus on George's feelings in these situations. If he avoided, the technique of gentle confrontation was used again, for example, "I asked you how you felt about that and you changed the subject, so can I ask you again." Thus, the aim of every session was to put George in touch with as much of his true feelings as he can bear (Malan, 2001). George started to describe feeling unwanted and uncared for and then acted this out by goading the therapist to reject him. The therapist reflected this behavior back and then responded by offering continued appointments that George accepted. George talked increasingly about the problems at home, and he gradually started to express more anger toward his parents session by session. He began to see that such feelings were justified and that it was appropriate to be more assertive at home. This was accompanied by a reduction in self-injurious behavior outside of the sessions and acting this out and other forms of avoidance in the sessions. In the psychodynamic model, this is described as an increase in activating affects and a reduction of inhibitory affects. George decided that he wanted to end therapy after nine months. By then, his strangulation behavior was very rare. Before and after therapy, George completed the Brief Symptom Inventory (BSI) and the Inventory of Interpersonal Problems (IIP). On both measures, he had very elevated scores at assessment, which had reduced to being in the nonclinical range after treatment. George agreed to attend for three and six months' follow-up appointments. At three months, he reported very infrequent strangulation, and by six months, this had ceased.

The Evidence Base

There is a belief that psychodynamic psychotherapy lacks scientific support or that it is less effective than other forms of treatment. There is also some hostility to evaluating the effectiveness of psychodynamic psychotherapy as practitioners feel that the process of evaluation interferes with the client–therapist relationship (Beail, 1995). However, there is considerable evidence to show the efficacy and effectiveness of psychodynamic psychotherapy with the general population (Shedler, 2010). Evidence for its effectiveness with people who have IDs is only emerging. There is an emergent body of knowledge built on clinical experience and theoretical development (see, e.g., De Groef & Heinemann, 1999; Sinason, 1992). There are also a small number of studies that have evaluated the effectiveness of this approach with adults who have IDs. These have been reviewed in Beail (2003) and Willner (2005). Since then, Beail *et al.* (2005) have published an open trial, and Newman and Beail (2005) have looked how people with IDs assimilate their problems during treatment. While research is limited, all studies suggest that people who have IDs make positive gains. Beail *et al.* (2007) also showed that significant gains can be made in shorter-term psychodynamic interventions of a few months. Merriman and Beail (2009) have also shown that recipients of psychodynamic psychotherapy value this provision.

Conclusions

Psychodynamic psychotherapy offers an alternative or preferred approach to the treatment of psychological distress and behavioral difficulties. The approach can be part of ID mental health service care pathways (Jackson, 2009). However, when used with people who have ID, the approach needs some adaptation to take account of the client's development. The approach we have described is more aligned to shorter-term psychodynamic psychotherapy. However, some clients may benefit from longer-term approaches. For George, the intervention helped him to stop engaging in a behavior that was not only harmful but also socially unacceptable. However, there were other issues not addressed such as his understanding of his disability, a topic that had remained unsaid. There was also the dysynchrony of his physical, cognitive, emotional, and sexual development and his emergent sexuality and sexual fantasies. George would need to engage in longer-term treatment for these to be addressed. It was his choice to end therapy when he felt he had made significant gains and that was respected. However, others value longer-term help (Merriman & Beail, 2009). Evidence is emerging to show that this approach can be effective, but research studies on the model's efficacy (i.e., controlled trials) with people who have ID have yet to be conducted, and such studies would need to make many compromises (Beail, 2010).

References

Beail, N. (1995). Outcome of psychoanalysis, psychoanalytic and psychodynamic psychotherapy with people with intellectual disabilities. *Changes, 13,* 186–191.

Beail, N. (2003). What works for people with mental retardation? Critical commentary on cognitive behavioural and psychodynamic psychotherapy. *Mental Retardation, 41,* 468–472.

Beail, N. (2010). The challenge of the randomized control trial to psychotherapy research with people with learning disabilities. *Advances in Mental Health and Learning Disabilities, 4,* 37–41.

Beail, N. & Jackson, T. (2009). A psychodynamic formulation. In P. Sturmey (Ed.) *Clinical case formulation: Varieties of approaches* (pp.251–290). Chichester: Wiley-Blackwell.

Beail, N., Kellett, S., Newman, D.W. & Warden, S. (2007). The dose-effect relationship in psychodynamic psychotherapy with people with intellectual disabilities. *Journal of Applied Research in Intellectual Disabilities, 20,* 448–454.

Beail, N. & Newman, D. (2005). Psychodynamic counselling and psychotherapy for mood disorders. In P. Sturmey (Ed.) *Mood disorders in people with mental retardation.* New York: NADD Press.

Beail, N., Warden, S., Morsley, K. & Newman, D.W. (2005). Naturalistic evaluation of the effectiveness of psychodynamic psychotherapy with adults with intellectual disabilities. *Journal of Applied Research in Intellectual Disabilities, 18,* 245–251.

Blagys, M.D. & Hilsenroth, M.J. (2000). Distinctive activities of short-term psychodynamic-interpersonal psychotherapy: A review of the comparative psychotherapy process literature. *Clinical Psychology: Science and Practice, 7,* 167–188.

Brown, D. & Pedder, J. (1991). *Introduction to psychotherapy.* London: Routledge.

Clarkson, P. (1993). *On psychotherapy.* London: Whurr Publishers.

De Groef, J. & Heinemann, E. (Eds.) (1999). *Psychoanalysis and mental handicap.* London: Free Associations Books.

Freud, S. (1912). The dynamics of transference. In J. Strachey (Ed.) *The standard edition of the complete psychological works of Sigmund Freud* (Vol. 12, pp.97–108). London: Hogarth.

Freud, S. (1940). *An outline of psychoanalysis. The standard edition of the complete psychological works of Sigmund Freud* (Vol. 23). London: Hogarth.

Hartmann, H. (1964). *Essays in ego psychology: Selected problems in psychoanalytic theory.* New York: International Universities Press.

Hollins, S. & Sinason, V. (2000). New perspectives: Psychotherapy, learning disabilities and trauma. *British Journal of Psychiatry, 176,* 32–36.

Jackson, T. (2009). Accessibility, efficiency and effectiveness in psychological services for adults with learning disabilities. *Advances in Mental Health and Learning Disabilities, 3,* 13–18.

Klein, M. (1975). *The writings of Melanie Klein* (Vol. 3). London: Hogarth Press.

Laplanche, J. & Pontalis, J.B. (1988). *The language of psychoanalysis.* London: Karnac Books.

Malan, D. (1979). *Individual psychotherapy and the science of psychodynamics.* London: Butterworths.

Malan, D.H. (2001). *Individual psychotherapy and the science of psychodynamics.* London: Butterworth.

Merriman, C. & Beail, N. (2009). Service user views of long term individual psychodynamic psychotherapy. *Advances in Mental Health and Learning Disabilities, 3,* 42–47.

Newman, D.W. & Beail, N. (2002). Monitoring change in psychotherapy with people with intellectual disabilities. The application of the assimilation of problematic experiences scale. *Journal of Applied Research in Intellectual Disabilities, 15,* 48–60.

Newman, D.W. & Beail, N. (2005). An analysis of assimilation during psychotherapy with people who have mental retardation. *American Journal on Mental Retardation, 110,* 359–365.

Newman, D.W. & Beail, N. (2010). An exploratory study of the defence mechanisms used in psychotherapy by adults who have intellectual disabilities. *Journal of Intellectual Disability Research, 54,* 579–583.

Perry, J.C. (1996). Defense mechanisms in impulsive versus obsessive-compulsive disorders. In J. Oldham & A.E. Skodol (Eds.) *Impulsive versus obsessive-compulsive disorders* (pp.195–230). Washington, DC: American Psychiatric Press.

Shedler, J. (2010). The efficacy of psychodynamic psychotherapy. *The American Psychologist, 65*, 98–109.

Sinason, V. (1992). *Mental handicap and the human condition: New approaches from the Tavistock*. London: Free Association Books.

Smith, D. (1987). Formulating and evaluating hypotheses in psychoanalytic psychotherapy. *The British Journal of Medical Psychology, 60*, 313–316.

Stiles, W.B., Elliott, R., Llewelyn, S.P., Firth-Cozens, J.A., Margison, F.R., Shapiro, D.A. *et al.* (1990). Assimilation of problematic experiences by clients in psychotherapy. *Psychotherapy, 27*, 411–420.

Willner, P. (2005). The effectiveness of psychotherapeutic interventions for people with learning disabilities: A critical overview. *Journal of Intellectual Disability Research, 49*, 75–85.

Chapter 16
Mindfulness-Based Approaches

Nirbhay N. Singh
Giulio E. Lancioni
Alan S.W. Winton
Angela D.A. Singh
Ashvind N.A. Singh
Judy Singh

Introduction

Our knowledge of psychological therapies for people with intellectual disabilities (ID) has grown exponentially in the last few decades. The closure of institutions and improved quality of life in community settings partially attest to the effectiveness of psychosocial interventions. Recently, mindfulness-based approaches have emerged as being clinically useful for alleviating pain and suffering, as well as for transforming our approach to life, and there is a small but growing body of research that attests to their effectiveness in assisting individuals with ID to self-manage their challenging behaviors. In this chapter, we briefly discuss mindfulness within the context of cognitive–behavioral therapy, methods currently used to measure the impact of mindfulness on psychosocial functioning, and its applications with individuals with ID.

Mindfulness Approaches in Cognitive–Behavioral Therapy

Many symptoms of psychological distress are rooted in an individual's irrational thinking that leads to problems in cognition, behavior, and affect. Cognitive–behavioral therapy subsumes a number of clinical approaches, such as self-management, self-monitoring, reality testing, and other cognitive restructuring approaches, that can be used by the individual to modify his or her irrational or negative thinking. The specific techniques chosen will depend on the nature of the psychological distress (e.g., psychiatric disorder, maladaptive behavior), and mediating and moderating variables (e.g., status of medical and psychological distress, cognitive level, motivation for therapeutic change, ability to shift the focus of one's attention). Mindfulness-based techniques are a recent addition to cognitive–behavioral therapy that generally aim to change the individual's relationship to thoughts and feelings instead of changing

Psychological Therapies for Adults with Intellectual Disabilities, First Edition.
Edited by John L. Taylor, William R. Lindsay, Richard P. Hastings, and Chris Hatton.
© 2013 John Wiley & Sons, Ltd. Published 2013 by John Wiley & Sons, Ltd.

the individual's response to irrational thoughts (Shapiro & Carlson, 2009). Like cognitive–behavioral therapy itself, mindfulness-based approaches encompass a wide range of techniques that are customized to the needs of the individual.

Mindfulness-based approaches have emerged in an unsystematic manner, with procedures being developed based on the theoretical orientation and personal practice of the researchers. However, in the Brownian motion of mindfulness research, two diffuse theoretical strands appear to be developing in the recent literature, one having roots in psychology and the other in wisdom traditions, chiefly Buddhism at the present time. For example, acceptance and commitment therapy emerged from behavior analysis and relational frame theory, which deals with language and cognition (Hayes *et al.*, 2001). Langer's (1989) research on mindfulness and its application to human behavior is firmly rooted in cognitive psychology. In this approach, specific psychological techniques are used to enhance mindfulness in individuals.

In contrast, the work of Kabat-Zinn (1990, 2003) on mindfulness-based stress reduction (MBSR) is based on Buddhist teachings and derives its psychological theory from these teachings. Mindfulness-based cognitive therapy (MBCT), which was informed by MBSR, also follows in this tradition (Segal *et al.*, 2002; Williams *et al.*, 2007). Mindfulness-based techniques are taught by experienced meditation practitioners who adhere to the spirit and substance of *dharma*, the teachings and instructions of Buddha. This approach has resulted in a proliferation of research that attests to replicable clinical findings across disorders and settings (Baer, 2006). Extant research on the use of mindfulness-based approaches with individuals with ID is also based on this tradition.

Mindfulness

Although there is currently no consensus on the actual definition of mindfulness, it has been described as "a bare awareness of thoughts, feelings, and perceptions as they occur" (Mingyur Rinpoche, 2007). In terms of clinical application of mindfulness, it may be useful to conceptualize it as both an outcome (i.e., awareness) and a process (i.e., practice). Shapiro and Carlson (2009, p. 4) have stated it in this way: "(a) *mindful awareness*: an abiding presence or awareness, a deep knowing that manifests as freedom of mind (e.g., freedom from reflexive conditioning and delusion) and (b) *mindful practice*: the systematic practice of intentionally attending in an open, caring, and discerning way, which involves both knowing and shaping the mind." The limited current research on the use of mindfulness-based approaches with individuals with ID incorporates very rudimentary forms of both types of mindfulness.

Assessment Methods

The lack of a coherent definition and process of mindfulness across studies means that measuring its outcome can be an interesting exercise, especially in Western science, which requires quantifiable, reliable, and valid measures. While there is agreement that the outcome is experiential, and perhaps transformational in the life of the practitioner, the way in which this experience is measured has taken different forms.

First, rating scales have been developed to measure different aspects of mindfulness, but these rating scales suffer from one or more forms of validity (Singh, Lancioni, Wahler *et al.*, 2008). Second, outcomes can be measured at neurophysiological levels, but they may not always be practical in most clinical outcome studies. Third, outcomes can be measured in terms of the effects of mindfulness practice on others. Fourth, the impact of training in mindfulness can be measured in terms of qualitative and quantitative changes in the dependent variable (e.g., on specific behaviors or disorders; Grossman *et al.*, 2004). Thus far, the third and fourth strategies have been used with individuals with ID.

Mindfulness in ID

Unlike traditional behavior modification procedures for individuals with ID, in which external agents (e.g., parents, caregivers, and teachers) administer the programmed contingencies, self-management strategies enable individuals to regulate their own behaviors and to achieve self-selected goals. They enable individuals to effectively establish control over their own behaviors. In addition, self-management procedures avoid problems of generalization and maintenance because the individuals are able to use the procedures in multiple settings, provide immediate self-reinforcement, and apply them to covert behaviors, thoughts, and feelings. The role of external agents is to assist the individuals to select appropriate self-management strategies that match their cognitive ability, teach the individuals how to use the strategies, provide support and encouragement, and generally be their cheerleaders as they learn, practice, and correctly use the selected techniques.

There is increasingly promising research on the use of cognitive–behavioral therapy in individuals with mild ID (e.g., Taylor *et al.*, 2005). It indicates that these individuals are able not only to accurately report their own emotional states, but also to respond appropriately to them (Rose *et al.*, 2000). For example, individuals with mild ID can use a number of self-management strategies, including relaxation training, self-instructional training, and problem solving (e.g., Benson, 1994). These studies strongly suggest that individuals with ID are capable of learning a variety of cognitive coping strategies that they can access when faced with emotionally arousing situations that may otherwise lead to socially unacceptable behavior.

Meditation on the Soles of the Feet (SoF)

SoF is a mindfulness-based strategy that has been used either alone or in combination with other strategies to self-manage anger, inappropriate sexual behavior, obesity, and smoking. It is likely that this procedure can be used as an effective intervention with other behaviors where the same or similar cognitive processes play a central role in their maintenance. SoF enables the individual to divert attention from an emotionally arousing thought, event, or situation to an emotionally neutral part of the body. The individual is able to stop, focus the mind back on the body, calm down, and then make a choice about how to react to the thought, event, or situation that triggered the arousal response. Once the procedure is mastered to the point of automaticity, the individual can use it in multiple contexts, whether sitting, standing, or walking slowly. It provides the individual with an internalized response that is transportable and easy to master, and can be accessed in almost any situation (Singh, Singh *et al.*, 2011).

Typically, training the mind includes one or more of the following: (a) a personal meditation practice based on concentration and/or contemplative meditation exercises, (b) behavioral practices (e.g., loving kindness, compassion, and generosity), (c) cognitive strategies (e.g., reflection on the transitory nature of events and the emptiness of self), and (d) empathic strategies (e.g., the alternate giving of happiness and taking of suffering (*tonglen* practice)). All of these techniques are viewed collectively as elements of training the mind. SoF falls squarely in this tradition but is modified for use by those who may not have a personal meditation practice. This meditation strategy was initially developed for people with severe mental illness and then used with other populations in the disabilities field generally.

The initial impetus was to teach individuals the traditional meditation on "letting go," a standard Buddhist meditation practice that focuses on our relationship with our thoughts. Letting go of thoughts requires understanding that we are not our thoughts, and that we can overcome or control the emotions that are associated with thoughts and avoid the terminal physical response. Thus, in an anger-producing situation, someone says something that we take objection to, it translates into an angry emotion, which in turn may translate into a physical action that would be called aggressive behavior. If individuals can train their mind to look at the first link of their behavior – the rising of the thought that they do not like what is being said – and let it go, then nothing else follows. They can do this by practicing a meditation on letting go of thoughts. Of course, they may not be able to do this if they do not already have a personal meditation practice. We reasoned that they could use a shortcut by moving their attention from the anger-producing thought to a neutral place, the soles of their feet, and contemplate on that for a few moments. By doing that, they are letting go of the anger-producing thought, and when their mind returns to the social interaction that produced the thought in the first place, they are ready to move on without the anger.

In terms of the four components of training the mind described earlier, they have used a short burst of concentration meditation (i.e., personal meditation practice) in a behavioral practice format (i.e., whenever an anger-producing thought arises, drop the mind to and concentrate on the soles of the feet). The link is that we practice loving kindness with ourselves (avoiding anger and angry behavior) by going to the soles of our feet. Practitioners can use cognitive strategies to affirm their knowledge that the rising of anger is transitory in nature and would dissipate without any action. There is a beginning, middle, and an end to any situation. There is no need for action, in terms of either thoughts or behavior. For those further advanced along this line of meditation, they may engage in *tonglen* practice and use empathic strategies to help the other person in the interaction reduce his or her anger.

Aggression

The first exploration of the use of SoF was with a 27-year-old man with mild ID and mental illness who had been institutionalized several times because he could not control his aggressive behavior in community settings (Singh *et al.*, 2003). His last admission to an inpatient hospital occurred when he seriously hurt one of his peers at his group home. He was admitted with an Axis I diagnosis of psychotic disorder not otherwise specified (NOS) and an Axis II diagnosis of mild mental retardation, and treated with psychotropic medications and behavior therapy. After 12 months as an inpatient without achieving much control of his verbal and physical aggression, he requested training using mindfulness-based strategies because he was frustrated with his progress and highly motivated to live in the community. He was taught a simple meditation procedure designed to increase his mindfulness of external and internal environments. Training was provided during 30-minute supervised role play and practice sessions held twice a day for five days. This was supplemented with homework practice assignments for another week before he was instructed to use the procedure to control his verbal and physical aggression.

He was initially taught to recognize situations that were triggers or precursors for verbal or physical aggression. Then, he was guided through the specific steps of the SoF meditation. These included finding a natural posture, breathing naturally while allowing the emotions and thoughts to flow without trying to stop or respond to them, and shifting his attention to the soles of his feet. He was guided to be mindful of the soles of his feet. This continued until calmness and clarity of the mind were established. The final step included walking away from the situation with an appropriate response, without engaging in verbal or physical aggression. Consistently practicing the SoF strategy increased his self-control of aggressive behaviors, and he met the community provider's requirement for six months of aggression-free behavior in the inpatient facility before being transitioned to the community. No aggressive behavior was observed during the 12-month follow-up after his community placement. This case study suggested that SoF may be a viable self-management strategy for individuals with ID and warranted further investigation.

In the first single-subject experimental study, three individuals with *moderate* mental retardation were taught within a multiple baseline design to use SoF to control their aggressive behavior. They were at risk of losing their community placements because of their aggressive behavior (Singh *et al.*, 2007). These individuals initially found the procedure difficult to comprehend because they could not easily visualize past anger-producing situations, a problem noted with young children, who lack cognitive maturity. However, they were able to master the SoF strategy when the trainers added *recreating the scene* as a mediational procedure (Van Houten & Rolider, 1988) and a discriminative stimulus on the soles of their feet (a dot sticker). They were able to self-manage their aggressive behavior by using the SoF strategy, and follow-up data showed that they managed their aggressive behavior in the community for at least two years and thus were able to retain their community placements.

In a somewhat larger experimental study, SoF was taught to six offenders with mild ID (Singh, Lancioni, Winton *et al.*, 2008). Results showed that physical and verbal aggression decreased substantially, no stat medication or physical restraint was required, and there were no staff or peer injuries. Benefit–cost analysis of lost staff workdays and cost of medical and rehabilitation due to injury caused by these individuals in the 12 months prior to and following mindfulness-based training showed a 95.7 percent reduction in costs. This study suggested that the SoF strategy might not only be clinically effective but also a cost-effective method of enabling adult offenders with ID to manage their aggression.

Recently, three adolescents with Asperger's syndrome were taught to use SoF to control their physical aggression in the family home and during outings in the community (Singh, Lancioni, Singh *et al.*, 2011). Prior to training in the mindfulness-based procedure, the adolescents had moderate rates of aggression. During mindfulness practice, their aggression gradually decreased, with no instances observed during the last three weeks of mindfulness practice. No episodes of physical aggression occurred during a four-year follow-up. A similar study evaluated the effectiveness of SoF in helping three adolescents with autism to manage their physical aggression (Singh, Lancioni, Manikam *et al.*, 2011). Incidents of aggression across the three adolescents ranged from a mean of 14 to 20 per week during baseline, 4 to 6 per week during mindfulness training, including zero rates during the last four weeks of intervention. Aggression occurred at a rate of about one per year during a three-year follow-up. These studies suggest that adolescents with Asperger's syndrome and autism may be able to successfully use a mindfulness-based procedure to control their aggressive behavior.

Finally, a young man who had previously been taught to successfully manage his aggressive behavior by using SoF (see Singh *et al.*, 2003) reported that he shared his mindfulness practice with his peers with ID. When requested by his peers, and without any training as a therapist, he began to teach this procedure to his peers for controlling their anger and aggressive behavior. Subsequently, Singh, Lancioni, Winton, Singh, Singh and Singh (2011) tracked the anger and aggressive behavior of three of the individuals he taught and the fidelity of his teaching of the procedure. According to self- and staff reports, anger and aggressive behavior of the three individuals decreased to very low levels within five months of initiating training and remained at very low levels for the two years during which informal data were collected. The fidelity of his teaching the procedure was high, if one allows for his idiosyncratic teaching methods. These findings suggest that individuals with mild ID, who have mastered an effective mindfulness-based strategy to control their aggressive behavior, may be able to teach their peers the same strategy to successfully control their anger and aggressive behavior to a level that is acceptable for community living.

Inappropriate sexual behavior

Of the few remediation modalities used with adult sexual offenders with ID, cognitive–behavioral approaches hold most promise (Lindsay, 2002a, 2002b). In a preliminary study, Singh, Lancioni, Winton, Singh, Adkins *et al.* (2011) assessed if three adult sexual offenders with ID could learn to control their deviant sexual arousal using mindfulness-based strategies. They serially assessed if the individuals could use two mindfulness-based strategies – a modified SoF and *Mindful Observation of Thoughts* – to manage their deviant sexual arousal when given relevant printed stimulus materials. The results showed that the individuals were minimally successful when they used their own self-control strategies, more effective with SoF, and most effective with the *Mindful Observation of Thoughts* meditation. Although this was a preliminary study, the data suggest that mindfulness-based procedures may be worthy of future investigation for adult sexual offenders with ID.

Obesity

Individuals with Prader–Willi syndrome have hyperphagia, a characteristic eating disorder defined by a marked delay in the satiety response when compared with controls. The relentless food-seeking and insatiable appetite in individuals with Prader–Willi syndrome leads to overeating, which, if uncontrolled, results in life-threatening obesity (Dykens, 2000). Although a small number of interventions have been developed for managing overeating and obesity in individuals with Prader–Willi syndrome, this eating disorder has been particularly difficult to control.

Using a single-subject changing criterion design, Singh, Lancioni, Singh, Winton, Singh, McAleavey *et al.* (2008) taught and evaluated the effectiveness of regular exercise alone, regular exercise plus healthy eating, and mindfulness-based strategies combined with exercise and healthy eating to an adolescent with this syndrome. The mindfulness-based strategies included mindful eating, visualizing and labeling hunger, and rapidly shifting attention away from hunger by engaging in SoF. On average, when compared with baseline levels, there were decreases in weight with regular exercise and exercise plus healthy eating, but the most consistent and sustained changes were evidenced when mindfulness training was added to exercise and healthy eating. The adolescent continued using the mindfulness-based health wellness program and further reduced his weight during the three-year follow-up period.

In a follow-up study, three individuals with Prader–Willi syndrome participated in a long-term, multicomponent mindfulness-based health wellness program to reduce their obesity by changing their lifestyle. The components included (a) physical exercise, (b) food awareness, (c) mindful eating to manage rapid eating, (d) visualizing and labeling hunger, and (e) a mindfulness procedure used as a self-control strategy against temptation to eat between meals (Singh, Lancioni, Singh *et al.*, 2011). All three individuals reached their desired body weights, reduced their body mass index (BMI) to within the normal range, enhanced their lifestyles, and maintained their desired body weights during the three-year maintenance period. When taken together, these two studies with individuals with Prader–Willi syndrome suggest that mindfulness-based health wellness programs may be effective in producing sustained lifestyle changes in individuals who are obese, including those with a biological predilection for excessive eating due to delayed satiety response.

Smoking

Individuals with or without ID have a similar propensity for smoking cigarettes. Its prevalence in individuals with ID varies from 2 percent to 36 percent, depending on the sample size, community versus institution versus clinical samples, living arrangements, age range, gender, degree of ID, and comorbid mental illness. Given the medical risk sequelae of smoking, it is critical that individuals have access to effective self-management strategies should they elect to stop smoking. However, the choices are extremely limited. In a recent single-subject experimental study, a 31-year-old man with mild ID was taught three mindfulness techniques (i.e., intention, you are not your thoughts, and SoF) as self-management strategies. He was able to eliminate his smoking habit and maintain nonsmoking during the four-year follow-up period (Singh, Lancioni, Winton, Singh, Singh & Adkins, 2011).

Strategies for Teaching Mindfulness to Individuals with ID

There are a number of things that clinicians and caregivers can do to support individuals with ID when they begin learning and using mindfulness-based coping strategies to transform their lives. These range from methods for teaching mindfulness to supporting them when they are trying to maintain new practices. To ensure fidelity of training, we use a SoF training manual (Singh, Singh *et al.*, 2011), but individualize the procedures to suit the cognitive capability of each individual.

Individuals with IDs need varying degrees of support when learning, practicing, and using a new skill. In our experience, we have found that using a multisystemic approach enables the individual to learn mindfulness-based strategies in a positive and supportive environment. The importance of attending to the multiple systems in which the individual functions (family, peers, paid caregivers) is critical to the outcome of the support provided. It behooves the clinician to enlist family members and other caregivers in multiple settings as "therapists" to help individuals correctly and appropriately use mindfulness-based strategies to enhance the probability of positive outcomes. In addition, using a multisystemic approach enables clinicians to sensitize family, peers, and caregivers to their own reactions to the individuals' behavior, and how their interaction may provide the setting for reinforcing the individuals' use of mindfulness-based strategies.

Training in mindfulness-based strategies typically includes a psychoeducational component. If individuals have elected to learn a mindfulness-based strategy to manage a maladaptive behavior or a disorder, clinicians or caregivers can enhance such learning by providing a context for the use of the selected strategy. For example, with individuals learning SoF to control their anger, clinicians can begin by providing information about anger and aggressive behavior, their antecedents, consequences, and a discussion of how individuals can use some of this information for self-management. Clinicians can emphasize that the concept of antecedents and triggers is important in SoF because it informs individuals when to begin using the SoF strategy. That is, individuals can begin practicing being in the soles of their feet the moment they feel anger arising. The best way clinicians can deliver the psychoeducational aspects of training is in an interactive manner, by engaging individuals in discussion of how the concepts apply to them, such as helping individuals remember specific instances of antecedents and triggers for their anger or aggressive behavior in the previous month. This kind of encouraging and supportive engagement helps individuals feel that the clinician understands them and is trying to tailor the supports to their unique needs.

Practice-based evidence suggests that clinicians working with individuals who have ID are very successful when they use techniques such as role plays and video modeling, and provide audio- or videotapes of the mindfulness-based strategies. Individuals with moderate levels of IDs often have difficulty remembering anger-producing situations from their recent past, a critical component of initial SoF training. This may require the clinician to improvise a different context for the training to increase the probability of the individual being able to learn and use SoF effectively.

The probability of an individual successfully controlling a maladaptive behavior through mindfulness-based strategies is enhanced by consistently and conscientiously practicing the procedures outside of formal teaching sessions, much like homework in cognitive–behavioral therapy. Individuals with ID are not noted for engaging in homework assignments without social support and reinforcement. However, unlike cognitive–behavioral therapy sessions with people in the general population where simply telling them that compliance with homework will enhance their wellness often increases adherence to the therapy, caregivers have to be much more supportive of individuals with ID and use selected interactions as the setting events for practicing mindfulness-based strategies. These interactions provide unique teaching moments during which caregivers can alert the individual to use his or her newly acquired mindfulness-based strategies. In addition, caregivers can use the individual's unique strengths and life goals to encourage adherence to mindfulness-based practice in real time.

Caregivers often assist individuals to use behavioral self-monitoring, such as behavior charts, to keep track of their target behavior in terms of frequency, intensity, and duration of the behavior. With individuals who are more capable, caregivers encourage them to work out the antecedents for their maladaptive behavior and then discuss how they could have handled the situation using a mindfulness-based strategy. Caregivers can follow this with a discussion of the consequences of engaging in the maladaptive behavior. Self-monitoring helps individuals to become more mindful of their own behavior. While most self-monitoring has focused on the maladaptive behavior itself, often reduced to a frequency count, it is also important to teach individuals with ID to self-monitor their emotion regulation. Caregivers can assist by cuing individuals when they observe emotional arousal (e.g., anger), thereby increasing the individuals' awareness of a possible precursor for the physical manifestation of their emotional arousal (i.e., aggressive behavior). In our clinical work, we often color code emotions for self-monitoring purposes, thereby providing visual cues as to how the individual's emotions vary with time.

Caregivers can also provide other forms of support to the individual. For example, if the individual's preferred or native language is not English, we have found it to be very helpful to have the step-by-step training directions audio- or videotaped in his or her native language and spoken by a native speaker. Caregivers have found that a dosage effect is also needed with some individuals. That is, some individuals need a higher dose of practice at the beginning of the training phase, with assistance being faded in later sessions. Finally, clinicians and caregivers are encouraged to build a strong therapeutic alliance with the individual because of its positive effects on clinical outcome. We have found that a number of mindfulness-based approaches can be used to build therapeutic alliances between individuals and their caregivers (Singh *et al.*, 2009).

We have found that the meditation practice of the therapist, parent, and support staff is a critical variable in the training and delivery of mindfulness interventions, and consequently, the outcomes for individuals with ID. Mindfulness is a multifaceted practice and without personal engagement in meditation, we may be unable to fully relate to the experiences of individuals with ID who are trying to master a mindfulness-based technique, and to provide informed feedback. Fortunately, training in SoF is a relatively simple endeavor, and most therapists, parents, and support staff report finding its practice to be very beneficial in their own lives.

Translating Research into Practice

One of the challenges of teaching mindfulness-based strategies to individuals with ID is their cognitive level, which acts as a moderator of support outcome. Cognitive level varies across individuals with ID, such that individuals of the same age may differ significantly with respect to their cognitive functioning. In the cognitive–behavioral therapy literature, clinicians are advised to adapt manualized interventions to the cognitive level of the participants, but the advice has rarely been accompanied by methodological suggestions as to how this may be achieved in real time.

While there is an abundance of literature on individuals with ID, there is paucity in terms of support and interventions that are aligned with the cognitive level of the individuals. For example, the plethora of current behavioral interventions is technique based, implemented mainly by caregivers, and seldom requires the support and interventions to be delivered at the cognitive level of the individual. Within the emerging mindfulness literature, there is nascent evidence suggesting that the cognitive level of the individual may determine what and how a procedure is taught. For example, if both parents and their children are taught mindfulness meditation techniques, the procedures and instructions used with parents have to be adapted to the cognitive level of their children (see Singh *et al.*, 2010). More specifically, the use of SoF provides a good illustration of this approach. While individuals who function at a mild level of ID have been taught the standard SoF procedure, those who function at a moderate level needed several modifications without which they failed to master the technique. Thus, clinicians should be aware that mindfulness-based strategies need to be customized to the cognitive level of the individual.

The small body of current research on the use of mindfulness-based strategies with individuals who have ID is based primarily on single-subject experimental designs. While these studies provide useful clinical information on the feasibility of using specific mindfulness strategies with specific individuals, this research effort has not been followed by group design studies to better inform general clinical practice. Group design studies may help assess the impact of moderating and mediating variables, the actuarial effects of different mindfulness-based strategies on the same behavior and effects of the same mindfulness-based strategy on different behaviors, the range of effects with manualized treatments, therapist variables, interaction with different functions of the behavior, and effects of varying degrees of impairment of the individuals. Furthermore, with the exception of using an alternating treatment single-subject design, it is only through group design studies that we will be able to establish the efficacy – the comparison of mindfulness against other viable therapeutic approaches – of mindfulness-based approaches in this population.

Of course, this is not to suggest that only group studies be undertaken, because group findings may not apply to specific individuals. The suggestion is that data from group studies be incorporated into clinical practice. First, knowledge of group findings may alert clinicians to specific mindfulness-based strategies that are salient for individuals at different levels of cognitive and social functioning, or who have comorbid conditions. Prior knowledge would enable clinicians to appropriately assess the individual and thus assist them to match the mindfulness technique that is most appropriate to the individual client. Second, in selecting the mindfulness-based strategy, group data may help the clinician to match a technique to the individual's preferred mode of learning (e.g., 1:1 demonstration, role play, video modeling). Thus, both individual and group studies are necessary to advance clinical application.

At present, we do not know much about who will benefit from using mindfulness-based approaches or who will drop out of treatment. However, we do know from the research literature that those who are highly motivated to change usually have much better outcomes than those who are reluctant participants. In terms of self-determination theory (Deci & Ryan, 1985; Ryan, 1995), which postulates five forms of motivation, from least to most motivated (i.e., external, introjective, identified, integrated, and intrinsic motivation), individuals with at least *identified* motivation seem to be able to control their emotional arousal and overt maladaptive behavior, and do even better if they have *integrated* or *intrinsic* motivation. While it has been difficult to empirically assess the level of motivation of individuals with ID in the extant studies of mindfulness, in our own studies, the participants have stated that using mindfulness-based approaches to control their maladaptive behavior is personally important and meaningful to them in terms of their desired quality of life, which is suggestive of *identified* motivation.

It is clear from the emerging literature that mindfulness-based interventions are beneficial in individuals with ID. In extant studies, the effects of mindfulness-based training have been measured in terms of clinically or socially relevant outcomes. No attempts have been made thus far to assess the construct of mindfulness itself in this population. We know from our clinical work that individuals with ID, at least those with mild ID, can learn to meditate using concentration (as opposed to contemplation) methods, but we know little of their understanding of mindfulness or, even at a more basic level, their understanding of meditation. Future studies may focus on developing a methodology for assessing these issues, because elucidating their understanding of mindfulness may enable clinicians to devise more effective mindfulness-based interventions not only for specific behaviors but also for personal transformation.

The issue of the effectiveness of SoF and other mindfulness-based procedures in supporting individuals to self-manage behaviors that are either biologically driven (e.g., Prader–Willi syndrome, Lesch–Nyhan syndrome) or are symptoms of certain psychiatric disorders that make behavior change very difficult (e.g., personality disorders, autism spectrum disorders) is yet to be explored. Our use of SoF with people with Prader–Willi syndrome (Singh, Singh *et al.*, 2011; Singh, Lancioni, Singh *et al.*, 2008) and sex offenders with ID (Singh, Lancioni, Winton, Singh, Adkins *et al.*, 2011) suggests that it may be possible to do so, but the current data are very limited. We suspect that it would be fairly challenging to devise mindfulness-based procedures that would overcome some of the core features of some psychiatric disorders, such as those inherent in antisocial and borderline personality disorders, in individuals with compromised cognitive ability.

Another important issue is the social validity of SoF and the behavioral changes that may accrue through its use by individuals with ID. That is, what is the clinical importance and acceptability of the treatment goals, procedures, and outcomes associated with the use of SoF (Kazdin, 1977; Wolf, 1978)? Extant studies of SoF have not formally assessed social validity, but there are anecdotal data from parents and carers attesting to the importance of the changes produced through SoF. For example, individuals with ID have been able to transition to and maintain their community placements through the use of SoF when previous interventions had failed (Singh *et al.*, 2003, 2007). Community providers, in particular, have noted broad changes that are clearly evident when individuals with ID use SoF in their daily lives. For example, when compared with their peers, those using SoF have far fewer disagreements with staff and coworkers in vocational settings, are more calm in emotionally arousing situations that would typically produce unacceptable social behavior, and more accepting of unanticipated changes in their daily schedules. Future studies should provide qualitative and quantitative data on the social validity of mindfulness-based procedures.

A further issue is whether community-based therapists can routinely use SoF procedures with individuals with ID. Current research indicates that when experienced researchers provide SoF training to individuals with ID, the individuals are able to effectively self-manage their maladaptive behaviors. One study investigated whether similar effectiveness would be found if community-based therapists provided the training to individuals with ID living in the community (Adkins *et al.*, 2010). Three adults with mild ID and mental illness were taught by a community-based therapist to use SoF to control maladaptive behaviors that included verbal aggression, disruptive behavior, and physical aggression. All three individuals were able to reduce their maladaptive behaviors to near-zero levels and maintain their community placement that they had been at risk for losing due to their maladaptive behavior. Thus, there is suggestive evidence that community-based therapists may be able to routinely utilize this mindfulness strategy in clinical settings.

If future independent research should confirm the social validity and importance of changes produced through mindfulness-based procedures, should we consider teaching SoF and related mindfulness-based procedures to children with or without ID as general skills that would enhance their resilience? We know from the experiences of those who have an effective personal meditation practice that they are capable of withstanding negative life events with more equanimity and less stress than those who do not (Trungpa, 1993), and anecdotally from the hundreds of individuals we have taught SoF that they find it easier to deal with changes in their personal lives with the use of SoF than with other coping strategies they employed in the past. This suggests that mindfulness-based procedures that are based on meditation practices may be effective in inoculating children and adolescents against the stresses and strains of daily life if they can be taught these procedures as general skills early in their lives.

Conclusions

Promising and emergent literature provides some support for the effectiveness of mindfulness-based procedures for individuals with ID. The research is limited to a few mindfulness-based procedures, and the outcomes have been evaluated using only single-subject experimental methodology. Much more well-controlled research is needed before we know if the various mindfulness-based strategies are truly effective in the daily life of individuals with ID, who they work for, and why or how the strategies work. However, extant research does indicate that individuals with ID can learn and effectively use mindfulness-based strategies to control some of their behaviors rather successfully. These findings are closely in line with our clinical experience and reports from individuals with ID who have been using these procedures on a daily basis in the community.

References

Adkins, A.D., Singh, A.N., Winton, A.S.W., McKeegan, G.F. & Singh, J. (2010). Using a mindfulness-based procedure in the community: Translating research to practice. *Journal of Child and Family Studies, 19,* 175–183.

Baer, R.A. (2006). *Mindfulness-based treatment approaches.* New York: Academic Press.

Benson, B.A. (1994). Anger management training: A self-control program for people with mild mental retardation. In N. Bouras (Ed.) *Mental health in mental retardation* (pp. 224–232). Cambridge, UK: Cambridge University Press.

Deci, E.L. & Ryan, R.M. (1985). *Intrinsic motivation and self-determination in human behavior.* New York: Plenum Press.

Dykens, E.M. (2000). Contaminated and unusual food combinations: What do people with Prader-Willi syndrome choose? *Mental Retardation, 38,* 163–171.

Grossman, P., Niemann, L., Schmidt, S. & Walach, H. (2004). Mindfulness-based stress reduction and health benefits: A meta-analysis. *Journal of Psychosomatic Research, 57,* 35–43.

Hayes, S.C., Barnes-Holmes, D. & Roche, B. (2001). *Relational frame theory: A post-Skinnerian account of human language and cognition.* New York: Plenum Press.

Kabat-Zinn, J. (1990). *Full catastrophe living: Using the wisdom of your body and mind to face stress, pain and illness.* New York: Delacorte.

Kabat-Zinn, J. (2003). Mindfulness-based intervention in context: Past, present, and future. *Clinical Psychology: Science and Practice, 10,* 144–156.

Kazdin, A.E. (1977). Assessing the clinical or applied importance of behavior change through social validation. *Behavior Modification, 1,* 427–452.

Langer, E.J. (1989). *Mindfulness.* Reading, MA: Addison-Wesley.

Lindsay, W.R. (2002a). Research and literature on sex offenders with intellectual and developmental disabilities. *Journal of Intellectual Disability Research, 46,* 74–85.

Lindsay, W.R. (2002b). Integration of recent reviews on offenders with intellectual disabilities. *Journal of Applied Research in Intellectual Disabilities, 15,* 111–119.

Mingyur Rinpoche, Y. (2007). *The joy of living: Unlocking the secret and science of happiness.* New York: Three Rivers Press.

Rose, J., West, C. & Clifford, D. (2000). Group interventions for anger in people with intellectual disabilities. *Research in Developmental Disabilities, 21,* 171–181.

Ryan, R.M. (1995). Psychological needs and the facilitation of integrative processes. *Journal of Personality, 63,* 397–427.

Segal, Z.V., Williams, J.M.G. & Teasdale, J.D. (2002). *Mindfulness-based cognitive therapy for depression: A new approach to preventing relapse.* New York: Guilford Press.

Shapiro, S.L. & Carlson, L.E. (2009). *The art and science of mindfulness.* Washington, DC: American Psychological Association.

Singh, J., Adkins, A.D. & Singh, A.N. (2009). *Mindfulness approaches to building therapeutic alliance.* Midlothian, VA: One Research Institute.

Singh, N.N., Lancioni, G.E., Manikam, R., Winton, A.S.W., Singh, A.N.A., Singh, J. *et al.* (2011). A mindfulness-based strategy for self-management of aggressive behavior in adolescents with autism. *Research in Autism Spectrum Disorders, 5,* 1153–1158.

Singh, N.N., Lancioni, G.E., Singh, A.D.A., Winton, A.S.W., Singh, A.N.A. & Singh, J. (2011). Adolescents with Asperger syndrome can use a mindfulness-based strategy to control their aggressive behavior. *Research in Autism Spectrum Disorders, 5,* 1103–1109.

Singh, N.N., Lancioni, G.E., Singh, A.N.A, Winton, A.S.W., Singh, A.D.A., & Singh, J. (2011). A mindfulness-based health wellness program for individuals with Prader-Willi syndrome. *Journal of Mental Health Research in Intellectual Disabilities, 4,* 90–106.

Singh, N.N., Lancioni, G.E., Singh, A.N., Winton, A.S.W., Singh, J., McAleavey, K.M. *et al.* (2008). A mindfulness-based health wellness program for an adolescent with Prader-Willi syndrome. *Behavior Modification, 32,* 167–181.

Singh, N.N., Lancioni, G.E., Wahler, R.G., Winton, A.S.W. & Singh, J. (2008). Mindfulness approaches in cognitive behavior therapy. *Behavioural and Cognitive Psychotherapy, 36,* 659–666.

Singh, N.N., Lancioni, G.E., Winton, A.S.W., Adkins, A.D., Singh, J. & Singh, A. (2007). Mindfulness training assists individuals with moderate mental retardation to maintain their community placements. *Behavior Modification, 31,* 800–814.

Singh, N.N., Lancioni, G.E., Winton, A.S.W., Singh, A.N., Adkins, A.D. & Singh, J. (2008). Clinical and benefit-cost outcomes of teaching a mindfulness-based procedure to adult offenders with intellectual disabilities. *Behavior Modification, 32,* 622–637.

Singh, N.N., Lancioni, G.E., Winton, A.S.W., Singh, A.N., Adkins, A.D. & Singh, J. (2011). Can adult offenders with intellectual disabilities use mindfulness-based procedures to control their deviant sexual arousal? *Psychology, Crime and Law, 17,* 165–179.

Singh, N.N., Lancioni, G.E., Winton, A.S.W., Singh, A.N., Singh, J. & Adkins, A.D. (2011). Effects of a mindfulness-based smoking cessation program for an adult with mild intellectual disability. *Research in Developmental Disabilities, 32,* 1180–1185.

Singh, N.N., Lancioni, G.E., Winton, A.S.W., Singh, J., Singh, A.N.A. & Singh, A.D.A. (2011). Peer with intellectual disabilities as a mindfulness-based anger and aggression management therapist. *Research in Autism Spectrum Disorders, 5,* 2690–2696.

Singh, N.N., Singh, A.N., Lancioni, G.E., Singh, J., Winton, A.S.W. & Adkins, A.D. (2010). Mindfulness training for parents and their children with ADHD increases the children's compliance. *Journal of Child and Family Studies, 19,* 157–166.

Singh, N.N., Singh, J., Singh, A.D.A., Singh, A.N. & Winton, A.S.W. (2011). *Meditation of the soles of the feet for anger management: A trainer's manual.* Raleigh, NC: Fernleaf Publishing.

Singh, N.N., Wahler, R.G., Adkins, A.D. & Myers, R.E. (2003). Soles of the feet: A mindfulness-based self-control intervention for aggression by an individual with mild mental retardation and mental illness. *Research in Developmental Disabilities, 24,* 158–169.

Taylor, J.L., Novaco, R.W., Gillmer, B., Robertson, A. & Thorne, I. (2005). Individual cognitive-behavioral anger treatment for people with mild-borderline intellectual disabilities and histories of aggression: A controlled trial. *The British Journal of Clinical Psychology, 44,* 367–382.

Trungpa, C. (1993). *Training the mind and cultivating loving kindness.* Boston, MA: Shambhala Publications.

Van Houten, R. & Rolider, A. (1988). Recreating the scene: An effective way to provide delayed punishment for inappropriate motor behavior. *Journal of Applied Behavior Analysis, 21,* 187–192.

Williams, M., Teasdale, J., Segal, Z. & Kabat-Zinn, J. (2007). *The mindful way through depression: Freeing yourself from chronic unhappiness.* New York: Guilford.

Wolf, M.M. (1978). Social validity: The case for subjective measurement or how applied behavior analysis is finding its heart. *Journal of Applied Behavior Analysis, 11,* 203–214.

Chapter 17

Psychological Therapies for Adults with Intellectual Disabilities:

Future Directions for Research and Practice

Richard P. Hastings
Chris Hatton
William R. Lindsay
John L. Taylor

This book has two ambitions: (1) to present and review the current evidence supporting the use of psychological therapies with adults with intellectual disabilities (and their supporters), and (2) to provide practical advice for practitioners about what expert authors have found to be effective in their practice. The primary motivation for producing this book was to contribute toward improving access to psychological therapies among people with intellectual disabilities. Our underlying assumption is that access might be improved if clinicians are more informed about the existing evidence, and have to hand practical advice and guidance to support their therapeutic work with their clients. In this chapter, we discuss a number of issues concerning the process of developing an evidence base to support clinical practice. We look at the development of the evidence for effective psychological therapies in the intellectual disabilities field to date and measure it against a proposed model of translation of scientific evidence into practice. In so doing, we are able to judge the status of the research effort to date, identify gaps in the evidence, and suggest priorities for taking forward the development of the evidence base.

Psychological Therapies in the Intellectual Disability Field: "The Translational Continuum"

There has been increasing international research on, and policy development and practice interest in, the translation of scientific evidence. A good deal of attention has been given to the translation of basic scientific evidence into some form of

Psychological Therapies for Adults with Intellectual Disabilities, First Edition.
Edited by John L. Taylor, William R. Lindsay, Richard P. Hastings, and Chris Hatton.
© 2013 John Wiley & Sons, Ltd. Published 2013 by John Wiley & Sons, Ltd.

application to help solve human problems, and also to the translation of evidence about efficacious/effective interventions into practice. Both of these steps have been described as "blocks" along a *translational continuum*.

A number of models of the translational continuum have been developed that describe a series of steps or phases that need to be considered when attempting to implement research findings in practice settings. For example, Thornicroft *et al.* (2011) described a model that links basic science discovery to practice through five phases that include three translational blocks along the way. We will use this schema to evaluate the current state of the evidence in relation to psychological therapies for adults with intellectual disabilities, and to identify future research and practice priorities.

Basic science research

The first phase (Phase 0) of Thornicroft *et al.*'s translational continuum model concerns basic scientific discovery. For the present context, this might include epidemiological research including a focus on etiology, critical appraisal and testing of relevant theories of mental health and well-being, considering research design and methodological issues, and identifying confounding variables. Within the field of intellectual disability, there are some examples of good quality epidemiological research on mental health in adults with intellectual disabilities (e.g., Cooper *et al.*, 2007). However, much of the available research on epidemiology in this field is weak in that it is does not involve whole populations (i.e., the research in most cases relies on selected samples of people referred to services), and lacks clear and valid definitions of intellectual disability supported by reliable assessment measures. More significantly, the mechanisms by which adults with intellectual disabilities develop psychological problems are not well understood. In particular, there is a lack of experimental and longitudinal research that allows conclusions about causal factors and mechanisms to be drawn. There has been some considered theorizing about the development of mental health problems in adults with intellectual disabilities and some correlational research evidence, but it remains the case that we have few direct data on causal mechanisms.

According to Thornicroft *et al.* (2011), the first potential translational block occurs in relation to the transfer of basic science into the development (in our case) of new interventions. Given the paucity of data on causal mechanisms, this block has not emerged as a problem when it comes to psychological therapies for adults with intellectual disability but only because basic science findings ready for translation are lacking. There are some exceptions in terms of significant basic science findings, relating to mental health in children with intellectual and developmental disabilities, our understanding of the role of social deprivation in mental health inequalities, the relationship between exposure to adverse life events, and the development of mental health problems (Wigham *et al.*, 2011).

Using data derived from national population-based research, it is clear that intellectual disability and autism are risk factors for mental health problems in children (Emerson & Hatton, 2007; Totsika, Hastings, Emerson, Lancaster *et al.*, 2011). In addition, inequalities in mental health for these groups of children emerge early in life (by the age of five years at the latest) (Emerson & Einfeld, 2010; Totsika,

Hastings, Emerson, Berridge *et al.*, 2011). An implication of these data is that psychological therapeutic interventions for individuals with intellectual disability need to start early (i.e., a more early intervention/prevention approach is needed). Although one could argue that these research findings are only recently available, there is little sign yet of these discoveries feeding new preventative interventions.

A similar argument can be made about the role of social deprivation in mental ill-health. Research focused on children (Emerson & Hatton, 2007; Totsika, Hastings, Emerson, Berridge *et al.*, 2011; Totsika, Hastings, Emerson, Lancaster *et al.*, 2011) and adults with intellectual disabilities (Emerson & Hatton, 2008) demonstrates that those from economically and socially impoverished backgrounds and/or with restricted social networks are more likely to be vulnerable to mental health problems or lower well-being. These data are congruent with evidence from the general population that these factors play a causal role in mental ill-health. Again, although this evidence has been available for some time, it is hard to pinpoint its impact on new interventions designed to address these potential causal factors in adults with intellectual disabilities.

While previous research has demonstrated an association between exposure to life events and psychopathology in people with intellectual disabilities, causal links have not been demonstrated using prospective study designs. Using a measure of trauma that was developed specifically for this population group, Wigham *et al.* (2012) found that adverse life events were predictive of levels of trauma in terms of behavioral changes, and frequency and severity of symptoms six months later. Unlike the findings of research involving nondisabled participants, social support was not predictive of trauma and did not moderate the relationship between life events and trauma. These are new findings that can guide the development of interventions in this area of need.

Early outcome studies of psychological interventions

Phases 1 and 2 of Thornicroft *et al.*'s translational continuum model refer to the identification of key intervention components and manualization of interventions, and then the initial testing of interventions in exploratory studies. Exploratory outcome studies might include randomized controlled trial (RCT) designs.

Psychological therapy outcome research involving adults with intellectual disabilities is working through these phases. Many of the chapters in this book describe therapeutic approaches and interventions that have been developed and evaluated using case study and case series descriptions, single case designs with some element of experimental control, and group design studies – often simple pre-post test designs, but including a number of controlled studies, especially for cognitive–behavioral therapy (CBT). If these phases can be likened to a journey, then there is still some way to go. First, more robust research designs (especially RCTs) are needed to demonstrate the efficacy of psychological therapies. Second, the field needs more carefully described and manualized interventions. Third, research designs need to incorporate active control intervention conditions. This third point is perhaps the most relevant to the current evidence base. The only conclusion that can be drawn with confidence from the material presented in this book is that psychological therapy is more effective than no intervention or "treatment as usual" (often likely to consist of no specific intervention). Although such data are important, we also need more evidence from more sophisticated controlled study designs demonstrating which therapeutic interventions tend to lead to better outcomes than others.

To take a small diversion at this point, in this book, we have steered away from debates about which types of psychological therapies (e.g., behavioral therapy vs. CBT vs. psychodynamic therapy) lead to better outcomes for adults with intellectual disabilities experiencing mental health and emotional problems. The reason for this decision, despite considerable debate on the topic (e.g., Beail, 2003; Lindsay, 2006; Sturmey, 2006; Taylor, 2005; Taylor *et al.*, 2008), is that it is clear that the evidence base as a whole in our field is not yet developed sufficiently to be able to draw any firm conclusions in this regard. Rather, the priority is for better defined and described psychological interventions with clearer evidence from more robustly designed research studies in order to start improving access to evidence-based therapeutic support for adults with intellectual disabilities.

It is important to recognize that there are particular problems in attempting to carry out large-scale RCTs of psychological therapy for people with intellectual disabilities. Chief among these include recruitment of sufficient numbers for statistical power purposes from an intrinsically small population (just 2 percent of the general population) that is heterogeneous in nature and in its presenting problems. These issues necessitate complex multicenter studies that are difficult to organize and expensive at a time when little funding is available for research with this largely disenfranchised population. Beyond these problems, putative researchers in this field have to contend with ethical considerations concerning obtaining valid consent from participants where mental capacity may be an issue, along with a paucity of therapists with the requisite skills and experience in providing high-fidelity psychological therapies to people with intellectual disabilities as part of a controlled trial.

Effectiveness and uptake in clinical settings

Thornicroft *et al.* (2011) identified a second translational block that can follow Phases 1 and 2 that involves evaluating whether interventions that have been shown to be *efficacious* in well-controlled large-scale studies (e.g., RCTs) are *effective* in routine clinical practice settings. Once again, at present, this particular translational block is not a major problem in the intellectual disabilities treatment outcome field since psychological interventions with potential efficacy have yet to be adequately examined using sufficiently rigorous research designs for the reasons described earlier.

Phase 3 of the Thornicroft *et al.* (2011) translational model describes how evidence is generated to deal with the translational block using large-scale well-controlled studies. Research in this fourth phase also involves comparing the effectiveness of interventions used in routine clinical settings with credible alternative treatments. This type of research is currently not available in the intellectual disabilities field. However, it is important not to be precipitous by attempting to address these questions without first laying the groundwork with solid evidence of efficacy as described in Phase 2 of the model. In this sense, it is appropriate that we do not have as yet good examples of Phase 3 research in our field. However, it is important to understand that such research will be required as evidence of efficacious interventions is developed through Phase 2 research. It would not be sufficient to stop the research cycle concerning specific psychological therapies following the completion of efficacy-focused RCTs.

The third translational block is described (Thornicroft *et al.*, 2011) at this stage; interventions with proven efficacy and effectiveness that become "approved" or "recommended" may still not be taken up in day-to-day clinical practice. Thus, the fifth phase of Thornicroft *et al.*'s model concerns implementation and relates to the field of implementation science. Phase 4 research is focused on understanding the factors that lead to the third translational block, or indeed the factors that may facilitate evidence-based interventions being incorporated into day-to-day clinical practice.

Our view is that the implementation of evidence-based interventions in routine care settings in the intellectual disability field is weak if not absent at present. We have been unable to locate any peer-reviewed research published on this third translational block relating to psychological therapies for adults with intellectual disabilities. Again, this may not be surprising given that currently there are no psychological therapeutic interventions for mental health problems that have attained Phase 3 evidence that are ready for large-scale implementation in routine clinical settings. However, it is important to bear in mind that implementation science in the field of intellectual disability will require attention since an understanding of how the available evidence affects the delivery of intellectual disability services will be needed in order to be proactive in implementing new psychological interventions as they are developed and pass through the research testing Phases 0–3 described earlier.

Special Case versus Mainstream Models, Interventions, and Evidence

Readers will have noted that there is a large but, so far, implicit assumption underlying the preceding critique and discussion. Our analysis is predicated on the assumption that evidence for the efficacy and effectiveness of psychological therapies for people with intellectual disabilities requires research that involves people with intellectual disabilities as study participants. It is beyond the scope of this chapter to provide an extensive discussion of the issues underlying this assumption. However, we maintain this is an important position to adopt, and we outline some of the arguments in support of this view in the following discussion.

The need for the development of "special" evidence to support effective psychological interventions specifically designed for people with intellectual disabilities is indicated by a number of observations. Good quality research evidence, including RCTs, supporting the efficacy and effectiveness of psychological therapies is very likely to have excluded adults with intellectual disabilities. Exclusion criteria concerning the participant's IQ levels are very common in psychotherapy outcome studies, and referral procedures in research trials are typically concerned with mainstream mental health services rather than specialist services for people with intellectual disabilities. Thus, although high-quality evidence for the efficacy and effectiveness of psychological therapies for mental health problems is available (see the National Institute for Health and Clinical Excellence (NICE) guidelines for mental health and behavioral problems; www.nice.org.uk/), generally this research does not include adults with intellectual disability and thus there is a question about whether the same evidence applies to this population.

Are there reasons to suppose that adults with intellectual disabilities will respond differently to psychological therapies shown to be effective with people without such disabilities? One issue is the extent of intellectual disability involved. Almost without exception, the psychological interventions described in this book have been applied to individuals with mild to moderate intellectual disability who make up more than 80 percent of the intellectually disability population as a whole. Is there any reason to presume that this group's mental health problems are qualitatively different to those experienced by the general population in terms of epidemiology, causative factors, and subjective experience? This brings us back to earlier parts of this chapter – because there is a lack of basic science research on the nature of, and causal factors underlying mental health problems in adults with intellectual disabilities, we cannot answer these questions with confidence. The limited basic science findings that are available to date (e.g., the early establishment of mental health inequalities, the role of deprivation in mental health, and a lack of buffering of the effects of trauma by social support) suggests that the experience of people with intellectual disabilities with mental health problems may be different to some extent.

In adapting and applying established evidence-based psychological interventions, it is assumed that these treatments operate and produce their effects in the same way when used with people with intellectual disability. For example, several treatments include visual imagery or metacognitive components. Can people with intellectual disability employ visual imagery and metacognition in the same way and to the same level of competence as those without intellectual disability? At present, there is a lack of basic research demonstrating that people with intellectual disability can indeed competently employ such techniques or that they can be successfully trained to do so.

Some basic research on therapeutic processes in intellectual disability is available. Researchers have identified difficulties in understanding of the relationships between cognition, emotion, and behavior among individuals with intellectual disability in experimental studies (e.g., Dagnan *et al.*, 2000; Sams *et al.*, 2006). However, in practice, CBT can be delivered with a high degree of fidelity to the cognitive–behavioral model (Jahoda *et al.*, 2009), and pilot data suggest that adults with intellectual disability can be trained to understand cognitive mediation processes (Bruce *et al.*, 2010). Also, the limited evidence available suggests that the effectiveness of psychological therapies for different disorders in people with intellectual disabilities is similar to the outcomes achieved when these interventions are used with people in the general population. However, more basic research on therapeutic processes is needed partly because the evidence accumulated over time will be a significant factor in the specialized versus adapted mainstream treatment debate.

A further reason for taking a "special case" approach and continuing to look for evidence to support the use of psychological therapies with people with intellectual disabilities is the work of theorists and practitioners who argue that one focus for psychological therapy for adults with intellectual disabilities is the person's response to his or her own disability and/or his or her experience of stigma (e.g., Hollins & Sinason, 2000; Jahoda *et al.*, 2006).

The benefits and costs associated with the special case approach need to be debated openly. For example, there is a long history in intellectual disability services of moving toward inclusion. From this perspective, mainstream mental health services, using evidence-based approaches, ought to be available to all adults whether or not they have intellectual disabilities. Thus, research and practice should be focused on improving access to mainstream services and on supporting clinicians in mainstream services to provide effective therapies for adults with intellectual disabilities who have mental health problems. Unfortunately, there is little research on service models that can achieve this access or provide the support required. A more informed discussion about the relative values of special case versus mainstream approaches is difficult without additional evidence about what improving access models might look like and how they would work. Thus, this is another research priority.

Conclusions

We propose that there are three priorities for future research concerning psychological therapies for adults with intellectual disability and mental health problems. The first is a need for basic science focused on mental health in adults with intellectual disabilities. Here, we need to develop more robust methods of assessing mental health in adults with intellectual disability along with high-quality research on the adaptation of mainstream assessment measures of mental health. Specialist assessments of mental health problems experienced by adults with severe and profound intellectual disabilities are also a research priority. With a wider variety of robust assessment tools, epidemiological research, and research on causal and maintaining factors, research in mental ill-health will be facilitated. Basic research is also needed on the cognitive skills and abilities required for successful engagement in psychological therapy and the extent to which these may be similar or different in adults with intellectual disability and those in the general population.

The second priority area is the need for large-scale, high-quality RCTs exploring both efficacy and then effectiveness of psychological therapies for adults with intellectual disabilities. These studies must also include direct comparisons with evidence-based alternative interventions; this might be pharmacological interventions and other forms of psychological therapy. The standards of evidence required in relation to clinical practice means that RCTs are needed to ensure formal recognition and recommendation of effective interventions in official guidelines (e.g., NICE) for this population. Researchers in the field will be doing a disservice to people with intellectual disabilities unless they take up, in collaboration with clinical colleagues, the challenge of high-quality controlled treatment outcome research.

Finally, a new area of research is needed with a clear focus on implementation science and service model design and evaluation. Direct research is required on the uptake of evidence-based approaches in intellectual disability practice. We also need research on the models of mental health service delivery that may lead to better outcomes for individuals with intellectual disability. In particular, are specialist intellectual disability services more effective in delivering evidence-based interventions than mainstream mental health services supported by colleagues with intellectual disability expertise?

Of course, the call for more high-quality research evidence has been made through-out this book. However, this is not an easy goal to achieve. It is much more difficult to recruit the large numbers of participants required for RCT studies when working with a relatively small and heterogeneous population like adults with intellectual dis-abilities. National and possibly international collaborations are probably required to overcome the significant recruitment issues in this field. Also, the additional work and resources involved in obtaining valid consent and training therapists with the specialist skills needed to work with this population is considerable. Significant funding is required for large-scale research such as RCTs. Following changes to research funding structures (in the United Kingdom at least), it has proven difficult for researchers in the intellectual disability field to obtain financial support for the types of research indicated as priorities here. This situation is unlikely to improve significantly in the near future given the current pressures on and cuts in public expenditure. As the intellectual disability field lags behind others in terms of its evi-dence base, then strategic arguments for the establishment of ring-fenced funding to pump prime a coordinated program of research for this patient population need to be developed.

A final point is that there is a debate in the broader psychological therapies field about the amount of variance in treatment outcomes that is accounted for by the particular type of therapy used as opposed to the quality of the relationship between the client and therapist (e.g., Lambert & Barley, 2001; Wilson, 1998). Research on the putative association between client–therapist relationship and outcomes for psychological therapies for people with intellectual disabilities has not yet been devel-oped. However, the results of such research could be important in terms of how we think about appropriate evidence and how we design mental health service delivery for adults with intellectual disabilities. What therapist qualities and competencies are required to work effectively with adults with intellectual disabilities and mental health problems? If such competencies and qualities can be clearly identified, a further ques-tion is how best to train these competencies.

We hope that this book is helpful to researchers and clinicians in thinking about their approach to developing and providing psychological therapies to clients with intellectual disabilities who experience mental health problems. In this final chapter, we have briefly identified some of the ongoing debates and strategic considerations involved in taking this effort forward in terms of further research and its implementa-tion in routine practice. While we have made some significant strides forward in the 15 years since the publication of the influential text by Stenfert Kroese and her col-leagues (1997) on CBT for people with learning disabilities, there is still some way to go and much work to do!

References

Beail, N. (2003). What works for people with mental retardation? Critical commentary on cognitive-behavioural and psychodynamic psychotherapy research. *Mental Retardation, 41*, 468–472.

Bruce, M., Collins, S., Langdon, P., Powlitch, S. & Reynolds, S. (2010). Does training improve understanding of core concepts in cognitive behaviour therapy by people with intellectual disabilities? A randomized experiment. *The British Journal of Clinical Psychology*, *49*, 1–13.

Cooper, S.A., Smiley, E., Morrison, J., Williamson, A. & Allan, L. (2007). Mental ill-health in adults with intellectual disabilities: Prevalence and associated factors. *The British Journal of Psychiatry*, *190*, 27–35.

Dagnan, D., Chadwick, P. & Proudlove, J. (2000). Toward an assessment of suitability of people with mental retardation for cognitive therapy. *Cognitive Therapy and Research*, *24*, 627–636.

Emerson, E. & Einfeld, S. (2010). Emotional and behavioural difficulties in young children with and without developmental delay: A bi-national perspective. *Journal of Child Psychology and Psychiatry, and Allied Disciplines*, *51*, 583–593.

Emerson, E. & Hatton, C. (2007). Mental health of children and adolescents with intellectual disabilities in Britain. *The British Journal of Psychiatry*, *191*, 493–499.

Emerson, E. & Hatton, C. (2008). Self-reported well-being of women and men with intellectual disabilities in England. *American Journal of Mental Retardation*, *113*, 143–155.

Hollins, S. & Sinason, V. (2000). Psychotherapy, learning disabilities and trauma: New perspectives. *The British Journal of Psychiatry*, *176*, 32–36.

Jahoda, A., Dagnan, D., Jarvie, P. & Kerr, W. (2006). Depression, social context and cognitive behavioural therapy for people who have intellectual disabilities. *Journal of Applied Research in Intellectual Disabilities*, *19*, 81–89.

Jahoda, A., Selkirk, M., Trower, P., Pert, C., Kroese, B.S., Dagnan, D. *et al.* (2009). The balance of power in therapeutic interactions with individuals who have intellectual disabilities. *The British Journal of Clinical Psychology*, *48*, 63–77.

Lambert, M.J. & Barley, D.E. (2001). Research summary on the therapeutic relationship and psychotherapy outcome. *Psychotherapy: Theory, Research, Practice, Training*, *38*, 357–361.

Lindsay, W.R. (2006). That poor laddie cannae tell his thoughts fae his actions: A reply to Sturmey. *Journal of Applied Research in Intellectual Disabilities*, *19*, 119–120.

Sams, K., Collins, S. & Reynolds, S. (2006). Cognitive therapy abilities in people with learning disabilities. *Journal of Applied Research in Intellectual Disabilities*, *19*, 25–33.

Stenfert Kroese, B., Dagnan, D. & Loumidis, K. (Eds.) (1997). *Cognitive-behaviour therapy for people with learning disabilities*. London: Routledge.

Sturmey, P. (2006). On some recent claims for the efficacy of cognitive therapy for people with intellectual disabilities. *Journal of Applied Research in Intellectual Disabilities*, *19*, 109–117.

Taylor, J.L. (2005). In support of psychotherapy for people who have mental retardation. *Mental Retardation*, *43*, 450–453.

Taylor, J.L., Lindsay, W.R. & Willner, P. (2008). CBT for people with intellectual disabilities: Emerging evidence, cognitive ability and IQ effects. *Behavioural & Cognitive Psychotherapy*, *36*, 723–733.

Thornicroft, G., Lempp, H. & Tansella, M. (2011). The place of implementation science in the translational medicine continuum. *Psychological Medicine*, *41*, 2015–2021.

Totsika, V., Hastings, R.P., Emerson, E., Berridge, D.M. & Lancaster, G.A. (2011). Behavior problems at five years of age and maternal mental health in autism and intellectual disability. *Journal of Abnormal Child Psychology*, *39*, 1137–1147.

Totsika, V., Hastings, R.P., Emerson, E., Lancaster, G.A. & Berridge, D.M. (2011). A population-based investigation of behavioural and emotional problems and maternal mental health: Associations with autism and intellectual disability. *Journal of Child Psychology and Psychiatry, and Allied Disciplines*, *52*, 91–99.

Wigham, S., Hatton, C. & Taylor, J.L. (2011). The Lancaster and Northgate Trauma Scales (LANTS): The development and psychometric properties of measures of trauma for people with mild to moderate intellectual disabilities. *Research in Developmental Disabilities, 32,* 2651–2659.

Wigham, S., Taylor, J.L. & Hatton, C. (2012). A prospective study of the relationship between adverse life events and trauma in adults with intellectual disabilities. Manuscript submitted for publication.

Wilson, T. (1998). Manual-based treatment and clinical practice. *Clinical Psychology: Science and Practice, 5,* 363–375.

Index

Psychological Therapies for Adults with Intellectual Disabilities, First Edition.
Edited by John L. Taylor, William R. Lindsay, Richard P. Hastings, and Chris Hatton.
© 2013 John Wiley & Sons, Ltd. Published 2013 by John Wiley & Sons, Ltd.

Printed in Great Britain
by Amazon